FISH REPRODUCTION:

Strategies and Tactics

FISH REPRODUCTION:
Strategies and Tactics

Edited by

G. W. Potts
Marine Biological
Association U.K., Plymouth

R. J. Wootton
Department of Zoology
University College of Wales

1984

ACADEMIC PRESS

Harcourt Brace Jovanovich, Publishers
London   Orlando   San Diego   New York   Austin
Toronto   Montreal   Sydney   Tokyo

ACADEMIC PRESS INC. (LONDON) LTD.
24–28 Oval Road
London NW1 7DX

U.S. Edition published by
ACADEMIC PRESS INC.
Orlando, Florida 32887

Copyright © 1984 by
ACADEMIC PRESS INC. (LONDON) LTD.
Second printing 1985

British Library Cataloguing in Publication Data

Fish reproduction.
  1. Fishes—Reproduction
  I. Potts, G. W.   II. Wootton, R. J.
  597'.01'6   QL639.2

ISBN 0–12–563660–1

LCCCN 83–71859

Filmset by Latimer Trend & Company Ltd, Plymouth
Printed in Great Britain by
St Edmundsbury Press, Bury St Edmunds, Suffolk

Contributors

Balon, E. K.: Department of Zoology, College of Biological Science, University of Guelph, Guelph, Ontario N1G 2WI, Canada.

Bye, V. J.: Ministry of Agriculture, Fisheries and Food, Fisheries Laboratory, Lowestoft, Suffolk, NR33 0HT, England.

Crandall, R. E.: Department of Physics, Reed College, Portland, Oregon 97202, U.S.A.

Crisp, D. T.: Freshwater Biological Association, Teesdale Unit, c/o Northumbrian Water Authority, Lartington Treatment Plant, Lartington, Barnard Castle, Durham, DL12 9DW, England.

Dando, P. R.: Marine Biological Association of the U.K., Citadel Hill, Plymouth, PL1 2PB, England.

Garrod, D. J.: Ministry of Agriculture, Fisheries and Food, Fisheries Laboratory, Lowestoft, Suffolk, NR33 0HT, England.

Giles, N.: Department of Life Sciences, The University College at Buckingham, Buckingham, MK18 1EG, England.

Gross, Mart R.: Department of Biological Sciences, Simon Fraser University, Burnaby, British Columbia V5A 1S6, Canada.

Hislop, J. R. G.: D.A.F.S. Marine Laboratory, P.O. Box 101, Victoria Road, Aberdeen, AB9 8DB, Scotland.

Horwood, J. W.: Ministry of Agriculture, Fisheries and Food, Fisheries Laboratory, Lowestoft, Suffolk, NR33 0HT, England.

Iles, T. D.: Marine Fish Division, Bedford Institute of Oceanography, Dartmouth, Nova Scotia, B2Y 4A2, Canada.

Mann, R. H. K.: Freshwater Biological Association, River Laboratory, East Stoke, Wareham, Dorset, BH20 6BB, England.

Marshall, N. B.: 6 Park Lane, Saffron Waldon, Essex, England.

McKaye, K. R.: Duke University Marine Laboratory, Beaufort, North Carolina 28516, U.S.A.

Miller, P. J.: Department of Zoology, University of Bristol, Woodland Road, Bristol, BS8 1UG, England.

Mills, C. A.: Freshwater Biological Association, River Laboratory, East Stoke, Wareham, Dorset, BH20 6BB, England.

Price, D. J.: Department of Biological Sciences, Plymouth Polytechnic, Plymouth, PL4 8AA, England.

Potts, G. W.: Marine Biological Association of the U.K., Citadel Hill, Plymouth, PL1 2PB, England.

Reay, P. J.: Department of Biological Sciences, Plymouth Polytechnic, Plymouth, PL4 8AA, England.

Shapiro, D. J.: Department of Marine Sciences, University of Puerto Rico, Mayaguez, Puerto Rico 00708, U.S.A.

Stacey, N.: Zoology Department, University of Alberta, Edmonton, Alberta, T6G 2E9, Canada.

Stearns, S. C.: Zoologisches Institut, Rheinsprung 9, CH-4051 Basel, Switzerland.

Ware, D. M.: Pacific Biological Station, Department of Fisheries and Oceans, Nanaimo, British Columbia, Canada.

Wootton, R. J.: Department of Zoology, University College of Wales, Aberystwyth, Dyfed, SY23 3DA, Wales.

Preface

In recent years, the analysis of the adaptive significance of reproductive patterns in both plants and animals has flourished. The teleost fishes are particularly suitable subjects for such an analysis both because of the wide variety of reproductive patterns that they show, and because such patterns are crucial in determining how a species will respond to exploitation by fishing or in aquaculture. The reproductive patterns that are observed in teleosts pose two major but related problems for the fish biologist. The first relates to the nature of the adaptive significance of an observed pattern, and the second, the causal mechanisms that produce those patterns. These two problem areas formed the central theme of an international symposium organized by the Fisheries Society of the British Isles with the title "Fish Reproduction: Strategies and Tactics". This symposium was held at Plymouth Polytechnic, 19–23 July, 1982. The contributions of the invited speakers at the symposium form the major portion of this volume. Other oral and poster papers played an important role in the success of the symposium and their titles are included at the back of this volume. Important features of the symposium were the international character of the participants, coming from many countries; and the way it brought together the academic research biologist and the fisheries scientist. These factors, together with the very different approaches to the subject of fish reproduction, led to a stimulating and productive symposium which we hope is reflected in this volume.

The book begins with a review of the applicability of modern evolutionary theory to the questions of strategies and tactics in fish reproduction. This is developed by the hypothetical deductions of the mathematical modeller and then expanded to consider how evolutionary processes bring about changes in fish populations and the genetic mechanisms by which these changes occur. The diversity of reproductive modes is examined in a series of reviews covering many different environments; the deep sea, tropical and temperate seas, and estuarine and freshwater conditions. While each subject tackles specific aspects of fish reproduction and development they also offer an important comparative approach that has great ecological and behavioural significance. The causal mechanisms are represented in work on the endocrine control of reproduction and complement the ethological contributions. Finally, some of the commercially important aspects of fish reproduction in aquaculture and fisheries biology are examined.

vii

The organization and coordination needed in planning the symposium and during the preparation of this book has involved many people. To all these people we offer our grateful thanks. Special mention should be made of the Fisheries Society of the British Isles Council who have provided help and advice during the preparatory stages and to the Society for financial assistance which enabled a number of students of fish biology to attend the meeting. A grant from the Royal Society defrayed some of the travel expenses of overseas speakers and is gratefully acknowledged. The smooth running of the symposium largely resulted from the administrative efficiency of the local committee under Dr P. J. Reay and included Dr D. J. Price (poster sessions), Mr M. M. Berkien (Residences Officer), Mr A. Littlejohn (Catering Manager) and other members of the Polytechnic staff. Their help was invaluable. Thanks should be given to Dr L. A. F. Heath who welcomed the Fisheries Society of the British Isles on behalf of Plymouth Polytechnic who had provided the facilities. The meeting was opened by Mr E. D. Le Cren (FBA and President of the FSBI) who with the Chairmen: Professor N. B. Marshall (London), Dr R. J. H. Beverton (Swindon), Dr M. E. Varley (Open University), Dr B. L. Bayne (IMER), Dr P. J. Miller (Bristol), Dr E. D. Le Cren (FBA) and Dr T. B. Bagenal (FBA) did so much to promote interested discussion and contribute to the sustained interest throughout the meeting. We are grateful also to Professor E. J. Denton (MBA) and Mr R. Glover (IMER) who kindly allowed delegates to look around their research institutes.

During the preparation of this book we have had much help from the individual contributors who not only provided manuscripts on time but were also quick in responding to minor changes as were needed. We are grateful to the anonymous referees whose help has contributed significantly to the final quality of the manuscripts. We should like to acknowledge the secretarial help of Miss Susan Gwynne and Mrs Iris Thomas and in particular Mrs Sylvia Marriott whose assistance in the compilation of the Species Index and whose willing help during the preparation of the final typescript was invaluable. Finally we offer our thanks to our wives who contributed in so many ways.

October 1983   G. W. POTTS and R. J. WOOTTON

Contents

1. Introduction: Strategies and Tactics in Fish Reproduction

R. J. WOOTTON

Department of Zoology, The University College of Wales, Aberystwyth, Wales, U.K.

Abstract: Although both are derived from military science, the words tactics and strategies are not synonyms. Strategy is the art of generalship, particularly the choice of operations to be attempted. Tactics is the art of handling troops in battle. Within a given strategy, a range of flexible tactics may be deployed depending on the battle situation. This distinction between strategies and tactics may be usefully retained when these terms are used as metaphors in the analysis of the reproductive patterns of fishes.

Within this military metaphor, natural selection can be regarded as an opportunistic general confronting an enemy, the environment, that is hostile, capricious but indifferent. A successful strategy for a taxon will be that which maintains the existence of that taxon in the next and subsequent generations. The components (or operations) of a reproductive strategy will include the age at which reproduction first starts, the post-breeding survivorship, size-specific fecundity, the organization of the reproductive behaviour and the timing of the breeding season.

These components will show tactical modifications as short term variations in the environment are experienced by the fish. Such tactical modifications may be minor or considerable, but they depend on the ability of individual fish in the taxon to detect the relevant environmental cues and have the physiological mechanisms to make the required tactical adjustments within the framework of the reproductive strategy.

The military metaphor provides a useful unifying theme in which genetical, physiological, behavioural and ecological studies can be linked within an evolutionary framework.

I. INTRODUCTION

In this introduction, I shall discuss a use of the terms "strategies" and "tactics" that I think can be valuable in the analysis of the reproductive biology of fishes. Other ways of using the term appear in this volume and elsewhere (e.g. Stearns, 1976; Cohen, 1977), and it is unlikely that these evocative words will ever be employed in a uniform way by biologists.

From its beginning, the Darwinian theory of evolution by natural selection

FISH REPRODUCTION
ISBN: 0–12–563660–1

has used terms that suggest conflict. The subtitle of "The Origin of the Species" is "The preservation of favoured races in the struggle for life" (Darwin, 1859). Natural selection provides a materialistic explanation for the appearance that living organisms have of being planned for the environments in which they live. This characteristic of organisms once provided strong justification for the belief that they had been created by a rational deity, and even today the niceties of some adaptations shown by organisms can fill the most dogmatic of neo-Darwinians with a sense of awe. The reproductive biology of fishes, in all its diversity (Breder and Rosen, 1966), is an area of study in which this awe can repeatedly be provoked, as many of the examples in this volume illustrate.

The notions that natural selection involves some form of conflict and that living organisms have the appearance of being planned entities are both retained by the use of the terms *strategies* and *tactics* in analyses of the adaptive significance of reproductive patterns. Both these terms have their origin in the art (or science) of warfare, but they are not synonyms. Strategy is the art of generalship, the planning of the military operations to be attempted, or the plan itself. In a wider context, strategy has come to mean the skilful planning and management of an enterprise and hence the plan that ensues. Tactics is the art of handling troops in battle and by extension, the operations on the battlefield. Within a given strategy, a range of tactics will be deployed depending on the immediate battle situation. The relationship between strategies and tactics is hierarchical, the tactics are at a lower level in the hierarchy of decisions than the strategies. This relationship is reflected in the strongly hierarchical organization of a modern army with its distinction between tactical units such as regiments and battalions and the strategic units such as corps and armies.

In game theory, the term strategy has a more restricted technical meaning. It designates a plan so complete that it cannot be upset by enemy action or Nature, note that it does not have to be a "successful" strategy (Williams, 1954). In population biology, this usage has led to the development of the concept of evolutionarily stable strategies (ESS), that is a strategy or mixture of strategies adopted by a population that is not susceptible to invasion by a hypothetical alternative (Maynard Smith, 1974). This concept has now been incorporated in some population genetics models of animal behaviour such as parent-offspring relationships (e.g. Parker and McNair, 1978). As yet, there are few biological situations which have been studied in sufficient quantitative detail to be convincingly analysed in the context of ESS, but recent studies on dwarf and sneaking males in centrachid and salmonid fishes have used the concept (Gross, 1982; Chap. 4, this volume).

Although the terms strategies and tactics imply rational planning, this implication is clearly inappropriate in the context of evolutionary biology (see also Ware, Chap. 19, this volume). The adaptiveness of reproductive strategies is a consequence of the action of natural selection, which can perhaps be thought of as an opportunistic general confronting an enemy, the environment, that is hostile, capricious but indifferent to the outcome. The goal of a reproductive strategy is to produce reproductively active offspring from each generation, but the global strategy adopted is almost invariably a strategy of attrition. Far more gametes are produced than achieve a successful fertilization and far more zygotes are produced than will reach maturity even under relatively benign conditions. The adaptive successes of natural selection are achieved through a carnage that makes the casualty rates of human wars pale into numerical if not ethical insignificance.

The reproductive strategy of a species of fish is that complex of reproductive traits that fish will attempt to manifest so as to leave some offspring. Such traits include age at first reproduction, size and age-specific fecundities, size and nature of the gametes, degree of parity, timing of the reproductive season, organization of reproductive behaviour and in some species traits such as sex change (see Shapiro, Chap. 7, this volume). An individual fish will be attempting to carry out a reproductive strategy in an environment that is more or less variable, and in face of changes in the environment, the fish must make tactical changes in the details of the reproductive strategy for that strategy to be successful. The reproductive strategy is the overall pattern of reproduction typically shown by individuals in a species, whereas the reproductive tactics are those variations in the typical pattern which fish make in response to fluctuations in the environment. It is assumed that both the overall strategy and the tactical variations are adaptive.

A major problem for population biologists is to show how particular reproductive strategies and tactics are adaptive in particular environmental circumstances. A second major problem is to elucidate the causal mechanisms that produce the observed patterns.

One technique for analysing the probable adaptive significance of reproductive strategies or tactics is the use of mathematical models such as those developed by Stearns and Crandell (Chap. 2, this volume) and Ware (Chap. 19, this volume). Such models provide a rigorous framework against which empirical observations can be interpreted. Experimental manipulations, unfortunately still rare, such as those described by Mann et al. (Chap. 10, this volume) for *Cottus gobio*, provide another powerful technique of analysis. However, in most cases the adaptive significance has to be inferred from correlations between reproductive strategy and environment. Such correlations emerge from comparisons within taxonomic groups such as those for gadoids, gobies and cichlids provided by Hislop (Chap. 17, this volume), Miller (Chap. 8, this volume) and McKaye (Chap. 14, this volume) respectively (see also Lowe-McConnell, 1975; Fryer and Iles, 1972). Similarities between different taxonomic groups living in the same environment are another source of such correlations (Dando, Chap. 9, this volume; Marshall, Chap. 6, this volume). Convergences in specific aspects of reproduction such as behaviour shown by different taxonomic groups are also valuable (see Potts, Chap. 13, this volume).

The analysis of the causal mechanisms involves genetical, physiological and behavioural studies (Price, Chap. 5, this volume; Iles, Chap. 18, this volume; Bye, Chap. 11, this volume; Stacey, Chap. 12, this volume). Physiological studies on the reproductive biology of fishes have concentrated on relatively few species, particularly some salmonids and cyprinids. Such studies have suggested both similarities but also some important differences such as that between spontaneous and reflex ovulators discussed by Stacey. Differences in the details of the physiological control of reproduction between strains or races within a species indicate the close relationship between the adaptations of the reproductive system and the environment (see Bye, Chap. 11, this volume).

Although some theoretical analyses of the adaptive significance of reproductive strategies either implicitly or explicitly assume that in a given environment an optimal strategy can be attained, in reality the predicted optimal strategy may not be available because of constraints on the reproductive traits imposed by the requirements of other adaptive traits such as defence against predators, efficient locomotion or food acquisition (Stearns, 1980; Wilz, 1971) (see also Giles, Chap. 15, this volume). The constraints on a reproductive strategy that it must be adaptive and compatible with non-reproductive adaptations suggest that there may be a restricted number of strategies that can be adopted (Balon, Chap. 3, this volume).

II. REPRODUCTIVE STRATEGIES OF CANADIAN FRESHWATER FISH

This possibility that only a limited number of types of reproductive strategy may be recognizable was explored by an analysis of the strategies of Canadian freshwater species. Details of these were obtained from Scott and Crossman (1973). This preliminary exploration was at a crude level and only the following traits were considered: length at sexual maturity, life span, usual spawning month, fecundity, egg diameter, time taken for eggs to hatch and whether the species was usually anadromous or confined to freshwater. Geographical variations in these traits within a species were not included at this stage of the analysis. Catadromous species were excluded.

The frequency distribution of length at maturity for 162 species is shown in Fig. 1. Species with lengths less than 30 mm or greater than 1000 mm were extremely rare. A relatively high proportion of species were small with lengths at maturity of less than 150 mm. No species had a life span of less than one year, a constraint presumably imposed by the strong seasonality of the

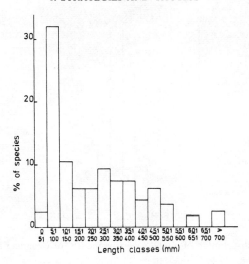

Fig. 1. Frequency distribution of lengths at maturity for Canadian freshwater fishes.

Canadian environment. The modal life span was between 7 and 9 years with almost as many species with a life span of 4–6 years, but many species had shorter or longer spans (Fig. 2). Spawning was largely confined to the late spring or early summer (April–July) or to the autumn months. This constraint on time of spawning (Fig. 3) was mirrored even more strongly by a constraint on the time of hatching (or emergence of alevins from the gravel). For most species hatching occurred over a period of about 100 days, a period which started about 100 days from the start of the year (Jan. 1) (Fig. 4). The relative

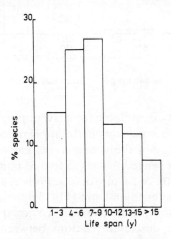

Fig. 2. Frequency distribution of life span for Canadian freshwater fishes.

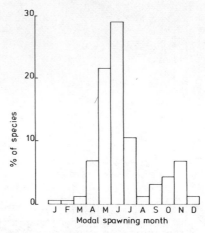

Fig. 3. Frequency distribution of modal spawning month for Canadian freshwater fishes.

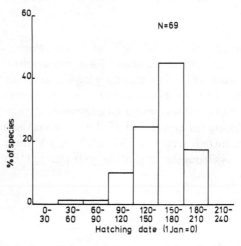

Fig. 4. Frequency distribution of hatching (or emergence) dates for Canadian freshwater fishes.

importance of availability of suitable food, swamping of predators or other factors which result in this synchrony in the appearance of young-of-the-year is not known. The ecology of the young stages has received comparatively little study. Egg diameter ranged from 0·75 to 6·55 mm, but two thirds of the species had an egg diameter of 2·0 mm or less. Fourteen per cent of the species had an egg diameter greater than 4 mm (Fig. 5).

The extent to which the reproductive traits covaried was crudely explored, firstly by calculating the simple correlations between them (Table I). The highest correlations were between length at maturity, life span and egg

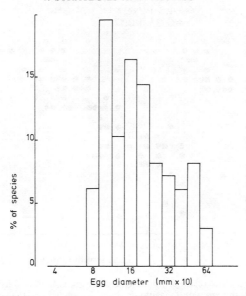

Fig. 5. Frequency distribution of egg diameters for Canadian freshwater fishes. Note logarithmic scale.

TABLE I. Simple correlation matrix for reproductive traits of Canadian freshwater fishes.

	Variables				
	1	2	3	4	5
1 = Length at maturity	1·00	0·52	0·25	0·22	0·55
2 = Life span		1·00	—	0·34	—
3 = Spawning month			1·00	−0·13	0·52
4 = Fecundity				1·00	−0·25
5 = Egg diameter					1·00

(Only correlations significant at the 0·05 level are shown.)

diameter. Egg diameter was also strongly correlated with modal spawning month. Although fecundity was significantly correlated with length at maturity, it was a relatively weak correlation. But when fecundity was expressed in terms of the total volume of eggs rather than their number, a strong relationship between total volume and length at maturity was found. When both of these variates were logarithmically transformed, the relationship was linear and three quarters of the variance in egg volume could be accounted for in terms of body length (Fig. 6). Total egg volume has two

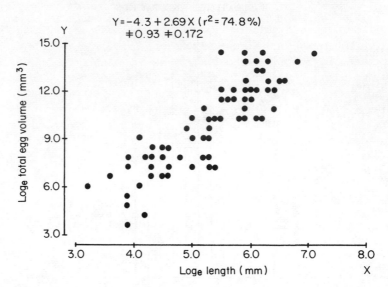

Fig. 6. Scatter diagram of relationship between total egg volume and fish length for Canadian freshwater fishes. Both axes with logarithmic scale. Parameters of the least-squares regression shown.

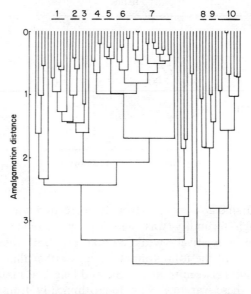

Fig. 7. Dendogram of cluster analysis of reproductive traits of Canadian freshwater fishes (see also Table II).

components, fecundity and the average volume of each egg, and the strong correlation between total egg volume and body size shows that there is only restricted scope for the independent variation of fecundity and egg size. Thus spawning in autumn was positively correlated with egg diameter and the latter was positively correlated with large body size, but given the constraints on total egg volume, the large egg size implied a relatively low fecundity.

The co-relationship of reproductive traits was also indicated by a cluster analysis which treated each species as a case (Dixon, 1981) (Fig. 7 and Table II). This analysis produced a cluster which contained only salmonid species, that is those species characterized by autumnal or winter spawning, large egg

TABLE II. Some species clusters based on reproductive traits of Canadian freshwater fishes. Clusters formed using a single linkage algorithm (Dixon, 1981).

CLUSTER 1
Micropterus salmoides
Stizostedion canadense
Micropterus domomieui
Catastomus macrocheilus
Thymallus arcticus

CLUSTER 2
Esox masquinongy
Catostomus catostomus
Esox lucius
Ictalurus punctatus

CLUSTER 3
Hiodon alosoides
Perca flavescens

CLUSTER 4
Dallia pectoralis
Richardsonius baleatus
Ictalurus nebulosus
Ictalurus melas

CLUSTER 5
Poxomis nigromaculatus
Lepomis gibbosus
Morone americana
Lepomis megalotis

CLUSTER 6
Esox americanus americanus
Esox americanus vermiculatus
Cottus asper
Esox niger
Erimyzon sucetta

CLUSTER 7
Gasterosteus aculeatus
Apeltes quadracus
Notropis rubellus
Pimephales notatus
Culea inconstans
Etheostoma exile
Percopsis ominiscomaycus
Etheostoma nigrum
Etheostoma blennioides
Percina maculata
Etheostoma caeruleum
Umbra limi

CLUSTER 8
Salmo trutta
Salvelinus fontinalis
Salvelinus namaycush

CLUSTER 9
Prosopium cylindriaceum
Prosopium williamsoni
Coregonus artedii

CLUSTER 10
Oncorhynchus keta
Oncorhynchus kisutch
Oncorhynchus nerka
Oncorhynchus twawytscha
Oncorhynchus gorbuscha
Salmo salar
Salvelinus alpinus
Salvelinus malma

size, large body size and a relatively low fecundity. A second cluster that emerged included the sticklebacks, some small cyprinids and small percids especially the genus *Etheostoma*. These species are characterized by small body size, relatively short life span, late spring or summer spawning and low fecundities. This last trait reflects the small body size of these species together with the constraints on minimum egg size that is adaptive in the Canadian environments (Fig. 5). Another cluster consisted of the related centrachids, *Lepomis* spp. *Morone* and *Poxomis*, although the larger centrachids belonging to the genus *Micropterus* clustered with the grayling *Thymallus arcticus* etc. (Table II).

These preliminary correlation and cluster analyses suggest that in a given geographical area only a restricted number of types of reproductive strategy will evolve. The constraints that restrict the number of strategies will include environmental factors, morphological design and phylogeny.

A problem that emerged during this initial analysis of the Canadian fauna was that there were still many species for which accurate basic data on their reproductive strategies are not available, and this in a country noted for the quality of its fishery research.

III. TACTICAL VARIATIONS IN A REPRODUCTIVE STRATEGY

The tactical variations that can be displayed within a reproductive strategy may be illustrated for the three-spined stickleback, *Gasterosteus aculeatus*, a species that is a member of the Canadian fish fauna. It is a hardy species, easy to breed in the laboratory and so has been widely used in experimental studies on fish reproduction.

Age at maturity is typically one year, but in some populations the fish may not mature until they are two years old (Wootton, 1976). Size at maturity is also variable, in some Canadian populations this variation has been correlated with the presence of fish predators (McPhail, 1977), but the chronic level of food abundance may also be a factor influencing the typical size of maturity.

Breeding occurs in late spring and early summer. If kept under constant but permissive conditions of photoperiod and temperature, sticklebacks cycle between a reproductive and a non-reproductive condition, but the temporal patterning of this cycle displayed under constant conditions would not synchronize the breeding with the appropriate season. This synchronization is achieved through an interaction between the neuro-endocrine system and the environmental cues of photoperiod and temperature (Baggerman, 1980; see also Bye, Chap. 11, this volume). Studies on the control of timing of breeding have used sticklebacks from the middle of the latitudinal range of the species, while Vrat (1949) noted that the start of the breeding season tended to be later in the year for the more northerly populations. The extent and the factors controlling such geographical variations in the timing of breeding are not known.

Within a breeding season, the female will spawn at intervals of a few days, usually producing 50–150 eggs at a spawning depending on her size. Tactical variations in total fecundity in response to the supply of food are achieved by variations in the number of spawnings. But at low food levels, a higher proportion of the energy content of the food consumed is channelled into egg production than at higher food levels (Wootton, 1977), a similar result was obtained for a small cyprinodont, *Oryzias latipes* (Hirshfield, 1980). The sensitivity of the female to food levels suggests that egg production during a breeding season tracks the food availability. Within a few weeks of hatching, young sticklebacks consume the same food items as the parental generation, so the food supply experienced by the adults may be a good predictor of the food supply that will be experienced by their offspring.

The male stickleback defends a territory during the breeding season and only a certain minimum territory size is acceptable (van den Assem, 1967). As the density of males in a given area increases, the number of males successfully acquiring a territory does not increase proportionately. Thus the territorial behaviour of the male tends to buffer the density of breeding males against fluctuations in the total density of males in the population. At a given density of males, the number acquiring a territory tends to be lower when food is in short supply (Wootton, 1982).

Although the tactical variations in the reproductive traits can be substantial, nevertheless they clearly lie within the framework of a particular strategy. In spite of marked variations in life-span, timing of reproduction, fecundity and other traits, the reproductive strategy of the stickleback is clearly that of a short-lived, small, early-summer breeding fish with complex reproductive behaviour.

IV. CONCLUSION

Strategies and tactics: the words evoke two images, warfare and rational planning to achieve a purpose. Strategies are the plans to achieve the purpose and tactics the detailed implementations and modifications of the plan in the face of immediate contingencies.

In the context of the reproductive biology of fishes, the term strategy emphasizes the co-relationships between reproductive traits so that the resulting reproductive pattern has the appearance of having been planned to achieve a goal in the face of a hostile environment. Particular reproductive traits are not linked together at random, but through the agency of natural selection display an arrangement that has adaptive significance which, in principle, can be identified.

The term tactics emphasizes that details within the reproductive strategy will depend on the interactions between the environment and the genetical, physiological, behavioural and ecological response of individuals attempting to manifest the reproductive strategy. The term focuses attention on the range of variation that reproductive traits show in the face of environmental variations, and on the mechanisms that mediate between the environmental variables and reproductive responses. The question of whether similar reproductive strategies show similar tactical responses to environmental fluctuations can also be posed. Environmental fluctuations may be imposed by man through his fishing or aquacultural activities, so the study of reproductive strategies and tactics is of practical as well as academic importance (Reay, Chap. 16, this volume; Garrod and Horwood, Chap. 20, this volume).

REFERENCES

Assem, J. van den (1967). *Behav. Suppl.* **16**, 1–164.
Baggerman, B. (1980). *In* "Environmental Physiology of Fishes" (M. A. Ali, ed.), pp. 533–567. Plenum Press, New York.
Breder, C. M. Jr and Rosen, D. E. (1966). "Modes of Reproduction in Fishes". Natural History Press, New York.
Cohen, J. (1977). "Reproduction". Butterworths, London.
Darwin, C. (1859). "The Origin of the Species by Means of Natural Selection". John Murray, London.
Dixon, W. J. (1981). "BMDP Statistical Software 1981". University of California Press, Berkeley.
Fryer, G. and Iles, T. D. (1972). "The Cichlid Fishes of the Great Lakes of Africa". Oliver & Boyd, Edinburgh.
Gross, M. R. (1982). *Z. Tierpsychol.* **60**, 1–26.
Hirschfield, M. F. (1980). *Ecology* **61**, 282–292.
Lowe-McConnell, R. H. (1975). "Fish Communities in Tropical Freshwater". Longman, London.
McPhail, J. D. (1977). *Hereditary* **38**, 53–60.
Maynard Smith, J. (1974). *J. Theor. Biol.* **47**, 209–221.
Parker, G. A. and McNair, M. R. (1978). *Anim. Behav.* **26**, 97–110.
Scott, W. B. and Crossman, E. J. (1973). "Freshwater Fishes of Canada". Fisheries Research Board of Canada, Ottawa.
Stearns, S. C. (1976). *Quart. Rev. Biol.* **51**, 3–47.
Stearns, S. C. (1980). *Oikos* **35**, 266–281.
Vrat, V. (1949). *Copeia* **1949**, 252–260.
Williams, J. D. (1954). "The Compleat Strategyst". McGraw Hill, London.
Wilz, K. J. (1971). *Z. Tierpsychol.* **29**, 1–10.
Wootton, R. J. (1976). "The Biology of the Sticklebacks". Academic Press, London.
Wootton, R. J. (1977). *J. Anim. Ecol.* **46**, 823–834.
Wootton, R. J. (1982). *In* "Proceedings International Symposium on Reproductive Physiology of Fishes" (C. J. J. Richter and T. J. Th. Goos, eds), pp. 210–219. Pudoc, Wageningen.

2. Plasticity for Age and Size at Sexual Maturity: A Life-history Response to Unavoidable Stress

STEPHEN C. STEARNS[1] and RICHARD E. CRANDALL[2]

[1]*Zoologisches Institut, Rheinsprung 9, CH-4051 Basel, Switzerland*
[2]*Department of Physics, Reed College, Portland, Oregon, U.S.A.*

Abstract: An organism encountering an unavoidable stress that results in slower growth should alter its age and size at maturity along a trajectory that minimizes the reduction in fitness caused by slower growth and smaller size. We constructed a life-history model to predict that trajectory. It assumes that r is the definition of fitness, that populations are in stable age distribution, that genetic constraints do not inhibit evolution near local optima, and that maturity is delayed either to gain fecundity or to reduce juvenile mortality. The model predicts that the trajectory should take one of at least four shapes that depend on whether slower growth is correlated with increases in juvenile or adult mortality, or with neither. Quantitative predictions of age-at-maturity were in good agreement with observation ($r = 0.91$, $P < 0.01$) in 19 populations of fish, and qualitative predictions were in agreement with the available evidence. This model provides a unified explanation for diverse observations whose relation had previously not been perceived. It resolves the controversy over whether organisms mature at a fixed size or a fixed age by pointing out that they do neither; they mature along a trajectory of age and size that depends on demographic conditions. It also resolves the controversy over whether age and size at maturity are genetically or environmentally determined; they are determined both by genes and by environment, and in a particular way that makes clear the separation of the two influences.

I. INTRODUCTION

This paper analyses how an organism encountering an unavoidable stress that results in slower growth should alter its age at maturity to keep fitness as high as possible despite slower growth. The analysis is anchored in life-history theory and is most clearly prefigured in Gadgil and Bossert (1970) and Schaffer and Elson (1975). The manner in which an organism alters age and size at maturity under stress can be predicted. The track along which age and

FISH REPRODUCTION
ISBN: 0–12–563660–1

size at maturity change as stress increases is called a *plastic trajectory* (Stearns, 1983; following Alberch *et al.*, 1979). This whole trajectory, and neither age at maturity nor size at maturity taken separately, may be considered the trait under selection.

These results have significance both for fisheries biology and for evolutionary theory. When fishing effort increases on an exploited stock, part of the response to reduced population density is increased growth. This analysis predicts how age and size at maturity should change. When conditions vary from year to year, or from place to place, as they do for almost all exploited stocks, this analysis predicts how age and size at maturity should change as growth rates change. Thus two types of fisheries data to which these ideas naturally apply are geographic variation and year class strength.

The impact of developmental plasticity on genetic change has not yet been completely analysed by evolutionary theory (Stearns, 1982). That developmental plasticity has specific, concrete consequences for life-history evolution is part of the answer to a quite general question: what do we need to know about the phenotype and its interactions with the environment to predict evolutionary change? These results suggest that we need at least to understand the general properties of plastic trajectories for life-history traits, the components of fitness.

Evidence bearing on these issues has been presented by fisheries biologists for many years. For example, Molander (1925) noted that witch flounder that grew faster also matured earlier and at a larger size than did conspecific populations growing more slowly. On the other hand, Pitt (1975) found that in plaice from the Grand Bank faster growing fish matured earlier but at the same size as more slowly growing fish; Grainger (1953) had noted the same pattern in Arctic char. In experimental studies, Donaldson and Olson (1955) found that the largest rainbow trout matured earliest, while Scott (1962), Bagenal (1969), and Wootton (1973) all noted that as food supply increased and their fish grew faster, age at maturity decreased in rainbow trout, brown trout and sticklebacks. However, Pinhorn (1969) reported that in Atlantic cod off Newfoundland, fish from one area matured earlier and at a smaller size than fish from another area.

This diversity of results is reflected in Alm's (1959) massive report and review on connections between maturity, age and size in fish. He noted some cases in which slower growing forms matured earlier and at a smaller size than faster-growing forms, and many more cases in which the opposite was true. He summarized the results of all his experiments by suggesting that fish mature along a single age–size trajectory — concave downward — as growth rates vary. In other words, Alm thought that as growth rates declined, fish would first delay maturity and mature at larger sizes, then further delay and mature at the same size, then finally, as growth rates became very small, delay maturity even further and mature at smaller sizes. The resulting relationship should describe an inverted "u" on a plot of age (x-axis) versus size (y-axis). However, this relationship was inferred from many experiments in which a number of fish were grown in each tank, not measured directly on individual fish.

A model that claims to explain variation under stress in age and size at maturity should accomplish at least three things. First, it should account for the diversity of observed trajectories as the different consequences of a single model that depend only on changes in parameter values, thus demonstrating the mechanism that unifies many apparently contradictory observations. There are three prominent patterns reported in the literature, and they refer to both inter- and intra-populational differences. Decreased growth brings with it either delayed maturity at a smaller size, delayed maturity at the same size, or, more rarely, delayed maturity at a larger size. One can also imagine that decreased growth could result in earlier maturity at a smaller size.

The first task is to show how one model can explain all four patterns. Secondly, the model should be not only qualitatively but quantitatively consistent with published observations. Thirdly, it should make possible a clear statement of the manner in which genes and environment interact to produce the patterns observed. The rest of this paper examines how well one model meets these goals.

II. ANALYSIS OF THE MODEL

A. Assumptions and definitions

This model belongs to a set of variational models of life-histories whose general properties are presented in Crandall and Stearns (1982). Like them, this one assumes that a population can be modelled as a set of asexual haploid clones, that the Malthusian parameter (r) is the definition of fitness, that there is no frequency-dependence or density-dependence, and that genetic co-variance does not constrain the course of evolution near local equilibria. Those assumptions seem restrictive, but they have led to reasonably successful predictions (e.g. Stearns and Crandall, 1981).

Like our other models of delayed maturity, this one assumes that maturity may be delayed either because it results in a gain in fecundity or because it results in reduced juvenile mortality, or both. It is distinctive in that it takes explicit account of growth. We assume that the primary impact of environmental stress is on growth rate, that changes in growth rate impose unavoidable changes in size at given ages, and that these changes in size have particular consequences for fecundity and for the juvenile mortality rates of the offspring produced. In addition, in some submodels we assume that changes in growth rate can serve as reliable *cues* to the direct impact of environmental change on juvenile and adult mortality, unmediated by size.

Our procedure is to define functions for death rates and birth rates in terms of age and size, then to assume stable age distributions and apply the Euler-Lotka relation. The Euler-Lotka relationship defines fitness (r) implicitly in terms of age-specific birth and death rates; from it, one can find the age-at-maturity that maximizes r for any given growth rate.

B. Technical aside

To be precise, we constructed a two-dimensional variational model indexed by the 2-vectors $v = (k,\alpha)$ — where k determines growth rate of the individual and α is age-at-maturity — consisting of the collection of function pairs $\{d_v, b_v\}$ where the death rate is:

$$d_v = \begin{cases} a(k) & ; \text{age } x \geq \alpha, \\ j(k,\alpha) & ; \text{age } x < \alpha. \end{cases}$$

This assignment indicates a qualitative difference between juvenile and adult mortality. The birth rate is discontinuous at α:

$$b_v = \begin{cases} M(k,x) & ; \text{age } x \geq \alpha, \\ 0 & ; \text{age } x < \alpha. \end{cases}$$

Note that adult mortality depends only on individual growth rate, not on age-at-maturity or post-maturational age.

We next analyse the Euler-Lotka relation:

$$1 = \int_\alpha^\infty b_v(x) l_v(x) e^{-rx} dx \tag{1.1}$$

where:

$$l_v(x) = \exp\left[-\int_0^x d_v(u) du \right]$$

in order to find an optimal α at which r is locally stationary; that is any value of α satisfying:

$$\partial r/\partial \alpha = 0 \text{ with } r > 0.$$

In the sense of Crandall and Stearns (1982), we are thus asking whether the model defined by the function pairs $\{d_v, b_v\}$ is an optimizable variational model (OVM). By differentiating the Euler-Lotka relation with respect to α and setting $\partial r/\partial \alpha = 0$, we find that:

$$0 = -b_v(\alpha)l_v(\alpha)e^{-r\alpha} + \int_\alpha^\infty e^{-rx}\partial/\partial\alpha\{b_v(x)l_v(x)\}dx \tag{1.2}$$

It turns out that the integral can be removed from this last condition of optimality, because for the model in question we have:

$$\partial/\partial\alpha\{b_v(x)l_v(x)\} = -b_v(x)l_v(x)\partial/\partial\alpha[\alpha(j-a)]$$

as is easily verified from the definitions for b_v, d_v. Therefore the integral in (1.2) is proportional to the Euler-Lotka integral, the latter being unity, and we arrive at a direct algebraic relation for maximal r in terms of the optimal α:

$$r_k = -\frac{1}{\alpha}ln\left[\frac{-\dfrac{\partial}{\partial\alpha}[\alpha(j-a)]}{b_v(\alpha)l_v(d)}\right] \tag{1.3}$$

This relation can be inserted back into the Euler-Lotka integral (1.1) to provide a complete solution to the problem of finding critical points (i.e. with $\partial r/\partial\alpha = 0$) in the sense that α is now the only variable on the right-hand side of the integral formula, and solution comes down to solving the resulting single-parameter implicit equation. Once a critical point exists, we also require that the rate r from (1·3) be positive, and finally that the critical point gives a locally maximal r, this last being determined by inspection of the second derivative.

We can now give necessary and sufficient conditions for a model to be an OVM. For convenience, we shall cast the remarks above in terms of auxiliary functions defined by:

$$f(k,\alpha) = -\frac{\partial}{\partial\alpha}\exp[\alpha(j(k,\alpha)-a(k))] \text{ (N.B., } f>0) \tag{1.4}$$

$$Q(k,\alpha) = f(k,\alpha)\exp[-\alpha(j(k,\alpha)-a(k))]/M(k,\alpha). \tag{1.5}$$

Theorem: *Let k be fixed. Assume that the model $\{d_v,b_v\}$ is an OVM with respect to variations in α only. Then the following three relations are satisfied at a locally optimal α:*

$$1 = \int_0^\infty dz\, Q^{1+z/\alpha}M(k,z+\alpha)\exp[-z(a(k)-j(k,\alpha))] \tag{1.6}$$

$$0 < Q\exp[\alpha j(k,a)] < 1 \tag{1.7}$$

$$(\partial/\partial\alpha - 1/\alpha)ln(f/M) < 0. \tag{1.8}$$

Conversely, for fixed k, if these three relations are satisfied at the point (k,α) then the model is an OVM and this α is locally optimal.

Condition (1.6) implies that there is an age-at-maturity at which the first derivative of r with respect to α is zero. Condition (1.7) requires that this r be positive, and condition (1.8) is equivalent to the statement that the second derivative is negative, assuring a local maximum.

The theorem represents a complete solution to the variational problem in the sense that the Malthusian parameter r has been entirely eliminated. In practice, we isolate optima by generating solutions alpha to (1.6), always checking (1.7), (1.8). Sometimes much time can be saved by first ruling out whole ranges of alpha values that obviously cannot satisfy (1.7) and (1.8). Indeed, certain models cannot be OVMs, meaning no optimal alpha exists, and conditions such as (1.7) and (1.8) are useful for removing these models from contention and therefore from the domain of costly computational tasks. Every alpha passing all tests is locally optimal and (1.3) will give the locally maximal, and positive-definite, r value.

C. Implementation

As defined above, the model will accommodate many alternative functions for mortality and fecundity rates and growth. To make a prediction, one specifies functions defining adult mortality, juvenile mortality, growth, and the size-fecundity relation. These in turn define $M(k,x)$, $f(k,\alpha)$, and $Q(k,\alpha)$. Then for each growth rate, one solves (1.6) numerically for a positive real α, and checks that (1.7) and (1.8) hold for that α. If all three steps are passed, then the point (k,α) is locally maximal, and one can increment or decrement k to find the behaviour of age-at-maturity as growth rate varies.

We specified the simplest functions that had worked in other contexts and whose parameters could easily be estimated from the types of data usually available. We assumed that fecundity grew linearly with size, and that the growth curve, or size-age relation, was defined by the Von Bertalanffy equation. We took adult mortality to be independent of age-at-maturity but possibly a function of growth rate. We also assumed that the juvenile mortality of the offspring produced by parents of a given age-at-maturity decreases as an inverse power of age-at-maturity, agreeing asymptotically (large α) with adult mortality rate. Specifically,

$$M(k,x) = FS(k,x) + H$$

$$S(k,x) = A(1 - Be^{-kx})$$

$$a(k) = a_o/k^\sigma$$

$$j(k,\alpha) = \lambda/\alpha^\rho + a_o$$

where F is the slope defining the rate at which fecundity increases with size, and H is the intercept for that line. $S(k,x)$ is size at a given age and growth rate, A is the limiting size in the Von Bertalanffy curve, $(1 - B)$ is size at birth as a proportion of limiting size, k is the growth rate, and x is age. $a(k)$ is the adult mortality rate, $j(k,\alpha)$ is the juvenile mortality rate, ρ is the power to which the inverse of age-at-maturity is raised, defining the shape of the juvenile mortality curve, and λ is a constant that shifts the curve up or down.

D. Sensitivity analysis

Extensive numerical analysis revealed that the model can produce at least four qualitatively different types of trajectories for age and size at maturity (Fig. 1). The trajectories represent the locus of points of age and size at maturity each of which is optimal for the given growth curve. Points in the upper left of the figure correspond to rapid growth, while those in the lower right correspond to slow growth.

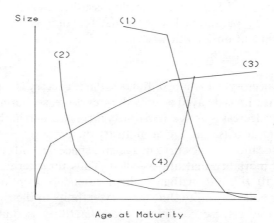

Fig. 1. The four qualitatively different types of age-size maturation trajectories predicted by the model. Every point on each line represents the optimal age and size at which to mature under the given assumptions. You should imagine that the plane is covered by a family of growth curves such that growth decreases from the upper left to the lower right. (1) Growth rates not correlated with juvenile or adult mortality. (2) Juvenile mortality increases slowly as growth rates decrease. (3) Juvenile mortality increases rapidly as growth rates decrease. (4) Adult mortality increases rapidly as growth rates decrease. In (1–3) maturity is delayed as growth rate decreases; only in (4) is maturity advanced when growth rate decreases. In (1) and (2), later maturity occurs at smaller sizes; in (3) and (4), later maturity occurs at larger sizes.

When neither juvenile nor adult mortality depends on growth rate, the trajectories look like a mirror-image of a sigmoid curve or some segment of such a curve. Thus when growth is rapid, changes in growth produce large changes in age-at-maturity but small changes in size-at-maturity, giving the impression that the organisms always mature at a fixed size. At intermediate growth rates, changes in growth produce very large changes in size at maturity but small changes in age at maturity, giving the impression that the organisms always mature at a fixed age. When growth is slow, changes in growth again produce large changes in age at maturity but small changes in size at maturity, giving the impression that the organisms always mature at a fixed size. As growth rates decrease, maturity is delayed and occurs at smaller sizes.

When adult mortality increases as growth rates decrease, which would be the case when environmental stress both slows growth and increases adult risk, the trajectory is J-shaped. Along the lower limb, organisms appear to mature at a fixed size, while along the upper limb they appear to mature at a fixed age. Here, as growth rates decrease and adult mortality rates increase, maturity occurs earlier at smaller sizes.

When juvenile mortality increases as growth rates decrease, which would be the case when environmental stress both slows growth and increases juvenile risk (but not adult risk), then the trajectory is either L-shaped or shaped like the upper half of a parabola. The particular function used to make juvenile mortality dependent on growth was

$$\lambda = \text{constant} \div k^{\sigma}.$$

If $\sigma \leq 1$, the trajectory is L-shaped. If $\sigma > 1$, the trajectory is a paraboloid. In either case, maturity is delayed as growth rates decrease, but in the first case, size at maturity decreases as age at maturity increases, and in the second case, size at maturity increases as age at maturity increases.

The actual location of the curve in age-size space depends on the levels of fecundity and mortality that are specified. Thus for intermediate levels of fecundity ($F = 10$, $H = 100$), with mortality rates independent of growth rates, increases in juvenile mortality shift the curve rapidly to the right (Fig. 2). In other words, under these conditions age-at-maturity is quite sensitive to juvenile mortality and increases rapidly as juvenile mortality increases.

Throughout the numerical analysis, age-at-maturity was much more sensitive to juvenile mortality, by a factor of 5–50, than it was to adult mortality rate or rate of fecundity gain with size. Because of the complex shapes of the trajectories (Fig. 1), description of the sensitivity of the predictions to changes in the parameters is difficult. Rather than give a complex table of sensitivity values that would be hard to interpret, we recommend that if you apply this model to a data set, you should check the sensitivity of the predictions to changes in the parameters in the vicinity of the actually observed points. In general, the estimate of juvenile mortality rate and the growth curve should be the most accurate, followed by the estimate of adult mortality rate and then the size-fecundity relationship. However, this comment cannot be taken as completely general because of the limitations of numerical analysis.

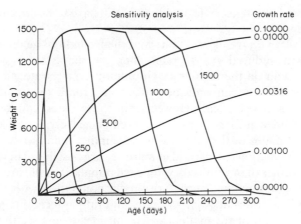

Fig. 2. An example of the type of sensitivity analysis carried out. Juvenile mortality increases in proportion with the numbers 50–1500 (values for λ, see text) that label the curves. The growth rate parameter, k, in the Von Bertalanffy growth equation is varied from 0·0001 to 0·1 to generate the growth curves. For moderate rates of fecundity gain with size, increases in juvenile mortality cause large delays in maturity.

E. Predictions

This model makes two different types of qualitative predictions. The first has to do with the *shape* of the trajectory followed by age and size at maturity as stress is applied (cf. Fig. 1). If increased stress not only slows growth but also increases adult mortality, then the trajectory should be J-shaped. If increased stress only affects growth, with no direct effect on mortality rates, the trajectory should be a mirror-image sigmoid curve. If increased stress not only slows growth but also increases juvenile mortality, then the trajectory should either be L-shaped or the upper half of a paraboloid. In testing these predictions, it is important to generate both very fast and very slow growth rates. Otherwise, only a segment of the trajectory will be observed, perhaps not enough of a segment to infer the shape of the whole curve.

The second type of prediction has to do with the relative *position* of the trajectory in age-size space, and results from sensitivity analyses of the sort presented in Fig. 2. Suppose you are dealing with two conspecific populations with different evolutionary histories, and you expose them to graded stresses in laboratory growth experiments. If one population has had higher adult mortality in the field than the other, its trajectory should lie to the left. If one population has had higher juvenile mortality than the other, its trajectory should lie to the right. If one population gains fecundity with size more rapidly than does the other, its trajectory should lie to the left, but the interpopulational difference in fecundity gain will have to be large to produce a small difference in the trajectories.

If both adult and juvenile mortality and the fecundity-size relationship are correlated with reduced growth rates, then the shape and position of the trajectory depend on the relative magnitude of the separate effects.

Often, populations can only be ranked according to juvenile or adult mortality rates in the field. However, if those rates can be measured accurately, if growth rates can be measured accurately, and if one can get reasonable estimates of the rate at which fecundity increases with size, then quantitative predictions of age and at maturity are possible. They consist of a single point, rather than a trajectory, for each population, and are obtained by calculating the optimal age at maturity for a population with the observed juvenile and adult mortality, growth rate, and rate of fecundity gain. This is the first type of test of the model carried out in the next section.

III. TESTS OF THE PREDICTIONS

A. Quantitative tests

We tested the capacity of the model to predict age and size at maturity on every suitable data set presented in the *Journal of Fish Biology* from 1969 to the second number in 1982, and on several data sets published elsewhere. We worked only with those data sets that contained estimates of growth rates, the fecundity-size relationship, estimates of adult and juvenile mortality rates or information from which they could be inferred, and measurements of age and size at maturity. If the parameters of the Von Bertalanffy growth curve were not presented in the paper, we calculated them from tables of size and age using the method of Fabens (1965). Direct estimates of juvenile mortality are hard to come by, and in most cases we had to settle for a rough estimate derived by assuming that on average two offspring survived to maturity and that population size was approximately constant.

For example, Mann (1974) presents detailed information on the life-histories of dace, *Leuciscus leuciscus*, living in the Rivers Stour and Frome in southern England. He reports that dace mature at 4–5 years in the Stour and 2–4 years in the Frome. We simplified by taking the observed ages at maturity to be four and three years, respectively. From the Von Bertalanffy growth curves that he presents, we calculated that dace matured at 129·8 mm in the Stour and 135·6 mm in the Frome, and, given the fecundity-length relationships he measured for the two stocks, that means that at maturity Stour dace produced 1147 eggs and Frome dace produced 1541 eggs. If two of those eggs survived to maturity, then the instantaneous juvenile mortality rate was 1·588 in the Stour and 2·216 in the Frome. Recall that the model assumes

$$j = \lambda/\alpha^2 + a_o.$$

(We set $\rho = 2$ because we had shown (Stearns and Crandall, 1981) that ρ must be greater than 1 for a solution to exist, and the next larger integer is 2.) Mann reports that adult mortality (a_o) was 0.594 in the Stour, but gives no figure for the Frome. We used 0.594 for both rivers. Thus $\lambda = 15.9$ for the Stour and 14.6 for the Frome. Given those estimates, the model predicts that Stour dace should mature at 4.06 years, and Frome dace at 3.50 years.

We repeated this sort of procedure for each of 19 populations of various species (Table I), and found that the correlation of prediction with observation was strongly positive ($r = 0.906$, $P < 0.01$). Stearns and Crandall (1981), using data on nine populations of lizards and salamanders, found slightly better agreement between prediction and observation ($r = 0.96$, $p < 0.01$). These predictions would be more convincing if juvenile mortality rates had been measured directly, and if the dependence of juvenile mortality on age-at-maturity of parent could be checked empirically. They embody the assumption that the rate at which fish are gaining potential fecundity with age as juveniles can be estimated from the size-fecundity relationship found in adult fish. This is probably usually an underestimate of the true relationship, but since the predictions are not very sensitive to the slope of that relation the inaccuracy in estimation is not serious.

Where possible, we calculated the observed age-at-maturity by taking the mean of the range of observed values. This accounts for decimal places in the observed ages-at-maturity of fish that breed seasonally. The model takes no account of seasonality. The effect of seasonality should be to make predictions less accurate for early-maturing species, and this does appear to be the case.

B. Qualitative tests

1. *Hawaiian mosquitofish.* Stearns (1983) has raised mosquitofish, *Gambusia affinis*, from two Hawaiian reservoirs, one stable (Twin Reservoir) and one fluctuating (Reservoir 33) in water level, through two generations in the laboratory. Individual fish were photographed at regular intervals for growth estimates, and each fish was kept in an individual 1.5 litre container, fed a measured amount of food three times a day, and kept at $25 \pm 0.5°C$. In the first generation, each brood was kept in the container in which it was born for ten days before the siblings were placed in individual containers. In the second generation, siblings were isolated on the day they were born. There was no other systematic difference between first and second generations. In the first generation, fish matured at about 80 days, and in the second at nearly the same size and at about 40 days. Thus crowding early in life considerably reduces growth rates in mosquitofish.

The age-length trajectories are defined only by two points, one for each

TABLE I. Predicted and observed ages at maturity for 19 populations of fish.

Species	Location	Reference	Observed	Predicted
Roach	R. Stour, England	Mann (1973)	3·5	5·6
Roach	L. Volvi, Greece	Papageorgiou (1979)	3·8	4·8
Pike	R. Stour, England	Mann (1976a)	2·3	2·7
Pike	L. Windermere, England	Kipling and Frost (1969)	3·5	3·2
Chub	R. Stour, England	Mann (1976b)	6·5	7·3
Dace	R. Stour, England	Mann (1974)	4·0	4·1
Dace	R. Frome, England	Mann (1974)	3·0	3·5
Red Salmon	Cultus Lake, B.C.	Foerster (1968)	4·0	3·5
Turbot	N.E. Atlantic	Jones (1974)	4·5	6·1
Mountain whitefish	Wyoming, U.S.A.	Hagen (1970)	3·5	5·2
Upland bully	New Zealand	Staples (1975a,b)	1·5	2·6
Arctic char	Baffin Island, Canada	Moore (1975)	11·0	11·1
Haplochromis intermedius	Lake Malawi, Malawi	Tweddle and Turner (1977)	2·2	1·3
Haplochromis mloto	Lake Malawi, Malawi	Tweddle and Turner (1977)	2·0	1·2
Lethrinops parvidens	Lake Malawi, Malawi	Tweddle and Turner (1977)	3·2	2·0
Gudgeon	R. Stour, England	Mann (1980)	2·1	3·0
Common bully	New Zealand	Stephens (1982)	0·7	1·1
Painted greenling	Seattle, U.S.A.	DeMartini and Anderson (1980)	3·2	5·2
Painted greenling	Monterey, U.S.A.	DeMartini and Anderson (1980)	3·0	4·7

generation. For females (Fig. 3a), the trajectory for the Reservoir 33 stock lies below and to the left of the trajectory for the Twin Res. stock. It slopes down to the right, whereas the trajectory for the Twin Res. stock slopes up to the right. If the model is correct, this means that Reservoir 33 females either gain fecundity more rapidly with size or have lower juvenile mortality than do Twin Reservoir females. Field data indicate that Reservoir 33 females do gain fecundity with size more rapidly than Twin Reservoir females, but we have no information as yet on differences in mortality rates.

For males (Fig. 3b), the trajectory for the Reservoir 33 fish lies below and to the left of the trajectory for the Twin Reservoir fish, intersecting it near its right terminus. Whereas Twin Reservoir males mature later at smaller sizes

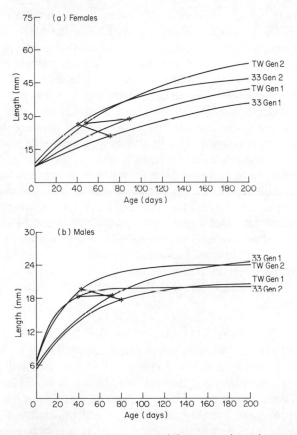

Fig. 3. Experimentally determined shifts in age and size at maturity under stress in mosquitofish from two populations exposed to different environments for the last 75 years. (a) Females. (b) Males. The relative location of the trajectories for the two populations is consistent with what is known of the rates of fecundity gain in the two populations in the field. It also suggests that juvenile mortality rates, which have not yet been measured in the field, should be higher in Twin Reservoir than in Reservoir 33.

under stress, Reservoir 33 males mature later at the same size. This could indicate that juvenile mortality increases as growth rates decrease in Reservoir 33 but not in Twin Reservoir, that Reservoir 33 males, like Reservoir 33 females, gain fecundity more rapidly with size than do Twin Reservoir males, or else have lower juvenile mortality rates.

This case suggests the strengths and weaknesses of our approach. Because so many factors can affect the position and shape of the trajectory, if two trajectories differ then one is left with a short list of possible causes rather than a single cause. This helps to suggest further research, but it does not constitute a test of the model except in the sense that demonstrating qualitative consistency can be considered a weak test.

2. *Male platyfish.* McKenzie *et al.* (1982) raised male platyfish (*Xiphophorus maculatus*) of two genotypes under an extreme range of conditions. One genotype matures later and at a larger size than the other genotype. McKenzie *et al.* plotted the ages and sizes at maturity for both genotypes in age-size space, and discovered that the data could be described by two L-shaped, non-overlapping envelopes, one centred at 84 days and the other at 140 days. The shape of the envelopes indicates that juvenile mortality probably increases as growth rates decrease in this species. The average distance between the trajectories cannot be accounted for by differences in juvenile mortality rates, since both types of males are inseminating females in the same populations. If the difference were to be accounted for simply by differences in fecundity, the model requires that the smaller and earlier-maturing genotype gain fecundity with size 10–15 times as fast as does the larger and later-maturing genotype. This seems implausible, since larger males should have access to mates as good as or better than small males. That leaves differences in adult mortality as a potential explanation. If the earlier-maturing males have significantly higher adult mortality, the observed pattern would be consistent with the predictions of the model. No one knows whether they do or not, but it would at least be plausible if they did.

3. *Rats and humans.* We could find only two cases in which other vertebrates had been raised with and without stress where ages and sizes at maturity had been recorded. Kennedy and Mitra (1963) raised normally fed and starved rats to maturity, and found that they matured later and at smaller sizes under stress. This is consistent with prediction if slower growth is not correlated with adult mortality and only weakly related to juvenile mortality. Frisch (1978) analysed the differences between well-fed modern Hutterite populations in the U.S.A. and food-stressed English and Scottish populations in the period 1850–1870. The Hutterite girls attained menarche at 12–13 years of age and were fit to conceive at 18; nineteenth-century British women attained menarche at 15–16 and were fit to conceive at 22. Capacity to bear children in humans coincides with the cessation of physical growth; thus Hutterite

women also stop growing earlier. Bongaarts (1980) cites several types of evidence that indicate that malnutrition has a substantial effect on delaying menarche. For example, age at menarche has declined by three years in Western societies since the end of the last century, and this decline has been associated with improved diet and larger body sizes. These patterns in humans are consistent with the predictions of these models if malnourished women bear fewer children that have higher juvenile mortality than well-fed women, as Frisch (1978) reports.

IV. DISCUSSION

Our model is in qualitative agreement with all the evidence presented, and in quantitative agreement with that portion of the evidence where enough parameters could be estimated to make a quantitative prediction meaningful. This does not mean that the model has been strongly validated, because none of the evidence was gathered for the specific purpose of probing the model's weakest points, such as its assumptions about the manner in which juvenile mortality of offspring varies with age-at-maturity of parent. Thus the success of the qualitative predictions is perhaps more impressive than that of the quantitative predictions.

To us, the most striking attribute of this model is its ability to provide a unified explanation for diverse phenomena that had not previously been seen as related. First, it does away with a disagreement one occasionally finds in the literature, a disagreement over whether organisms mature at a fixed size or at a fixed age. It does so by revealing that neither age nor size at maturity need be considered the trait under selection; instead, selection operates on the shape of the age-size maturation trajectory. Over some portions of such trajectories, organisms appear to mature at a fixed size; over other portions of such trajectories, organisms appear to mature at a fixed age. Only by considering maturation events occurring across a wide range of growth rates can the shape of the whole trajectory be perceived.

Secondly, it suggests that instead of a single general trajectory, as Alm (1959) believed, there are at least four types of trajectories (Fig. 1), and that these correspond to particular demographic conditions. For example, when reduced growth rates are strongly correlated with increased adult mortality, then organisms should mature earlier at smaller sizes, and the trajectory is J-shaped. This result agrees with our intuition about what an organism should do if a change in the environment increases adult mortality without altering juvenile mortality. Because the adult is "worth" less, it should mature early and convert its biomass into offspring, whose chances of survival are better. Similar intuitive explanations can be readily constructed for the other types of trajectories.

Thirdly, it unifies genetic and environmental explanations of variation in age and size at maturity. These have not always been seen as components of a single explanation in the literature. For example, in constructing his review of factors which influence the maturation of Atlantic salmon, Gardner (1976) chose to organize his material by contrasting "environmental" and "genetic" hypotheses, as though they were mutually exclusive. In our model, the environment imposes changes in growth rates and, at times, in juvenile and adult mortality rates. We assume that the populations have encountered these changes over evolutionary time, and that particular trajectories of age and size at maturity have evolved in each population and represent the genetically fixed and adaptive component of the organisms' response.

Fourthly, Mann (personal communication) has noted in dace that as stress increases, gonadosomatic index remains the same but fewer, larger eggs are produced. Only when stress becomes extreme does gonadosomatic index decline. This observation was certainly not predicted by our model, but it is consistent with it if larger eggs result in lower juvenile mortality. In all simulations, the age-size maturation trajectory was much more sensitive to changes in juvenile mortality than to changes in fecundity, and the same was true for the sensitivity of the Malthusian parameter. Mann's observation suggests that the primary response to stress is a change in egg size that reduces juvenile mortality; reduction in the proportion of biomass allocated to reproduction is a secondary response. Clearly, more than one trait can be conceived as having a plastic trajectory in response to stress. How a number of such traits interact to produce an appropriate, coordinated response to stress that reflects the demographic history of the population is an open, and a challenging, problem.

Models are often limited by the range of conditions in nature that correspond plausibly to the assumptions used. In this model, we have assumed that the Malthusian parameter defines fitness, that populations are in stable age distribution (i.e., the Euler-Lotka relation applies), and that adaptations represent responses to average conditions, not to the variance in conditions. Since it was the life-histories of fish that originally suggested (Murphy, 1968) that adaptations to unpredictability are important, these features may seem particularly restrictive to fisheries biologists. Thus an important extension of this work will be the examination of other fitness definitions applied to populations in which mortality rates are random variables.

ACKNOWLEDGEMENTS

The senior author thanks the Fisheries Society of the British Isles for the opportunity to present this work and for travel support. Comments by Bob Wootton, N. Lloyd, Jim Murray, and David Policansky improved the presentation. This research was supported by NSF DEB 78-22812, by an NIH Biomedical Research Support Grant, and by a Vollum Junior Sabbatical awarded by Reed College to the senior author.

REFERENCES

Alberch, P., Gould, S. J., Oster, G. F. and Wake, D. B. (1979). *Paleobiology* **5**, 296–317.

Alm, G. (1959). *Rept. Inst. Freshw. Res., Drottningholm* **40**, 1–145.

Bagenal, T. B. (1969). *J. Fish. Biol.* **1**, 176–182.

Bilton, H. T., Alderdice, D. F. and Schnute, J. T. (1982). *Can. J. Fish. aquat. Sci.* **39**, 426–447.

Bongaarts, J. (1980). *Science, N.Y.* **208**, 564–569.

Bowering, W. R. (1976). *J. Fish. Res. Bd., Can.* **33**, 1574–1584.

Crandall, R. E. and Stearns, S. C. (1982). *Theor. Pop. Biol.* **21**, 11–23.

DeMartini, E. E. and Anderson, M. E. (1980). *Env. Biol. Fish.* **5**, 33–47.

Donaldson, L. R. and Olson, P. R. (1955). *Trans. Am. Fish. Soc.* **85**, 93–101.

Drickamer, L. C. (1981). *Behav. Neur. Biol.* **31**, 82–89.

Fabens, A. (1965). *Growth* **29**, 265–289.

Foerster, R. E. (1968). "The Sockeye Salmon, *Onchorhynchus nerka*". Queen's Printer, Ottawa.

Frisch, R. E. (1978). *Science, N.Y.* **199**, 22–30.

Gadgil, M. and Bossert, W. (1970). *Am. Nat.* **104**, 1–24.

Gardner, M. L. G. (1976). *J. Fish Biol.* **9**, 289–327.

Grainger, E. H. (1953). *J. Fish. Res. Bd., Can.* **10**, 326–370.

Hagen, H. K. (1970). *In* "Biology of Coregonid Fishes" (C. C. Lindsey and C. S. Woods, eds), pp. 399–415. University of Manitoba Press, Winnipeg.

Jones, A. (1974). *J. mar. biol. Ass. U.K.* **54**, 109–125.

Kennedy, G. C. and Mitra, J. (1963). *J. Physiol. (Lond.)* **166**, 408–418.

Kipling, C. and Frost, W. E. (1969). *J. Fish Biol.* **1**, 221–237.

Kneib, R. T. (1978). *Copeia* **1978**, 164–178.

Mann, R. H. K. (1973). *J. Fish Biol.* **5**, 707–736.

Mann, R. H. K. (1974). *J. Fish Biol.* **6**, 237–253.

Mann, R. H. K. (1976a). *J. Fish Biol.* **8**, 179–197.

Mann, R. H. K. (1976b). *J. Fish Biol.* **8**, 265–288.

Mann, R. H. K. (1980). *J. Fish Biol.* **17**, 163–176.

McKenzie, W., Crews, D., Kallman, K. D., Policansky, D. and Sohn, J. J. (1982). *Copeia* (in press).

Molander, A. R. (1925). *Publs. Circonst. Cons. perm. int. Explor. Mer.* **85**, 15.

Moore, J. W. (1975). *J. Fish Biol.* **7**, 143–151.

Murphy, G. I. (1968). *Am. Nat.*, **102**, 390–404.

Papageorgiou, N. K. (1979). *J. Fish Biol.* **14**, 529–538.

Pinhorn, A. T. (1969). *J. Fish. Res. Bd., Can.* **26**, 3133–3164.

Pitt, T. K. (1975). *J. Fish. Res. Bd., Can.* **32**, 1383–1398.

Schaffer, W. M. and Elson, P. F. (1975). *Ecology* **56**, 577–590.

Scott, D. P. (1962). *J. Fish. Res. Bd., Can.* **19**, 715–731.

Staples, D. J. (1975a). *J. Fish Biol.* **7**, 1–24.

Staples, D. J. (1975b). *J. Fish Biol.* **7**, 25–46.

Stearns, S. C. (1982). *In* "Evolution and Development" (J. T. Bonner, ed.), pp. 237–258. Springer Verlag, Berlin, Heidelberg, and New York.

Stearns, S. C. (1983). *Am. Zool.* **23**, 65–76.

Stearns, S. C. and Crandall, R. E. (1981). *Evolution* **35**, 455–463.

Stephens, R. T. T. (1982). *J. Fish Biol.* **20**, 259–270.

Tweddle, D. and Turner, J. L. (1977). *J. Fish Biol.* **10**, 385–398.

Wootton, R. J. (1973). *J. Fish Biol.* **5**, 89–96.

APPENDIX

{This program is written in PASCAL.
It calculates the optimal age and size at which to mature given the growth rates defined
in the program.}

```
program  mass (input, output);
const     eps = 0.01;        {sets tolerance for estimate of optimal r}
          a0 = 0.01;         {defines adult mortality as a constant for this run}
          delta = 0.001;     {defines the increment used in calculating derivatives}
          A = 1500;          {defines limiting size in the Von Bertlanffy equation}
          B = 0.999;         {defines size at birth as 0.001 × limiting size}

var       alpx,rho,malp,der,k,alp,test0,test1,test2,inc,lam,laml,H,F:real;
```

{alpx and alp are both estimates of optimal age at maturity. The program
first tries to estimate that age using a convergence algorithm in procedure
"alpha0". If that procedure fails, as it must if there is a discontinuity in r
when alp is varied, then the program tries to estimate optimal alpha simply
by incrementing alpha and calculating r. This is done in procedure
"alpha1". rho is the power to which alpha is raised in defining the juvenile
mortality function, malp is mass-at-maturity, der is a derivative, k is
growth rate, the test0, test1, test2 variables are used to test for proximity to
a solution, lam is the numerator in the function defining juvenile mortality,
H is the intercept of the fecundity size relation, and F is the slope of the
fecundity-size relation.}

```
          logic1,logic2,logic3:boolean;
```

{The logic variables are used to test for the satisfaction of the three
conditions necessary and sufficient to define an optimal alpha. These
conditions are given as Equations 1.5, 1.6, and 1.7 in the preceeding paper.}

```
          i,switch:integer;
function  a:real;
          begin
                    a: = a0;
          end;
```

{function a defines adult mortality rate. A constant is used here, but any desired
function can be substituted. It was by redefining this function that we made adult
mortality a function of growth rate.}

```
function  j(alp:real):real;
          begin
                    j: = lam*exp( − rho*ln(alp)) + a;
          end;
```

{function j defines juvenile mortality as a function of age-at-maturity, alp, and two
parameters, lam and rho. lam scales juvenile mortality up or down, and rho changes
the shape of the hyperbola. Juvenile mortality is asymptotically equal to adult
mortality for large age-at-maturity.}

```
function  mass (k,x:real):real;
```

```
var        test:real;
           begin
                    test:=H+F*(A*(1.0−B*(exp(−k*x))));
                    if not (test>0) then test:=0.00000001;
                    mass:=test;
           end;
```

{function mass defines fecundity as a linear function of size at a given age, x. H and F are the intercept and slope of the linear relation of fecundity and size, and A, B, and k are the parameters of the Von Bertalanffy growth curve.}

```
function   f(alp:real)real;
var        term1,term2:real;
           begin
                    terml:= − exp(lam*exp(ln(alp)*(1.0−rho)));
                    term2:=(1−rho)*lam*exp(−ln(alp)*rho);
                    f:=terml*term2;
           end;
```

{function   f(alp:real):real;
           begin
                    f:=lam/sqr(alp)*exp(lam/alp);
           end;}

```
function   q(k,alp:real):real;
var        term:real;
           begin
                    term:=(rho−1.0)*lam*exp(−ln(alp)*rho);
                    term:=term/mass(k,alp);
                    q:=term;
           end:
```

{function   q(k,alp:real):real;
           begin
                    q:=(lam/sqr(alp))/mass(k,alp);
           end;}

{functions f and q correspond to equations 1.4 and 1.5 of the paper. We give two forms for each function. The first form is general, and allows the user to vary the value of rho, which is the exponent to which age-at-maturity is raised in the juvenile mortality function. The second form, given here inside curly braces {}, assumes that rho=2. This assumption was used in making the predictions for 19 fish populations in the paper.}

```
function   g(k,alp:real):real;
           begin
                    g:= − ln(f(alp)/mass(k,alp));
           end;
```

{functions f and q correspond to equations 1.4 and 1.5 of the paper. We give two forms calculating a derivative.}

```
function   alpha0 (k:real):real;
var        n:integer;
           lowlim,uplim,numer,denom,test,testlast:real;
```

```
begin
        n: = 0;
        lowlim: = 0·0001;
        uplim: = 10000.0;
        repeat
                n: = n + 1;
                alp: = (lowlim + uplim)/2.0;
                numer: = q(k,alp)*mass(k,alp);
                denom: = − ln(q(k,alp))/alp + k + a − j(alp);
                test: = numer/denom;
                if (test < 0) and (testlast > 0) then alpx: = alp;
                testlast: = test;
                if test > 1 then lowlim: = alp;
                if test < 1 then uplim: = alp
        until (abs(test − 1.0) < eps)or(n = 50);
        alpha0: = alp;
        if n = 50 then alpha0: = − 1
end;
```

{function alpha0 estimates optimal age-at-maturity using a convergence algorithm. It will not be successful if there is a discontinuity in the relationship between r and age-at-maturity. If successful, it returns the value of age-at-maturity. If not, it returns the value − 1.}

```
function    alphal(k:real):real;
var         numer,denom,test:real;
begin
        alp: = alpx;
        repeat
                alp: = alp + 0.01;
                numer: = q(k,alp)*mass(k,alp);
                denom: = − ln(q(k,alp))/alp + k + a − j(alp);
                test: = numer/denom;
        until (abs(test − 1.0) < eps)or(alp = 500.0);
        alphal: = alp;
        if alp = 500.0 then alphal: = − 1
end;
```

{function alphal calculates optimal age-at-maturity simply by incrementing age-at-maturity and calculating the corresponding value for r under the given conditions. If successful, it returns the proper age-at-maturity. If not, it returns the value − 1.}

```
begin                                   {mainline}
        read(laml,F,H,rho);
        writeln(laml:8:3,F:8:3,H:6:0,rho:6:2);
        inc: = − 0.5;
        for i: = 1 to 10 do begin        {start loop varying growth rate}
                inc: = inc − 0.5;
                k: = exp(ln(10.0)*inc);
                lam: = 0.00316228*laml/k;        {let juvenile mortality
                                                      vary with k}
                alp: = 999999.0;
                logicl: = true;
```

```
logic2: = true;
logic3: = true;
test0: = 0;
test1: = 0;
alpx: = 0.0;
test0: = alpha0(k);        {try first algorithm for
                                optimal alpha}
if test0 > 0 then alp: = test0;
if test0 = − 1 then test1: = alpha1 (k);        {try second
                                                    algorithm}
if test1 > 0 then alp: = test1;
if (test0 = − 1)and(test1 = − 1) then logic1: = false;
test2: = q(k,alp)*exp(alp*j(alp));
if (logic1)and(not(test2 > 0)and(test2 < 1)) then logic2: = false;
der: = (g(k,alp + delta) − g(k,alp))/delta;
der: = der − g(k,alp)/alp;
if (logic1)and(logic2)and(not(der > 0)) then logic3: = false;
```

{if logic1 = false, then there is no positive real age-at-maturity at which the first derivative of r equals zero. If logic2 = false, then the derivative equals zero but r is negative. If logic3 = false, then the second derivative is not negative, and we have no assurance of a local maximum.}

```
malp: = A*(1.0 − B*exp( − k*alp));
```

{calculate mass-at-maturity}

```
if logic1 then switch: = 1;
if (not (logic2))and(logic1) then switch: = 2;
if ((logic1)and(logic2))and(not(logic3)) then switch: = 3;
writeln(k:12:6,malp:12:3,alp:12:3,switch:4,' 0')
```

{write out results}

```
        end;
end.
```

3. Patterns in the Evolution of Reproductive Styles in Fishes

E. K. BALON

Department of Zoology, College of Biological Science, University of Guelph, Ontario, Canada

Abstract: Reproductive styles of fishes exhibit distinct patterns which can be classified in a system of reproductive guilds. Such guilds are evolutionary trends, i.e. viable steady states within reproductive and developmental variations separated by saltatory nonviable thresholds. Within each guild significant variations permit the selection of vital adaptations to changing environments and associations and form the main basis for the evolution of new reproductive styles.

I. INTRODUCTION

The term "style" encompasses the meanings of "programme" (Dawkins, 1982), "strategy" and "tactics" (Cohen, 1977), and although used in the same sense does not replace them since I believe that epigenesis should be considered an equal partner to gene programmes (Balon, 1983a). For reproductive styles (and also for life history and evolution) early ontogeny is at least as important as, for example, courtship and mating behaviour, oogenesis, spermiogenesis, parental care or fertilization. The development of a classification devoted to reproductive styles in fishes started with Kryzhanovsky's proposals on the definitions and groupings of these styles (Kryzhanovsky's, 1948, 1949). This classification was completed by incorporating all known reproductive styles of marine and freshwater taxa (Balon, 1962, 1964a,b, 1965, 1975a,c, 1978, 1981c; Balon *et al.*, 1977). Later, the importance of early ontogeny for the formation of structures and events in later ontogeny was proposed (Balon, 1981a, 1983a), and these investigations led to a re-examination of the significance of life-history phenomena such as hatching, parturition and larvae (Balon, 1975c, 1977, 1980, 1981a; Noakes and Balon, 1982). In this paper I should like to concentrate on evolutionary patterns of reproductive styles, recapitulating the scattered earlier data with a new perspective.

FISH REPRODUCTION
ISBN 0–12–563660–1

II. PATTERNS AND MODELS: A RECAPITULATION

A. The theory of saltatory ontogeny

The concept of saltatory development was first applied in animals to the ontogeny of fishes (Vasnecov, 1953; Kryzhanovsky *et al.*, 1953), following its use in plants (Medvedev, 1969). Our present understanding and application of the complex theory of saltatory ontogeny differs significantly from those of the past (Balon, 1984).

Changes in structures and functions during ontogeny have usually been regarded as gradual processes, which may proceed at various rates at different times (Brody, 1945; Martin, 1949), so that development is interpreted as proceeding via a continuous, inconspicuous accumulation of small changes. Rapid changes in form and function are recognized only rarely when a dramatic metamorphosis occurs. During this the animal, which in an earlier ontogenic interval looks nothing like its parents, changes rapidly into a parent-like juvenile. Some larval forms, which typically require metamorphosis to change into small adults, were first described as separate organisms, e.g. the echinoderm pluteus, hemichordate tornaria, lamprey ammocoetes, eel leptocephalus, chaetodontid tholichthys, acanthurid acronurus, brotulid exterilium, and tunicate and amphibian tadpoles.

Since development was perceived as a continuous succession of growth and small changes most investigators felt justified in selecting "normal stages" to represent ontogeny and assumed that, except for some variable rates, nothing of importance can be missed between such stages. Metamorphosis, if present, had to be attended to separately (Etkin and Gilbert, 1968).

Saltatory processes in ontogeny, however, are more than variable developmental rates. Structures which together form a system (organ) align their rates of development to become simultaneously functional (Carey and Noakes, 1981) and initiate a new function — e.g. photoresponse, change of substratum, nutrition — at a highly accelerated rate (Fig. 1). This "high speed" switch is what I call a threshold, a rapid transition from one state to another of the organism–environment interaction. Depending on the number of coinciding structures and functions and their adaptive or developmental significance, the "height" of thresholds will vary, as will the preceding and following life-history intervals. The recognition of thresholds is often difficult (McElman and Balon, 1979, 1980; Balon, 1979a, 1981a) because competing functions obscure the clear relationships between form and function (Bock, 1980, 1981).

Nevertheless, the recognition of ontogeny as saltatory will have an important and decisive effect on the way experiments are designed, data interpreted and conclusions drawn. The various rates in time of "stasis" and the existence of intervening thresholds should not be ignored, for no arbitrary representation can replace the existence of natural boundaries between steady

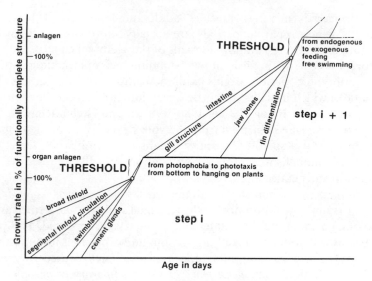

Fig. 1.   Two consecutive steps bordered by thresholds in early ontogeny of the zope, *Abramis ballerus* (after Balon, 1959).

state intervals of ontogeny. In other words, we can no longer assume a simple correlation between variables of two consecutive stages. In addition, recognizing "... the saltatory origin of key features (around which subsequent adaptations may be moulded) and marked phenotypic shifts caused by small genetic changes that affect rates of development in early ontogeny with cascading effects thereafter" (Gould, 1982b, pp. 88–89), we may better understand the epigenetic mechanisms of evolution (Alberch, 1980).

B. A life-history model

A basic set of unambiguous terms applicable to a saltatory model of ontogeny for at least all vertebrates, was *defined* (Balon, 1975c) and some earlier terms, exclusive to fishes, had to be abandoned because of their vague and confused meanings and because of their limitation to "egg and larval" fish taxonomy, which failed to integrate these terms into the basic science of developmental biology. Hatching and parturition, for example, are rarely natural thresholds (Noakes, 1978, 1981) and therefore, insignificant in the life-history model. Also, the "yolksac larva" was superseded by an epigenetic understanding of what an embryo actually entails.

The saltatory model of ontogeny is a hierarchial system of intervals — periods, phases and steps. Stage refers to an instantaneous state of ontogeny and should not be confused with an interval. The entire ontogeny, from beginning (Balon, 1981a) to end, consists of four or five periods — embryonic, larval (sometimes missing), juvenile, adult and senescent (Table I). The thresholds which separate periods are usually more distinct than those separating the shortest saltatory intervals of ontogeny called steps. They are, therefore, easier to distinguish, notwithstanding their epigenetic significance.

The embryonic period begins with activation (or, to be less exact, fertilization) which initiates the cortical reaction and bipolar differentiation, etc. (for details see Balon, 1975c, 1980, 1981a), and is characterized by an *exclusively endogenous nutrition* from the yolk of the ovum or, in viviparous fishes, nutrition via special absorptive organs from an ovarian secretion or embryonic cannibalism and/or a combination of yolk and secretion (as explained in the next section).

The larval period commences with the transition to *exogenous feeding* and usually lasts until metamorphosis, when an axial skeleton has formed and the (embryonic) median finfold is differentiated or has disappeared. This period often begins with a step of mixed endogenous and exogenous feeding, a safety adaptation against asynchronous appearance of prey caused by environmental perturbations. The *persistence of some temporary embryonic organs*

TABLE I.   The opposite ends of evolutionary trends of the life-history model and the hierarchy of intervals in ontogeny based on natural saltatory boundaries (bottom half of the table).

Periods and phases	
Generalist (altricial)	Specialist (precocial)
Embryonic	Embryonic
cleavage egg	cleavage egg
embryo	embryo
free embryo (eleutheroembryo)	free embryo
Larval	Juvenile
finfold larva (apterolarva)[a]	
finformed larva (pterolarva)[a]	
Juvenile	Adult
Adult	
(Senescent)	Senescent

Period: the longest interval of ontogeny separated by the strongest thresholds.
Phase: the next longest interval into which periods are divided as morphophysiological units for identification purposes but of lesser saltatory significance — the phases of embryonic period are: cleavage, embryonic and free embryonic (or eleutheroembryonic); of larval period (if present): finfold larva (apterolarva) and finformed larva (pterolarva); juvenile period, e.g. in anadromous salmonids can be divided into: parr, smolt and juvenile.
Step: the shortest natural interval of ontogeny separated by thresholds, the most important homeostatic state of epigenesis (Balon, 1983a).
Stage: an instantaneous state of ontogeny; should not be used to denote interval.

[a] After Rass (1968).

(e.g. respiratory plexuses) and the *development of special larval temporary organs* (e.g. respiratory vessels in fins, in gill covers, various spines, flaps and filamentous appendages) also characterize this period. Those transient features (Oppenheim, 1981) disappear when their functions become unnecessary or are replaced by different definitive organs with identical functions. This period can be extremely long in some fishes (e.g. eels) but is truncated or ultimately entirely eliminated in fishes with a large reproductive cost (Miller, 1979; Bell, 1980) and large young at the time of transition to exogenous feeding (see figures in the next section). In short, a larval period is present mostly in fishes with distinct metamorphoses but is absent in fishes which develop definitive organs throughout the embryonic period (Cohen, 1977).

The juvenile period begins when the fins are fully differentiated and all the significant *temporary organs* have been replaced by *definitive organs*. The transition from larva to juvenile (i.e. metamorphosis) involves mostly extensive and relatively rapid changes from unfishlike into adultlike forms (Wilbur and Collins, 1973; Smith-Gill and Berven, 1979). When the larval period is eliminated and a juvenile immediately follows the embryonic period, the onset of exogenous feeding is the period's boundary. The juvenile period lasts until the maturation of the first gametes and may be characterized by rapid growth and a specific juvenile coloration.

The adult period commences with maturation of the first gametes and is characterized by a spawning run, spawning concentration or by special behaviour accompanied by changes in colour and/or morphology. Spawning — being a series of courtships, matings and gamete depositions (in oviparous fishes) — can be repeated in seasonal or circannual rhythms (iteroparous), in alternate years, less often (Bull and Shine, 1979), or performed only once (semelparous). Somatic growth often decreases substantially, or as in the case of semelparous fishes, becomes completely arrested. Because of changes in growth rates, period boundaries can be established using relative growth indices (Balon, 1964c, 1974).

The senescent period begins when the reproduction rate of cells in most tissues has reached its limits (see also Woodhead, 1979; Oppenheim, 1981, pp. 95–96). Growth slows considerably, stops permanently, or even becomes negative. Gametes, if produced, are inferior (personal unpublished observations in *Cyprinodon* spp.). This period lasts for years (e.g. sturgeons) or days (e.g. semelparous annuals and Pacific salmons).

The basic saltatory intervals are steps (Fig. 1, Table I). Phases, subdivisions of each period, are merely a convenient means of morpho-physiological identification but are of little saltatory relevance (Balon, 1975c; Balon and Noakes, 1980). Names given to various stages of fishes at different intervals of ontogeny may be based on phases, hence — cleavage eggs, embryos, free embryos, finfold and finformed larvae, alevins, parrs, smolts, juveniles — all unambiguous biological terms applicable to fishes but understood by specialists in other vertebrates also. Various reproductive styles in fishes will markedly differ in the duration, character and even presence of successive periods (e.g. larval) in ontogeny.

III. CLASSIFICATION OF REPRODUCTIVE STYLES

Reproductive styles in fishes, as far as we know from the several hundred cases studied (Breder and Rosen, 1966), form distinct patterns. Kryzhanovsky (1948) had an idea that using some combined features of early development and reproduction (Gerbilsky, 1956), ecological groupings of fishes would be possible, and constructed a classification based on selected spawning features, environmental factors and ontogenetic characters (Kryzhanovsky, 1949; Kryzhanovsky *et al.*, 1951). Greek or Latin names denoted the different groups according to their respective spawning substrata. This system, however, was restricted mainly to freshwater fishes of a certain geographical area. Since then only Disler *et al.* (1965), Holčik and Hruška (1966) and Kuznetsov (1977) have made attempts to add other groups.

Kryzhanovsky's idea was expanded into an evolutionary classification of reproductive guilds thereby attempting to encompass all known reproductive trends in fishes, plotting additional characters (Balon, 1975a,b). Further additions and amendments were recently published (Balon, 1981a,c).

The concept of reproductive guilds rests on the assumption that it should reflect evolutionary trajectories. In this hierarchial system (Table II) the succession of guilds in each ecological group and the succession of groups

TABLE II. Classification of reproductive styles of fishes in order of putative evolutionary trajectories (as per Fig. 1 in Balon 1981b).

ETHOLOGICAL SECTION	A. NONGUARDERS
Ecological group	A.1 Open substratum egg-scatterers
Guild	Representative species
A.1.1 Pelagic spawners	*Clupeonella delicatula*
A.1.2 Rock and gravel spawners with pelagic larvae	*Stizostedion vitreum*
A.1.3 Rock and gravel spawners with benthic larvae	*Catostomus commersoni*
A.1.4 Nonobligatory plant spawners	*Rutilus rutilus*
A.1.5 Obligatory plant spawners	*Cyprinus carpio*
A.1.6 Sand spawners	*Gobio gobio*
A.1.7 Terrestrial spawners	*Galaxias maculatus*

TABLE II — *continued*

	Ecological group	A.2 Brood hiders
A.2.1	Beach hiders	*Leuresthes tenuis*
A.2.2	Annual fishes	*Cynolebias bellotti*
A.2.3	Rock and gravel hiders	*Salvelinus namaycush*
A.2.4	Cavity hiders	*Astyanax mexicanus*
A.2.5	Hiders in live invertebrates	*Rhodeus sericeus*

ETHOLOGICAL SECTION   B. GUARDERS

	Ecological group	B.1 Substratum choosers
B.1.1	Pelagic tenders	*Anabas testudinosus*
B.1.2	Above water tenders	*Copeina arnoldi*
B.1.3	Rock tenders	*Chromis chromis*
B.1.4	Plant tenders	*Leucaspius delineatus*

	Ecological group	B.2 Nest spawners
B.2.1	Froth nesters	*Macropodus opercularis*
B.2.2	Miscellaneous substratum nesters	*Lepomis gibbosus*
B.2.3	Rock and gravel nesters	*Micropterus dolomieui*
B.2.4	Gluemaking nesters	*Gasterosteus aculeatus*
B.2.5	Plant material nesters	*Amia calva*
B.2.6	Sand nesters	*Abbottina rivularis*
B.2.7	Hole nesters	*Neogobius melanostomus*
B.2.8	Anemone nesters	*Amphiprion chrysopterus*

ETHOLOGICAL SECTION   C. BEARERS

	Ecological group	C.1 External bearers
C.1.1	Transfer brooders	*Corydoras aeneus*
C.1.2	Auxiliary brooders	*Kurtus gulliveri*
C.1.3	Mouth brooders	*Labeotropheus trewavasae*
C.1.4	Gill-chamber brooders	*Amblyopsis spelaea*
C.1.5	Pouch brooders	*Syngnathus abaster*

	Ecological group	C.2 Internal bearers
C.2.1	Facultative internal bearers	*Oryzias latipes*
C.2.2	Obligate lecithotrophic internal bearers	*Poecilia reticulata*
C.2.3	Matrotrophous oophages and adelphophages	*Lamna cornubica*
C.2.4	Viviparous trophoderms	*Zoarces viviparus*
C.2.5	Viviparous yolksac placentals	*Mustelus canis*

within the three ethological sections — A: nonguarders; B: guarders; and C: bearers — follow trends from less to more protective styles (Balon, 1981b). Because the main trends of reproductive guilds may be shaped by something akin to "species selection" (Eldredge and Gould, 1972; Stanley, 1975, 1979; Gould and Eldredge, 1977; Gould, 1982a,b; Levinton and Simon, 1980), it is highly relevant to first examine some of the trends among guilds. The variation repeatedly reinstated by reproduction and enhanced by epigenesis will form the *real* substrate for natural selection of complex reproductive steady states (Dawkins, 1978, 1982). We shall consider this variation elsewhere (Balon, 1983a), together with the processes which both stabilize and modify the reproductive guilds.

Most fishes are nonguarding, egg-scattering pelagic spawners characterized by small, nutrient-poor ova produced in high numbers, delayed embryonic differentiation and a long larval period terminated by metamorphosis (Fig. 2). This reproductive style seems to be the ancestral condition of reproductive styles in fishes and agrees with what is apparently the most plausible theory for the origin of chordates. It must have been the reproductive style of an adult tunicate with a ciliated, auricularia-like larva which through paedomorphosis eliminated its sessile lophophore-feeding adult period to become a pelagic spawning fish (Garstang, 1894, 1928). The guild of pelagic spawners consequently remained the most suitable style for the dominant marine environment. This style might also have been best suited, as Barlow (1981) emphasized, for dispersal, a feature of excellent survival value and therefore

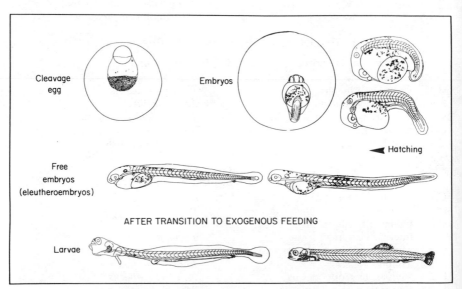

Fig. 2.   Early ontogeny of a nonguarding egg-scattering pelagic spawner (A.1.1) — *Clupeonella delicatula* (after Kryzhanovsky, 1956); state of differentiation in phases of the embryonic period and immediately thereafter (at first exogenous feeding).

selected for, irrespective of ancestral position. If so, the dispersal value was traded in for other values during the evolution of derived guilds, or most probably, the dispersal lost its initial value after new habitats were invaded.

The following example clearly indicates the value of the pelagic style. When the walleye, *Stizostedion vitreum*, evolved from some ancestral marine serranid (Collette and Banarescu, 1977) and invaded freshwater fluvial systems, its scattering of eggs on rocks and gravel in rivers enhanced their survival because invertebrate predators were scarce in comparison with similar marine habitats (Balon *et al.*, 1977). Embryonic differentiation could have been accelerated by increase of yolk volume in order to produce larger young at the first exogenous feeding; instead the pelagic larva was retained (Fig. 3) as a food gathering vegetative interval but the size at that transition remained too small for utilization of available food particles in the new system. Free embryos must drift to reach a planktonic "soup" with appropriate food particles (McElman and Balon, 1979).

Although it makes sense to escape invertebrate predation on cleavage eggs and on embryos by invading a freshwater environment (Kryzhanovsky, 1949; Soin, 1968), further escape from predation and more effective feeding of fishes can only occur if larger free embryos and larvae are produced. Salmonids evolved denser and larger ova from which more developed and larger young could be produced, and compensated for their higher energy value and lower numbers by hiding them under gravel (Smirnov, 1975; Balon, 1980). Concurrently, more and denser yolk, and larger embryos allowed the

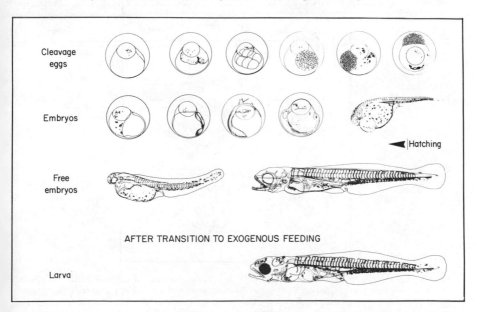

Fig. 3. Early ontogeny of a nonguarding egg-scattering rock and gravel spawner with pelagic larvae (A.1.2) – *Stizostedion vitreum* (after McElman and Balon, 1979).

formation of embryonic respiratory structures (both temporary circulatory plexuses and carotenoids, see Balon, 1979b, 1980) which compensated for the decreased availability of oxygen in hiding (Fig. 4). Accelerated (truncated) differentiation of embryos (adultation), necessary to produce competent young upon emergence from hiding, eliminated the true larval period and metamorphosis (Fig. 5).

Hiding, however, was not the only possible style of protecting zygotes with high investments. It must have been replaced or supplemented early by parental guardings. In principle any guild of nonguarding egg-scattering spawners could have evolved into guarders, but having the clutch concentrated in hiding might have been an advantage or prerequisite (Baylis, 1981). If increased guarding became worthwhile, the trends (relating to yolk amount and yolk density, and to the differentiation rate, size and developmental state of the young at first exogenous feeding) evident earlier in the trajectory from egg-scatterers to hiders should be more pronounced (Fig. 6).

Often additional unusual features develop; for example, the evolution of specific embryonic, larval and juvenile electric discharges enabling individuals of the species *Marcusenius* to communicate with their guarding parents (Kirschbaum and Westby, 1975, pp. 1291–1292).

A further step in evolution must have been a switch towards even more specialized measures, from guarding a clutch on a selected or prepared

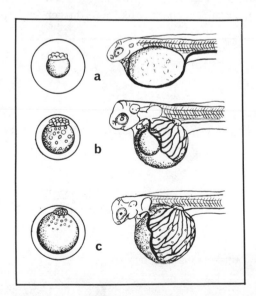

Fig. 4.   Cleavage eggs and embryos of a pelagic spawner *Caspialosa volgensis* with colourless yolk (a), rock and gravel spawner *Coregonus lavaretus* with yellow yolk (b), and rock and gravel hider *Thymallus arcticus* with an orange yolk (c) (after Soin, 1968). Note the increase in size of the vitelline respiratory plexuses (Balon, 1981c).

substratum, to bearing it on or inside the parent's body (e.g. Wake, 1980). Bearing further decreased the exposure of zygotes to predators and eliminated adverse environmental perturbations (e.g. water level fluctuations, Baylis, 1981) because the clutch was carried along (Fig. 7).

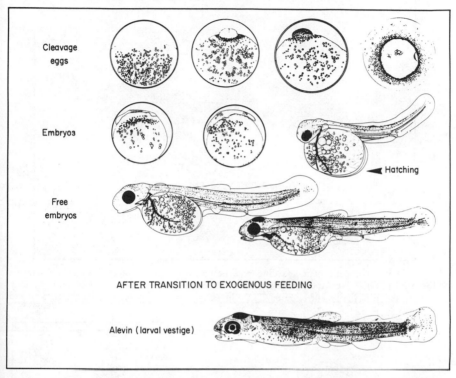

Fig. 5.   Early ontogeny of a nonguarding, zygote hiding rock and gravel spawner (A.2.3) — *Salvelinus namaycush* (after Balon, 1980). Note the truncated differentiation and the vestige of a larva only.

The evolution of mouthbrooding in general (Balon, 1981b), and specifically in cichlids (Thys van den Audenaerde, 1970) is probably polyphyletic (Noakes and Balon, 1982), but the over-estimation of the significance of hatching led Peters and Berns (1982a) to misinterpret the evolution of this style. There is little reason to judge solely from the time and developmental state of hatching alone that so-called "larvophilous" and "ovophilous" mouthbrooders had separate evolutionary origins from the substrate tenders. All the other evidences, however (regression of cement glands and both parent brooding or alternate and single parent brooding, Peters and Berns, 1979, 1982a,b) are incidental for survival (as explained below) and do not exclude the evolution

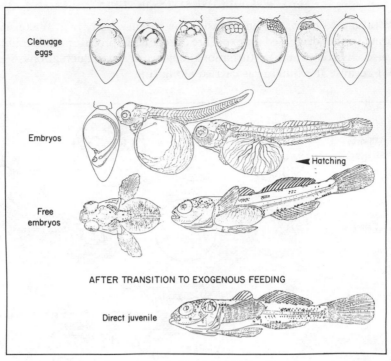

Fig. 6. Early ontogeny of a guarding hole nester (B.2.7) — *Neogobius melanostomus* (after Moskalkova, 1967). Note the strongly truncated differentiation, e.g. of the finfold, and resultant direct development of embryo into juvenile, without a larval intermediary.

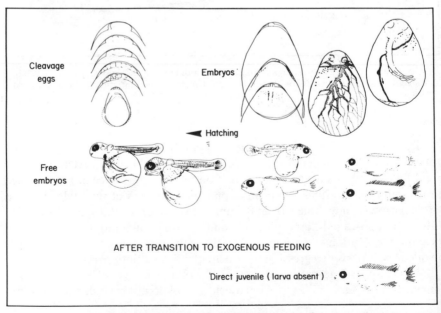

Fig. 7. Early ontogeny of an external mouthbrooding bearer (C.1.3) — *Labeotropheus fuelleborni* (after Balon, 1977). Note the extremely truncated differentiation in embryonic period.

of complete (ovophilous) mouthbrooders either directly from substrate tenders or via the intermediate (larvophilous) mouthbrooders. The changes in time and developmental state at hatching are probably developmental antecedents of only little significance for the organism–environmental interactions. At best they are the result of transient demands; for example, the availability of dissolved oxygen is lower for the brood when taken up into the mouth than it was during parental fanning, so there has to be compensation for this reduction. The comparatively accelerated hatching in intermediate mouthbrooders and delayed hatching in complete mouthbrooders (Fig. 8) can be due to an acquisition of a supplementary endogenous oxydative metabolism by the latter. The yolk of complete mouthbrooders contains more carotenoids which have been shown to serve as an endogenous source of oxygen (Balon, 1977, 1979b, 1980, 1981c).

In contrast, the valuable gain, which has clear survival consequences, is the increase in size and specialization at the time of first exogenous feeding, which

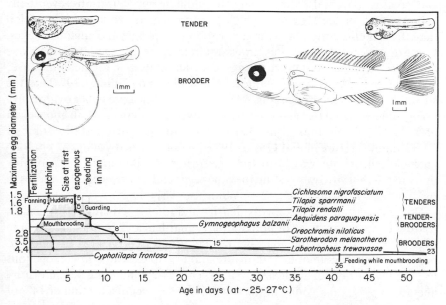

Fig. 8. The evolution of reproductive styles in cichlid fishes from tenders of clutch on a substrate, via intermediate initial substrate tenders and subsequent mouthbrooders, to mouthbrooders with immediate uptake of ova after or prior to fertilization. Fish figures represent the sizes and forms of substrate tender *Cichlasoma nigrofasciatum* and complete mouthbrooder *Labeotropheus trewavasae* at the time of hatching (left) and first exogenous feeding (right). In the diagram below tenders on a substrate are represented by *Cichlasoma nigrofasciatum* (after Balon, 1960), *Tilapia sparrmanii* and *Tilapia rendalli* (Philippart and Ruwet, 1982; Trewavas, 1982); intermediate mouthbrooders by *Aequidens paraguayensis* and *Gymnogeophagus balzanii* (Peters and Berns, 1982a); complete mouthbrooders by *Oreochromis niloticus*, *Sarotherodon melanotheron* (Philippart and Ruwet, 1982; Trewavas, 1982), and *Labeotropheus trewavasae* (after Balon, 1977); *Cyphotilapia frontosa* represents the most advanced style with exogenous feeding already during mouthbrooding (Balon, 1981c). Buccal uptake and brooding until the first release are represented by the dotted screen.

coincides with the release from huddling or brooding. Therefore, the emphasis is not on hatching but on time of first exogenous feeding. The increase of yolk volume and density (and of carotenoid content) supports further the illustrated sequence of evolution, but is ultimately also a consequence of initial behavioural changes in reproductive style which most likely preceded all the other changes. Over and above the developmental constraints imposed by the size and density of yolk, a further increase in size at release, i.e. at the first exposure to predators, had been achieved in *Cyphotilapia frontosa* by exogenous feeding during mouthbrooding. This example shows the importance of having a realistic life-history model based on comparative ontogeny and epigenetic principles (Balon, 1975c, 1984), when interpreting evolutionary patterns.

The only improvement left was to also eliminate the exposure of gametes; this was accomplished by internal fertilization. To compensate for the inevitable limitations in numbers of young, the scope of endogenous feeding expanded in a fascinating variety of ways (Table II). Livebearing trophoderms and yolksac placentals, while being the ultimate specializations, eventually compromised on steady states which produce smaller young at parturition than the evolutionarily simpler matrotrophous oophages and adelphophages. Using *Latimeria chalumnae* as an example to represent the latter case: one female 163 cm long contained 19 eggs, each about 9 cm in diameter and over 300 g in weight (Anthony and Millot, 1972; Millot and Anthony, 1974), i.e. the size and colour of an orange (Fig. 9a). Another female bore in her oviduct five highly differentiated free embryos, with an average length of 32 cm and weight of 550 g (Fig. 9b) (Smith *et al.*, 1975). After an estimated gestation time of 10–13 months (Hureau and Ozouf, 1977), a fully formed young, 42 cm long and 800 g in weight was born (released) (Fig. 9c, Balon, 1977), probably nurtured to that size by ingesting the other eggs and less developed embryos in the oviduct (Wourms *et al.*, 1980; Wourms, 1981).

Data concerning egg sizes, yolk density and total length at first exogenous feeding of some examples of nonguarders, guarders and bearers are given in Fig. 10. For example, the guarding nesters progressed through brooders to bearers from a zygote of 62% moisture and 6% lipids, and a first exogenous feeding juvenile 7% of adult size, to a larger zygote containing 52% moisture and 45% lipids and a young at the transition to exogenous feeding of 14% of average adult size.

In conclusion, ontogenies with larval periods and metamorphoses represent the ancestral condition, and ontogenies lacking both larval periods and metamorphoses and descendant steady states of evolutionary trends in reproductive styles. The salient features characterizing the two extremes are listed in Table III (see also Bonar, 1978).

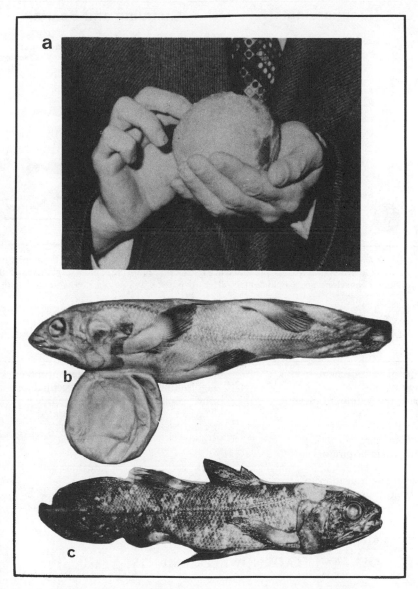

Fig. 9.   An egg, free embryo and a freshly released juvenile of an internal bearer, matrotrophous oophage – *Latimeria chalumnae* (photo a by K. Hensel, photos b and c by the author).

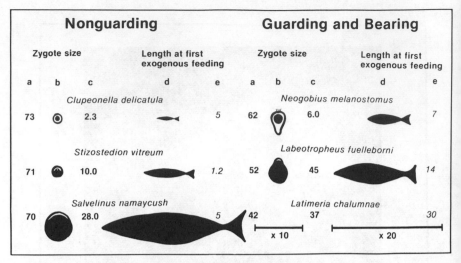

Fig. 10. Zygote sizes, densities and lengths at first exogenous feeding in selected examples of nonguarders, guarders and bearers, presented in Figs 2–7. a: % moisture content; b: relative size of ● yolk and O envelopes; c: % lipid content; d: relative size; e: in % of an average adult length.

TABLE III. Some properties marking the opposite ends of evolutionary trends in reproductive styles.

Type of development	metamorphic	ametamorphic
Type of egg	oligolecithal	polylecithal
Consistency/amount of yolk	watery/small	dense/large
Differentiation	delayed	accelerated
Larva	present	absent
Parental care	absent	present
Embryonic respiratory structures	weak	extensive
Size at the transition to exogenous feeding	small	large

ACKNOWLEDGEMENTS

David L. G. Noakes and my wife, Christine Flegler-Balon, stimulated several of the concepts and illustrations, and their comments or suggestions helped to attain more clarity. I thank Jeffrey Baylis (who also contributed the more apt term "tenders"), David Lavigne, Michael Paine, Susan Mahon and Joan Cunningham for several useful comments on the manuscript. The studies on which this work is based were supported by grants from the National Science and Engineering Research Council and University of Guelph.

REFERENCES

Alberch, P. (1980). *Am. Zool.* **20**, 653–667.
Anthony, J. and Millot, J. (1972). *C.r. Acad. Sci. Paris, Sér. D.* **224**, 1925–1927.
Balon, E. K. (1959). *Biologické práce* **5**, 1–87.
Balon, E. K. (1960). *Věst. Čs. spol. zool.* **24**, 199–214 (in Slovak).
Balon, E. K. (1962). *Biológia, Bratisl.* **17**, 283–296 (in Slovak).
Balon, E. K. (1964a). *Polskie Arch. Hydrobiol.* **12**, 233–251 (in Polish).
Balon, E. K. (1964b). *Hydrobiologia* **24**, 441–451.
Balon, E. K. (1964c). *Věst. Čs. spol. zool.* **28**, 369–379.
Balon, E. K. (1965). *Čs. Ochrana Prírody* **2**, 135–160 (in Slovak).
Balon, E. K. (1974). *In* "Lake Kariba: A Man-Made Tropical Ecosystem in Central Africa" (E. K. Balon and A. G. Coche, eds), pp. 249–676. Junk Publ., The Hague.
Balon, E. K. (1975a). *J. Fish. Res. Bd Can.* **32**, 821–864.
Balon, E. K. (1975b). *Verh. int. Verein. theor. angew. Limnol.* **19**, 2430–2439.
Balon, E. K. (1975c). *J. Fish. Res. Bd Can.* **32**, 1663–1670.
Balon, E. K. (1977). *Envir. Biol. Fish.* **2**, 147–176.
Balon, E. K. (1978). *Envir. Biol. Fish.* **3**, 149–152.
Balon, E. K. (1979). *Envir. Biol. Fish.* **4**, 97–101.
Balon, E. K. (1980). (ed.) "Charrs: Salmonid Fishes of the Genus *Salvelinus*". Junk Publ., The Hague.
Balon, E. K. (1981a). *Am. Zool.* **21**, 573–596.
Balon, E. K. (1981b). *Envir. Biol. Fish.* **6**, 129–138.
Balon, E. K. (1981c). *Envir. Biol. Fish.* **6**, 377–389.
Balon, E. K. (1982). *Proc. Intn. Symposium on Arctic Charr*, Winnipeg (in press).
Balon, E. K. (1983a). *Can. J. Fish. Aquat. Sci.* **40**, (in press).
Balon, E. K. (1984). *Trans. Am. Fish. Soc.* **113**, (in press).
Balon, E. K. and Noakes, D. L. G. (1980). "Principles of Ichthyology: Supplements to Lectures and Laboratory Exercises". Department of Zoology, Guelph.
Balon, E. K., Momot, W. T. and Regier, H. A. (1977). *J. Fish. Res. Bd Can.* **34**, 1910–1921.
Barlow, G. W. (1981). *Envir. Biol. Fish.* **6**, 65–85.
Baylis, J. R. (1981). *Envir. Biol. Fish.* **6**, 223–251.
Bell, G. (1980). *Am. Nat.* **116**, 45–76.
Bock, W. J. (1980). *Am. Zool.* **20**, 217–227.
Bock, W. J. (1981). *Am. Zool.* **21**, 5–20.
Bonar, D. B. (1978). *In* "Settlement and Metamorphosis of Marine Invertebrate Larvae" (F. Chia and M. E. Rice, eds), pp. 177–196. Elsevier, New York.
Breder, C. M. Jr and Rosen, D. E. (1966). "Modes of Reproduction in Fishes". Natural History Press, Garden City.
Brody, S. (1945). "Bioenergetics and Growth with Special Reference to the Efficiency Complex in Domestic Animals". Van Nostrand, New York.
Bull, J. J. and Shine, R. (1979). *Am. Nat.* **114**, 296–303.
Carey, W. E. and Noakes, D. L. G. (1981). *J. Fish Biol.* **19**, 285–296.
Cohen, J. (1977). "Reproduction". Butterworths, London.
Collette, B. B. and Banarescu, P. (1977). *J. Fish. Res. Bd Can.* **34**, 1450–1463.
Dawkins, R. (1978). *Z. Tierpsychol.* **47**, 61–76.
Dawkins, R. (1982). "The Extended Phenotype". W. H. Freeman, Oxford.
Disler, N. N., Reznitchenko, P. N. and Soin, S. G. (1965). *In* "Theoretical Principles of Fisheries", pp. 119–128. Nauka Press, Moscow (in Russian).
Eldredge, N. and Gould, S. J. (1972). *In* "Models in Paleobiology" (T. J. M. Schopf, ed.), pp. 82–115. W. H. Freeman, San Francisco.
Etkin, W. and Gilbert, C. I. (ed.). (1968). "Metamorphosis". North Holland, Amsterdam.

Garstang, W. (1894). *Zool. Anz.* **17**, 122–125.
Garstang, W. (1928). *Q. J. microsc. Sci.* **72**, 51–187.
Gerbilsky, N. L. (1956). *Trudy karel'. Fil. Akad. Nauk SSSR* **5**, 6–12 (in Russian).
Gould, S. J. (1982a). *Science, N.Y.* **216**, 380–387.
Gould, S. J. (1982b). *In* "Perspectives of Evolution" (R. Milkman, ed.), pp. 83–104. Sinauer Associations, Sunderland.
Gould, S. J. and Eldredge, N. (1977). *Paleobiology* **3**, 115–151.
Holčik, J. and Hruška, V. (1966). *Věst. Čs. spol. zool.* **30**, 22–29.
Hureau, J. C. and Ozouf, C. (1977). *Cybium* **2**, 129–137.
Kirschbaum, F. and Westby, G. W. M. (1975). *Experientia* **31**, 1290–1293.
Koshelev, B. V. (1978). *In* "Ecomorphological and Ecophysiological Studies of Fish Development" (B. V. Koshelev, ed.), pp. 3–9. Nauka Press, Moscow (in Russian).
Kryzhanovsky, S. G. (1948). *Isv. tikhookean. nauchno-issled. Inst. ryb. Khoz. Okeanogr.* **27**, 3–114 (in Russian).
Kryzhanovsky, S. G. (1949). *Trudy Inst. Morf. Zhivot.* **1**, 5–332 (in Russian).
Kryzhanovsky, S. G. (1956). *Trudy Inst. Morf. Zhivot.* **17**, 1–225 (in Russian).
Kryzhanovsky, S. G., Smirnov, A. I. and Soin, S. G. (1951). *Trudy Amur. Icht. Eksp. 1945–1948* **2**, 5–222 (in Russian).
Kuznetsov, V. A. (1977). *Zool. Zh.* **56**, 1503–1509.
Levinton, J. S. and Simon, C. M. (1980). *Syst. Zool.* **29**, 130–142.
Martin, W. R. (1949). Univ. Toronto Studies 58, *Publ. Ont. Fish. Res. Lab.* **70**, 1–73.
McElman, J. F. and Balon, E. K. (1979). *Envir. Biol. Fish.* **4**, 309–348.
McElman, J. F. and Balon, E. K. (1980). *Envir. Biol. Fish.* **5**, 191–224.
Medvedev, Z. A. (1969). "Rise and fall of T. D. Lysenko". Columbia University Press, New York.
Miller, P. J. (1979). *Symp. zool. Soc. Lond.* **44**, 263–306.
Millot, J. and Anthony, J. (1974). *Sci. Nat., Paris* **121**, 3–4.
Moskalkova, K. I. (1967). *In* "Morphological Analysis of Fish Development", pp. 48–75. Nauka Press, Moscow (in Russian).
Moskalkova, K. I. (1978). *In* "Ecomorphological and Ecophysiological Studies of Fish Development" (B. N. Koshelev, ed.), pp. 72–88. Nauka Press, Moscow (in Russian).
Noakes, D. L. G. (1978). *In* "The Development of Behaviour: Comparative and Evolutionary Aspects" (G. M. Burghardt and M. Bekoff, eds), pp. 103–125. Garland STPM Press, New York.
Noakes, D. L. G. (1981). *In* "The Interdisciplinary Study of Early Development" (K. Immelmann, G. W. Barlow, L. Petrinovitch and M. Man, eds), pp. 491–508. Cambridge University Press, Cambridge.
Noakes, D. L. G. and Balon, E. K. (1982). *In* "The Biology and Culture of Tilapias" (R. S. V. Pullin and R. H. Lowe-McConnell, eds), pp. 61–82. ICLARM Conf. Proc. 7, Manila.
Oppenheim, R. W. (1981). *In* "Maturation and Development: Biological and Psychological Perspectives" (K. J. Connolly and H. F. R. Prechtl, eds), pp. 73–109. J. P. Lippincott, Philadelphia.
Peters, H. M. and Berns, S. (1979). *Mitt. hamb. zool. Mus. Inst.* **76**, 506–508.
Peters, H. M. and Berns, S. (1982a). *Z. zool. Syst. Evolut.-forsch.* **20**, 18–52.
Peters, H. M. and Berns, S. (1982b). *TI (Tatsachen und Informationen aus der Aquaristic*, Tetra) **58**, 19–22.
Philippart, J.-Cl. and Ruwet, J.Cl. (1982). *In* "The Biology and Culture of Tilapias" (R. S. V. Pullin and R. H. Lowe-McConnell, eds), pp. 15–59. ICLARM Conf. Proc. 7, Manila.
Rass, T. S. (1968). *In* "Symposium on the Ecology of Pelagic Fish Species in Arctic

Waters and Adjacent Seas (R. W. Blacker, ed.), pp. 135–137. Cons. Per. Int. l'Expl. Mer. Rapp. Proc.-Verb. Réun. 158, Copenhague.

Smirnov, A. I. (1975). "Biology, Reproduction and Development of Pacific Salmons". Moscow University Press, Moscow (in Russian).

Smith, C. L., Rand, C. S., Schaeffer, B. and Atz, J. W. (1975). *Science, N.Y.* **190**, 1105–1106.

Smith-Gill, S. J. and Berven, K. A. (1979). *Am. Nat.* **113**, 563–585.

Soin, S. G. (1968). "Adaptive Principles of Fish Development". Moscow University Press, Moscow (in Russian).

Stanley, S. M. (1975). *Proc. natn. Acad. Sci. U.S.A.* **72**, 646–650.

Stanley, S. M. (1979). "Macroevolution: Pattern and Process". W. H. Freeman, San Francisco.

Thys van den Audenaerde, D. F. E. (1970). *Rev. Zool. Bot. Afr.* **77**, 285–300.

Trewavas, E. (1982). *In* "The Biology and Culture of Tilapias" (R. S. V. Pullin and R. H. Lowe-McConnell, eds), pp. 3–13. ICLARM Conf. Proc. 7, Manila.

Vasnecov, V. V. (1953). *In* "Otcherky po obshtch. vopr. ichtiol." (E. N. Pavlovsky, ed.), pp. 207–217. Acad. Nauk SSSR Press, Moskva-Leningrad (in Russian).

Wake, M. H. (1980). *Copeia* **1980**, 193–209.

Wilbur, H. M. and Collins, J. P. (1973). *Science, N.Y.* **182**, 1305–1314.

Woodhead, A. D. (1979). *Symp. zool. Soc. Lond.* **44**, 179–205.

Wourms, J. P. (1981). *Am. Zool.* **21**, 473–515.

Wourms, J. P., Stibling, M. D. and Atz, J. W. (1980). *Am. Zool.* **20**, 962.

4. Sunfish, Salmon, and the Evolution of Alternative Reproductive Strategies and Tactics in Fishes

MART R. GROSS

Department of Biological Sciences, Simon Fraser University, British Columbia, Canada

Abstract: Most current models of the evolution of reproductive strategy are based on optimization theory. Optimization theory does not allow for the dynamic interplay among behavioural phenotypes which are in competition. When fish reproduction involves competition, a more appropriate form of analysis is game theory. Game theory searches for Evolutionarily Stable Strategies (ESS's) (Maynard Smith, 1982) rather than "best" strategies.

The first section of this paper explains how alternative reproductive tactics and strategies may be evolutionarily stable within the same environment. Theoretical examples of alternative reproductive tactics and strategies are given with their corresponding fitness solutions. Understanding these solutions is a prerequisite for selecting the fitness criteria necessary for empirical measurements. In the second section, a game theoretic analyses is applied to the evolution of discrete alternative reproductive tactics in North American sunfishes and Pacific salmon. Both fishes have precocial males — termed cuckolders in sunfish, jacks in salmon — which use alternative behavioural tactics to achieve mating success. The analysis shows that it is theoretically possible for precocial male phenotypes to enjoy fitness equal to late maturing males — long considered the only "normal" phenotype.

I. INTRODUCTION

It is commonly thought that animal species should have a "best" reproductive strategy. Consequently, most models of fish reproduction are based on optimization theory (Schaffer, 1979; Stearns, 1980; Ware, 1982). However, in many fish species alternative male reproductive behaviours have evolved. These alternative behaviours are used in competition with conspecifics and coexist in the same environment with the so-called "normal" phenotype (Table I). While some of these alternative behaviours are facultative and can

FISH REPRODUCTION
ISBN 0–12–563660–1

be changed depending on circumstances, others are associated with discrete life histories—for example, precocial maturity.

In the present paper I use game theory (Maynard Smith, 1982) to show how alternative reproductive tactics and strategies may be evolutionarily stable. The first section contrasts predictions from optimality theory to those from game theory. Theoretical examples of alternative reproductive strategies are given and are resolved into mutually exclusive game theory categories. A brief discussion of why such alternative strategies may be a common phenomenon in fishes follows. In the second section I review my work on alternative tactics and strategies in North American sunfishes (*Lepomis*: Centrarchidae) and Pacific salmon (*Oncorhynchus*: Salmonidae). These fishes differ greatly in their ecology, life history and behaviour, and exhibit a variety of alternative reproductive behaviours which include precociousness, cuckoldry, and female mimicry. This behavioural diversity, combined with the biological differences shown by these fishes, render them excellent groups for comparative studies.

II. THEORY

A. Optimization theory versus game theory

An analysis of reproductive strategy evolution may be approached through either optimization or game theory. To date, most models have employed optimization theory, and a large literature is available on the use of this technique (e.g. Maynard Smith, 1978; McCleery, 1978). In its simplest form the theory proceeds as follows (see Fig. 1). For any given level of investment made by an organism (the organism's "cost") there will be an accompanying return in "benefit" or fitness which can be described using a cost-benefit function. The cost-benefit function can be solved to yield the level of

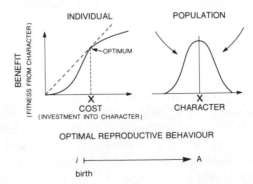

Fig. 1.   Schematic summary of optimization theory applied to reproductive strategy evolution (see text for further details).

investment which *maximizes* the net rate of fitness return. For the hypothetical organism in Fig. 1 the rate of return is maximized at "x" units of investment. Since theoretically this is the best investment an organism can make, the character should be approximately normally distributed about "x" in the population, with normalizing selection acting against *deviants*. Under such conditions, the evolution of alternative strategies is highly unlikely.

Optimization theory as a means for understanding reproductive strategy evolution has an important shortcoming: it does not take into account the interactive aspects of animal behaviour. Unlike most life-history traits, the behavioural components of reproduction can be highly variable, dynamic, and used opportunistically by individuals to compete with conspecifics. It may often be the case that the most appropriate tactic to adopt depends on what others are doing. The incorporation of such behavioural dynamics into an analysis of evolution is permitted by the theory of games. Developed to analyse human economic conflicts (Von Neumann and Morgenstern, 1944), this theory assumes that in contest situations strategies will emerge which maximize winnings (Rapoport, 1973). Game theory therefore finds a logical structure in evolutionary biology through genetics and natural selection. The incorporation of game theory into evolutionary biology has been pioneered by Maynard Smith (Maynard Smith and Price, 1973; Maynard Smith, 1976, 1979, 1982).

Game theory shows that if fitness payoffs depend *both* on the strategy adopted by an individual and on those employed by other members of the population, the strategy which evolves need not be optimal. Instead, it must be an Evolutionarily Stable Strategy (ESS) (Maynard Smith, 1982), a strategy which, when adopted by a critical proportion of the population, yields an individual fitness which exceeds that of all alternative strategies when these are rare in the population. Sex ratio, for example, has probably evolved as an ESS. Pay-offs depend largely upon what other individuals (particularly females) in the population are doing. Large winnings can be achieved by overproducing the limited sex, and great losses can result from overproducing the common sex. The strategy which has evolved for many populations is equal allocation, 50% sons and 50% daughters, a ratio where each sex is of equal value. Since no alternative sex ratio can do better when rare, this is an ESS.

That an "ESS" may yield lower fitness than an "optimal" strategy is illustrated by the hawk-dove game (Maynard Smith, 1976). Let us assume that individual reproductive success may achieve its maximum in a population of peaceful cohabitors (doves). Such a population is susceptible to invasion by cheaters (hawks) which hoard resources to increase their reproductive success. In order to obtain some success, doves are thus forced into conflict over resources even though such behaviour reduces energy available for repro- duction. Thus, the evolution of a resource acquisition strategy will incorporate fighting behaviour (at either the individual or population level, see below) irrespective of whether such behaviour yields optimal fitness. The most important consequence of a "hawk-dove" resource acquisition strategy is that no alternative can yield a higher fitness. It is, then, an ESS and such "unbeatable" strategies should predominate in nature.

It is necessary to define the terms "strategy" and "tactic". Here, a *strategy* is considered to be a genetically determined life history or behaviour program which dictates the course of development, or action throughout an organism's life. Mathematically it is a specification of what an individual will do in any situation in which it finds itself (*sensu* Maynard Smith, 1976). Strategies are composed of *tactics* — decision rules and methods for achieving the behaviour and life history programs. The difference between strategies and tactics is that strategies are in "evolutionary" competition with one another and tactics are the way they compete, that is, the "proximate" levels of competition. Therefore, strategies are subject to natural selection and they evolve through alterations in their tactics.

B. Theoretical reproductive strategies

In Fig. 2, I have summarized theoretical alternative reproductive strategies into pure, conditional and mixed "game theoretic" categories. A *pure* strategy is composed of one tactic which is genetically fixed. In this instance a tactic is equivalent to a strategy. *Conditional* strategies are composed of more than one tactic. The tactics provide unequal fitness, reflect individual competitive ability, and are genetically facultative. A *mixed* strategy also has more than one tactic. However, the tactics provide equal fitness, they may not reflect competitive ability, and they are genetically facultative or genetically stochastic. Finally, mixed *strategies* exist at the *population* level, when two or more of the above strategies coexist with equal fitness. Alternative mixed strategies at the population level are mathematically equivalent to alternative tactics at the individual level in a mixed strategy.

Alternative reproductive tactics may be further reduced to two basic fitness types: subordinate or equivalent, which occurs is dependent upon the type of selection operating on the organism. Subordinate tactics evolve to provide animals with the opportunity to make the Best of a Bad Situation (BBS) and are responses to competitive displacement. Since some natural variance in competitive ability exists in all populations, individuals will be placed in contest with superior conspecifics on some occasions and inferior competitors on others. Behavioural modifications which take into account the status of competitors (e.g. "if smaller flee, if bigger fight") should help maximize individual reproductive success, and evolve into a conditional strategy.

If alternative behavioural phenotypes are subject to frequency dependent advantage, they may in theory become equivalent (Fig. 3, see also Rubenstein, 1980). Equivalency, or equal fitness, can occur for tactics at the individual

THEORETICAL BEHAVIOURAL ONTOGENIES IN REPRODUCTION

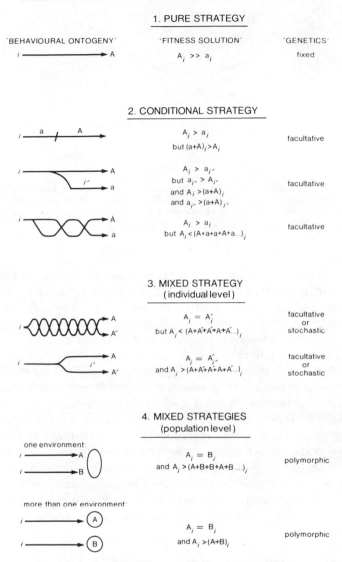

1. PURE STRATEGY

'BEHAVIOURAL ONTOGENY'   'FITNESS SOLUTION'   'GENETICS'

$i \longrightarrow A$ $A_i \gg a_i$ fixed

2. CONDITIONAL STRATEGY

$A_i > a_i$
but $(a+A)_i > A_i$ facultative

$A_i > a_{i'}$
but $a_{i'} > A_{i'}$
and $A_i > (a+A)_i$ facultative
and $a_{i'} > (a+A)_{i'}$

$A_i > a_i$
but $A_i < (A+a+a+A+a...)_i$ facultative

3. MIXED STRATEGY
(individual level)

$A_i = A'_i$ facultative
but $A_i < (A+A'+A'+A+A'...)_i$ or
stochastic

$A_i = A'_{i'}$ facultative
and $A_i > (A+A'+A'+A+A'...)_i$ or
stochastic

4. MIXED STRATEGIES
(population level)

one environment:
$i \longrightarrow A$
$i \longrightarrow B$ $A_i = B_i$
and $A_i > (A+B+B+A+B....)_i$ polymorphic

more than one environment:
$i \longrightarrow (A)$
$i \longrightarrow (B)$ $A_i = B_i$
and $A_i > (A+B)_i$ polymorphic

Fig. 2. Theoretically, a variety of reproductive behaviour ontogenies may evolve—some of which are presented here. These ontogenies may be organized into 4 game theory categories: pure, conditional, mixed and alternative. Both upper and lower case A symbolize tactics; A' denotes a tactic of equal fitness to A while a one of unequal fitness. B represents a different strategy. The fitness solutions indicate the success of the tactics or strategies for an individual i and are those conferring stability on the behavioural ontogeny. The genetical structure of the tactics may be fixed, facultative, stochastic or polymorphic: fixed means that individuals are genetically coded without contingency for adjustment of their tactics or strategy; facultative implies individuals may alter their tactics; stochastic indicates that they vary tactics in a genetically predetermined random or probabilistic fashion, finally, polymorphic denotes two or more genetically different groups of individuals.

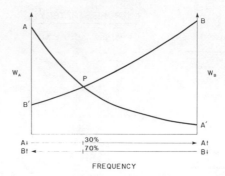

FREQUENCY

Fig. 3. Frequency-dependent advantage can result in 2 strategies, A and B, both providing bearers within the same population equal fitness. The strategies will coexist in an Evolutionarily Stable State (ESSt) with an equilibrium frequency P. For the hypothetical population shown here, P occurs at 30% type A and 70% type B. W is fitness.

level (mixed ESS), or for strategies at the population level (mixed ESS's). The latter is more likely when an individual showing both behaviours is inferior to specialists $(A_i = B_i,$ but $A_i > (A + B + B + A...)_i,$ Fig. 2). A fitness equilibrium derived from frequency dependence has, as shown in Fig. 3, several interesting properties. (1) Local perturbations from the equilibrium will with time return to their equilibrium frequencies. (2) The equilibrium is globally stable. This means that for a population composed entirely of type A individuals, any mutant or immigrant of type B will rapidly invade the population until the equilibrium is reached. Strictly speaking, neither strategy A nor B are an ESS — rather, the strategies exist in an Evolutionarily Stable State (ESSt). (3) The equilibrium frequency, P, is determined by the environmental properties or behaviours which give rise to the frequency-dependent success of the phenotypes. If, for example frequency-dependence operates through the relative availability of rock refuges, habitats differing in rock number will have correspondingly different P values. Frequencies of phenotypically similar strategies may thus differ greatly among neighbouring populations.

C. Alternative reproductive tactics and strategies in fishes

In fishes, alternative male mating behaviours are relatively common (Table I). These behaviours presumably contribute to the reproductive success of their bearers and can be viewed as tactics. The prevalence of alternative tactics in fishes is probably due in part to the competitiveness of their mating systems and widespread occurrence of external fertilization (Gross and Shine, 1981). External fertilization usually involves guarding a territory for defense of paternity. However, maintaining territorial boundaries is physically difficult

TABLE I. Alternative male mating behaviours are a common and taxonomically widespread phenomenon in fishes. Listed here are some examples of fertilization stealing (FS), female mimicry (FM), cuckoldry (C, the fertilization of eggs which are cared for by another male), and precociousness [P, the attainment of reproductive maturity (viable sperm) at an unusually early age].

Family	Species	Common name	Alternative behaviour	Reference
Gasterosteidae	*Pungitius pungitius*	10-spine stickleback	FM,C[a]	Morris (1952)
	Gasterosteus aculeatus	3-spine stickleback	FM,C	Assem (1967)
	Apeltes quadracus	4-spine stickleback	FM,C	Rowland (1979)
Tripterygiidae	*Tripterygion tripteronotus*	—	FM?,C	Wirtz (1978)
Nandidae	*Polycentrus schomburgki*	leaf fish	FM,C	Barlow (1967)
Cichlidae	*Acarichthys heckeli*	—	P,C[a]	Cichocki (1976)
Percidae	*Etheostoma caeruleum*	rainbow darter	FM?,FS	Reeves (1907)
Poeciliidae	*Poeciliopsis occidentalis*	gila topminnow	FS	Constantz (1975)
Cyprinodontidae	*Cyprinodon* sp.	pupfish	FS	Kodric-Brown (1977)
Gobiidae	*Pomatoschistus norvegicus*	Norway goby	C[a]	Gibson and Ezzi (1981)
				P. J. Miller (pers. comm.)
Labridae	*Crenilabrus melops*	corkwing	P,FM,C	Dipper (pers. comm.)
	Thalassoma bifasciatum	wrasse	P,FM?,FS	Warner and Robertson (1978)
Scaridae	*Scarus croicensis*	striped parrotfish	P,FS	Warner and Downs (1977)
Centrarchidae	*Lepomis megalotis*	longear sunfish	C	Keenleyside (1972)
	Lepomis macrochirus	bluegill sunfish	P,FM,C	Gross (1979, 1982)
				Dominey (1980)
	Lepomis gibbosus	pumpkinseed sunfish	P,C	Gross (1979)
Salmonidae	*Salmo trutta*	sea trout	P,FS	Jones and Ball (1954)
				B. Jonsson (pers. comm.)
	Salvelinus alpinus	Arctic charr	F,S	Jonsson and Hindar (1982)
	Salmo salar	Atlantic salmon	P,FS	Jones (1959)
				R. Naiman (pers. comm.)
	Oncorhynchus nerka	sockeye salmon	P,FS	Hanson and Smith (1967)
	Oncorhynchus kisutch	coho salmon	P,FS	Gross and Van Den Berghe (in prep.)

[a] Behaviour not interpreted as such by author.

in a multidimensional space, especially as it must be combined with the owner's own sperm release. This difficulty in guarding eggs from rival sperm, combined with the natural variance in male competitive ability, creates a situation favourable to the invasion of alternative reproductive tactics.

If the alternative reproductive tactics arising in a population are subject to frequency-dependent selection, indeterminate growth may contribute to the evolution of discrete alternative life history pathways. Under indeterminate growth, additional energy expenditures such as precocial maturity will result in smaller body size. When the success of a strategy is dependent upon body size, males employing alternative tactics will, as a consequence of their reduced growth, be competitively inferior. The alternative tactics may thus be incompatible within an individual. When equivalent fitness is possible, selection may allow genetic differences to accumulate with specialization into alternative routes.

III. EVOLUTION OF ALTERNATIVE REPRODUCTIVE STRATEGIES AND TACTICS IN SUNFISH AND SALMON

North American sunfishes and Pacific salmon have precocial males which are known as "cuckolders" (Gross, 1979) and "jacks" respectively. In this section I describe their reproductive behaviour and life history tactics, and explicitly state the conditions under which these males will be evolutionarily stable. My primary objective is to determine if their alternative tactics are evolutionarily stable as a BBS, or if they have equivalent fitness with a frequency-dependent equilibrium. Evidence assessing these conditions is presented for both groups.

A. Alternative reproductive tactics in sunfish and salmon

1. *Sunfish.* Sunfish are freshwater, iteroparous fishes occupying the slow-moving warmer waters of N.E. North America (Scott and Crossman, 1973; Carlander, 1977). Their reproductive behaviour includes male nest-building and subsequent care of young. Nests are constructed in the shallow littoral zone of their habitat and are arranged in aggregations or colonies (Breder, 1936; Miller, 1963; Avila, 1976). Some males, however, mature early and attempt to cuckold these nest-building individuals (Keenleyside, 1972; Gross, 1979, 1980; Dominey, 1980). In bluegill sunfish, for example, males have three distinct mating behaviours which I have termed parental, sneaker, and satellite (Fig. 4). *Parental* males build nests to which they attract females (Fig. 4a). After spawning, males remain at the colony and provide the parental care characteristic of all centrarchids. These males are relatively large (172 ± 11 mm, $n = 70$) and old (8.5 ± 1.0 years, $n = 67$). By contrast, *sneakers* fertilize eggs by darting into nests of parental males during oviposition (Fig. 4b). Such

opportunities are awaited from concealed or cryptic positions near the nest border. Sneaker males are small (73 ± 9 mm, $n=46$) and relatively young ($2 \cdot 7 \pm 1$ year, $n=45$). *Satellite* males mimic females and release sperm while pairing simultaneously with true females and parental males (Fig. 4c). Both the size (95 ± 9 mm, $n=32$) and age ($4 \cdot 2 \pm 0 \cdot 7$ years, $n=30$) of these males is intermediate to that of parentals and sneakers. Although parental males attempt to defend their paternity by aggressively chasing any cuckolders detected by the nest, the specialized behaviour of sneakers and satellites ensures that they too fertilize eggs (Gross, 1982).

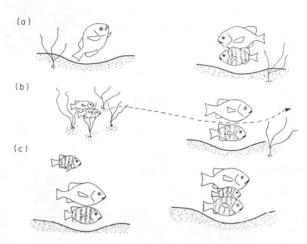

Fig. 4. Schematic representation of male mating behaviour in bluegill sunfish (*Lepomis macrochirus*). A: Parental; B: sneaker; C: satellite. See text and Gross (1982) for details.

In an analysis of reproductive strategy evolution it is first necessary to determine the ontogenetic structuring of the tactics. This is important since fitness from competing strategies is determined by the success accrued from all component tactics and because it is necessary to ascertain at what level the competition between tactics occurs. Bluegill mating behaviour could, for example, be accounted for by cuckoldry and parental care existing as sequential behaviours performed during the lifetime of a single male. Alternatively, two life histories, one specialized for cuckoldry and the other for parental care, might describe the ontogeny. There could even be three distinct life histories, corresponding to the three behavioural and age categories.

By combining information on the age at first reproduction for cuckolder and parental males (marked by a sharp decrease in growth and recorded on scale annuli patterns) with population demography data, I have found that the reproductive behaviours observed for male bluegill result from two alternative life history pathways (Gross, 1982). In one pathway are males that mature early and use sneaking and satellite behaviour to cuckold, in the other pathway are males that delay maturity to build nests and show parental care (Fig. 5a). Cuckoldry and parental care are therefore discrete reproductive tactics.

(a) Reproductive life histories : Bluegill sunfish

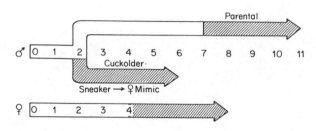

(b) Reproductive life histories : Coho salmon

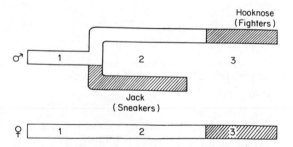

Fig. 5.   (a) Male bluegill have two alternative life history pathways: one leading to cuckoldry, the other to parental care (see text for further details). These data are from Gross (1982) and describe a bluegill population in Lake Opinicon, Ontario. Hatched areas indicate reproductive maturity. (b) Salmon males have two alternative life history pathways: jacks and hooknoses. The data are for coho salmon (Gross and Van Den Berghe, in press), the numbers indicate age in years.

The genetics underlying the alternative pathways in sunfish are not yet known. Hence, it cannot be determined whether the behaviours are alternative tactics at the level of the individual, or alternative strategies at the level of the population (see Fig. 2). However, the theoretical analysis of their coexistence is, as we will see, relatively independent of this problem.

2. *Salmon.*   The natural history of Pacific salmon contrasts sharply with that of sunfish. These are anadromous and semelparous fishes, with adults maturing in temperate waters of the Pacific ocean and homing to breed in their natal freshwater streams (Foerster, 1968). The reproductive behaviour of salmon is characterized by female nest building, territoriality, and subsequent guarding of eggs; males enter the nest to fertilize eggs during oviposition and then depart.

For many populations and species of salmon an inspection of adult body size on the breeding grounds would show that the distribution of female size is approximately normal while that of males is bimodal (Fig. 6). This bimodal distribution in males is due to the presence of small, precociously mature "jack" males which return to their home stream after only one year in the ocean. By contrast to jacks, "hooknose" males return after several years in the ocean and therefore are larger in body size. Hooknose males are more colourful than jacks, and possess a kype (angular protrusion of the snout) with enlarged teeth. There are thus two "types" of males competing for females on the breeding grounds.

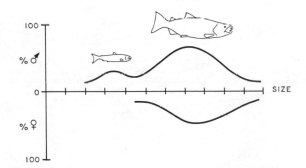

Fig. 6.   Schematic representation of the distribution of adult salmon body size on the spawning grounds.

A female digging her nest is usually surrounded by more than one, and sometimes as many as 10 or 12, males. These male aggregations include both jack and hooknose males competing for access to the female. When oviposition commences, these males rush into the nest and release sperm. As fertilization success is correlated with order of nest entry — the greatest proportion of eggs being fertilized by the first male (Schroeder, 1981) — distance from the nest is probably an important determinant of male reproductive success. Invariably, the male closest to the nest enters first, and the remaining males follow in a sequence corresponding to their distance from the nest.

It has generally been thought that jacks are a "sick" or "inferior" male, and hooknoses the "normal" phenotype in salmon. This interpretation of jacks would be correct if they were unsuccessful at fertilizing eggs. However, several studies suggest that precocial males are successful spawners (e.g. Jones and King, 1952; Hanson and Smith, 1967; Gross and Van Den Berghe, in prep.). In coho (Gross and Van Den Berghe, in prep.), jack success was primarily attributed to their specialization in an alternative behavioural tactic: sneaking. Proximity to the female can be achieved either through fighting with competitors or by sneaking around them (Fig. 7). Hooknoses acquired 91% of their matings through fighting while 82% of the matings of jacks were obtained through sneaking. That the males are specialized for these alternative tactics is apparent from their morphological development. The kype in hooknoses is a specialized weapon evolved to aid in male–male fighting, while the absence of a kype and the cryptic colouration of jacks is an aid for sneaking. Jackness is therefore an evolved alternative life history pathway for a specialized mating tactic (Fig. 5b).

COHO MATING STRUCTURE

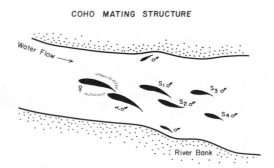

Fig. 7. The mating system of coho salmon involves multiple males attempting to fertilize the eggs of each female. Fighting males form a linear dominance hierarchy with an alpha (α) male closest to the female and the subordinates (S_1, S_2, . . .) more distant. Males which sneak use refuges to escape fighters and occupy positions outside the dominance hierarchy.

As in sunfishes, the genetics underlying these alternative pathways are poorly understood. There is some suggestion of a genetic component to precocial jack maturity (Ellis and Nobel, 1961; Ricker, 1972; Schroeder, 1981), and there is also evidence for larger members of the smolt cohort entering the jack pathway (e.g. Bilton et al., 1982). These data suggest that becoming a jack is probably determined by a genotype-environmental interaction (sensu Falconer, 1962), but conclusive evidence requires further study.

There is striking similarity in the male reproductive strategies of sunfish and salmon. Both groups have a phenotypic bifurcation placing males into discrete, alternative behavioural pathways to compete over the same set of eggs. In the next section we examine how these alternative pathways may be evolutionarily successful.

B. Evolutionary stability

Male cuckolders and jacks can be evolutionarily stable through either *equal* or *unequal* fitness to parental and hooknose males (Fig. 8). If cuckoldry and jackness are subordinate reproductive tactics at the individual level, they may be evolutionarily stable as a BBS. As equivalent tactics they may be evolutionarily stable as a mixed ESS at the individual level, or as mixed alternative strategies with an Evolutionarily Stable State (ESSt) at the population level. To be equivalent tactics or strategies, their success should be frequency-dependent.

ALTERNATIVE REPRODUCTIVE PATHWAYS: SUNFISH AND SALMON

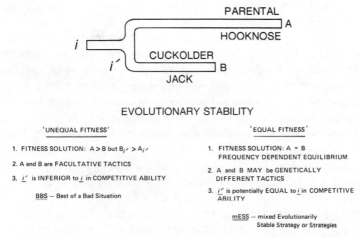

Fig. 8.   North American sunfish and Pacific salmon have a phenotypic life history bifurcation which leads to alternative reproductive behaviours among males. Three theoretical solutions exist to the evolutionary stability of these pathways: Best of a Bad Situation (BBS), mixed Evolutionarily Stable Strategy (mixed ESS), or an Evolutionarily Stable State (ESSt). As the fitness solution is identical for a mESS and an ESSt, these are grouped for consideration. Conditions for stability under the alternative solutions are shown.

1. *A BBS?*   Several lines of evidence suggest that cuckoldry and jackness are not BBS tactics. For sunfish, there is no difference in body size between males at the time the cuckolder and parental pathways are entered (Gross, 1982). A significant difference would be expected under the conditions of a BBS. Furthermore, there is no field evidence for females discriminating against

cuckolder sperm. Such discrimination should occur if these males were competitively inferior. In salmon, some evidence suggests precociousness involves a genotype-environmental interaction. This genetic contribution, if further substantiated, would make it improbable for jackness to exist as a subordinate tactic since the genes could not be maintained in the gene pool. Also, the positive correlation between males entering the jack route and male body size is opposite to that expected from a BBS.

2. *Mixed ESS or evolutionary stable state?* (a) Sunfish. Mating success for sunfish cuckolder males is influenced by the physical environment and the social interactions occurring at the nest site (Gross, in prep.). In weedy areas where cover is high, cuckolders are most successful in competition with parental males when alone. A single cuckolder can position himself close to a nest and intrude upon most spawnings — additional cuckolders only reduce individual success by increasing sperm competition. In nest sites without cover additional cuckolders increase individual intrusion frequency by distracting the parental male and allowing cuckolders a closer approach to the nest edge. The greater intrusion frequency outweighs costs of sperm competition until an "optimal" cuckolder number is reached (Fig. 9a). Beyond this, the increase in intrusion frequency does not outweigh sperm competition.

With a knowledge of how the physical environment and cuckolder frequency interact to determine reproductive success, and the frequency distribution of environments in Lake Opinicon, Ontario, I have analysed for frequency-dependent mating advantage in cuckolder fitness (Gross, in prep.). This was achieved through theoretical calculations of maximum and minimum fitnesses. Maximum fitness was determined by assuming that cuckolders (1) possessed "perfect knowledge" of their success rates at colonies having different degrees of cover, and of the number of cuckolders in the population relative to parental males, (2) that they payed no cost for this knowledge, and (3) that they adjusted their frequencies among colonies to maximize their mating success. This calculation provided cuckolders with the best fitness possible in competition with parentals. I contrasted the worst fitness cuckolders could achieve to this "best" fitness. The "worst", or theoretical minimum fitness, would occur if cuckolders behaved randomly at colonies, not adjusting their numbers or their behaviour to reflect their changing success rate. "True" fitness should lie within the area bounded by these two success curves. For both the ideal and random situations, it is found that cuckolder fitness decreases relative to that of parental males as cuckolder frequency increases in the population (Fig. 9b). Therefore, fitness through the cuckolder pathway is negatively-frequency dependent, and an equilibrium between cuckolders and parentals is a theoretical possibility.

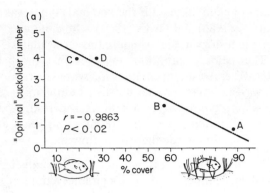

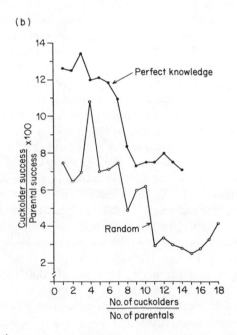

Fig. 9.   (a) The "optimal" cuckolder number at a nest site, from a cuckolder's viewpoint, is that number which maximizes their individual success rate. This optimal number varies among colonies depending upon the degree of cover present at the nests. Data shown are averaged from 4 colonies in Lake Opinicon, Ontario (Gross, in prep.). (b) Theoretical bounds for mating success of cuckolder males, relative to parental males, at different cuckolder frequencies. "Perfect knowledge" symbolizes the theoretical best fitness of cuckolders; "random" is the theoretical worst. True success rates are bounded by the curves. As survivorship of males in the 2 pathways will be relatively independent of their frequency, the curves represent "fitness". Figure modified slightly from Gross (in prep.).

This possibility of equal fitness for the two male types was investigated by Gross and Charnov (1980) and Gross (1982), who conducted a test of fitness by developing a life history model which reduced the analysis to behavioural observations. The major assumptions involved in using behavioural data were: (1) that the observed sperm competition would be random, and (2) that the population was stationary (stable age distribution and size). The test was conducted on seven colonies over a two year period, and the observed fertilization success averaged over the colonies and years gave qualitative agreement with equal fitness for the two pathways.

(b) Salmon.   Male mating success in salmon, as in sunfish, is influenced by both the physical environment and the social interactions at the mating site. Large males are clearly at an advantage when access to females involves fighting and they invariably head the dominance hierarchies (Fig. 10a). By contrast, when access to females is dependent upon sneaking behaviour, the most successful individuals are the smallest as they are (1) less apparent to competitors and (2) able to utilize refuges unavailable to the larger males. These "refuges" may be debris or shallow areas close to the nest site where sneaking males can hide, or escape aggression from larger conspecifics. Since only two mating tactics, fighting and sneaking, occur on the breeding grounds, middle size males should be least successful in competition for proximity to females. This hypothesis is supported by field data (Fig. 10a).

The disruptive selection which acts on male body size during mating (Fig. 10a) is probably responsible for driving males into the two observed life histories and size classes. This is evidenced by the close overlap between the size observed to separate jacks and hooknoses in a coho population, and the size threshold where disruptive selection operates on breeding males (Fig. 10a). But, can sneaking and fighting provide jacks and hooknoses with equal fitness? At present only a rough estimate of male success, based on average proximity to females, can be made. This reveals that jacks closely equal hooknoses in average female proximity (Fig. 10b).

These behavioural data cannot incorporate life-time survivorship, and they assume random sperm competition and a stationary population. Jacks are likely to have a higher ocean survivorship as a consequence of their earlier maturity, and reduced susceptibility to fishing pressure (Foerster, 1968). This therefore suggests that jacks would not have to fertilize as many eggs as hooknoses to achieve equal fitness. On the other hand, the lifespan of jacks on the spawning grounds is significantly shorter than that of hooknoses (Gross and Van Den Berghe, in press). Whether these factors cancel each other out cannot yet be determined. Since the testes of hooknose males are physically larger than those of jacks, they may release more sperm. However, it is known that salmon males release only a small proportion of their sperm at any mating event, and jacks make a relatively larger investment into sperm production

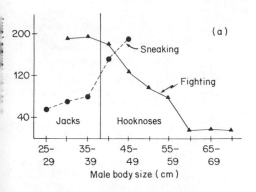

	F	S	x̄
J	197(11)	71(13)	129(24)
H	90(111)	170(6)	94(117)

Fig. 10.   (a) The distance between a coho male and a female during mating varies with male body size and behavioural tactic. Larger males do best when they fight, smaller males when they sneak. There exists a threshold above which males do better fighting, and below which they do better sneaking; males in the middle size range have the lowest success. The vertical line indicates the size division between early maturing jack males and late maturing hooknose males as observed on the spawning grounds. Figure modified from Gross (in prep.). (b) Fighting (F) and sneaking (S) are alternative behavioural tactics employed by jacks (J) and hooknose (H) males, and accord different proximities to the female, as shown. Each cell in the matrix is statistically different from its neighbour ($P<0.05$), except for the average distance (x̄) of jacks and hooknoses to females ($P=0.05$) (data in cms, sample sizes bracketed).

(Robertson, 1957; Kazakov, 1981). Jacks may also assume positions closer to the eggs because of their smaller size (Jones, 1959). The assumption least likely to influence the behavioural data presented here is that of a stationary population, since the population under study was chosen for its stability.

A perhaps more powerful test for fitness equality between jacks and hooknoses is made by examining frequency-dependent mating success (Krebs, 1980). To successfully sneak matings, jacks depend upon refuges from hooknose aggression. These refuges are relatively fixed within the breeding environment and with increasing jack frequency their relative availability will diminish. As a consequence, the probability of jacks being forced into direct competition with hooknose males increases. When placed in competition with hooknoses, jacks will be forced to assume the most distant positions from females. Assuming such a scenario, I have theoretically examined how jack population frequency influences jack mating success. This was achieved by incorporating male frequency into the data presented in Figure 10. My calculation allows for decreasing competition among hooknoses, and increasing competition between hooknoses and jacks, as jack frequency increases. For the population modelled (Deer Creek Jr, Washington) a fitness equilibrium is found when jacks comprise about 12% of the breeding males [Fig. 11a,b; this was also the observed frequency (18 of 147 males)]. The important point is that deviations from this equilibrium are subject to strong negative

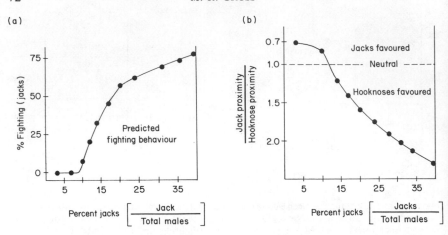

Fig. 11. (a) Theoretical prediction of jack fighting behaviour under different jack frequencies, for a coho population studied by Gross and Van Den Berghe (in prep.). (b) Theoretical proximities to females for jacks and hooknoses for different jack frequencies (based on Fig. 10b). The results show an equilibrium at approximately 12% jacks. Here the average proximity to females of jacks and hooknose males is equal.

frequency-dependent selection. Therefore, assuming the correctness of my scenario, jack fitness may be held equal to that of hooknose males.

3. *Summary of evolutionary stability.* The present analysis summarizes the known fitness potentials of cuckolder and jack males relative to parental and hooknose males. Many of these data are qualitative in nature. The fitness tests are conducted on only a single population, and important assumptions remain to be substantiated. However, there is considerable evidence favouring an hypothesis that cuckolders and jacks are equally fit alternative reproductive tactics to parentals and hooknoses. The behavioural data show that precocial males have the potential for obtaining equal reproductive success. The lack of evidence for competitive disadvantage combined with the morphological and behavioural specializations of the males, further support such a conclusion: in both groups reproductive success is strongly negatively frequency-dependent, a primary condition of evolutionarily stable alternative reproductive tactics through a fitness equilibrium. I therefore conclude that cuckolders and jacks may be part of a mESS at the individual level, or mESS's with an ESSt at the population level. The genetical evidence would suggest that jack salmon are favoured at the population level, but only further empirical study will tell.

IV. CONCLUSIONS

Alternative reproductive tactics and strategies are an adaptive phenomenon in sunfishes and salmon. Several factors suggest that we should expect such adaptiveness to be a more widespread phenomenon in fishes. The examples in Table I give evidence of the potential diversity of alternative mating behaviours in a wide variety of families. As has been shown here, the evolution of these behaviours is not necessarily dependent upon parental care or mating system (e.g. male care in sunfish, female care in salmon), life history (iteroparity in sunfish, semelparity in salmon), or ecology. The primary requisites are only that competition occurs among individuals for access to mates, that this competition may be partially (BBS) or entirely (ESS) circumvented by alternative behaviours, and that the success of these alternatives depends upon the activities of other members of the population.

If the success from alternative tactics is negatively-frequency dependent then the tactics may provide equal fitness and evolve as a mixed ESS or mixed ESS's. This appears to be the situation in sunfish, salmon and hermaphrodites (Warner and Hoffman, 1980; Charnov, 1982). In many other species alternative tactics will not provide equal fitness, and thus evolve as a BBS (e.g. arctic charr; Jonsson and Hindar, 1982). Irrespective of how they may evolve, such alternative tactics are evolutionarily stable. While I have stressed male reproductive behaviours, similar game theory analyses can provide an understanding of female competition.

ACKNOWLEDGEMENTS

I wish to acknowledge the kind help of Nancy L. Gerrish who discussed with me the concepts appearing here, edited the manuscript and drew many of the figures. Eric Van Den Berghe introduced me to the salmon population in Deer Creek Jr, and together with his family made my stay there most comfortable. The sunfish research has benefited from the facilities of Queen's University Biological Station at Lake Opinicon, Ontario (R. J. Robertson, Director). I also thank E. Charnov, E. Brannon, L. Dill, K. Groot, P. Harvey, B. Jonsson, J. Maynard Smith, P. Miller, R. Peterman, S. Rohwer, S. Schroeder, M. Slatkin, S. Stearns and R. Wootton. This study was supported by grant UO244 of the Natural Sciences and Engineering Research Council of Canada.

REFERENCES

Assem, J. van den (1967). *Behaviour Suppl.* **16**, 1–164.
Avila, V. L. (1976). *Am. Midl. Nat.* **96**, 195–206.

Barlow, G. W. (1967). *Am. Midl. Nat.* **78**, 215–234.

Bilton, H. T., Alderdice, D. F. and Schnute, J. T. (1982). *Can. J. Fish. aquat. Sci.* **39**, 426–447.

Breder, C. M. (1936). *Zoologica, N.Y.* **21**, 1–48.

Carlander, K. D. (1977). "Life History Data on Centrarchid Fishes of the United States and Canada". Iowa State University Press, Ames.

Charnov, E. L. (1982). "The Theory of Sex Allocation". Princeton University Press, Princeton.

Cichocki, F. P. (1976). "Cladistic history of cichlid fishes and reproductive strategies of the American genera *Acarichthys*, *Biotodoma* and *Geophagus*". Vol. 2, Ph.D. Thesis, University of Michigan, Ann Arbour.

Constantz, G. D. (1975). *Ecology* **56**, 966–973.

Dominey, W. (1980). *Nature, Lond.* **284**, 546–548.

Ellis, C. H. and Nobel, R. E. (1961). *Wash. State Fish. Dep. Ann. Rep.* **70**, 72–75.

Falconer, D. S. (1962). "Quantitative Genetics". Ronald Press Company, New York.

Foerster, R. E. (1968). *Bull. Fish. Res. Bd Can.* **162**, 1–422.

Gibson, R. N. and Ezzi, I. A. (1981). *J. Fish Biol.* **19**, 697–714.

Gross, M. R. (1979). *Can. J. Zool.* 1507–1509.

Gross, M. R. (1980). "Sexual selection and the evolution of reproductive strategies in sunfishes (Lepomis: Centrarchidae)". No. 8017132, 1–319. University Microfilms Int., Ann Arbour.

Gross, M. R. (1982). *Z. Tierpsychol.* **60**, 1–26.

Gross, M. R. and Charnov, E. L. (1980). *Proc. natn. Acad. Sci. U.S.A.* **77**, 6937–6940.

Gross, M. R. and Shine, R. (1981). *Evolution* **35**, 775–793.

Hanson, A. J. and Smith, H. D. (1967). *J. Fish. Res. Bd Can.* **24**, 1955–1977.

Jones, J. W. (1959). "The Salmon". Harper and Row, New York.

Jones, J. W. and Ball, J. N. (1954). *Brit. J. Anim. Behav.* **2**, 103–114.

Jones, J. W. and King, G. M. (1952). *Proc. zool. Soc. Lond.* **122**, 615–619.

Jonsson, B. and Hindar, K. (1982). *Can. J. Fish. aquat. Sci.* **39**, 1404–1413.

Kazakov, R. V. (1981). *J. Fish Biol.* **18**, 1–8.

Keenleyside, M. H. (1972). *Copeia* **1972**, 272–278.

Kodric-Brown, A. (1977). *Evolution* **31**, 750–766.

Krebs, J. R. (1980). *In* "Evolution of Social Behaviour: Hypotheses and Empirical Tests" (H. Markl, ed.), pp. 205–218. Weinheim: Verlag Chemie GmbH, Berlin.

Maynard Smith, J. (1976). *Am. Scient.* **64**, 41–45.

Maynard Smith, J. (1978). *Ann. Rev. Ecol. Syst.* **9**, 31–56.

Maynard Smith, J. (1979). *Proc. R. Soc. Lond.* B **205**, 475–488.

Maynard Smith, J. (1982). "Evolution and the Theory of Games". Cambridge University Press, Cambridge.

Maynard Smith, J. and Price, G. R. (1973). *Nature, Lond.* **246**, 15–18.

McCleery, R. H. (1978). *In* "Behavioural Ecology, an Evolutionary Approach" (J. R. Krebs and N. B. Davies, eds), pp. 377–410. Sinauer Assoc., Sunderland, Mass.

Miller, H. C. (1963). *Behaviour* **22**, 88–151.

Morris, D. (1952). *Behaviour* **4**, 233–261.

Rapoport, A. (1973). "Two-Person Game Theory". University Michigan Press, Ann Arbour.

Reeves, C. D. (1907). *Biol. Bull. Woods Hole* **14**, 35–59.

Ricker, W. E. (1972). *In* "The Stock Concept in Pacific Salmon" (R. C. Simon and P. A. Larkin, eds), pp. 27–160. University of British Columbia, Vancouver.

Robertson, O. H. (1957). *Cal. Fish Game* **43**, 119–130.

Rowland, W. J. (1979). *Am. Nat.* **114**, 602–604.

Rubenstein, D. (1980). *In* "Limits to Action: the Allocation of Individual Behaviour" (J. Stadden, ed.), pp. 65–100. Academic Press, New York.

Schaffer, W. M. (1979). *Symp. zool. Soc. Lond.* **44**, 307–326.
Schroeder, S. L. (1981). "The role of sexual selection in determining overall mating patterns and mate choice in chum salmon". Ph.D. Thesis, College of Fisheries, University of Washington, Seattle.
Scott, W. B. and Crossman, E. J. (1973). *Bull. Fish. Res. Bd Can.* **184**, 1–966.
Stearns, S. C. (1980). *Oikos* **35**, 266–281.
Von Neumann, J. and Morgenstern, O. (1944). "Theory of Games and Economic Behaviour". Princeton University Press, Princeton.
Ware, D. M. (1982). *Can. J. Fish. aquat. Sci.* **39**, 3–13.
Warner, R. R. and Downs, I. (1977). *Proc. 3rd Int. Symp. Coral Reefs* **1** (Biol), 275–282.
Warner, R. R. and Hoffman, S. G. (1980). *Evolution* **34**, 508–518.
Warner, R. R. and Robertson, D. R. (1978). *Smithsonian Contr. Zool.* **254**, 1–27.
Wirtz, P. (1978). *Z. Tierpsychol.* **48**, 142–174.

5. Genetics of Sex Determination in Fishes—A Brief Review

DAVID J. PRICE

Department of Biological Sciences, Plymouth Polytechnic, U.K.

Abstract: Sexuality in fishes is characterized by its diversity. Hermaphroditism, unisexuality and bisexuality all occur. Hermaphroditism is usually considered to be mainly a process of sex differentiation rather than sex determination. The involvement of possible genetic factors is not well understood. Unisexual fish are known whereby females produce only female offspring, either by gynogenesis or hybridogenesis.

The majority of fishes reproduce bisexually. This review is therefore mainly concerned with the genetics of sex determination in gonochorists. A variety of approaches have been used to elucidate the mechanisms involved, and these are discussed.

Relatively few fish species have been examined cytologically. Instances of morphologically distinct chromosomes are even fewer, but examples of male heterogamety, female heterogamety and various multiple sex chromosome mechanisms have been found. Sex associated differential staining of chromosomes has also recently been reported. In most species, the existence of either male or female heterogamety has been inferred from genetic rather than cytological evidence.

Polygenic sex factors located on autosomes may also be involved in sex determination. Usually sex chromosome genes are epistatic, but occasionally the autosomal genes may override these. Relative chromosome strengths in determining sex may vary between species, and various models have been proposed to account for results obtained from breeding experiments. In some species, sex determination may be entirely polygenic.

Determination of sex by environmental factors after conception is rare in gonochorists. However, in one atherinid, sex determination is under the control of both genotype and temperature.

Certain species may be characterized by more than one mode of sex determination, or at the very least, by a sex chromosome polymorphism. It is certain that several closely related species may exhibit different mechanisms of sex determination. Aspects of the evolution and adaptive significance of sex determining mechanisms are discussed.

I. INTRODUCTION

Fishes stand out amongst vertebrates in the range of sexuality which they

FISH REPRODUCTION
ISBN: 0–12–563660–1

exhibit. The various strategies employed include hermaphroditism, unisexuality and bisexuality. As a consequence of this diversity fishes have been
used in many studies into the problems of sex determination and sex
differentiation (Yamamoto, 1969).

II. HERMAPHRODITE FISHES

Hermaphrodites may be synchronous (simultaneous) when both eggs and
sperm mature at the same time, or asynchronous (consecutive) when the fish
functions as either male or female at any one time. Among the latter, both
protandrous and protogynous forms are known (Atz, 1964; Yamamoto, 1969;
Chan, 1970; Smith, 1975; Shapiro, Chap. 7, this volume). Occasionally,
hermaphrodites may occur in species which are normally bisexual, e.g. in
certain domesticated strains of *Xiphophorus helleri* (Lodi, 1979). Hermaphroditism is usually considered to be mainly a process of sex differentiation rather
than of sex determination (Gold, 1979; Kirpichnikov, 1981). Any possible
genetic basis for sexuality in these fishes is not well understood. Nevertheless,
genetic factors have been implicated.

Lepori (1980) considers that the most important feature of the gonad in
hermaphrodites is a genetic factor which makes the primary sexualizing
substances produced by the male and female parts of the gonad "non-
diffusable". This enables gonadal hermaphroditism to occur by preventing any
interaction between ovarian and testicular tissue. Chan *et al*. (1975) proposed
a scheme to account for natural sex reversal in *Monopterus*. This involved an
endocrine control behind which there was an underlying genetic control. In
the bisexual *Xiphophorus maculatus* genes which control sexual maturation
through hormonal control have been identified (Kallman and Schreibman,
1973).

In scarid fishes, Choat and Robertson (1975) have suggested that the
occurrence of different sexual identities in various mating systems may be
genetically determined. The fish *Rivulus marmoratus* is a hermaphrodite
capable of self-fertilization (Harrington, 1961). In natural populations it
forms genetically different groups of homozygous, isogenic individuals
(Kallman and Harrington, 1964; Harrington and Kallman, 1968). Harrington
(1967) found that low temperature tended to transform hermaphrodites into
males. However, this transformation is also dependent on the fishes genotype:
certain clones produce a greater percentage of males than others (Harrington,
1975).

Where environmental factors cause a switch from one sex to another, there
may exist genetic variation in the threshold level which results in the change-
over. Such a situation occurs in map turtles where sex is dependent upon the
temperature at which eggs are incubated. Bull *et al*. (1982) demonstrated a

high heritability for variation in the primary sex ratio at intermediate temperatures.

Hermaphroditism occurs in several orders of fish (Atz, 1964). This, together with the different forms of the gonad which are observed, indicates that hermaphroditism has evolved several times independently (Smith, 1975). It is usually considered to have evolved from bisexual or gonochoristic species (Lepori, 1980), although some workers have suggested that, at least in certain groups, hermaphroditism is the primitive type (e.g. Smith, 1959).

The evolutionary significance of hermaphroditism has often been speculated upon (e.g. Chan, 1970; Smith, 1975; Gold, 1979). It is commonly held that the reproductive strategies employed by fishes are adaptive. This implies that such systems evolved by natural selection. If this is true, then there must have been, at least in the past if not at present, genetic variation with respect to those strategies (see Dawkins, 1982). This argument is also of course pertinent to unisexual and bisexual fishes.

III. UNISEXUAL FISHES

Unisexuality in fishes is rarer than hermaphroditism, but examples are known whereby females produce only female offspring. This may be accomplished by either gynogenesis or hybridogenesis. In gynogenesis, sperm of a closely related species is used to trigger development of the egg nucleus but does not fuse with it. The male nucleus makes no contribution to the developing embryo. In hybridogenesis, gametic fusion occurs and the paternal genome is expressed, but only the haploid female genome is transmitted to the ovum.

The first unisexual fish was described by Hubbs and Hubbs (1932). *Poecilia (Mollienesia) formosa* mates with male *P. latipinna* or *P. mexicana* but reproduces gynogenetically to produce only female offspring. Natural gynogenesis also occurs in certain triploid populations of both *Poeciliopsis* species and *Carassius auratus gibelio*. Hybridogenesis has so far been described only in the genus *Poeciliopsis* where various hybridogenetic forms have been identified (Schultz, 1971). Reviews of the development of work with this genus, and the possible adaptive significance of hybridogenesis, have been given in a series of papers by Schultz (1971, 1977, 1980).

IV. BISEXUAL FISHES

The majority of fishes reproduce bisexually. The remainder of this review will therefore be concerned with sex determination in gonochoristic fish. Several different mechanisms exist in these fish and a variety of approaches have been used to investigate the genetic basis of these mechanisms. They include the following: (a) segregation analysis using sex-linked marker genes; (b) analysis of sex ratios in intraspecific crosses; (c) analysis of sex ratios in interspecific crosses; (d) inferences from fish produced either by artificial gynogenesis or artificial polyploidy; (e) inferences drawn from so-called "sex-reversals"; (f) analysis of offspring from fish artificially sex-reversed; (g) cytological analysis of both chromosomes and chromatin.

V. POLYGENIC SEX DETERMINATION

In some fish, sex determination is said to be polygenic, i.e. sex is determined by a number of minor genes distributed throughout the chromosome complement. There are no sex chromosomes as such. A zygote's sex is usually considered to be the result of a balance between the sum of male and female determining genes (Yamamoto, 1969). This viewpoint has been criticized by Kallman (1965). Criteria and possible models for the analysis of polygenic sex determination have been given by several authors (e.g. Kosswig, 1964; Scudo, 1967; Bulmer and Bull, 1982). Evidence for polygenic sex determination is provided by variable sex ratios and the "inheritability" of this trait (Scudo, 1967). In analysing biased sex ratios, one should exclude differential mortality and differential production of genotypes as a cause. Farr (1981) has recently shown that biased sex ratios in some laboratory strains of *Poecilia reticulata* are the result of differential production of XX and XY genotypes.

The best known example of probable polygenic sex determination occurs in *Xiphophorus helleri*. Breider (1935a) reported results from different females mated with the same male. Sex ratios in progeny from any one female were variable. Some females however consistently produced a lower frequency of males in different broods (e.g. 13–42%) whereas other females gave a consistently higher figure (e.g. 67–87%). Similarly, Kosswig (1964) has shown that different males also vary in this manner. Thus, different fish vary in the strength of the sex determining genes which they carry. Other examples of possible polygenic sex determination include *Poecilia (Limia) caudofasciata* (Breider, 1935b) and *Macropodus concolor* (Schwier, 1939).

Polygenic sex determination is considered to be the most primitive mechanism from which a sex chromosome system gradually evolved (Ohno, 1967; Kirpichnikov, 1981). This does not mean that all fish with polygenic sex determination should be considered primitive. Several workers have suggested conditions under which sex ratios may deviate from unity (e.g. Hamilton, 1967). When a 1:1 sex ratio is apparently not necessary (and an excess of females may even be an advantage) then the sex determining system may possibly evolve into a new specialized system (Kallman, 1965). Kallman (1965) suggests that this may be true in *Xiphophorus helleri* — the polygenic system representing an advanced condition that arose from an XX–XY

chromosome system. He considers that this viewpoint accords better with the fact that *Xiphophorus helleri* is the most widespread, ecologically diverse and specialized member of the genus (Rosen, 1960).

VI. GENOTYPE–ENVIRONMENT INTERACTION

An interesting case of possible polygenic involvement occurs in the atherinid *Menidia menidia*. Conover and Kynard (1981) have demonstrated that sex determination is under both genetic and environmental control during a critical phase of larval development. Sex ratios in progeny from different females are highly skewed, highly variable and differ in their responsiveness to temperature. Sex in this species, once determined, appears to be irreversible. This determination of sex by environmental factors after conception is a relatively rare phenomenon among bisexual animals. It is the first reported case among fishes.

VII. SEX CHROMOSOMES

A. Identification of heterogamety

In most bisexual fish which have been investigated there is some sort of sex chromosome involvement in sex determination. Often the evidence is indirect, but both male heterogamety (e.g. *XX* female–*XY* male) and female heterogamety (e.g. *WZ* female–*ZZ* male) occurs. Sex chromosomes are in a primitive state of evolution in fishes (Ohno, 1967), and are morphologically indistinguishable from the autosomes in the majority of species. Hence methods other than cytological ones have to be used to demonstrate sex chromosomes.

The earliest approach to this problem involved the use of sex-linked pigment genes as in Winge's work on *Poecilia reticulata* in the 1920s and later. Winge demonstrated male heterogomety in this species and his work has been well summarized elsewhere (Dodd, 1960; Bacci, 1965; Mittwoch, 1967; 1973). Species exhibiting these sex-linked marker genes are few in number. It is possible that the use of electrophoretic techniques may demonstrate the existence of sex-linked genes in other species. Avtalion and Mires (1976) have recently demonstrated a sex-specific protein in *Sarotherodon* (*Tilapia*) *aureus* using electrophoresis.

Without marker genes, other approaches must be adopted. Golovinskaya (1969) artificially induced gynogenesis in *Cyprinus carpio*. All the offspring were female which implies that, in this species, the female is the homogametic sex. Stanley (1976) obtained similar results with *Ctenopharyngodon idella*. Purdom and Lincoln (quoted in Purdom, 1972) obtained both sexes among gynogenetic *Pleuronectes platessa*, thus suggesting that female plaice are heterogametic. Wolters *et al.* (1982) artificially induced triploidy in *Ictalurus punctatus* eggs and obtained a 1:1 male:female ratio in the triploid fish. This suggests that females are the homogametic sex since then both *XXX* and *XXY* triploids would be expected to occur. If females were the heterogametic sex (*WZ*) and males homogametic (*ZZ*), then all the resulting fish would have been *WZZ* and female.

Another technique is to use fish artificially sex-reversed by hormone treatment. Jalabert *et al.* (1974) treated fry of *Sarotherodon niloticus* with methyltestosterone. Complete and functional sex reversal was achieved. Some of the experimental males when crossed with normal females produced all-female offspring. This means that they must have had a female *XX* genotype and thus demonstrates female homogamety. Similar work has also demonstrated female homogamety in *Carassius auratus* (Yamamoto and Kajishima, 1968), *Sarotherodon mossambicus* (Clemens and Inslee, 1968), and *Salmo gairdneri* (Okado *et al.*, 1979). Male homogamety was demonstrated in *Sarotherodon aureus* (Guerrero, 1975).

Where two related species have different sex chromosome mechanisms, hybridization may allow the detection of heterogamety. If a female from a female homogametic species (*XX*) is crossed with a male from a male homogametic species (*ZZ*), then all-male offspring result. The reciprocal cross (*WZ* female x *XY* male) yields both male and female offspring. This approach has been used to examine sex determination in tilapia (see Balarin, 1979) and will be discussed further below.

B. The platyfish system

The most extensively studied system involving natural populations is in the platyfish *Xiphophorus maculatus*. Early domesticated stocks of unknown origin were shown to exhibit female homogamety (Bellamy, 1928). Later it was found that samples from Mexico were *XX* female–*XY* male (Gordon, 1947) whereas Belize populations were *WY* female–*YY* male (Gordon, 1951). Further investigations by Kallman (1965, 1970, 1973) showed that the *W* and *X* chromosomes may be present together in populations covering 90% of the species range. In some populations, three female genotypes (*WY*, *WX* and *XX*) and two male genotypes (*XY* and *YY*) may be found (Kallman, 1973). Thus, in this fish there is a polymorphism for sex chromosomes. Two (*W*,*X*) determine female sex whilst one, the *Y*, is male determining.

In the related species *X. variatus*, *X. milleri* and *X. pygmaeus*, sex chromosomes are homologous with *X. maculatus* and of the *XX–XY* type (Kallman and Atz, 1966; Zander, 1968). It is suggested therefore that the *XX–XY* mechanism is the original type and that the *W* evolved later. Both the *XX–XY* and *WY–YY* systems occur among other poeciliid fish and they may have arisen several times independently.

W chromosomes in females from wild populations often possess wild-type alleles for dull colour at the pigment loci, unlike the X chromosomes which possess both wild-type and alleles for colour. Kallman (1970, 1973) suggests that there would be selection against coloured XX females. However, X chromosomes carrying alleles for colour in the males would be selected for since brightly coloured poeciliid males have greater mating success (Endler, 1978). The W chromosome carrying alleles for dull colour would not be selected against since it only occurs in females. Also dull coloured WY females have more offspring than females with the sex-linked colour patterns. WY and WX females are therefore fitter than XX females and the chromosome polymorphism should be transient (Kallman, 1970). However, this ignores the effect of male fitness. Orzack et al. (1980) performed mating competition experiments which showed that XY males are better than YY males at inseminating females. They further show that, providing these same conditions hold in natural populations, a stable polymorphism would result with all three chromosomes (W, X and Y) being maintained in the populations (Orzack et al., 1980).

In *Xiphophorus maculatus* there are also instances of atypical sex determination where the phenotypic sex does not agree with the chromosomal sex. Of the six possible combinations of sex chromosomes, all but the YY can differentiate into either male or female. It seems that genes for both male- and femaleness are on the W and X but that the Y carries predominately male determining genes.

In mammals the indifferent gonad becomes a testis in the presence of H–Y antigen and an ovary in its absence. Male–female graft rejection has been reported in an inbred strain of platies (Miller, 1962) and the H–Y antigen has been demonstrated in XY males of *Oryzias latipes* (Pechan et al., 1979). Apparently, in fish from more primitive orders (Isopondyli and Ostariophysi), absorption of H–Y antibody is similar in gonads of both males and females (Müller and Wolf, 1979), suggesting that H–Y genes may be present on both sex chromosomes in these fish (Wachtel and Koo, 1981).

C. Autosomal influences

Kallman (1968) presented evidence for the existence of sex transformer genes located on the autosomes to account for the so-called "sex-reversals" which occurred in laboratory stocks of platies. There is no evidence that these genes act additively (as they would in polygenic sex determination). Rather they seem to act epistatically and preferentially through the W chromosome. This is interesting since the W chromosome is usually considered to be more strongly female determining than the X (see below).

Oktay (1959a,b) also demonstrated the existence of autosomal genes affecting sex in an inbred line of platies. She obtained XX males which when outcrossed to normal females produced all female offspring as expected.

When interbred, both sexes were produced in extremely variable proportions. Possible mechanisms are discussed by Kosswig (1964), but it is not possible to demonstrate epistasis here.

Other evidence for interactions between autosomes and sex chromosomes has come from work on hybrids between *Xiphophorus maculatus* and *X. helleri* — a fish with no sex chromosomes. Sengün (1941) crossed *WZ* female platies with swordtails (*xx*). All the resulting *Wx* fish were females. When *XX* female platies were crossed with swordtails (*xx*), both sexes resulted among the *Xx* offspring. Thus, the *W* is stronger than the *X* in determining femaleness, and the *Xx* males are the result of polygenic male-determining genes from *X. helleri*. Similar results are discussed by Kosswig (1964) who points out that depending on which species are used in these crosses, either the polygenic or sex chromosome species may be epistatic.

Yamamoto (1969) provides a model to illustrate the type of "polyfactorial" sex determination with epistatic genes located in the sex chromosomes. Occasional "sex reversals" are considered as fish where the balance of male and female determining genes in the autosomes is altered by, say, recombination, and overrides the sex chromosome constitution to determine sex. Kallman (1965) has, however, cast considerable doubt upon the idea that sex determination is simply dependent upon the strength of a large number of male and female factors. Any models of autosomal influence must therefore be regarded as tentative.

D. Tilapia hybrids

In 1960 Hickling produced all-male offspring by crossing what he thought were two different strains of *Sarotherodon mossambicus*. They were later shown to be different species and various interspecific crosses with tilapia since have resulted in a high percentage of male offspring (Balarin, 1979). Preliminary studies on the sex-determining mechanism were produced by Chen (1966, 1969) who suggested that some species were male heterogametic (*XX–XY*) and others female heterogametic (*WZ–ZZ*).

Not all observed results can be explained on the above hypothesis. Possible reasons for this include contamination of parental stocks by other species (Avtalion *et al.*, 1976), differential mortality, or autosomal influence. A detailed model of autosomal influence has been suggested (Avtalion and Hammerman, 1978; Hammerman and Avtalion, 1979) to account for the results of crosses between *S. mossambicus* and *S. hornorum*. They suggest 18 different genotypes each having a pair of autosomes (*AA*, *Aa* or *aa*) and two sex chromosomes (*WX*, *WY*, *WW*, *XY*, *XX* or *YY*). By using a series of directed graphs showing the relative strength of chromosome pairs and developed from Chen's sex ratio results, the sex of the different genotypes was determined. The theory predicts eight different sex ratios (0:1, 1:3, 3:5, 1:1,

9:7, 5:3, 3:1, 1:0, female:male) of which three (5:3, 9:7, 3:5) are not predicted by the $WXYZ$ theory. In the following genotype pairs — ($AaWY$, $aaWY$), ($AaXY$, $aaXY$), ($AAWW$, $AaWW$) — the first genotype is male, the second female, thus showing the importance of the autosomes.

The above theory succeeds in explaining all of Chen's (Chen, 1969) results, including those not predicted by the $WXYZ$ theory. It also explains many of Jalabert *et al.* (1971) results with *S. macrochir* and *S. niloticus*, although here the relative strength of the W chromosome differs from that in the *mossambicus-hornorum* system. As Kallman (1965) has pointed out, almost any sex ratio can be explained by assigning arbitrary valences to chromosomes and genes. Nevertheless, Hammerman and Avtalion's scheme does explain observed results. Furthermore, the theory makes predictions which are testable. Experiments currently being undertaken by Hammerman and Avtalion should determine its validity.

E. Cytological heterogamety

Although only comparatively few species have been examined cytologically (perhaps 2–3%, Gold, 1979), most fish do not possess morphologically distinct sex chromosomes. Ebeling and Chen (1970) list three criteria for the confirmation of heterogamety. These are — (1) the invariable occurrence of a heteromorphic pair in one but not the other sex, (2) the presence of an atypically behaving bivalent at meiosis, and (3) the presence of two different haploid karyotypes in secondary spermatocytes. All these criteria are rarely met, but evidence for cytological heterogamety has been reported in more than 50 species of fish from 27 different families (Kirphichnikov, 1981).

The first report was by Nogusa (1955) who demonstrated male heterogamety of the XX–XY type in a gobiid species, *Mogrunda obscura*. Other reported types of male heterogamety include XX–XO (e.g. *Galaxias platei*, Campos, 1972) and three kinds of multiple sex chromosome mechanisms. These are $X_1X_1X_2X_2/X_1X_2Y$ (e.g. filefish *Stephanolepis cirrhifer*, Murofushi *et al.*, 1980), $X_1X_1X_2X_2/X_1X_1X_2$ (e.g. cichlid *Callichromous bimaculatus*, Rishi 1976a), and XX/XY_1Y_2 (e.g. erythrinid *Hoplias* sps., Bertollo, 1978).

Female heterogamety is less common and is usually of the WZ–ZZ type (e.g. anguilloid *Astroconger myriaster*, Park and Kang, 1979). Other reported cases include a ZO/ZZ type (e.g. belodontiidid *Colisa lalius*, Rishi, 1976b) and one example of a multiple sex chromosome mechanism of the W_1W_2Z/ZZ kind (paradontiidid *Apeirodon affinis*, Filho *et al.*, 1980).

There are technical problems in working with fish chromosomes. They tend to be small, numerous, and the karyotype may be symmetrical. This makes it difficult to distinguish individual chromosomes. The application of newer chromosome staining techniques which cause differential staining of chromosomes may help overcome these problems. In the mudminnow *Umbra limi*, a sex-associated differential fluorescence of mitotic chromosomes and of spermatozoa has been demonstrated (Howell and Bloom, 1973). In the killifish *Fundulus diaphanus*, differential staining of nucleolar organizer regions located on the sex chromosomes has been achieved (Howell and Black, 1979). The technique of G-banding has been used to confirm female heterogamety in *Colisa fasciatus* (Rishi, 1979).

Staining of constitutive heterochromatin (C-banding) in the sex chromosomes of *Fundulus* has allowed Kornfield (1981) to make deductions concerning the evolution of sex chromosomes in this genus. Ueda and Ojima (1978) have also used C-banding to investigate chromosomal characteristics in *Carassius auratus*. In some *C. auratus* subspecies they found that females had a pair of chromosomes which had intensely stained C-bands. In males, only one chromosome of the pair stained intensely. Similar sex chromosome markers were found in other subspecies but not all (Ojima and Tekai, 1979; Ojima *et al.*, 1979).

Mehl and Reinboth (1975) were able to demonstrate sex chromatin in interphase cells of female but not male *Haplochromis burtoni*. This suggests that these fish have a *XX–XY* or possibly *XX–XO* sex determining mechanism. Haider (1973) was however unable to demonstrate sex chromatin in interphase cells of *Salmo gairdneri*—a species where heteromorphic sex chromosomes have since been demonstrated cytologically (Thorgaard, 1977).

F. Evolution

Even with the above examples, it is clear that the sex chromosomes of fishes are relatively unspecialized and in a primitive state of evolution. This is supported by the fact that crossing over may still occur between the different sex chromosomes (e.g. Kallman, 1970). The number of genes located on the sex chromosomes which are involved in sex determination is not known. The position of these genes has however been mapped in *Xiphophorus maculatus* to a location close to the centromere (Anders *et al.*, 1973).

The mechanisms by which sex chromosomes may evolve have been considered by Ohno (1967). To develop heteromorphic sex chromosomes, some sort of isolation during meiosis is required in order to accumulate the sex determining factors, i.e. crossing over needs to be restricted. This seems to have occurred in *Oryzias latipes* where in *XY* male fish there is limited crossing over. If these fish are sex-reversed, the amount of crossing over between the *X* and *Y* chromosomes increases, thus showing the dependence upon the testicular environment (Yamamoto, 1961). Isolation need not involve all the chromosome. In *Poecilia reticulata*, there is crossing over between some sex-linked genes but not others (see Ohno, 1967).

Gold (1979) has pointed out that some studies (e.g. Chen, 1969; Ebeling and Chen, 1970) suggest a cytological progression towards increasing heteromorphy. In the majority of cases however it is not known whether chromosome heteromorphy represents isolated instances or is an early step in the continuing evolution of sex chromosomes in those groups of fishes.

VIII. CONCLUSIONS

It is clear that fishes represent an extremely heterogeneous group, not only in their range of sexuality, but also in the genetic mechanisms of sex determination which they have evolved. The existence of different mechanisms among closely related species is a common feature. This suggests two possibilities. First, that the various mechanisms have evolved independently several times, and second, that such mechanisms are adaptive.

REFERENCES

Anders, A., Anders, F. and Klinke, K. (1973). In "Genetics and Mutagenesis of Fish" (J. H. Schröder, ed.), pp. 53–63. Springer Verlag, Berlin.
Atz, J. W. (1964). In "Intersexuality in Vertebrates Including Man" (C. N. Armstrong and A. J. Marshall, eds), pp. 145–232. Academic Press, New York and London.
Avtalion, R. R., Duczyminer, M., Wojdani, A. and Pruginin, Y. (1976). Aquaculture 7, 255–265.
Avtalion, R. R. and Mires, D. (1976). Aquaculture 7, 391–394.
Avtalion, R. R. and Hammerman, I. S. (1978). Bamidgeh 30, 110–115.
Bacci, G. (1965). "Sex Determination". Pergamon Press, Oxford.
Balarin, J. D. (1979). "Tilapia — a guide to their biology and culture in Africa". University of Stirling.
Bertollo, L. A. C. (1978). Estudos citogenéticos no gênero Hoplias Gill, 1903 (Pisces, Erythrinidae). Doctoral Thesis. Universidade de São Paulo. 164 pp.
Bellamy, A. W. (1928). Genetics 13, 226–232.
Breider, H. (1935a). Z. wiss. Zool. 146, 383–416.
Breider, H. (1935b). Z. indukt. Abstamm. u. VererbLehre 72, 80–87.
Bull, J. J., Vogt, R. C. and Bulmer, M. G. (1982). Evolution 36, 333–341.
Bulmer, M. G. and Bull, J. J. (1982). Evolution 36, 13–26.
Campos, H. H. (1972). Copeia 1972, 368–370.
Chan, S. T. H. (1970). Phil. Trans. R. Soc. Lond. B 259, 59–71.
Chan, S. T. H., O, W. and Hui, S. W. B. (1975). In "Intersexuality in the Animal Kingdom" (R. Reinboth, ed.), pp. 201–221. Springer Verlag, Berlin.
Chen, F. Y. (1966). In "Report of the Tropical Fish Culture Research Institute", pp. 43–47. Batu Berendam, Malacca.
Chen, F. Y. (1969). Verh. int. Verein. theor. angew. Limnol. 17, 719–724.
Chen, T. R. (1969). Postilla 130, 1–29.
Choat, J. H. and Robertson, D. R. (1975). In "Intersexuality in the Animal Kingdom" (R. Reinboth, ed.), pp. 263–283. Springer Verlag, Berlin.
Clemens, H. P. and Inslee, T. (1968). Trans. Am. Fish. Soc. 97, 18–21.
Conover, D. O. and Kynard, B. E. (1981). Science N.Y. 213, 577–579.
Dawkins, R. (1982). "The Extended Phenotype". W. H. Freeman, Oxford.

Dodd, J. M. (1960). *Mem. Soc. Endocr.* **7**, 17–44.
Ebeling, A. W. and Chen, T. R. (1970). *Trans. Am. Fish. Soc.* **99**, 131–138.
Endler, J. A. (1978). *Evol. Biol.* **11**, 319–364.
Farr, A. J. (1981). *Heredity* **47**, 237–248.
Filho, O. M., Bertollo, L. A. C. and Galetti, P. M. (1980). *Caryologia* **33**, 83–91.
Gold, J. R. (1979). *In* "Fish Physiology" (W. S. Hoar, D. J. Randall and J. R. Brett, eds), Vol. VIII, pp. 353–405. Academic Press, New York and London.
Golovinskaya, K. A. (1969). *In* "Genetics, Selection and Hybridization of Fish" (B. I. Cherfas, ed.), pp. 74–78. Israel Program for Scientific Translations, Jerusalem, 1972.
Gordon, M. (1947). *Genetics* **32**, 8–17.
Gordon, M. (1951). *Zoologica N.Y.* **36**, 127–134.
Guerrero, R. D. (1975). *Trans. Am. Fish. Soc.* **104**, 342–348.
Haider, G. (1973). *Indian J. Zool.* **1**, 71–76.
Hamilton, W. D. (1967). *Science N.Y.* **156**, 477–488.
Hammerman, I. S. and Avtalion, R, R. (1979). *Theor. Appl. Genet.* **55**, 177–187.
Harrington, R. W. (1961). *Science N.Y.* **134**, 1749–1750.
Harrington, R. W. (1967). *Biol. Bull., Woods Hole* **132**, 174–199.
Harrington, R. W. (1975). *In* "Intersexuality in the Animal Kingdom" (R. Reinboth, ed.), pp. 249–262. Springer Verlag, Berlin.
Harrington, R. W. and Kallman, K. D. (1968). *Am. Nat.* **102**, 337–343.
Hickling, C. F. (1960). *J. Genet.* **57**, 1–10.
Howell, W. M. and Black, D. A. (1979). *Copeia* **1979**, 544–546.
Howell, W. M. and Bloom, S. (1973). *Nature Lond.* **245**, 261–263.
Hubbs, C. L. and Hubbs, L. C. (1932). *Science N.Y.* **76**, 628–630.
Jalabert, B., Kammacher, P. and Lessent, P. (1971). *Annls Biol. anim. Biochim. Biophys.* **11**, 155–165.
Jalabert, B., Moreau, J., Planquette, P. and Billard, R. (1974). *Annls Biol. anim. Biochim. Biophys.* **14**, 729–739.
Kallman, K. D. (1965). *Zoologica N.Y.* **50**, 151–190.
Kallman, K. D. (1968). *Genetics* **60**, 811–828.
Kallman, K. D. (1970). *Zoologica N.Y.* **55**, 1–18.
Kallman, K. D. (1973). *In* "Genetics and Mutagenesis of Fish" (J. H. Schröder, ed.), pp. 19–28. Springer Verlag, Berlin.
Kallman, K. D. and Atz, J. W. (1966). *Zoologica N.Y.* **51**, 107–135.
Kallman, K. D. and Harrington, R. W. (1964). *Biol. Bull., Woods Hole* **126**, 101–114.
Kallman, K. D. and Schreibman, M. P. (1973). *Gen. Comp. Endocrinol.* **21**, 287–304.
Kirpichnikov, V. S. (1981). "Genetic Bases of Fish Selection". Springer Verlag, Berlin.
Kornfield, I. (1981). *Copeia* **1981**, 916–918.
Kosswig, C. (1964). *Experientia* **20**, 190–199.
Lepori, N. G. (1980). "Sex Differentiation, Hermaphroditism, and Intersexuality in Vertebrates Including Man". Piccin, Padua.
Lodi, E. (1979). *Experientia* **35**, 1440–1441.
Mehl, J. A. P. and Reinboth, R. (1975). *In* "Intersexuality in the Animal Kingdom" (R. Reinboth, ed.). Springer Verlag, Berlin.
Miller, L. (1962). *Transplantn. Bull.* **30**, 147–149.
Mittwoch, U. (1967). "Sex Chromosomes". Academic Press, New York and London.
Mittwoch, U. (1973). "Genetics of Sex Differentiation". Academic Press, New York and London.
Müller, U. and Wolf, U. (1979). *Differentiation* **14**, 185–187.
Murofushi, M., Oikawa, S., Nishikawa, S. and Yosida, T. H. (1980). *Japan. J. Genet.* **55**, 127–132.

Nogusa, S. (1955). *Cytologia* **20**, 11–18.

Ohno, S. (1967). "Sex Chromosomes and Sex-linked Genes". Springer Verlag, Berlin.

Okado, H., Matumoto, H. and Yamazaki, F. (1979). *Bull. Jap. Soc. scient. Fish.* **45**, 413–419.

Öktay, M. (1959a). *Istanb. Üniv. Fen. Fak. Mecm. Seri. B.* **24**, 75–92.

Öktay, M. (1959b). *Istanb. Üniv. Fen. Fak. Mecm. Seri. B.* **24**, 224–233.

Ojima, Y. and Takai, O. (1979). *Proc. Japan Acad.* **55** (Ser. B.), 346–350.

Ojima, Y., Ueda, T. and Narikawa, T. (1979). *Proc. Japan Acad.* **55** (Ser. B), 58–63.

Orzack, S. H., Sohn, J. J., Kallman, K. D., Levin, S. A. and Johnston, R. (1980). *Evolution* **34**, 663–672.

Park, E. H. and Kang, Y. S. (1979). *Cytogenet. Cell Genet.* **23**, 33–38.

Pechan, P., Wachtel, S. S. and Reinboth, R. (1979). *Differentiation* **14**, 189–192.

Purdom, C. E. (1972). *Heredity* **29**, 11–24.

Rishi, K. K. (1976a). *Ciênc. Cult.* **28**, 1171–1173.

Rishi, K. K. (1976b). *Nucleus* **19**, 95–98.

Rishi, K. K. (1979). *Copeia* **1979**, 146–149.

Rosen, D. E. (1960). *Bull. Fla St. Mus. biol. Sci.* **5**, 57–242.

Schultz, R. J. (1971). *Am. Zool.* **11**, 351–360.

Schultz, R. J. (1977). *Evol. Biol.* **10**, 277–331.

Schultz, R. J. (1980). *In* "Polyploidy: Biological Relevance" (W. H. Lewis, ed.), pp. 313–340. Plenum Press, New York.

Schwier, H. (1939). *Z. indukt. Abstamm.-u. VererbLehre* **77**, 291–335.

Scudo, F. M. (1967). *Monitore zool. ital.* **1**, 1–21.

Sengün, A. (1941). *Istanb. Üniv. Fen. Fak. Mecm. Seri. B.* **6**, 33–48.

Smith, C. L. (1959). *Pap. Mich. Acad. Sci.* **44**, 111–119.

Smith, C. L. (1975). *In* "Intersexuality in the Animal Kingdom" (R. Reinboth, ed.), pp. 295–310. Springer Verlag, Berlin.

Stanley, J. G. (1976). *J. Fish. Res. Bd Can.* **33**, 1372–1374.

Thorgaard, G. H. (1977). *Science N.Y.* **196**, 900–902.

Ueda, T. and Ojima, Y. (1978). *Proc. Japan Acad.* **54** (Ser. B), 283–288.

Wachtel, S. S. and Koo, G. C. (1981). *In* "Mechanisms of Sex Differentiation in Animals and Man" (C. R. Austin and R. G. Edwards, eds), pp. 255–299. Academic Press, London.

Wolters, W. R., Libey, G. S. and Chrisman, C. L. (1982). *Trans. Am. Fish. Soc.* **111**, 102–105.

Yamamoto, T. (1961). *J. exp. Zool.* **146**, 163–179.

Yamamoto, T. (1969). *In* "Fish Physiology" (W. S. Hoar and D. J. Randall, eds), Vol. III, pp. 117–175. Academic Press, New York and London.

Yamamoto, T. and Kajishima, T. (1968). *J. exp. Zool.* **168**, 215–222.

Zander, C. D. (1968). *Molec. Gen. Genetics* **101**, 29–42.

6. Progenetic Tendencies in Deep-Sea Fishes

N. B. MARSHALL

6 Park Lane, Saffron Walden, Essex, U.K.

Abstract: Progenesis is the precocious assumption of sexual maturity before an animal has attained its complete development. Such "larvalization" is common in midwater fishes of the deep ocean, particularly in those of the bathypelagic zone, but is rare in bottom-dwelling species, whether benthopelagic or benthic.

At both mesopelagic and bathypelagic levels progenetic tendencies are well shown by the species of *Cyclothone*, the simplest and commonest genus of oceanic fishes. Larval features are present in the skeleton (weak ossification), below the skin (wide subdermal spaces), eyes, swimbladder, fins and axial muscles. Among the other progenetic midwater fishes the ceratioid angler-fishes are particularly prominent.

Progenetic deep-sea fishes are much more simply organized than are their fully developed relatives. Thus, mesopelagic species of *Cyclothone*, to take the best represented taxa, are able to live on a restricted diet and achieve, like non-progenetic, migrating mesopelagic fishes of comparable size, an annual life cycle. In the longer living and larger fishes of bathypelagic regions, a simple progenetic organization should enable them to subsist in food-poor surroundings and develop the fecundity needed for especially hazardous ontogenetic migrations.

I. INTRODUCTION

While tracing the development of the swimbladder in deep-sea fishes (Marshall, 1960), I was soon led to consider the entire organization of each species and its environmental setting. In many upper midwater (mesopelagic) fishes, such as the smaller stomiatoids and lantern-fishes, there is a gas-filled swimbladder: in others, most of which are relatively large and predatory, the swimbladder is markedly regressed or absent, which is true also of all the lower midwater bathypelagic fauna (e.g. ceratioid angler-fishes and black *Cyclothone*). However, contrary to this trend, close to the deep-sea floor, nearly all members of the diverse benthopelagic fauna (e.g. macrourids, morids, ophidiids, halosaurs, notacanths and synaphobranchid eels) have a well developed swimbladder. Benthic forms, such as sea-snails (Liparidae), eel-

FISH REPRODUCTION
ISBN: 0-12-563660-1

pouts (Zoarcidae) and tripod-fishes, etc. (Bathypteroidae) are without a swimbladder.

It soon became clear that the species with a capacious gas-filled swimbladder can, above all, carry well developed muscles and a firmly ossified skeleton at neutral buoyancy. In forms without a swimbladder these two systems and others are markedly reduced (Marshall, 1960). Indeed, an assessment of their buoyancy balance sheets showed that it is largely through such muscular and skeletal reduction that such mesopelagic fishes (e.g. *Xenodermichthys* and *Gonostoma elongatum*) come close below neutral buoyancy (Denton and Marshall, 1958).

Certain midwater species with reduced organ systems and no swimbladder retain larval or youthful features in their adult organization. In the 1960 Discovery Report I drew attention to such features without qualifying them as "neotenous". My main intention was to suggest that economies in the organization of deep-sea fishes, particularly in bathypelagic species, should enable them to live in food-poor surroundings. However, in a paper on the giganturid fishes, Walters (1961) remarked that they show "evidence of having become neotenic or larvalized" in such features as a poorly ossified and reduced skeleton, absence of scales, much gelatinous subdermal tissue and non-segmented fin rays. Walters also considered how far economies in the metabolic organization of the giganturids are an adaption for life in deserted surroundings. Cohen (1960) also found larval features in a mesopelagic argentinoid fish (*Dolichopteryx*). Aphyonid fishes are also markedly neotenic (Nielsen, 1969).

The retention of larval characters in deep-sea fishes is more pervasive than I recently recognized (Marshall, 1979). Thus, the present intention is first to look more closely at such features and then to see how far they are ecologically adaptive, especially during the reproductive phase of the life history. Moreover, for the rest of this paper I shall be following Gould (1977) in using progenesis to describe precociously mature animals that retain larval or juvenile features. The term is due to Giard, who realized that many parasitic animals are progenetic. As Gould (1977) quotes from Giard's 1887 paper: "We say that an animal exhibits progenesis when sexual reproduction occurs in a more or less precocious fashion, that is to say when the sexual products . . . form and mature before the animal has attained its complete development." Gould traces neoteny to Kollmann (1885), who applies the term to adult animals that retain larval features after a long period of maturation. The Mexican axolotl is a paradigm of neoteny.

II. PROGENETIC FEATURES IN DEEP-SEA FISHES

We can do no better than start with *Cyclothone*, a genus of stomiatoid fishes (family Gonostomatidae). Fishes of this genus, which range from about 25 to 70 mm in standard length, are the most ubiquitous, and among the simplest in organization, of all deep-sea fishes. In depth they range from epipelagic to bathypelagic levels and from subarctic to antarctic latitudes. There are four or five transparent species that live at mesopelagic levels. Eight black species extend from lower mesopelagic to deep bathypelagic parts of the water column (800–4000 m).

Like nearly all midwater fishes of the deep ocean, *Cyclothone* spp. pass their larval life in the productive epipelagic zone. Here they stay and feed on small zooplankters until ready for metamorphosis and descent to the adult environment. As larvae, *Cyclothone* spp. have much the same organization as the corresponding stages of their gonostomatid relatives of the same adult size. For instance, the larvae of both *Cyclothone* and *Vinciguerria*, when about 10–15 mm in length, have well formed vertical fins, prominent eyes and otic capsules, and a small swimbladder set about two-thirds of the way along the intestine. The stomach and liver are little more than anlagen (Fig. 1).

During metamorphosis in both genera there is a slight reduction in length, a

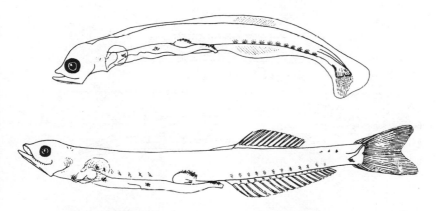

Fig. 1.   Postlarval stages of *Cyclothone braueri*. Above, 4·8 mm; below, 13·2 mm. Note the swimbladder over the posterior part of the intestine (from Marshall, 1979).

marked alteration in shape and changes towards the adult jaws and dentition. The development of the photophores and pigmentation is also well advanced. After metamorphosis the most trenchant differences between *Cyclothone* and *Vinciguerria* involve the development of the eyes, the swimbladder, the kidneys, the subdermal spaces and probably the muscle fibre complex of the myotomes. In *Vinciguerria* the oval larval eyes have increased in size and changed into the more rounded form of the adult: in *Cyclothone* there is little or no change in the eyes and those of the adult are more or less postlarval in size, form and fine structure. Locket (1977) examined the eyes of adult *Cyclothone braueri* and *C. pseudopallida*, and besides the disproportionately large lens, found anomalies in the relatively thick retina. During a recent visit to Dr Locket in the Department of Anatomy, Adelaide University, I was able to see his excellent preparations of the eyes in these two species. We both concluded that their eyes were more or less larval in form and fine structure.

Concerning the swimbladder, during metamorphosis that of *Vinciguerria* grows forward and increases markedly in capacity, its growth being matched by that of the rete and gas gland (see Fig. 2 and Ozawa, 1973). In *Cyclothone* there are no such changes and in the transparent species the adult swimbladder has much the same relative size and position as in the postlarvae. Moreover, the rete, which is about 1·5 mm long in *C. braueri*, feeds an active gas gland. Thus, the adults of transparent *Cyclothone* have both a larval and functional, gas-filled swimbladder (see Fig. 2). In the adults of black *Cyclothone* spp. the swimbladder is completely regressed (Marshall, 1960, 1979).

The kidneys of *Vinciguerria* also grow in size and complexity during and

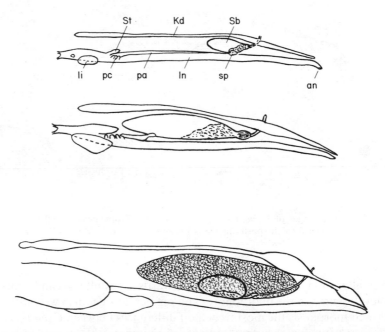

Fig. 2. The swimbladder in relation to other viscera (kidney and gut) in a postlarval and metamorphosing stage of *Vinciguerria nimbaria* (uppermost and middle, respectively and redrawn from Ozawa, 1973) and in an adult *Cyclothone braueri*. Note the rapid growth of the swimbladder during metamorphosis in the first species and the larval-sized swimbladder (about 1 mm in length and surrounded by a fat body) in the adult of the second. an: anus; in: intestine; kd: kidney; li: liver; pa: pancreas; pc: pyloric caeca; sb: swimbladder; sp: spleen; st: stomachs.

after metamorphosis (see Ozawa, 1973, Fig. 6), but in *Cyclothone* there is much less change. Indeed, the entire adult kidney system consists of two tubules only, each headed by a glomerulus, and which extend side by side along the body cavity to unite at the bladder (Owen, 1938). Despite their mesonephric resemblances Owen suggested, particularly because of the extreme anterior location of the glomeruli, that they may be ". . . modified pronephric glomeruli, associated posteriorly with a pronephric duct which has undergone modification into a typical secretory tubule". Jollic (1962) interpreted this as "a case of neoteny in a fish which looks like a larva in many respects".

As in larval fishes, there are relatively large subdermal spaces in adult *Cyclothone*, which are taken up with fat sinuses (see Marshall, 1960). There are also fat bodies around the swimbladder and mesenteries. Recently Smith and Laver (1981) have measured the respiration of three female *Cyclothone acclinidens*, caught off Southern California. They also analysed their energy stores (total lipid was 4·82–6·84%), and estimated (assuming a respiratory quotient of 0·72) that these fishes could survive on their own energy reserves for a period of up to 70 days. In *Vinciguerria* and other swimbladder-bearing mesopelagic fishes there is little space between the skin and myotomes.

The extensive subdermal sinuses in *Cyclothone* fill up space that would be given, as it were, to myotomes in *Vinciguerria*. Indeed, in cross section the myotomes of *Cyclothone* are almost entirely composed of muscle fibres with the same diameter, as in larval fishes. After metamorphosis there is no mosaic of smaller newly formed fibres among the larger larval fibres. In *Cyclothone* the white fibres presumably increase in diameter after metamorphosis but there is little increase in their number. Indeed, the depth of the myotomes in a metamorphosed *Cyclothone pygmaea* is much the same as that in a 10 mm postlarva. The same ratio in corresponding stages of *Vinciguerria* is about four. Lastly, the skeleton of an adult *Cyclothone* has a number of larvalized features. The vertebrae are but slightly constricted about a persistent notochord and the neurocranium is poorly ossified.

Using *Cyclothone* as a model of progenetic tendencies in midwater fishes, we turn to other instances and first to the Giganturidae, a family of mesopelagic fishes. As already mentioned, Walters (1961) studied their larval features and he concluded that the adults have certain features that are associated with early developmental stages in other teleost groups: the anterior setting of the kidney, non-segmented fin rays; subdermal spaces filled with mesenchymal jelly, the absence of scales and the persistence of a cartilaginous endocranium.

In the argentinoid genus *Dolichopteryx*, which is mesopelagic, Cohen (1960) found characters in sexually mature individuals that are also found in immature forms of the related *Bathylychnops*: poorly developed body muscles, scales vestigially present, paired fins on prominent peduncles and lack of pigmentation (skin mostly transparent). Compared to their relatives the ophidiids, fishes of the family Aphyonidae, which seem to live between bathypelagic and benthopelagic levels, have the following progenetic tendencies according to Nielsen (1969); the vertebral centra are barely constricted; the skeleton is lightly ossified; there are no scales; the pectoral fins have prolonged peduncles (in *Aphyonus, Nybelinia, Sciadonus* and *Leucochlamys*); the lamellae on the first gill arch are reduced, and these fishes are sexually mature when small (<100 mm).

There are also eel-like forms with progenetic features. Thus, Castle (1977) in describing a new genus and species of cyemid eel, *Neocyema erythrosoma*, which contains relatively well developed ovaries, refers to its leptocephalus-like appearance and much reduced skeleton (no primary upper jaw, opercular series, pectoral girdle and fin supports and the rather gelatinous nature of the body). He also refers to other observations on eel larvae (e.g. *Cyema*) with precocious gonads. There are also the most reduced and larval-looking of all deep-sea fishes, the Monognathidae, certain of which have developing gonads when very small (Raju, 1974).

Turning now to the largest group of bathypelagic fishes, the ceratioid angler-fishes (there are about 100 species), we think first of the dwarf males which certainly metamorphose when very small. Bertelsen (1951) concluded that larval life in ceratioids probably lasts less than two months. Then comes a relatively rapid metamorphosis. After metamorphosis, the slow growth rate of female ceratioids and the development of the ovaries suggests that they take several years to reach maturity. "Males that are not parasitic on the females are progenetic", and as I continued (Marshall, 1979) drawing on Bertelsen's observations:

> Such males, which are found in *Melanocetus, Himantolophus, Gigantactis* and some oneirodids, have large testes, even in late larval and metamorphosis stages. Not long after metamorphosis, when they are a few centimetres in length and ready to mate, they have developed pincer-like jaws, likely means, it is thought to nip on the skin of a female during breeding. Progenesis in males that become parasitic on the female (ceratiids and linophrynids) is not elicited until they become attached.

When mature, both male and female ceratioids may retain the following larval features: large subdermal spaces (filled with gelatinous tissue); and partly developed lateral muscles and skeleton. In an adolescent female of *Gigantactis longicirra*, Waterman (1948) drew attention to the larval appearance of the neurocranium.

> In its basic structure, lack of roofing elements anterior to the otic capsule and the dominance of the inner ear and capsule and absence of optic and nasal skeletal parts, the neurocranium of *Gigantactis* is shown to have a striking similarity to the developing chondrocranium of *Salmo fario*.

Lastly, the eyes of female ceratioids seem to be more or less postlarval in development. The eyes grow during larval life but only slowly after metamorphosis, when they tend to sink below the skin. The same is true of the eyes of certain male ceratioids (e.g. gigantactids) but in male linophrynids the eyes enlarge and become tubular or bowl-shaped in ceratiids. In metamorphosed males of caulophrynids, melanocetids, himantolophids and oneirodids the eyes are relatively large with an aphakic space (Bertelsen, 1951).

Thus, the ceratioid angler-fishes are markedly progenetic. Indeed, Rosenblatt has suggested that they are ". . . neotenic derivatives of benthic coastal forms via extended pelagic larval or juvenile stages . . ." (Moser, 1981). As Moser observes, the mature males are distinctly "larvoid" in appearance, which is true also of male *Idiacanthus*, a mesopelagic genus of stomiatoid fishes.

There are also a number of midwater fishes with lesser progenetic tendencies. For instance, in the Melamphaidae there are certain lower mesopelagic species with tiny (larval) eyes, poorly ossified bones and weakly developed spiny parts of the skeleton (Ebeling and Weed, 1973). Among the alepisauroids there are also certain progenetic forms. In the Scopelarchidae the genus *Benthalbella* is more progenetic (in its transparency, and reduced myotomes) than its relatives. Of the notosudids, the species of *Ahliesaurus* are unique and larvalized in having a weakly ossified skeleton, much reduced axial muscles (hypaxial and epaxial muscle masses remote from each other along the ventral and dorsal midlines) and the body wall thin and transparent (Bertelsen *et al.*, 1976).

To complete this survey we turn to progenetic tendencies in bottom-dwelling deep-sea fishes. The benthopelagic fauna, which lives near the deep-sea floor, is about as diverse as that of mesopelagic levels. All members are neutrally buoyant, whether by virtue of a well developed gas-filled swimbladder (macrourids, morids, ophidiids, halosaurs, notacanths, etc.), or through a squalene-charged liver (squalomorph sharks), or through tissue reductions (alepocephalids). Of these forms only the last would seem (with their gelatinous skin, subdermal spaces and their weakly developed skeleton and lateral muscles), to have progenetic traits.

Benthic deep-sea fishes have no swimbladder and their habit is to rest on the bottom. The most diverse forms are sea-snails (Liparidae), eel-pouts (Zoarcidae) and bathypteroids (tripod-fishes, *Ipnops*, etc.). The eel-pouts and tripod-fishes have no obvious progenetic features but most deep-sea liparids have ". . . a very loosely attached, fragile skin which is probably separated (in life) from the musculature of the fish by a gelatinous tissue or liquid" (Stein, 1978). Perhaps these tendencies have a progenetic basis.

Even so, it is clear that progenetic tendencies in deep-sea fishes are very largely confined to the midwater species. In the mesopelagic fauna many individuals are progenetic largely because species of *Cyclothone* are so abundant. For instance, out of more than 17 000 midwater fishes caught (by

RMT8) during a survey in the eastern North Atlantic down to a level of 2000 metres, about 6500 were of the mesopelagic species *Cyclothone braueri* (Badcock and Merrett, 1976), and as a rough estimate it seems that the individuals of this species alone form half of the mesopelagic fish fauna. But non-progenetic fishes are markedly predominant in numbers of species. Thus, about a third of the mesopelagic fauna consists of lantern-fishes (Myctophidae: there are about 250 species). Many species have a well developed swimbladder: in others this organ is reduced or absent and there is generally a high lipid content. However, whatever their buoyancy relations, two features of lantern-fishes are of interest in the present context: in no species is there any evident sign of progenesis and nearly all species commute daily between their midwater levels and the epipelagic zone where they must find most of their food.

Concerning the bathypelagic fauna, we have only to think of black *Cyclothone* species (much the most abundant compared to all other taxa) and the ceratioid angler-fishes (by far the most diverse; over 100 species) to realize that progenetic trends are almost universal (the exceptions include most of the whale-fishes (Cetomimiformes)).

III. ADAPTIVE SIGNIFICANCE OF PROGENESIS

As the transparent species of *Cyclothone* are so widespread and dominant in the mesopelagic zone, how far do their progenetic features contribute to their success? First, though, we need to consider their life history and here we are indebted to Badcock and Merrett (1976) who have closely studied *Cyclothone braueri* in the eastern North Atlantic. Their data indicate that its life span covers a single spawning only, which is true also of many other mesopelagic fishes of comparable size. Present evidence, which is reviewed by Childress *et al.* (1980), shows that in the tropics and subtropics (the reproductive headquarters of deep-sea fishes) the dominant mesopelagic migrators seem to be annual fishes. Moreover, these annual species are smaller than their nearest relatives in temperate regions which live more than one year. For instance, the lantern-fish *Benthosema glaciale*, a dominant mesopelagic fish in the North Atlantic north of 35°N, reaches maturity at two or three years and a maximum size of 7 cm in about four years (Gjøsaeter, 1981).

The progenetic features of *Cyclothone* species contribute largely to their simple organization (compared to that of relatives of the same size, such as *Valenciennellus* and *Vinciguerria*). In the oceanic water column, where food supplies decrease exponentially with depth, metabolic economies that are compatible with a viable life history should be advantageous (Marshall, 1960, 1979). In the eastern North Atlantic (at 30°N, 23°W) *Cyclothone braueri* certainly has a viable life history for it was the most abundant of all midwater fishes caught during Badcock and Merrett's (1976) survey. Here the populations are concentrated between depth of 400 and 600 m. Of the other dominant fishes at this position *Valenciennellus tripunctulatus* lives above *C. braueri* between 200 and 400 m. At much the same levels as *braueri* there are dominant lantern-fishes (*Hygophum hygomi, Benthosema suborbitale* and *Notolychnus valdiviae*). Overlapping with the depth range of *C. braueri* there is the deeper-living *C. microdon* (500–2000 m) (see Badcock and Merrett, 1976).

Considering the potential competitors of *Cyclothone braueri*, (and the species just listed are of much the same size (30–35 mm) and probably eat much the same food), we should note that these most numerous neighbours either undertake extensive migrations (the lantern-fishes) or are partial migrators (the hatchet-fish). *Cyclothone braueri*, like others of its genus, is not a migrator. If the dominant mesopelagic species are both migrators and annual fishes, this suggests that night-time feeding in the productive epipelagic zone enables small fishes (<7 cm) to grow quickly enough and complete their life cycle in a year. Lantern-fishes, nearly all of which are daily migrators, have by far the greatest biomass of all midwater fishes. Mesopelagic *Cyclothone* would thus seem to be faced with rapidly growing competitors. If they had, for instance, a two year life cycle their mortality until they reached the adult stage might be too much to sustain a viable life history. Hence, the suggestion is that progenesis in mesopelagic *Cyclothone* provides an organization that is simple enough to become mature in less than a year in the absence of vertical migrations. Moreover, the fecundity of *Cyclothone braueri* ranging from 24 to 29 mm in standard length was 218–416 eggs (Badcock and Merrett, 1976), which compares well with 191–484 eggs in two myctophids of length from 31 to 40 mm (Gjøsaeter, 1981). This is coming close to Gould's (1977) contention that "... progenesis is selected not primarily for morphology but by the need for precocious maturation as a life-history strategy".

Bathypelagic *Cyclothone* differ from their mesopelagic relatives in two outstanding respects: they are larger and more fecund. For instance, *C. microdon* attain a standard length of about 60 mm and a fecundity of 2184–3301 eggs in 48–52 mm individuals; in *C. braueri*, as we have seen, the corresponding figures are 38 mm and a fecundity range of 218–416 in 24–29 mm fishes (Badcock and Merrett, 1976). As I wrote elsewhere, (Marshall, 1979)

A fecundity of two or three thousand eggs in *Cyclothone microdon*, which is presumably much the same as its other bathypelagic congeners, seems relatively modest, but below 1000 metres these are much the commonest fishes.

The hypothesis was that the lengthy ontogenetic migrations from the bathypelagic zone to the surface waters and back again (eggs spawned at depth float upwards and hatch into larvae that feed in the epipelagic zone until metamorphosis when there is a return to the adult environment) require a relatively high fecundity (mortality is likely to be very heavy during the upward migration and the larval life history). Thus, if spawning in *C. braueri* is centred at 600 m and in *C. microdon* at 1200 m, the two-fold difference in depth is associated with a ten-fold difference in fecundity. But the population density of the former is about twice that of the latter, judging from Badcock and Merrett's (1976) figures. Thus, less numerous and larger fishes would seem to need all their bulk to be adequately fecund. Relative data are limited but these available are suggestive: a 600 mm gulper-eel, *Eurypharynx pelecanoides*, with 33 000 well developed ova (0·9 mm in diameter) and anglerfishes of the following sizes and fecundity: *Ceratias holboelli*, 650 mm, 5 million immature eggs; *Edriolychnus schmidti*, 63 mm, 9100 eggs; and *Dolopichthys longicornis*, 114 mm, about 10 800 ripening eggs and about the same number of immature eggs (see Marshall, 1979). As I concluded:

> There is thus evidence of increased fecundity in both small and large fishes of the bathypelagic zone, which must find enough nourishment in an impoverished environment to provide food reserves for thousands of developing eggs. Even so, their somatic organization is so economically integrated that a higher proportion of their limited energy budget can be diverted to gonadal development than in fishes from more productive environments.

Moreover, bathypelagic fishes in the subtropical and tropical regions take longer (one or more years) to reach maturity than do the smaller and less fecund fishes that live above them in the mesopelagic zone.

Concerning the above discussion, it is interesting to look at the recent work of Childress *et al.* (1980) on the metabolic relations and reproduction of midwater fishes off Southern California. In particular they stress that through greatly reduced metabolic rates bathypelagic fishes have increased their growth efficiencies: they grow relatively quickly to a large size. Even so, their maintenance costs in energy are low relative to their size. Moreover, reproduction is delayed until the end of their lives. In the present context a simple organization attained through progenesis would seem to be a fitting structural basis for such metabolic economies.

REFERENCES

Badcock, J. and Merrett, N. R. (1976). *Prog. Oceanogr.* **7**, 3–58.
Bertelsen, E. (1951). *Dana Rep.* **39**, 1–276.
Bertelsen, E., Krefft, G. and Marshall, N. B. (1976). *Dana Rep.* **86**, 1–114.
Castle, P. J. H. (1977). *Arch. Fischwiss* **28** (2/3), 69–76.
Childress, J. J., Taylor, S. M. and Cailliet, G. M. (1980). *Mar. Biol.* **61**, 27–40.
Cohen, D. M. (1960). *Copeia* **1960**, 147–149.
Denton, E. J. and Marshall, N. B. (1958). *J. mar. biol. Ass. U.K.* **37**, 753–767.
Ebeling, A. W. and Weed, W. H. (1973). Order Xenoberyces (Stephanoberyciformes).

In "Fishes of the Western North Atlantic", Part 6, Mem. Sears Foundation for Marine Research. Number 1, pp. 397–478. New Haven, Yale University.

Giard, A. (1887). *Bull. Scient. Fr. Belg.* **18**, 1–28.

Gjøsaeter, J. (1981). *Fisk Dir. Skr. Sene Havunders* **17**, 79–108.

Gould, S. J. (1977). "Ontogeny and Phylogeny." Harvard University Press, Cambridge, Mass.

Jollie, M. (1962). "Chordate Morphology." Rheinhold, New York.

Kollman, J. (1885). *Verh. naturf. Ges. Basel* **7**, 387–398.

Locket, N. A. (1977). *In* "The Visual System in Vertebrates" (F. Crescitelli, ed.), pp. 67–192. Handbook of Sensory Physiology Vol. 7/5. Springer Verlag, Berlin.

Marshall, N. B. (1960). *Discovery Rep.* **31**, 1–122.

Marshall, N. B. (1979). "Developments in Deep-Sea Biology." Blandford Press, Poole, Dorset.

Moser, H. G. (1981). *In* "Marine Fish Larvae" (R. Lasker, ed.), pp. 90–131. Washington Sea Grant Program.

Nielsen, J. G. (1969). *Galathea Rep.* **10**, 7–88.

Owen, B. B. (1938). *Biol. Bull., Woods Hole* **74**, 349–363.

Ozawa, T. (1973). *Mem. Fac. Fish. Kagoshima Univ.* **22**, 127–141.

Raju, N. S. (1974). *Fish. Bull.* **72**, 547–562.

Smith, K. L. and Laver, M. B. (1981). *Mar. Biol.* **61**, 261–266.

Stein, D. L. (1978). *Occ. Pap. Cal. Acad. Sci.* **127**, 1–55.

Walters, V. (1961). *Bull. Mus. comp. Zool. Harv.* **125**, 297–319.

Waterman, T. H. (1948). *J. Morph.* **82**, 81–149.

7. Sex Reversal and Sociodemographic Processes in Coral Reef Fishes

DOUGLAS Y. SHAPIRO

Department of Marine Sciences, University of Puerto Rico, Mayaguez, Puerto Rico

Abstract: Adult female-to-male or male-to-female sex reversal is a highly successful reproductive strategy among fishes: it has evolved independently in Stomiatioids (Salmoniformes), Synbranchiformes, Scorpaeniformes, and at least seven families of Perciformes. These fishes represent highly diverse combinations of life history traits. The one trait that these fishes share, gender switching, must be sufficiently fundamental and adaptable to harmonize successfully with variations in virtually all other features of life history. Sex reversal provides a special means to individuals of these varied fishes for improving reproductive success whenever circumstances allow, regardless of the point in life at which these circumstances occur. Significant intrapopulation variation in the size at which individuals of coral reef fishes change sex results from variability in occurrence of the circumstances favouring sex change. When early or late sex change is reliably associated with recognizable features of microhabitat, secondary life-history adaptations may be favoured, e.g. a specific size of social group a maturing fish should occupy, or a specific dispersion pattern of groups over the reef. In general, individuals are unlikely to change sex in isolation from other conspecifics. A species-dependent minimum number of like-sexed individuals are needed for one to change sex. These and other details of the proximal mechanism controlling sex change provide clues to the costs and benefits of sex reversal and render variation in the time of life at which individuals change sex comprehensible. Finally, I argue that the size-advantage model for the evolution of protogyny makes restrictive assumptions preventing its application to species with behavioural induction of sex change and/or with significant intrapopulation variation in size at sex change, and I suggest the terms of a more applicable model.

I. INTRODUCTION

Protandric and protogynous fishes are numerous and diverse (Atz, 1964; Reinboth, 1970; Smith, 1975). They include: species that are herbivores, zooplanktivores and piscivores; monagamous, polygamous and promiscuous; large- and small-bodied; solitary, paired, or occupants of single-male, single-female, multimale or multifemale bisexual groups; species that live in deep or shallow water; maintain monospecific or interspecific aggregations;

FISH REPRODUCTION
ISBN: 0–12–563660–1

reside in variant or invariant social systems; produce pelagic or sessile eggs; defend individual or group territories, or defend no territory; migrate diurnally over or off the reef or remain permanently residential; reproduce daily or monthly, throughout most of the year or during short, well-defined spawning seasons, in a lunar cycle or not. The one trait that these fishes share, gender switching, must be sufficiently fundamental and adaptable to harmonize successfully with variations in virtually all other features of life history. In this paper I argue that sex reversal provides a special means to individuals of improving reproductive success whenever circumstances allow, regardless of the point in life or the moment in time or space at which those circumstances occur. To support this view, first, I present evidence of significant variation in the time of life at which individuals within protogynous species change from female to male. Secondly, I argue that when early or late sex change is reliably associated with recognizable features of microhabitat, it influences processes of juvenile recruitment and of social-group formation. Thirdly, I describe details of operation of the only known mechanism for initiation of sex change, behavioural induction. I contend that these details provide clues to the costs and benefits of sex reversal and render variation in the time of life at which individuals change sex comprehensible. Finally, I argue that the size-advantage model for the evolution of protogyny makes restrictive assumptions preventing its application to species with behavioural induction of sex change, and I suggest the terms of a more applicable model.

The nature of the costs and benefits of female-to-male sex reversal can be outlined, although they have not yet been fully measured in any species (Jones, 1980; Warner and Hoffman, 1980). Benefits relate primarily to the opportunity for males to mate with multiple females. Overall female-to-male sex ratios in protogynous fishes generally exceed 1:1, with much higher ratios among monandric species. In diandric species, containing two ontogenetic types of males — primary males maturing as males initially and secondary males that have changed from female to male gender — ratios of females to secondary males substantially exceed unity (Choat and Robertson, 1975; Robertson and Warner, 1978; Warner and Robertson, 1978; Shapiro, 1977a). Whereas, females spawn once daily or less, secondary males may spawn up to 100 times per day, and even relatively disadvantaged secondary males spawn more frequently than females (Warner and Hoffman, 1980). Costs of sex reversal involve, at a minimum, (1) a metabolic expenditure of energy to alter gonadal cell types (Reinboth, 1962), induce new enzyme systems for the biosynthesis of different steroid hormones (Chan and Phillips, 1969), change the bodily mosaic of colour pigments (Shapiro, 1981b), alter types and frequencies of behavioural activities (Robertson, 1974; Warner and Hoffman, 1980; Shapiro, 1981c,d), and probably increase body size and change body composition (Shapiro, 1981a); (2) loss of reproductive time during sex reversals occurring in the breeding season; and (3) an increased risk of mortality during sex change, resulting either from (a) predation on individuals made temporarily more conspicuous than normal males or females by transitional alteration in colouration (Shapiro, 1981b) or behaviour (Shapiro, 1981c,d), or (b) disease in individuals weakened temporarily by the energy demands of sex change. Finally, differential mortality rates between the sexes may serve either as an advantage or a disadvantage of sex reversal, depending on the size and direction of the difference.

II. VARIATION IN SIZE AT SEX CHANGE

For fishes, age and size are incompletely, but directly related. In literature on sex reversal, size has been a more consistent correlate of aspects of sex change than age (Wenner, 1972; Warner, 1975a,b; Jones, 1980; Shapiro, 1981a). In this paper, I use relative size, in the life of an individual, as a rough indication of the individual's age.

There are two ways to determine the size at which individuals change sex within a population. The direct way is to measure individuals at the time they begin to change sex. This method can only be used for species with clear external or internal signs indicating onset of sex change. The second method is less direct and involves examining size ranges of males and females within a sample. In most protogynous species, females occupy all small size ranges; males occupy large size ranges, and there is a zone of overlap between sizes of males and females (Fig. 1). Sex-changing individuals generally fall within this overlap zone (Shapiro, 1981a; Robertson and Justines, 1982). The overlap zone, then, can be used to estimate the size range in which individuals change sex. If one extracts the number of individuals, male or female, from within the

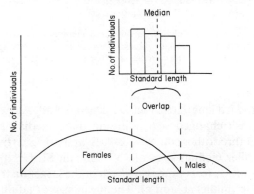

Fig. 1. Schematic representation of overlap in the size distributions of males and females. The number of males and females in the overlap zone are extracted to form a new size-frequency distribution (above).

106   D. Y. SHAPIRO

overlap zone and plots them as a size-frequency distribution (Fig. 1), multiple samples can then be compared statistically and the results will tell us whether sex reversal occurs at the same size in all samples.

Four hundred and fifty-four protogynous redband parrotfish, *Sparisoma aurofrenatum*, were collected from five sites along a 17 km portion of the southwestern coast of Puerto Rico and from Desecheo Island 25 km offshore (Clavijo, 1982). Size-frequency distributions of individuals in the overlap zone were not statistically similar at all sites nor among the five coastal sites (Fig. 2; Kruskal-Wallis one-way analysis of variance, $P<0.001$, two-tailed). The largest median size at which females changed sex, according to these estimates,

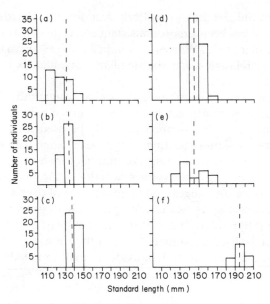

Fig. 2. Estimated size range in which *S. aurofrenatum* changes sex at six sites in Puerto Rico. Vertical dotted lines represent median values. Data taken from overlap zones in the size-frequency distributions of males and females (from Clavijo, 1982).

was 194 mm standard length (SL) on Desecheo Island. At two coastal sites (d and e, Fig. 2), fish changed sex at intermediate median sizes of 144 and 145 mm, while at three other coastal sites (a, b and c, Fig. 2) fish changed sex at significantly smaller median sizes of 132–138 mm SL ($P<0.025$, one-tailed, Kolmogorov-Smirnov test comparing each of the larger distributions d, e and f with each of the smaller, b and c). The mean size of adult males and adult females was the same for all sites, indicating that adults probably lived equally long at all sites. Thus, even though the size range of fish was the same at all sites, individuals changed sex sooner and spent a greater part of adult life as a male at some sites than at others. Intrapopulation variation in size at sex reversal among sites is also known in several labrids (Warner and Robertson, 1978).

Three to five female *S. aurofrenatum* share a common territory with one male, with whom they spawn. When a female changes sex it leaves its territory and becomes a wandering male until it establishes a territory of its own or enters an already-established territory containing females (Clavijo, 1982). If we assume that the delay between sex reversal and occupying a territory and spawning with multiple females is of similar duration at all sites, then individuals at sites where sex reversal occurs relatively early in life will have a greater lifetime reproductive output than they would have at a site where sex reversal occurs later in life. It then becomes advantageous for an individual to settle initially at, or migrate to, a site with early sex reversal. Migration between sites is thought likely to occur (Clavijo, 1982).

The serranid *Anthias squamipinnis* occupies groups ranging in size from one to thousands of individuals and containing one to many males (Shapiro, 1977a). The median female-to-male ratio in 45 such groups was eight (Shapiro, 1977b). Females change sex and males spawn individually with multiple females within the group. Removal of one male from any group induces a female to change sex (Shapiro, 1981a). In most groups, all males are larger than all females and it is the largest female that changes sex following male removal (Shapiro, 1981a).

In this species, differences between sites in the size at sex reversal are even more striking than in the redband parrotfish. Two sites separated by 650 m on the same fringing reef on Aldabra Island (Shapiro, 1981a) differed significantly (Kolmogorov-Smirnov test, $P < 0.0005$, one-tailed) by 15·0 mm SL in the median overlap estimate of sex-reversal size (Fig. 3). Size at sex reversal

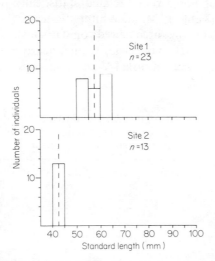

Fig. 3.   Estimated size ranges in which *A. squamipinnis* changes sex at two sites on Aldabra Island. Vertical dotted lines represent median values. Data taken from overlap zones in the size-frequency distributions of males and females (from Shapiro, 1981a).

also varies from one group to the next. In a population in the Gulf of Eilat, 79 neighbouring groups were separated by a distance of 11.8 ± 4.1 m ($\bar{x} \pm$ s.d.; Shapiro and Boulon, in prep.). Since all individuals could not be caught and measured in all groups, I estimated the size at sex reversal by measuring the size of the largest female within each of 58 bisexual groups. Sex reversal occurred in the size range 50–74 mm SL in nine groups, at 75–99 mm in 32 groups, and at ≥ 100 mm in 17 groups. Thus, in adjacent groups the size at which an individual changed sex might differ by more than a factor of two.

III. INFLUENCE OF SIZE VARIATION ON SETTLING AND GROUP SPACING

If *A. squamipinnis* groups can be identified by settling juveniles as producing early, rather than late sex change, there may be a reproductive advantage for settling juveniles to enter and remain in such groups. Each group in the Gulf of Eilat population occupied a fixed position over a "home rock" of coral. When groups were divided into three categories of sex-reversal size, both volume and horizontal area, i.e. cross-sectional surface areas as seen from above, of the home rock increased directly and significantly with size at sex reversal (Table I; Kruskal-Wallis one-way analysis of variance, $P < 0.001$, two-tailed, for both area and volume). Groups with small sex-reversal size occupied rocks of smaller volume than groups of intermediate sex-change size (Mann-Whitney U-test, $P < 0.001$, one-tailed) and groups with small and intermediate sex-change size occupied rocks of smaller volume than groups with large sex-change size (Mann-Whitney U-test, $P < 0.001$ and $P < 0.05$, one-tailed). Horizontal area of home rocks related statistically to sex-change size in identical fashion (Table I; Mann-Whitney U-tests, $P < 0.001$, < 0.001 and < 0.05, one-tailed, for the three paired comparisons). Neither bottom depth nor number of individuals in the group related clearly or significantly to size at sex reversal (group size: Kruskal-Wallis, one-way analysis of variance,

TABLE I. Median values of volume, horizontal area[a], and depth of home rock, and of number of individuals resident in the group, for *A. squamipinnis* groups with different size at sex reversal.

	Size at sex reversal (mm)			
	50–74	75–99	100+	No. groups
Volume (m^3)	2·6	16·0	40·0	39
Horizontal area (m^2)	2·5	7·1	20·0	39
Depth (m)	7·5	8·0	7·0	57
No. individuals	31	45	63	58

[a] See text for definition.

$P > 0.20$; depth: Kruskal-Wallis, $P < 0.02$, two-tailed, but Mann-Whitney U-tests failed to show significant differences between all pair combinations of the three categories of groups and median values formed no clear trend; Table I). Thus, horizontal area and volume of the home rock are available as cues to the size at which settling juveniles can expect to change sex later in life.

The recruitment process can also be examined from the point of view of the adults joined by settling juveniles, and again we find that social induction of sex reversal is of considerable importance. Two events have been discussed that may induce a female to change sex: loss of a male, with subsequent sex reversal tending to maintain a constant number of males in a population, and exceeding a threshold female-to-male ratio by the recruitment of females (Fishelson, 1970; Robertson, 1972; Shapiro, 1979). The latter process would increase the number of males in a growing population and, in monandric species, where all males are sex-reversed females, and in diandric populations with small proportions of primary males, would tend to maintain a constant sex ratio. Shapiro and Lubbock (1980) suggested that both means of inducing sex change, by loss of a male and by exceeding a threshold sex ratio, could be mediated by a common behavioural mechanism. In species like Anthiines that live in discrete groups (Shapiro, 1977a), sex reversal occurs always within the group and it is the sex ratio of the group, not the population, that would determine when a female group member changes sex. Theoretically, the more rapidly juvenile females enter a social group, the more rapidly the female-to-male sex ratio would exceed threshold value, and the more rapidly adult females would change sex. A female occupying a group that is successful at attracting juveniles can thus expect to change sex earlier in life than if it occupied a group less successful at attracting juveniles. Again, assuming that life expectancy and the delay between sex reversal and successful spawning are the same for all groups, a female changing sex early in life will produce more offspring than if she changed sex later. It is, thus, beneficial to an adult female to occupy a group that is more successful at attracting juveniles than are other groups. In effect, adult groups should compete with one another to attract juveniles.

Shapiro and Boulon (in prep.) have demonstrated that, when the rate of settlement and entry of juveniles into established groups is independent of the number of groups in an area and has some constant mean value, a group can be expected to receive a larger proportion of juveniles settling over an area of reef if it is far from its nearest neighbour than if it is close to its neighbour. Intergroup competition for juveniles might be expected, then, to produce an even distribution of groups spatially over the reef. Shapiro and Boulon (in prep.) demonstrated regular spacing by measuring the nearest-neighbour distance of 79 groups in a 65×1600 m area of reef in the Gulf of Eilat. Mean nearest-neighbour distance (11·8 m) was significantly greater than that expected (10·7 m) if groups were randomly distributed over the reef (Simber-loff, 1979, correction to Clark and Evan's test, $P < 0.02$, one-tailed) and the difference was in the direction of regularity. Thus, regular spacing of social groups can be perceived as a consequence of the ability of females to influence the time in their life at which they change sex by settling preferentially in aggregations at locations far from nearest neighbours. Alternative possible explanations for regular spacing are discussed elsewhere (Shapiro and Boulon, in prep.).

Variation in the time of life at which sex change occurs can also have an evolutionary effect on choice of which size social group an individual should occupy and the process of group formation. Some protogynous wrasses form single-male, multifemale units in which the number of females varies from group to group. In *Labroides dimidiatus* a female changes sex either if the group's male disappears, in which case the largest female becomes male, or if the group's male substantially alters the frequency or pattern of interactions with a female on the periphery of the group (Robertson, 1972, 1974). In the latter case, the peripheral female, smaller than the group's central female, becomes male. If male mortality rate is independent of group size (it may not be, but this has not been studied), a medium-sized female is more likely to change sex sooner in a large group, where the large number of females may force the male eventually to alter its interactions with peripheral females, than in a smaller group, where the male may more easily interact frequently and in consistent pattern with all females, central and peripheral. The advantage accrued by a medium-sized individual changing sex under these circumstances will depend upon its ability to attract females with whom to live and spawn, and that will depend on the processes of group formation.

Little is known about group formation in labrids generally (Warner and Robertson, 1978). In *L. dimidiatus*, maturing individuals emigrate from groups in which they originally settled as juveniles (Robertson and Choat, 1974). Since isolated adults are rare (Potts, 1973; Robertson, 1974), young adults leaving one group must quickly form a pair or enter an existing group. If the probability of sex change is a function of group size, as argued above, there should be differential advantages to entering groups of different size.

Groups of *A. squamipinnis* vary widely in size and sex ratio (Shapiro, 1977a, 1979). Shapiro and Lubbock (1980) demonstrated that, when sex reversal is induced both by male loss and by exceeding a threshold female-to-male ratio, males would generally have access to a greater average number of females in small than in large groups. Hence, it would be to the advantage of males to leave large groups and form or enter smaller groups. Such an advantage would explain the apparent fissioning of a large parent group into two or three small subgroups, some of which may become fully independent (Shapiro, 1977a, 1979). The effect of differential reproductive advantage in groups of different size on group fissioning is a direct consequence of plasticity in the time of life at which individuals change sex.

IV. BEHAVIOURAL INDUCTION AND COST-BENEFIT ANALYSIS

With the exception of environmental influences on hermaphroditic development in *Rivulus marmoratus* (Harrington, 1971), circumstances inducing sex
change are currently known only for species in which sex reversal is under
social control. From work on these species, several principles are beginning to
emerge. First, individuals are unlikely to change sex, or do so very slowly, in
isolation from conspecifics. When 24 mature females of the protandric
Amphiprion bicinctus were removed from their male partners, 18 of the
isolated males changed sex, but only after being joined by subadult males. Six
males that remained solitary did not change sex. When 12 males were forcibly
isolated, oocyte production increased more slowly in their gonads than when
males were paired, and the evidence suggests that the isolates may have not
completed their sex change (Fricke and Fricke, 1977). Eleven female
Thalassoma duperrey, a protogynous species, did not change sex when
removed from the reef and isolated in cages in the sea. In contrast, when 52
females were caged as 26 pairs, the large female changes sex in 81% of pairs
(Ross, 1982a). In protogynous *L. dimidiatus*, sex change could be judged by
the ratio of number of spermatogenic crypts to the number of oocytes in the
gonads. In the presence of other female group members, a sex-change fish
required 4–5 days for this ratio to exceed the usual female range of values.
When eight females were each isolated by removing all other group members,
the ratio did not exceed female values for 33 days (Robertson, 1974).

Secondly, the minimum number of similar-sexed individuals needed for one
of them to change sex is species-dependent. In *T. duperrey* and *A. bicinctus*, the
minimum number is two (Ross, 1982a; Fricke and Fricke, 1977). In *A.
squamipinnis*, it is four to five (Shapiro and Boulon, 1982). The minimum
number of similar-sexed individuals may well relate to the costs-benefits
balance of changing sex. There is no clear advantage for an isolated fish to
change sex. Regardless of gender, it can not reproduce. Furthermore, once an
isolated fish has changed sex it has lost its flexibility to adapt to circumstances.
Prior to sex reversal, a protogynous female can reproduce if either a male or a
second female appears (by changing sex). After it has changed sex, it can only
reproduce when a female appears. Thus, even if sex reversal contained no
concomitant risks, e.g. increased mortality during sex change, the physiological cost and loss of flexibility would probably render sex reversal by an
isolated fish disadvantageous.

In *A. squamipinnis*, only adult females contribute to the minimum number
(Shapiro and Boulon, 1982). The number of juvenile females does not affect
the initiation of sex change. This makes sense since juveniles will not be able to
spawn with a recently sex-changed male until they mature, and hence, can

only have a delayed effect on a male's reproductive output. In other species, the influence of juveniles remains untested.

Thirdly, the minimum number of females sufficient to initiate sex change may depend on the circumstances leading to the production of that number. In *A. squamipinnis*, substantial numbers of groups have been found containing juvenile and adult females, but no male. In the Sudanese Red Sea, 20% of 45 groups (Shapiro, 1977b), and in the Gulf of Eilat, 35% of 127 groups were all-female (Shapiro, in prep.). Most of these groups consisted entirely of juveniles, or juveniles and fewer than three adult females. Sixteen groups, however, contained four or more adult females, i.e. the minimum number. A male appeared in seven of these 16 groups during 46–90 days of observation, a rate that is significantly lower (44%) than the 84% rate of sex change in 38 bisexual groups, containing four or more adult females and from which a male had been removed, in the same populations ($X^2 = 7·28$, $P < 0·01$, two-tailed; from Shapiro, in prep.). Thus, male absence differed from male removal, and the rate of obtaining a sex reversal in groups containing more than the minimum number of adult females depends on whether the aggregation of females was a longstanding, all-female group or a recent consequence of male removal. Males do appear in all-female groups, but at low rates, with prolonged delays (Shapiro, in prep.).

Fourthly, in monandric species, and in diandric populations with small proportions of primary males, in which sex change is behaviourally controlled, the sex ratio of the population is determined by the nature of the mechanism initiating sex change, and by local rates of such demographic factors as juvenile recruitment, growth, and male and female mortalities. This conclusion follows immediately from recognition that males can only be produced by sex change initiated by male disappearance (or female loss in protandric species) or recruitment of a threshold number of new females. The average sex ratio of a population may be taken to represent the average number of females required by an average potential male for the reproductive benefits of sex change to outweigh the costs. The minimum numbers of females to produce sex reversal following male removal in *A. squamipinnis* and *T. duperrey*, four to five and two, are lower than the average female-to-male sex ratios of corresponding populations, 8·4 (Shapiro, 1977a) and 3·3–7·7 (Ross, 1982b). In both species, the minimum numbers were derived from experiments in which, after male removal, no additional male was present, potentially to compete with a future, sex-reversed male. Both social systems, however, contain mulitmalc as well as single-male units. In presence of competing males, a larger ratio of females may be required to offset the cost of sex reversal than when only one male was present, and this may explain the difference between minimum number of females, in these experiments, and average sex ratio on the reef.

Several questions concerning sex change remain partially or totally unanswered. Most known sex-changing species breed seasonally. Is it equally valuable to change sex within the spawning season as outside it? Year-round gonadal collections have generally demonstrated most frequent sex changes after the conclusion of breeding (Gunderman, 1972; Warner, 1975a; Jones, 1980; Clavijo, 1982). This pattern might suggest that changing sex in the midst of breeding would create an unnecessary loss of breeding time not counterbalanced by early resumption of multiple spawning as a male. On the contrary, I tend to think this seasonal pattern is an epiphenomenon, without direct selective import, resulting, in species with behavioural induction, from post-spawning increases in adult mortality and juvenile recruitment, which generally peaks one to two months after peak spawning.

As in other species, most *A. squamipinnis* females change sex outside the breeding season (Gunderman, 1972; Fishelson, 1975). Yet, *A. squamipinnis* is equally capable of changing sex, following male removal, year-round in the field and in the laboratory, regardless of whether fish are spawning or not. The onset and completion times for these sex changes do not differ between seasons or times of the year. Seasonal sex change results, therefore, from seasonal differences in occurrence of initiating conditions, not from seasonal alterations in physiological preparedness or from seasonal attainment of a critical size or internal state. Similar conclusions have been derived for *T. duperrey* (Ross, 1982b). Two possible explanations for the continuing readiness to change sex are apparent. (1) Sex change is equally valuable in or out of the breeding season provided the same, basic conditions occur, e.g. male disappearance in presence of a minimum number of adult females. (2) Sex change is not equally valuable at all seasons, but nevertheless occurs whenever basic conditions are met. If strong selection pressures maintained a simple mechanism for inducing sex change, minor disadvantages incurred by the chance of changing sex during a less favourable season may not be sufficient to alter the basic mechanism or to turn it on and off in different seasons.

There is evidence, in several species, that all males do not have equal spawning success (Popper and Fishelson, 1973; Warner and Hoffman, 1980; Ross, 1982b). Loss of a male that spawns infrequently may offer less of a reproductive "opening" in the mating system than loss of a highly successful spawner. Do all males, then, have equal replacement value if lost? The Gulf of Eilat contains a number of unusual *A. squamipinnis* groups composed of several thousand fish with a relatively low female-to-male sex ratio. These groups have two behaviourally distinct types of male, one of which maintains station in the upper parts of the group, interacts actively with, courts and spawns with females. The second type of male clusters at the bottom of the fish aggregation, does not court, interact or spawn with females, and has filamentous, degenerative gonads (Popper and Fishelson, 1973; Fishelson, 1975). One would not expect males of the second type to have a high replacement value.

One can test for equality of replacement value by removing each type of male from separate groups and looking for equal rates of subsequent sex reversal. Ten males of the first type were removed from each of two groups, and ten males of the second type were removed from each of three groups. A statistically similar proportion of removed males were succeeded by sex-changing females for each of the two male types (Shapiro, in prep.). It thus appeared as though replacement value did not play a role in determining whether females change sex or not. No information is available, however, on whether the sex-changed fish assumed the same behaviour or spatial location as the males they succeeded.

The behavioural mechanism initiating sex reversal seems to be staunchly maintained. Given a basic set of minimum conditions, e.g. loss of a male and minimum number of adult females, sex change is initiated regardless of size of the sex-changing fish, season, time of year, and perhaps even regardless of replacement value of the lost male. Relentless operation of this mechanism is also suggested by a recent experiment on *T. duperrey* (Ross, 1982b). When a large female was removed from the social system and caged alone, it did not change sex ($n = 11$), but when paired with a small female, the large female did change sex ($n = 13$). When a large female was similarly removed and paired with a small, initial-phase male whose colouration was identical to that of all females, the large female also changed sex, resulting in a pair of males ($n = 7$). There is no obvious advantage to changing sex in the latter circumstance. We can probably safely assume that the initiating mechanism generally provides a reproductive advantage to the sex-changing fish under a particular set of conditions. However, when these conditions are mimicked by others, as in this experiment, the mechanism continues to operate even if it offers no apparent advantage to the individual changing sex.

V. GENERAL EVOLUTIONARY CONSIDERATIONS

Two questions may be asked. (1) What advantage led to the initial selection of hermaphroditism in the evolutionary past? No answer has yet been given, although protogyny in serranid fishes, and simultaneous hermaphroditism among Aulopiform fishes, are both sufficiently old that a number of species have evolved away from a hermaphroditic state and become secondary gonochorists (Smith, 1975; Price, Chap. 5, this volume). (2) What present-day selective pressures maintain sex reversal in current populations? Causal circumstances initiating sex change can be carefully analysed. Costs and benefits of changing sex under these, but not under other circumstances can then be studied. If benefits exceed costs only under conditions that actually induce sex change, it may then be argued that sex change under those conditions has evolved in consequence of the net positive balance of benefits over costs. Most current literature on evolution of sex change address this second question.

Behavioural induction of sex reversal provides individuals with the flexibility to enhance reproductive output whenever environmental circumstances make it possible. Given the wide, intrapopulation variation in size at sex reversal, for individuals of some species, at different reef locations or within different social groups, it is clear that these circumstances do not occur at the same time of life for all individuals in the population. It is quite likely in these species that if individuals changed sex at a genetically inherited size or time of life, without regard to local social or environmental conditions, costs of sex change would often outweigh benefits, and the results would be generally maladaptive. Social induction is known or claimed for at least 12 species of fish (Shapiro, 1982). There is currently no clear evidence in any protogynous or protandric species of which I am aware, for any other mechanism for inducing sex change, e.g. one genetically programmed to size or development.

According to present evidence, then, any general explanation for the adaptive function of sex reversal should be compatible with a behavioural mechanism for its initiation and with its consequence: intrapopulation variation in the size or time of life at which sex change occurs. Ghiselin (1969) proposed a size-advantage model in which sex reversal would be favoured over gonochorism whenever individuals reproduced better as one sex when small and as the opposite sex when large. This model has since been formulated mathematically (Warner et al., 1975; Warner, 1975b; Leigh et al., 1976) and extended to establish the proper age/size to change sex by assuming that populations consist of individuals genetically programmed to change sex, or not, at particular sizes or ages. When male fertility at a given size exceeds female fertility at the same size, the model demonstrates that an allele producing sex change is favoured over an allele producing gonochores, and that an allele producing sex change at the appropriate age/size is favoured over an allele producing sex change at any other age/size. This formulation could apply to any species in which age/size at sex reversal were controlled genetically and in which there is no significant intrapopulation variation in the distribution of sex-change ages/sizes. To date, no species is known to control sex-change size genetically. Furthermore, size at sex change varies significantly among populations on neighbouring reefs, whose proximity renders their resident populations unlikely to be genetically distinct, for several labrids (Warner and Robertson, 1978) and at least one scarid (Clavijo, 1982) and serranid (Shapiro, 1981a). Greater variability will undoubtedly be discovered as more scientists begin looking for it.

Even the test species for these formulations of the size-advantage model, *Thalassoma bifasciatum*, varies in apparent size of sex change, as estimated by distributions of size overlap between initial-phase and terminal-phase fish, from reef to reef (Warner and Robertson, 1978, Fig. 10; Kolmogorov-Smirnov test, comparing overlap zones, reef I vs reef II, $P<0.0005$; reef II vs reef III, $P<0.0005$; reef I vs reef III, $P<0.01$, all tests one-tailed). Furthermore, sex change in *T. bifasciatum* is apparently not under genetic but social control (Warner *et al.*, 1975). Thus, there seems *prima facie* evidence to doubt that the size-advantage model applies even to the one species specifically chosen to exemplify it.

The size-advantage model is claimed to apply to species with behavioural control of sex change, provided the environment is constant, so that ". . . an animal that changes sex in response to external influences should do so at the same age as an animal that changes sex at a genetically-fixed stage of development" (Warner *et al.*, 1975, p. 635.). As the evidence in this paper demonstrates, behavioural initiation of sex change is preeminently a mechanism adapting individuals to environmental changes that may occur at any time. Furthermore, for the size-advantage model to apply, not only must the environment be constant, but its sex-reversal inducing components, e.g. male and female mortality, growth and recruitment rates, must also be set at precisely the correct level so that sex change occurs at the precise size/age predicted by the model. Such a conjunction of circumstances is highly improbable.

In summary, the assumptions of the size-advantage model are too restrictive to permit unequivocal application of the model, according to present knowledge, to any known species, particularly those in which sex reversal is behaviourally initiated. Ghiselin's original formulation could be made applicable to behavioural initiation and concomitant variation in size at sex change by paraphrasing him (Ghiselin, 1974) thus: if an animal in one circumstance can reproduce more effectively as one sex, and under a different circumstance can reproduce more effectively as the other sex, then it becomes advantageous for an individual to switch gender as it changes circumstance. The independent variable becomes circumstance, meaning the number of co-resident males and females, the pattern of interaction between those fish, and the historical, sociodemographic events producing these conditions, and size/age drops from the formulation entirely.

ACKNOWLEDGEMENTS

I thank G. Brecken, D. Hensley and M. Leighton-Shapiro for helpful reviews of the manuscript. Work was supported by NSF grant RIM78-17075 and NIH grant 2 SO6 RR 08103-09.

REFERENCES

Atz, J. W. (1964). *In* "Intersexuality in Vertebrates Including Man" (C. N. Armstrong and A. J. Marshall, eds), pp. 145–232. Academic Press, London and New York.

Chan, S. T. H. and Phillips, J. G. (1969). *Gen. Comp. Endocrinol.* **12**, 619–636.

Choat, J. H. and Robertson, D. R. (1975). *In* "Intersexuality in the Animal Kingdom" (R. Reinboth, ed.), pp. 263–283. Springer Verlag, Berlin and New York.

Clavijo, I. (1982). "Aspects of the reproductive biology of the redband parrotfish *Sparisoma aurofrenatum*". Ph.D dissertation, Department of Marine Sciences, University of Puerto Rico, Mayaguez.

Fishelson, L. (1970). *Nature* **227**, 90–91.

Fishelson, L. (1975). *In* "Intersexuality in the Animal Kingdom" (R. Reinboth, ed.), pp. 284–294. Springer Verlag, Berlin and New York.

Fricke, H. and Fricke, S. (1977). *Nature, Lond.* **266**, 830–832.

Ghiselin, M. T. (1969). *Q. Rev. Biol.* **44**, 189–208.

Ghiselin, M. T. (1974). "The Economy of Nature and the Evolution of Sex". University of California Press, Berkeley.

Gunderman, N. (1972). "The reproductive cycle and sex inversion of *Anthias squamipinnis* (Peters)". M.Sc. thesis, Department of Zoology, Tel-Aviv University (in Hebrew).

Harrington, R. W. Jr (1971). *Copeia* **1971**, 389–432.

Jones, G. P. (1980). *Copeia* **1980**, 660–675.

Leigh, E. G. Jr, Charnov, E. L. and Warner, R. R. (1976). *Proc. nat. Acad. Sci. U.S.A.* **73**, 3656–3660.

Popper, D. and Fishelson, L. (1973). *J. Exp. Zool.* **184**, 409–424.

Potts, G. W. (1973). *Anim. Behav.* **21**, 250–291.

Reinboth, R. (1962). *Zool. Jahrb., Abt. Allg. Zool. Physiol. Tiere* **69**, 405–480.

Reinboth, R. (1970). *Mem. Soc. Endocrinol.* **18**, 515–543.

Robertson, D. R. (1972). *Science N.Y.* **177**, 1007–1009.

Robertson, D. R. (1974). "A study of the ethology and reproductive biology of the labrid fish, *Labroides dimidiatus*, at Heron Island, Great Barrier Reef". Ph.D. dissertation, Queensland University.

Robertson, D. R. and Choat, J. H. (1974). *Proc. 2nd Int. Coral Reef Symp.*, Brisbane, 217–225.

Robertson, D. R. and Justines, G. (1982). *Env. Biol. Fish.* **7**, 137–142.

Robertson, D. R. and Warner, R. R. (1978). *Smithson. Contrib. Zool.* **255**, 1–26.

Ross, R. M. (1982a). *Proc. 4th Int. Coral Reef Symp.*, Manila (in press).

Ross, R. M. (1982b). "Sex change in the endemic Hawaiian labrid *Thalassoma duperrey* (Quoy and Gaimard): a behavioral and ecological analysis". Ph.D dissertation, University of Hawaii.

Shapiro, D. Y. (1977a). *Proc. 3rd Int. Coral Reef Symp.*, Miami, 571–577.

Shapiro, D. Y. (1977b). "Social organization and sex reversal of the coral reef fish *Anthias squamipinnis* (Peters)". Ph.D dissertation, University of Cambridge.

Shapiro, D. Y. (1979). *Adv. Study Behav.* **10**, 43–102.

Shapiro, D. Y. (1981a). *J. Zool. (Lond.)* **193**, 105–128.

Shapiro, D. Y. (1981b). *Bull. Mar. Sci.* **31**, 383–398.

Shapiro, D. Y. (1981c). *Anim. Behav.* **29**, 1185–1198.

Shapiro, D. Y. (1981d). *Anim. Behav.* **29**, 1199–1212.

Shapiro, D. Y. (1982). *Int. Symp. Comp. Endocrinol.*, *Ninth*, *Hong Kong* (in press).

Shapiro, D. Y. and Boulon, R. H., Jr (1982). *Horm. Behav.* **16**, 66–75.

Shapiro, D. Y. and Lubbock, R. (1980). *J. Theor. Biol.* **82**, 411–426.

Simberloff, D. (1979). *Ecology* **60**, 679–685.

Smith, C. L. (1975). *In* "Intersexuality in the Animal Kingdom" (R. Reinboth, ed.), pp. 295–310. Springer Verlag, Berlin.

Warner, R. R. (1975a). *Fish. Bull.* **73**, 262–283.

Warner, R. R. (1975b). *Am. Nat.* **109**, 61–82.

Warner, R. R. and Hoffman, S. G. (1980). *Evolution* **34**, 508–518.

Warner, R. R. and Robertson, D. R. (1978). *Smithson. Contrib. Zool.* **254**, 1–27.

Warner, R. R., Robertson, D. R. and Leigh, E. G. (1975). *Science N.Y.* **190**, 633–638.

Wenner, A. M. (1972). *Am. Nat.* **106**, 321–350.

8. The Tokology of Gobioid Fishes

P. J. MILLER

Department of Zoology, University of Bristol, Bristol, U.K.

Abstract: Use of the term "tokology" for reproductive biology is explained. The tokology of gobioid fishes is reviewed from four aspects: mode, machinery, dynamics and fitness with most attention paid to the last two. Mode concerns sexuality, sex-ratios, and occurrence of hermaphroditism. Machinery comprises gonad structure, including special endocrine and exocrine glands of the testis and sperm duct, secondary sexual dimorphism, behavioural organization, and neuroendocrine control of reproduction, although the ethology and endocrinology of reproduction are not considered here in detail. As dynamics, the temporal pattern of energy and material deployment for reproduction is examined under the topics of reproductive effort, developmental phasing, frequency, bestowal, timing and consequences for the reproducer. The adaptiveness of reproductive strategies, for maximizing fitness, is discussed with special reference to ecotopic predictability and also in relation to resource factors and intrinsic influence of body size.

I. INTRODUCTION

Traditionally, though with little modern usage, "tocology" (Ryan, 1828) is the science of parturition, but, from the same Greek root, are derived words with such meanings as "begetting", "bearing produce, broods or offspring" and even "usury" (Liddell and Scott, 1940). Thus, tokology can be employed as an apt term for the study of both the mechanics and the profitability of reproduction in living organisms. Although the biosyntheses of reproduction come within the province of phenology (as discussed by Miller, 1979a), equally significant areas of tokology will be the work done by reproducers, and the qualitative aspects of structural and physiological specialization within the organism for this purpose. It should be appreciated that the author's use of words such as tokology and phenology is not just an indulgence in logodaedelic adoxography or in logomachic proselytism. By so designating new limits around basic biological themes, progress should be helped by the unifying effect of gathering together conventionally well-separated viewpoints.

FISH REPRODUCTION
ISBN: 0–12–563660–1

The tokology of gobioid fishes is of interest because of the great systematic diversity and ecotopic radiation of these predominantly small teleosts. The Gobioidei form a suborder of percoid acanthopterygians, which, in number of species (1300–1700), may comprise 10% of all recent teleosts (Hoese, 1971; Nelson, 1976). Gobioid classification has been reviewed by Miller (1973b) and Miller et al. (1980), while a recent summary of the group is provided by Fritzsche (1982).

Tokological study of gobioid fishes concerns four major aspects of reproductive strategy. These are (i) mode, (ii) machinery, (iii) dynamics and (iv) fitness.

II. MODE

The gobies are typically gonochoristic, although a few cases of protogynous hermaphroditism are on record for small tropical marine species (Lassig, 1976, 1977; Robertson and Justineu, 1982). Little is known about the genetics of sex determination. Heterogamety has been reported in a few genera, but the evidence for widespread occurrence within the group remains inconclusive (Nishikawa et al., 1974; Manna and Prasad, 1974; Webb, 1980). Races of the mudskipper Periophthalmus vulgaris may be either "undifferentiated" or "differentiated" in sexual development (Eggert, 1931, 1933; Yamamoto, 1969). Modification of the phenotype in various Japanese species has been achieved by hormone treatment (Egami, 1960).

Adequate sex-frequency data is available for at least 26 species. Most do not depart significantly from a 1:1 ratio. During the breeding season of several species, there is an apparent marked reduction in the proportion of males, which, protecting eggs under shells or stones, are less likely to be caught by drag net (Duncker, 1928; Swedmark, 1958; Miller, 1963b, 1982; Healey, 1971a; Lee, 1974; Hesthagen, 1975, 1977). In some species, a modest but significant preponderance of one sex is found (Miyazaki, 1940; Wiley, 1973, 1976; Staples, 1975a), and, in certain cases, apparent differential survival between the sexes (Kostyuchenko, 1970; Gibson and Ezzi, 1978, 1981).

III. MACHINERY

A. Primary structure

1. *Gametogenesis.* Gametogenesis proceeds according to the general pattern for teleosts (Harder, 1975; Hilge, 1975). Important histological accounts for both sexes are those by Eggert (1931), Pilati (1950) and Mackay (1973a,b),

for spermatogenesis by Stanley *et al.* (1965) and Moiseyeva and Ponomareva (1973), and for oogenesis by Baimov (1962), Rajalakshmi (1966), Sriramalu and Rajalakshmi (1966) and Le Menn (1979). Donato *et al.* (1975) provide cytochemical and histological details of oogenesis in the Mediterranean *Deltentosteus quadrimaculatus*. The temporal pattern of gametogenesis within the gonad sex cell population is typically asynchronous or group-synchronized, as a basis for the usual occurrence of repeat-spawning within a breeding season.

2. *Male genitalia* (Fig. 1). In male gobies, testis structure and the associated sperm-duct glands display features unusual among teleosts. The testis is of the "lobular" type, with closely packed seminiferous lobules. In many species, the testis possesses surprisingly abundant interstitial tissue between the bases of the lobules, often as a reddish or brownish band along the testis edge, in strong contrast to the white mature lobules (Fig. 1a,b,g). This interstitial tissue has been described by Eggert (1931), Vivien (1939a, 1941), Coujard (1941), Pilati (1950), and as the so-called "cell mass" by Saksena and Bhargava (1975). Histochemistry and ultrastructure have been investigated by Stanley *et al.* (1965) and Colombo and Burighal (1974), who regard the cells as equivalent to the endocrine Leydig cells of the mammalian testis. The interstitial tissue of *Gobius* species can be cultured and testosterone output measured (Bonnin, 1975). Biochemical studies (Colombo *et al.*, 1970; Colombo *et al.*, 1977) have suggested that relatively large amounts of water-soluble steroid conjugates may originate from these cells and serve as sexual pheromones. If these substances play a role in species recognition, then the reduction of interstitial tissue in the testes of several *Pomatoschistus* species (Fig. 1h), and in *Lebetus* (Miller, 1963a) may correlate with a greater complexity in sexual colouration than is seen in *Gobius*.

Relatively prominent hyaline appendages from the sperm duct behind the testis, usually called "seminal vesicles" are of virtually universal occurrence throughout the suborder (Egami, 1960; Arai, 1964). A better term, without functional connotation, is "sperm-duct glands". Overall size increases with sexual maturation (Weisel, 1949; Miller, 1961; Moiseyeva and Ponomareva, 1973). In a number of gobies, an additional discrete glandular mass is present at the rear corner of each main gland, immediately before union of the sperm-ducts (Fig. 1c,d,f). This accessory sperm-duct gland is similar in structure to the main gland and has been found in *Pomatoschistus* species (Miller, 1963b) and certain Japanese forms (Arai, 1964). In *P. minutus* and *P. microps*, the accessory gland is very small but, in *P. pictus*, becomes enormous (Fig. 1c) and may extend the length of the abdominal cavity at maturity. Secretion in the lumen of the sperm-duct gland lobules is a viscous colloidal fluid, PAS + ve and rich in secondary proteases (Young and Fox, 1937; Moiseyeva and

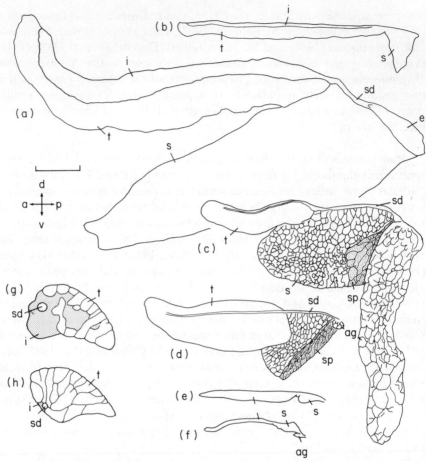

Fig. 1.   a–f. Testes and sperm-duct glands (median view) in *Gobius paganellus* (a) mature (lobules omitted from gland), (b) immature, from Poyll Brein, Isle of Man (other data in Miller, 1963b); *Pomatoschistus pictus* (c) mature, 45+8 mm, from Plymouth Sound, (f) immature, 26·5+5 mm, off Port Erin, Isle of Man; and *P. microps* (d) mature, (e) immature, from Silver Burn, Isle of Man (other data in Miller, 1963b). g, h. Transverse sections through ripe testis of *G. paganellus* and *P. microps* respectively, other data as above. a: anterior (for a–f), median (for g and h); ag: accessory sperm-duct gland; d: dorsal; e: common duct; i: interstitial tissue (fine stipple); p: posterior (lateral for g and h); s: sperm duct gland; sd: sperm duct; sp: posterior region of sd; t: testis (seminiferous lobules); v: ventral. Scale (for a–f) 2·5 mm.

Ponomareva, 1973). In *Pomatoschistus* species, the main gland is divisible into two regions, a narrow part along the rear border contrasting in tinctorial properties with the rest (Miller, 1963b, Fig. 1c,d).

Most recent observers have been unable to show that the sperm-duct glands act as true seminal vesicles for sperm storage. Suggested roles for these glands have been the promotion of sperm viability (Eggert, 1931; Weisel, 1948), enhancing the contact of sperm with the eggs (Vivien, 1938a) and even the cementing of nest walls (Moskalkova, 1967). The function of the sperm-duct glands still requires detailed experimental study but nest preparation by male

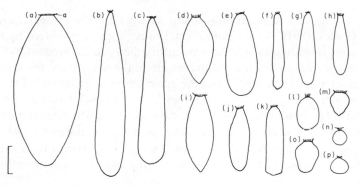

Fig. 2.   Egg capsule (chorion) during development of embryo in gobioid fishes. a, attachment filaments.

Species and source: (a) *Mesogobius batrachocephalus* (Georghiev, 1966); (b) *Acanthogobius flavimanus* (Dotu and Mito, 1955a); (c) *Pterogobius zacalles* (Shiogaki, 1981); (d) *Eviota abax* (Dotsu *et al.*, 1965); (e) *Clariger cosmurus* (Shiogaki and Dotsu, 1972b); (f) *Bathygobius soporator* (Tavolga, 1950); (g) *Rhinogobius giurinus* (Dota, 1961a); (h) *Gobius niger* (Padoa, 1953); (i) *G. paganellus* (Padoa, 1953); (j) *Expedio parvulus* (Shiogaki and Dotsu, 1971); (k) *Elacatinus oceanops* (Feddern, 1967); (l) *Periophthalmus cantonensis* (Kobayashi *et al.*, 1972); (m) *Gobiusculus flavescens* (Le Danois, 1913); (n) *Sicyopterus japonicus* (Dotu and Mito, 1955b); (o) *Pomatoschistus microps* (Petersen, 1891); (p) *Hypseleotris klunzingeri* (Lake, 1967b). Scale 1 mm.

gobies often entails rubbing the abdomen and urogenital papilla over a cleaned surface prior to egg deposition, and "sperm trails" have been noted by Auty (1978) over the nesting surface of *Hypseleotris compressus*. Perhaps functional division of the relatively complex male genitalia possessed by the gobies involves provision of gametes and pheromones by the testes, and of a substrate-coating by the sperm-duct glands.

Both sexes in the gobioid fishes possess an erectile urogenital papilla, between anus and anal fin origin. The external shape of this organ has been reviewed by Egami (1960) and Arai (1964) for many Japanese gobies. In the male, it is typically conical, more or less tapering with a terminal slit, but in a few forms (Egami, 1960; McDowall, 1965), width may be comparable to that in females.

3. *Female genitalia.*   The gobioid ovary is of the cystovarian pattern usual for teleosts (Brock, 1878; Eggert, 1931). The possible occurrence of viviparity among the gobies, in certain mudskippers (Mayer, 1929; Harms, 1935) and the nektonic *Sufflogobius bibarbatus* of the Benguela current (O'Toole, 1978), requires confirmation. In female gobioids, the urogenital papilla is usually broad, with a wide, more or less fimbriate tip bearing a terminal or subterminal transverse opening (Egami, 1960; Arai, 1964).

4. *Egg capsule.*   For all gobioids studied, a feature of later oogenesis is the formation, between follicle granulosa and oocyte chorion (zona radiata), of a layer of filaments, which coalesce into a network attached to a thickening of the chorion around the micropyle (Eggert, 1931; Wickler, 1962; Riehl, 1978; Takahashi, 1978). On extrusion, the filaments reflect away from the elongating

zona radiata, and form an attachment network for the demersal egg (Holt, 1890; Guitel, 1891). After fertilization, the egg capsule produced by the zona radiata is typically non-spherical, a feature dicussed by Breder (1943). Since the eggs are attached usually to the ceiling of the nest cavity, the gobioid egg normally hangs downwards from the attached, micropylar end. The range in size and form of capsule is shown in Fig. 2. Breder (1943) could see no obvious reason for the evolution of non-spherical eggs in teleosts. Khryzhanovski and Ptchelina (1941) believed that this shape permitted a more compact patch of eggs easier for the male parent to fan. An elliptical, pyriform, or cylindrical capsule might also shed sediment more readily, and promote water-flow from fanning.

B. Secondary organization

1. *Structural and other attributes.*   Secondary structural dimorphism between the sexes is displayed by most gobies, and may involve body size, body proportions, fin-ray length, pigmentation, dermal tubercles and dentition (Collett, 1878; Egami, 1960; Lee, 1974; Miller, 1963a, 1982; Petersen, 1919). For *Microgobius gulosus*, Baird (1966) suggested that sexual dimorphism in body length and proportions, including jaw size, all greater in adult males, permitted resource subdivision between the sexes and the possibility of niche expansion for the species, since males were able to eat larger food items. As well as in visual stimuli, the sexes may also differ in scent (Macginitie, 1939; Tavolga, 1954, 1956; Colombo et al., 1977), and sound (Tavolga, 1956, 1958; Kinzer, 1960).

2. *Reproductive behaviour.*   The essential reproductive behaviour of gobioid fishes concerns the deposition of demersal eggs on a nest-sheltered substrate and brood care by usually the male parent until hatching. The basic pattern may be divided into five phases (Reese, 1964). These are (i) establishment of territory; (ii) nest preparation, based on use of a relatively smooth undersurface of an immobile object, usually a shell or stone, or within a burrow, self-excavated or that of a symbiont; (iii) pre-spawning or courtship behaviour; (iv) spawning, on the nest ceiling or walls, with eggs deposited in a single-layered patch; and (v) parental care of eggs, chiefly by fanning and aggressive behaviour towards intruders. Between the gobioid species, there is much variety in emphasis on homologous parts of these behaviour patterns, and on the stimuli utilized, relative to ecotope and environmental resources, such as substrate, presence of potential symbionts, etc. Reviews of gobioid reproductive behaviour have been made by Kinzer (1960) and Reese (1964), with much information listed by Breder and Rosen (1966). Among numerous recent accounts, important contributions include those by Mashiko (1976a,b)

for the eleotrine *Odontobutis obscurus*, and a detailed analysis of nest building in *Pomatoschistus microps* (Vestergaard, 1976). Hudson (1977) has described an aberrant pattern of brood care in the coral reef species, *Signigobius biocellatus*, with alternate sealing and reopening of nest burrows, and perhaps survival of only one offspring per batch.

C. Control mechanisms

Many endocrine and neuroendocrine studies on gobioid fishes suggest that the proximal control mechanisms underlying the activation and maintenance of gametogenesis, and ancillary reproductive processes, are not radically different from the general plan seen in teleosts and fully reviewed elsewhere. According to de Vlaming (1972e), the work by Vivien (1938b, 1939b, 1941), involving *Gobius paganellus*, founded our present understanding of the relationship between pituitary and gonad in fishes.

IV. DYNAMICS

Operation of the reproductive machinery involves a cyclical demand for energy and material. This fuelling of reproduction shows a temporal pattern in amplitude, frequency and direction, within the overall reproductive strategy. Elements in the dynamics of bioenergetic expenditure for this purpose are (i) *reproductive effort*: the quantity of energy and material devoted to reproduction (Williams, 1966) compared to other metabolic needs; (ii) *developmental phasing*: time of onset, and point in growth pattern, for sexual maturation, within life-span and limiting size; (iii) *frequency*: the number of reproductive events during life; (iv) *bestowal*: subdivision of reproductive effort per offspring, and resulting fecundity; (v) *timing*: correlation of breeding with environmental seasonality; and (vi) *consequences*: effect of reproduction on the reproducers.

A. Reproductive effort

Reproductive effort in gobies (Fig. 3) may be divided into (i) a "primary" sector, involving prezygotic maturation biosyntheses and storage within the gametes, most obviously seen in oocyte size and number, and (ii) a "secondary" sector, itself divisible into (a) the anabolism of secondary sexual characters, including dimorphism in growth, body proportions, finnage, colouration, and perhaps in pheromone output, and (b) the catabolism of reproductive behaviour, involving the work done in territoriality, nidification, courtship, spawning and brood care, as well as any preliminary migration to

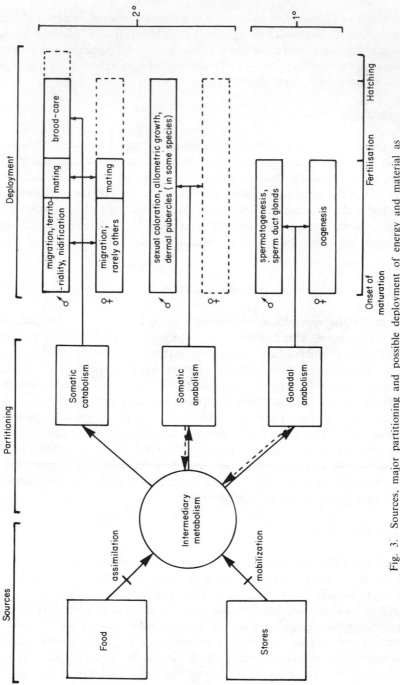

Fig. 3. Sources, major partitioning and possible deployment of energy and material as reproductive effort in gobioid fishes; rare occurrence denoted by broken lines; reclaim facility arrowed on broken lines; 1°, 2°, primary and secondary sectors.

breeding areas. Of these aspects, gonad maturation and mating are obvious necessities, but the gobies show a range of emphasis in the different components of reproductive effort.

As a further complication, in *Pomatoschistus* (Miller, 1963b; Lee, 1974; Gibson and Ezzi, 1981), there is evidence for alternative tactics within a species in male reproductive effort, perhaps as another example of cuckolding or sneaking by "satellite" or "type 2" males described for certain percoids (Gross, Chap. 4, this volume; Dipper, pers. comm.). A proportion of males, within the *Pomatoschistus* species, are found during the breeding season to be of small size and lacking in nuptial colouration, but possessing very large testes and genital papilla. Saving on secondary male features, including territoriality, courtship and brood care, may thus augment the primary sector of reproductive effort. However, confirmation of the reproductive activities of these small males is still required.

Primary reproductive effort in fish is usually denoted by gonadosomatic index (GSI), the percentage of ripe gonadal to somatic or total weight. Data for ovaries are given in Fig. 4, showing GSI against maximum standard length and the distribution of GSIs calculated in terms of both total and somatic (total less gonad) body weight. Values from the first method of calculation range from about 5 to over 28%, but most lie between 12–25%. These are all based on wet weights; after drying at 105°C, average GSI for two species, *Gobius paganellus* and *Pomatoschistus microps*, differed greatly at about 24 and 47% respectively (Miller, 1979b). Another method for comparing primary reproductive effort between females is to calculate total volume of mature eggs from fecundity and oocyte-size data. These data are available for more gobioids than are direct ovary weights, and are shown in Fig. 5, plotted against body length. Since the gobies vary in body attenuation, conclusions about GSI from such results must be tentative, and species may differ in yolk composition and calorific value. However, it is evident that species of similar size can differ in total egg volume by more than an order of magnitude. Evidence from GSI and egg volume would thus suggest a wide range in primary commitment by the female among gobioid species. In the case of male gobies, GSI is considerably less, ranging from about 0·3 to 3·6 (de Vlaming, 1972b; Healey, 1972a). In some cases, it is not clear whether or not sperm-duct glands are included in GSIs. In *Neogobius melanostomus*, for which Mois-eyeva and Ponomareva (1973) have calculated separate indices, testes (2·85) are about four times sperm-duct gland weight (0·79) at maturity, although, in another species, *Gillichthys mirabilis*, these glands may be twice as heavy as the testes of the mature male (Weisel, 1949).

Nearly all gobies practise repeat-spawning, in some cases at least several times in a season (see below). Thus, for the average female *Gobius paganellus* spawning twice per season, total ovarian expenditure over two months is rather less than half somatic weight while, in *P. microps*, with a

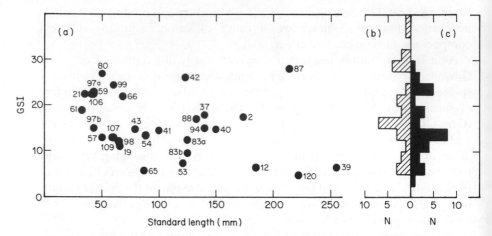

Fig. 4.   Gonadosomatic indices (GSI) and body size in female gobioid fishes; (a) GSI for total weight (ovary weight/somatic and gonad weight × 100) against maximum standard length for species; (b) and (c) frequency distribution (2·5% groups) of somatic weight GSI (ovary weight/somatic weight × 100) (b), and total weight GSI (c) for species of (a).

Species and sources are listed as follows (numbered in alphabetical order for all species cited in graphs of Figs 4–7: 2: *Acanthogobius flavimanus* (Miyazaki, 1940); 12: *Boleophthalmus dussumieri* (Mutsaddi and Bal, 1970); 19: *Chaeturichthys sciistius* (Okada and Suzuki, 1955); 21: *Clevelandia ios* (Brothers, 1975); 37: *Gillichthys mirabilis* (de Vlaming, 1972b); 39: *Glossogobius giuris* (Doha, 1974); 40: *G. olivaceus* (Senta and Hoshino, 1970); 41: *Gobiomorphus breviceps* (Staples, 1975a); 42: *G. cotidianus* (Stephens, 1982); 43: *G. huttoni* (McDowall, 1965 and unpub.); 53: *Gobius niger* (Le Menn, 1979); 54: *G. paganellus* (Miller, 1979b and unpub.); 57: *Hypseleotris galii* (Mackay, 1973a); 59: *Ilypnus gilberti* (Brothers, 1975); 61: *Knipowitschia caucasica* (Baimov, 1963); 65: *Lepidogobius lepidus* (Grossmann, 1979); 66: *Lesueurigobius friesii* (Gibson and Ezzi, 1978); 80: *Mugilogobius abei* (Kanabashira et al., 1980); 83: *Neogobius melanostomus* (a: Moiseyeva, 1972; b: Kovtun, 1977); 87: *Odontoamblyopus rubicundus* (Dotu, 1957e); 88: *Odontobutis obscurus* (Dotu and Tsukahara, 1964); 94: *Percottus glehni* (Kirpichnikov, 1945); 97: *Pomatoschistus microps* (a: Miller, 1979b and unpub.; b: Healey, 1972a); 98: *P. minutus* (Healey, 1972b; Hesthagen, 1977); 99: *P. norvegicus* (Gibson and Ezzi, 1981); 106: *Quietula y-cauda* (Brothers, 1975); 107: *Rhinogobius flumineus* (Mizuno, 1960); 109: *Rh. similis* (Mizuno, 1960); 120: *Trypauchen vagina* (Dandekar, 1965).

likely six spawnings in three months, total expenditure could reach above $2\frac{1}{2}$ times average adult female weight (reproductive effort of 0·6 per month) (Miller, 1979a,b). Differences in gonadosomatic index, and in spawning frequency, may thus lead to considerable disparity in quantity and intensity of primary reproductive effort between species. Although the testes and associated structures form a much smaller proportion of male body weight than do ovaries in females, male primary expenditure could be greater than indicated. Frequency of reproductive acts by an individual male may be much higher than the usual number of spawnings by females, since egg patches can be composite and destruction of a brood can be followed by rapid replacement from other females.

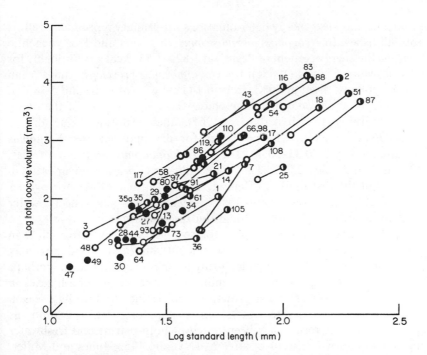

Fig. 5. Total ripe oocyte volume (oocyte volume × fecundity) in relation to standard length for gobioid fishes; open and semiclosed circles, values for extremes of adult female size using fecundities calculated from regression equation; closed circles, values for individual females.

Species and sources (for oocyte volume and fecundity respectively, if different) as Fig. 4, otherwise: 1: *Aboma lactipes* (Dotu, 1959); 2: *Acanthogobius flavimanus* (Dotu and Mito, 1955a; Miyazaki, 1940); 3: *Acentrogobius masago* (Dotu, 1958a); 7: *Apocryptodon bleekeri* (Dotu, 1961c); 9: *Barbulifer ceuthoecus* (Böhlke and Robins, 1968); 13: *Caspiosoma caspium* (Vladimirov and Kubrak, 1972); 14: *Chaenogobius castanea* (Dotu, 1954); 17: *Ch. urotaenia* (Dotu, 1955c; Takeuchi, 1971); 18: *Chaeturichthys hexanema* (Dotu et al., 1955); 21: *Clevelandia ios* (Prasad, 1959); 25: *Ctenotrypauchen microcephalus* (Dotu, 1958b); 27: *Elacatinus evelynae* (Böhlke and Robins, 1968); 28: *E. louisae* (Böhlke and Robins, 1968); 29: *E. oceanops* (Valenti, 1972); 30: *E. prochilos* (Böhlke and Robins, 1968); 34: *Eutaeniichthys gilli* (Dotu, 1955a); 35: *Eviota abax* (Dotsu et al., 1965); 35a: *Eviota zonura* (Dotsu et al., 1965); 36: *Expedio parvulus* (Shiogaki and Dotsu, 1971); 44: *Gobiopterus chuno* (Pillay and Sarojini, 1950); 47: *Gobiosoma pallens* (Böhlke and Robins, 1968); 48: *G. robustum* (Springer and McErlean, 1961); 49: *G. saucrum* (Böhlke and Robins, 1968); 51: *Gobius cobitis* (Oppenheimer, 1954; Gibson, 1970); 58: *Hypseleotris klunzingeri* (Lake, 1967b); 61: *Knipowitschia caucasica* (Baimov, 1962, 1963); 64: *Lebetus scorpioides* (Miller, 1963a); 73: *Luciogobius saikaiensis* (Dotu and Mito, 1958); 80: *Mugilogobius abei* (Kanabashira et al., 1980); 83: *Neogobius melanostomus* (Moskalkova, 1967; Kovtun, 1977); 86: *Nes longus* (Böhlke and Robins, 1968); 91: *Paleatogobius uchidae* (Dotu, 1957a); 93: *Parioglossus taeniatus* (Dotu, 1955e); 97: *Pomatoschistus microps* (Miller, 1963b); 98: *P. minutus* (Lee, 1974; Healey, 1971b); 105: *Pterogobius zonoleucus* (Dotu, 1955d); 108: *Rhinogobius giurio* (Dotu, 1961a); 110: *Sicyopterus japonicus* (Dotu and Mito, 1955b); 116: *Triaenopogon barbatus* (Dotu, 1957f); 117. *Tridentiger nudicervicus* (Dotu, 1958c); 119: *Tr. trigonocephalus* (Dotu, 1958c).

So far, there are few energy determinations for primary reproductive effort in gobioid fishes. In *Neogobius melanostomus*, Skazkina and Kostyuchenko (1968) give the energy content of "eggs" at $1\cdot824$–$1\cdot833$ kcal g^{-1}, probably for wet tissue, while Staples (1975c), for *Gobiomorphus breviceps*, found mean values for gonads, dried at 70°C, to be $6\cdot14$ kcal g^{-1} (ovaries) and $5\cdot73$ kcal g^{-1} (testes). If *N. melanostomus* eggs have the water content of the ovary ($62\cdot5\%$ according to Moskalkova, 1967), their calorific value dry is $4\cdot858$–$4\cdot876$ kcal g^{-1}. In kJ, the values for dry material are: *Neogobius melanostomus* eggs, $20\cdot33$–$20\cdot40$ kJ g^{-1}; *Gobiomorphus breviceps* ovaries, $25\cdot69$ kJ g^{-1}; and testes, $23\cdot97$ kJ g^{-1}. The value for *G. breviceps* ovaries lies in the middle of the distribution of energy content in teleost eggs or ovaries (Wootton, 1979). The lower value for *N. melanostomus* may reflect a water content for spawned eggs greater than that used above.

No quantitative data are available for secondary reproductive effort in gobioid fishes. Territoriality, intermittent courtship, and brood care may impose a heavy burden on the male during a long breeding season, perhaps comparable to the high primary expenditure by the female — both sexes in *Pomatoschistus microps* suffer a growth check during the breeding season (Miller, 1975). In temperate waters, an inshore breeding migration, as temperatures rise in spring, has been noted in both marine and freshwater forms, sometimes with ascent of streams (Nyman, 1953; Jones and Miller, 1966; Dotu, 1961a; Tamura and Honma, 1969, 1970a,b; Fonds, 1973). Such activity requires metabolic outlay, including osmoregulatory changes in energy expenditure.

Closely linked with reproduction is the phenology of storage (Miller, 1979a). Pianka (1976) noted that hoarding of storage materials permits transfer of ecosystem productivity, foraged in one part of the year or area of distribution, for expenditure at another time or place, when conditions exist for optimal reproductive success but not for support of reproductive metabolism by direct feeding. For gobies, information on such depot strategies is available for a few species, in which the liver has been shown to play the leading role in storage during the annual breeding cycle (Shulman, 1967; de Vlaming, 1971; Lee, 1974; Shih, 1979). During vitellogenesis, mobilization of reserves sees the appearance of two yolk proteins in the liver, serum and ovaries of *Gobius niger* (Le Menn, 1979); two such lipoproteins in the serum of maturing and spawning female *Neogobius* diminish after reproduction (Kulikova, 1977).

After expenditure of ripe gametes in the last spawning of the season, resorbtion of oocytes undergoing vitellogenesis, and spermatocytes and later stages in spermiogenesis takes place. This presumably results from diminished gonadotrophin secretion (de Vlaming, 1974). In females, the appearance and subsequent fate of ovarian corpora atretica has been described in a number of species (Vivien, 1939a,b; Miller, 1961; Miller, 1963b; Rajalakshmi, 1966;

Tamura and Honma, 1970a; de Vlaming, 1972b; Saksena and Bhargava, 1972; Mackay, 1973a; Belsare, 1975).

Feeding to a varying extent does occur during the breeding season, and food deficiency may cause gonadal regression at that time (de Vlaming, 1971). Using values adopted by Healey (1972b) for the energy of food intake and gonad growth, conversion efficiency for the latter process in *Pomatoschistus minutus* may be estimated at 17·25% (0-group) to 23·02% (I-group) for ripening females, 10·83% for this sex during the breeding season, and for males, 1·75% (O) or 0·46% (I). This discrepancy between males and females probably reflects a much greater catabolic expenditure by the former in reproductive activities. In *Neogobius melanostomus* breeding season conversion efficiency is 5·7–11·3% over three age-groups of females (Skazkina and Kostyuchenko, 1968).

B. Developmental phasing

At the outset of modern interest in life-history theory, Cole (1954) emphasized the significance of age at maturity as a major determinant of reproductive rate. A prerequisite for reproduction is the ontogenetic development of a body organization able to support maturation and use of the gonads. Within a species, age at maturity can therefore be influenced by growth rate, itself subject to environmental determinants. Although high growth rate may be advantageous, by earlier attainment of size for reproduction, a smaller limiting size and higher likelihood of mortality are fecundity and fitness penalties which may be incurred as a result (Beverton and Holt, 1959). However, ability to reproduce at small absolute size must be part of the evolutionary decrease in body size which forms an important feature of adaptive radiation of the teleosts and especially the gobies (Miller, 1979b).

For the gobioid fishes, age at maturity ranges from a few months to at least three years. Within a population, variation in age at maturity has been noted in *Gobiomorphus breviceps* (Staples, 1975a), and in *Chaenogobius isaza* has been attributed to individual variation in growth rate to minimum size at maturity (Nagoshi and Kojima, 1976). A latitudinal effect, found in *Gobiusculus flavescens* by Johnsen (1945), with delay towards northern limits of distribution, may be due partly to slower growth but whether maximum age is also extended was not ascertained. Individuals in the same population can differ in size at sexual maturity (Prasad, 1959; Mutsaddi and Bal, 1970; Staples, 1975a; Brothers, 1975) and, during a long breeding season, a decline may be seen in length for maturation within the same year-class (Miller, 1963b). Sexual dimorphism in age and size at maturity is especially manifest in *Neogobius melanostomus* (Kostyuchenko, 1961) and *Gobiomorphus breviceps* (Staples, 1975a); in both species most females mature at two years, males a year later.

In the evolution of small size, the present group is of special significance in that gobioid structure seems best suited of any among teleosts for sexual maturation in the tiniest vertebrate frame (Miller, 1979b; Winterbottom and Emery, 1981). The usual examples cited are *Mistichthys luzonensis*, with maturity at 11 mm in both sexes, and *Pandaka pygmaea* (males at 7·5, females at 10 mm) (Miller, 1979b) but the record smallest female gobies (and vertebrates) are now known to be those of *Trimmatom* species from the western Indian Ocean, described by Winterbottom and Emery (1981), who have found examples of 8 mm with fully developed eggs. Other species maturing at very small size include *Lythrypnus* forms (from 9 mm), and *Risor ruber* (10 mm) (Smith and Tyler, 1972), as well as a number of *Eviota* (Lachner and Karnella, 1978).

Early maturation at small size in the diminutive nektonic aphyine gobies is associated with gonadal heterochrony (Gould, 1977). Postlarval characters, retained in such genera as *Aphia*, *Crystallogobius*, *Gobiopterus*, *Leucopsarion* and *Mistichthys*, include body transparency and lateral compression, as well as a functional swimbladder and, in some instances, reduced finnage (Miller, 1973a, 1979b). The aphyines may be derived from estuarine postlarvae comparable to those of the sicydiine gobies (Miller, 1973a).

C. Frequency

Cole (1954) designated as "semelparous" those life-histories involving only a single reproductive event, followed by death, and as "iteroparous" those in which reproduction occurs on more than one occasion during life-span. Examples of both kinds are seen among gobies.

Truly semelparous forms may be found among the aphyine genera, a group exhibiting progenetic features (Miller, 1973a; see above). One of these, the temperate Japanese ice-goby, *Leucopsarion petersi*, is anadromous and death occurs after a short May breeding season (Tamura and Honma, 1969), presumably with only a single spawning by individual fish. Collett (1878) described the aphyines *Aphia minuta* and *Crystallogobius linearis* as both "annual fish", with breeding seasons from May to August, or March to August, in the cold-temperate Oslofjord, but there has been no confirmation of how many times the individual fish may spawn within the single breeding season of life. However, more recently, Mancini and Cavinato (1969) report that breeding by *Aphia minuta* in the Adriatic is restricted to May, a brief period for gobies in a warm-temperate environment and perhaps indicative of single spawning. A related tropical species, *Gobiopterus chuno*, appears to produce only one batch of eggs (Pillay and Sarojini, 1950).

The majority of gobies are potentially iteroparous but display a wide range in length of reproductive life (Section V). Two kinds of iteroparity may be recognized in species whose reproduction is seasonal, and these can be termed "abbreviate" and "protracted". Abbreviate iteropares display a long breeding season with several to many spawnings by individual fish but adult life-span is short and covers only one to a few breeding seasons. The protracted iteropares are longer-lived species, with frequently not more than two spawnings in a season, at up to 60 day intervals. They may, however, participate in two to over ten seasons. Examples of abbreviate and protracted iteroparity are considered in Section V. The eleotrine *Gobiomorphus breviceps*, the large Ponto-Caspian *Mesogobius batrachocephalus*, and the mudskipper, *Boleophthalmus dussumierei*, are unusual among gobies in spawning only once per season (Staples, 1975a,b; Moiseeva, 1970, 1971; Mutsaddi and Bal, 1970).

The facility of "repeat-spawning" within a season, seen in most gobies, is reflected in a characteristic size-frequency distribution of oocytes within the mature ovary where, as well as a batch completing vitellogenesis or already ripened, there is also a comparably numerous group at mid-vitellogenesis which will provide the next spawning. In addition, a reserve of mostly non-vitellogenic oocytes is normally present. This pattern of size distribution was illustrated by Miller (1961) for *Gobius paganellus*, and has been reported for many gobies. Repeat-spawning, over a more or less extended breeding season, is believed to have originated in relation to the availability of plankton in warmer seas for most of the year (Qasim, 1956; Cushing, 1959). This pattern of productivity would support not only planktotrophic offspring but also adult dietary needs for repeated gametogenesis and secondary reproductive activities (see below).

Within a species, number of spawnings in a season, and duration of the latter, may vary over geographical range, becoming more limited in cooler temperate conditions (Miller, 1961; Munroe and Lotspeich, 1979). Frequency of spawning is certainly subject to proximate environmental influences, such as temperature (Fonds, 1973; Kulikova and Fandeeva, 1976), food (Kovtun, 1977), and conditions of captivity (Macginitie, 1939).

D. Bestowal

1. *Egg size.*   Gobies exhibit a wide range in egg size (bestowal per offspring) in keeping with ecotope diversity (Fig. 6). Most of those examined possess eggs ranging in volume from 0.07 to 0.27 mm^3, but the extremes of bestowal stretch from $9.2 \times 10^{-3} \text{ mm}^3$ (diameter 0.26 mm) in the freshwater *Hypseleotris compressus*, whose eggs must be among the smallest known in teleosts, to 7.49 mm^3 (2.43 mm) for the large Ponto-Caspian *Mesogobius batrachocephalus*, three orders of magnitude greater in yolk volume.

Minimal bestowal is found in (i) riverine and stream-dwelling freshwater species whose tiny larvae are swept downstream to grow in estuaries and coastal waters before ascending to the parental habitat (the sicydiines, *Eleotris oxycephalus*, *Leucopsarion petersi*, etc.); (ii) other freshwater gobies spawning

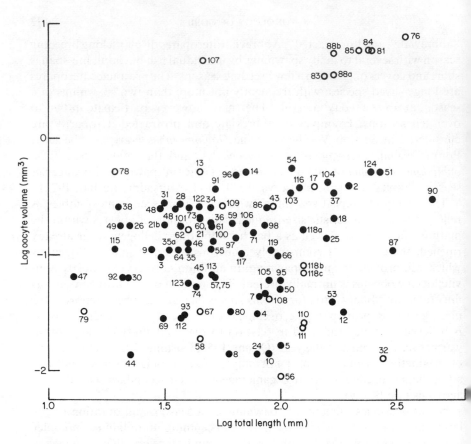

Fig. 6. Volume of ripe oocyte in relation to maximum total length for gobioid fishes. Open circles, breeding habitat in freshwater for at least some populations.

Species and sources as Figs 4 and 5, otherwise: 4: *Acentrogobius neilli* (Aiyar, 1935); 5: *A. ornatus* (Vijayaraghvan, 1973); 8: *Asterropteryx semipunctatus* (Dotu and Mito, 1963); 10: *Bathygobius fuscus* (Dotu, 1955b); 21b: *Clevelandia ios* (Brothers, 1975); 24: *Ctenogobius stigmaticus* (Kuntz, 1916); 26: *Elacatinus atronasum* (Böhlke and Robins, 1968); 31: *E. xanthiprora* (Böhlke and Robins, 1968); 32: *Eleotris oxycephalus* (Dotu and Fujita, 1959); 37: *Gillichthys mirabilis* (Weisel, 1947); 38: *Ginsburgellus novemlineatus* (Böhlke and Robins, 1968); 45: *Gobiosoma bosci* (Kuntz, 1916); 46: *G. ginsburgi* (Dahlberg and Conyers, 1973); 50: *Gobius bucchichii* (Gordina, 1973); 53: *G. niger* (Ballard, 1969); 54: *G. paganellus* (Miller, 1961); 55: *Gobiusculus flavescens* (Miller, unpubl.); 56: *Hypseleotris compressus* (Auty, 1978); 57: *H. galii* (Anderson *et al.*, 1971); 58: *H. klunzingeri* (Anderson *et al.*, 1971); 60: *Inu koma* (Shiogaki and Dotsu, 1974a); 62: *Knipowitschia longecaudata* (Georghiev, 1966); 67: *Leucopsarion petersi* (Tamura and Honma, 1970a); 69: *Lubricogobius exiguus* (Dotu and Fujita, 1963); 71: *Luciogobius guttatus* (Dotu, 1957d); 74: *Lythrypnus dalli* (Wiley, 1976); 75: *L. zebra* (Wiley, 1976); 76: *Mesogobius batrachocephalus* (Georghiev, 1966); 78: *Microgobius lacustris* (Blanco, 1947); 79: *Mistichthys luzonensis* (Te Winkel, 1935); 81: *Neogobius cephalargoides* (Georghiev, 1966); 84: *N. ratan* (Georghiev, 1966); 85: *N. syrman* (Georghiev, 1966); 88: *Odontobutis obscurus* (a, Dotu and Tsukahara, 1964; b, Mashiko, 1976b); 90: *Oxyeleotris marmorata* (Tan and Lam, 1973); 92: *Pandaka lidwilli* (Dotu, 1957c); 95: *Periophthalmus cantonensis* (Kobayashi *et al.*, 1972); 96: *Pomatoschistus marmoratus* (Georghiev, 1966); 97: *P. microps* (Miller, 1963b); 98: *P. minutus* (Lee, 1974); 100: *P. pictus* (Miller, 1972b); 101: *P. tortonesei* (Miller, 1982); 103: *Pterogobius elapoides* (Dotu and Tsutsumi, 1959); 104: *Pt. zacalles* (Shiogaki, 1981); 110: *Sicyopterus extraneus* (Manacop, 1953); 112: *Silhouettea dotui* (Dotu, 1958d); 113: *Stigmatogobius javanicus* (Nair, 1961); 115: *Tigrigobius gemmatum* (Böhlke and Robins, 1968); 118: *Tridentiger obscurus* (Kishi, 1979; a, estuarine; b, riverine; c, lacustrine); 122: *Zonogobius boreus* (Shiogaki and Dotsu, 1974b); 123: *Z. semidoliatus* (Sonoda and Imai, 1971); 124: *Zosterisessor ophiocephalus* (Pilati, 1950).

in temporarily flooded areas where rapid development and hatching is necessary before desiccation (*Hypseleotris* spp.), and (iii) a number of mostly small marine species, from nektonic shoalers (*Gobiopterus chuno*, *Parioglossus taeniatus*) to an epibenthic sand-dweller (*Silhouettea dotui*) and various cryptobenthic forms (*Lubricogobius exiguus*, *Asterropteryx semipunctatus*, etc.).

Maximum bestowal is seen among the Ponto-Caspian genera *Neogobius* and *Mesogobius*, large species of slow rivers, lagoons and brackish coastal waters, whose young do not pass through a planktonic stage. In the Far East, the entirely lacustrine *Rhinogobius flumineus* produces large eggs (1·4–2·1 mm diameter, average 4·84 mm^3) in contrast to those of the closely related, but amphidromous, *Rh. brunneus* whose eggs do not exceed 0·8 mm (0·27 mm^3) (Mizuno, 1960). Other gobiids with relatively large eggs include (i) a further group of phyletically unrelated freshwater species (*Caspiosoma caspium*, *Chaenogobius urotaenia*, *Microgobius lacustris*, *Odontobutis obscurus*, *Oxyeleotris marmorata*, etc.), (ii) the Mediterranean brackish *Zosterisessor ophiocephalus*, sister group to the Ponto-Caspian forms already mentioned, and (iii) marine species from a variety of ecotopes, such as high shore-pool (*Gobius cobitis*), epibenthic (*Acanthogobius flavimanus*), nektonic (*Pterogobius* spp) and cryptobenthic (*Gobius paganellus*) environments.

There is no clear relationship between egg volume and maximum body length. Opposing trends in bestowal are not related to simple habitat differences, such as salinity, and it seems that relatively larger or smaller eggs have been achieved in several evolutionary lines as similar end products caused by different arrays of selective forces. Divergence in this respect between species may be seen within *Gobius* and *Pterogobius*, and has been discussed by Kishi (1979) as a possible factor in speciation of *Rhinogobius*. Intraspecific variation in bestowal has been noted between different geographical populations (Prasad, 1959; Baimov, 1963; Brothers, 1975), as well as reduction in egg size during the breeding season (Kulikova and Fandeeva, 1975) or in captivity (Shiogaki, 1981).

In 49 species for which data can be obtained, volume of yolk at fertilization and size of resulting young on hatching show fair correlation ($r = 0.76$), if the former is compared with the cube of larval length as an indication of body weight. There is a wide range in length at hatching. Young of several freshwater species, mostly known to be anadromous, hatch at less than 1·5 mm, with larvae of *Dormitator latifrons* being merely 0·8–0·9 mm (Todd, 1975). Again, in fresh water, but under lacustrine or otherwise stagnant conditions, size at hatching, in species with large eggs, reaches 7·8 mm, in *Chaenogobius castanea* (Dotu, 1954).

2. *Fecundity.* For a fixed ovarian biomass, fecundity has an inverse relationship with bestowal. Fecundity is here regarded as the number of eggs produced in a single spawning, comprising the entire batch of ripe oocytes present in the mature ovaries, but excluding the following group at mid-

vitellogenesis. With ovary growth a function of body growth, and oocyte size more or less fixed (within limited seasonal or size-related trends), instantaneous fecundity typically increases with body size of female, although the direction of change in relative fecundity will depend on allometry between ovary weight and body size.

In the present study, fecundity has been compared only with standard length although differences between species in body proportions may lead to considerable disparity in weight at similar lengths. In the majority of gobioids examined, fecundity increases with body length, with correlation coefficients of over 0·9 in two-thirds of the 31 species for which this value can be calculated. Regression equations, obtained for 35 species, are mostly power functions of length, as is usual for teleosts, although in some cases the functions are linear. A few species, such as *Chaenogobius scrobiculatus* (Dotu, 1961b), show little correlation between body length and fecundity.

Fecundity between similar sized gobies may differ between species by two orders of magnitude. Thus, 224 960 eggs reported from a *Sicyopterus japonicus* at 105 mm (Dotu and Mito, 1955b) may be compared with about 1600 in *Neogobius melanostomus* of the same length (Kovtun, 1977).

Fecundity is maximized, with reduced bestowal, in the presence of suitable food resources for the fry. These resources can be available either in a water body contiguous with the spawning habitat or located down-drift from the latter. Heavy but predictable mortality for postlarval fish in the plankton is met from the reserves of offspring embodied in high fecundity. The sicydiines and many marine species exemplify such tactics. Within an ecosystem which does not permit nutrition of a free-living developmental stage, or presents other conditions reducing survival at this stage, selection must favour larger young, with increased bestowal but lowered parental fecundity. Evolution of lacustrine gobies under brackish or freshwater conditions has included this trend in the case of the various Ponto-Caspian gobies belonging to *Benthophilus*, *Caspiosoma*, *Mesogobius* and *Neogobius*, as well as the smaller *Rhinogobius flumineus* from Japan (Khryzhanovskii and Ptchelina, 1941; Mizuno, 1960; Kishi, 1979).

Miller (1979b) noted considerable differences in relative fecundity (eggs g^{-1} body) between *Pomatoschistus microps* (2364) and *Gobius paganellus* (687), where smaller oocytes are combined with higher gonadosomatic index in the former species, as well as between *Lesueurigobius friesii* (2663) and *G. paganellus*, of comparable gonad size but with much smaller eggs in *L. friesii* (0·563 vs 0·099 mm^3). Lower fecundity in old (2+) individuals of the short-lived *P. minutus* was noted by Healey (1971b), together with an increase in relative fecundity over the breeding season in I+ fish of similar size. Preliminary studies in *P. microps* (Miller, unpublished) suggest that increased relative fecundity over this period is due to reduced bestowal, rather than increased primary reproductive effort. A similar effect on fecundity is also evident in *Neogobius melanostomus* (Kulikova and Fandeeva, 1975).

Because of repeat-spawning, total fecundity achieved by a female, which survives to the end of a breeding season, will be greater than the instantaneous values discussed above. Thus, with higher relative fecundity and more frequent spawning, a female *Pomatoschistus microps*, averaging 3·5 cm and 0·55 g, would produce about 7800 eggs by spawning six times in a season, over two-thirds of the seasonal total of about 11 000 eggs from an average female *Gobius paganellus*, much larger in size at 7·5 cm and 8·0 g, spawning twice. The same biomass of female *microps*, spawning six times, would deposit over ten times the number of eggs produced in two spawnings by the *paganellus*, and four times the total from an equal number of spawnings by the latter.

E. Timing

Successful reproduction entails the production of young when physical and biotic conditions are most likely to promote their survival. A basic aspect of life-history in most gobioids is the occurrence of a planktonivorous postlarval stage, exploiting a different ecosystem to that of the usually demersal adult but needing to coincide with an adequate supply of planktonic food organisms. Spawning thus becomes limited to times of the year when such a resource for the young is likely to be available when the latter exhaust yolk nutrient, at or shortly after hatching. Another breeding requirement among the majority of gobies is that food supply for adults must support the succession of gonad maturations and activities in repeat-spawning.

Breeding seasons for many gobioid species have been listed by Darcy (1980). Under tropical conditions, breeding may occur for all or most of the year (Manacop, 1953; Marquez, 1960; Bhowmick, 1965), or be limited to a shorter period, often a wet season (Hora, 1936; Mutsaddi and Bal, 1970; Sircar and Har, 1975). Timing and change with geographical distribution in more temperate areas are discussed by Miller (1961), Dahlberg and Conyers (1973), and Munroe and Lotspeich (1979), while Takagi (1966) has summarized information about the breeding seasons of certain Japanese cold-temperate species. The nature of environmental cues for maturation has been investigated by de Vlaming (1972a,b,c,d), Mackay (1974) and Moiseyeva and Rudenko (1978).

F. Consequences

With expenditure of material and energy on reproduction, a corresponding reduction in that available for other metabolic needs, such as maintenance and growth, can be expected to influence the functional efficiency and viability of the reproducer. In addition, reproductive activities may increase risk of predation. There is thus a negative causal relationship between reproductive effort at a particular stage in life-history, and the subsequent residual reproductive value of the individual, in terms of fecundity (Calow, 1979).

Present reproductive effort may be expected to influence future reproductive value in a number of ways relevant to the mechanisms of gobioid reproduction. Indirectly, diversion of material away from growth will retard or halt this process. Smaller adult size could reduce fecundity in females, because of the dependence of egg number on body size, and, in males, perhaps by influencing aspects of their reproductive behaviour. Reduction in growth rate during the breeding season has been noted in *Pomatoschistus* species by Miller (1963b; 1979a) and Lee (1974), with strong growth compensation after breeding is completed, a response which would have selective value if further fecundity is thereby increased for the few individuals surviving into the next season (Miller, 1979a). Differences in time of breeding between *P. minutus* and *P. pictus*, in comparison to *P. microps*, are reflected in adult growth patterns and occurrence of scale annuli (Miller, 1963b, 1975; Lee, 1974). In captivity, markedly better growth by *P. microps* at low photoperiod was attributed by Miller (1973c) to limited gonad maturation. Conversely, the higher growth rate shown by males of various *Neogobius* species, leading to sexual dimorphism in size, may contribute to their death after only one season, in contrast to the longer life of slower-growing females (Beverton and Holt, 1959; Bilko, 1971; Kostyuchenko, 1961).

Reproductive activities by gobies are likely also to demand an increase in somatic maintenance expenditure. If capability for maintenance suffers, reproducer vitality could be diminished, with inadequate mating behaviour or brood care, and, later, viability itself will suffer. In *Pomatoschistus microps*. Fouda (1979) has shown that scale loss occurs more frequently during the breeding season, at the end of which the adults (I +) have lost an average of over 50% of their original scales, and in some individuals, over 90% of caudal peduncle scales at this time are replacements. In juvenile *Gobius paganellus* of the same age, little more than 20% of scales had been lost, although in adults of 4–10 years at least two-thirds had been replaced. Scale loss could be due to territory defence, nest construction, and vigorous courtship, and scale replacement must be viewed as an essential part of maintenance anabolism. A further sign of resource limitation for somatic use in the breeding season is given by the formation of a translucent otolith ring at this time in *G. paganellus* (Miller, 1961) and *Lepidogobius lepidus* (Grossmann, 1979), indicative of reduced protein incorporation, and otolith erosion has been noted (Bilko, 1971). An increasing loss of maintenance capability is seen in breeding males of *Neogobius melanostomus*, which, during this period, do not feed, draw on body reserves, and become emaciated, with skin ulceration (Kostyuchenko,

1961, 1970). At the end of the season, their bodies are washed up along the strand line or taken in the trawl. Similar deterioration in males of *N. fluviatilis* is reported by Dmitrievna (1966).

These cases within *Neogobius* furnish examples of the association between reproduction and mortality, but short lifespan is also to be found among many early maturing, abbreviate iteroparous, repeat-spawning gobies, such as the species of *Pomatoschistus* and *Knipowitschia*, and aphyines, including the semelparous *Leucopsarion petersi*, whose body changes prior to death have been described by Tamura and Honma (1969, 1970a,b). In the latter, and probably other gobies, such as *Gobiosoma robustum* (Springer and McErlean, 1961), death occurs immediately after the spawning season. However, for *Pomatoschistus microps*, there is a period of vigorous growth by adults after breeding, despite the fact that most of these will disappear within a few months in their second autumn of life (Miller, 1963b, 1975, 1979a). Predation is unlikely to be responsible for this apparent mortality and it may be caused by some slower, more insidious effect of reproduction on viability. A possible correlation between life-span and reproduction emerges from Waddensee observations by Creutzberg and Fonds (1971). After the abnormally cold winter of 1962/63, a greatly increased proportion of adult (I +) *Pomatoschistus minutus* survived into the autumn of 1963, perhaps as a result of a temperature-induced delay in maturation and later onset of breeding in that year, with fewer individual spawnings. Stephens (1982) recorded substantial mortality after the first spawning season in the eleotrid *Gobiomorphus cotidianus*, but found survival more likely in fish which had spawned only once. There is some evidence from sex-ratios that males and females of certain species may differ in adult longevity (Gibson and Ezzi, 1978, 1981). In females, the process of spawning may even induce some risk, if egg retention leads to ovarian necrosis (Juszczyk, 1976).

As yet, there seems to be no data concerning the likelihood of increased predation on adult gobies as a result of the activities connected with reproduction. Defence of territory by males in nuptial colouration and movement among territories by ripe females may both be expected to become more frequent with greater reproductive commitment, and would both increase risk from predators.

V. FITNESS

The reproductive strategy of a species, as an integration of mode, machinery and dynamics to maximize fitness, displays a pattern which may be regarded as having evolved in relation to ecotope. The forces of selection which mould reproductive traits can be viewed as either stochastic or deterministic, contrasting views on this subject having been summarized and discussed by Stearns (1976, 1977). In this section, the dynamic aspects of gobioid tokology are considered chiefly in relation to ecotope predictability.

To achieve fitness, reproductive strategy must maximize both the reproductive potential of adults, and the survival of their offspring to maturity. In the gobies, typically with a "complex" life-history, spanning planktonic and demersal ecosystems, two aspects of ecotope predictability appear to exert major influences. These relate to, first, the occurrence of deleterious situations which reduce the reproductive value of adults, most abruptly by death, and secondly, the level of resource supply both for survival of young and for their transfer into the adult habitat.

Apart from extreme vagaries in the physical environment, the chief stochastic source of mortality for a group composed essentially of small fish must be predation. It is a semipredictable factor for planktonic stages, but the level of this risk for reproducers has a profound influence on their strategies for multiplication. Miller (1979b) classified ecotopes for small fish on the basis of physical cover in the adult trophic habitat, as influencing the likelihood of predation. Thus nektonic, epibenthic, and cryptobenthic conditions were recognized, in decreasing order not only of risk but also in overt availability of small food. All three have been successfully exploited by gobies.

The evolutionary response expected under conditions of less predictable adult survival is earlier sexual maturation and higher reproductive effort, with diminished need to promote the uncertain residual reproductive value of the individual. Frequent spawning after maturity will enhance reproductive effort, which may be condensed from abbreviate iteroparity into true semelparity. This kind of reproductive history is exemplified by several small epibenthic members of the eastern Atlantic-Mediterranean genus *Pomatoschistus*, occurring on finer deposits from estuaries to offshore shelf and known to experience a high degree of predation as important intermediates in food webs (Miller, 1979b; Koefoed, 1979). Species investigated are *P. microps* (Miller, 1963b; Healey, 1972a; Pethon, 1975; Fouda and Miller, 1981), *P. minutus* (Swedmark, 1958; Healey, 1971a,b, 1972b; Lee, 1974; Hesthagen, 1977), *P. pictus* (Miller, 1972b), and *P. norvegicus* (Gibson and Ezzi, 1981). All these forms display early maturation, after the first winter of life in boreal waters, with numerous broods and average to high primary reproductive effort per spawning. Reproductive life is short, usually a single, long breeding season, and life-span is thus one or two years. Planktotrophic postlarvae are relatively well endowed (Fig. 6) and spend no more than several weeks in the plankton. In other areas, many small epibenthic gobiids exhibit similar reproductive strategies to the *Pomatoschistus* species. These include the related *Knipowitschia* species of Ponto-Caspian origin, often figuring prominently in the diet of larger fish (Koblitskaya, 1961; Baimov, 1963; Miller, 1972a; Gandolfi, 1972). Short reproductive lives, after early maturation, are

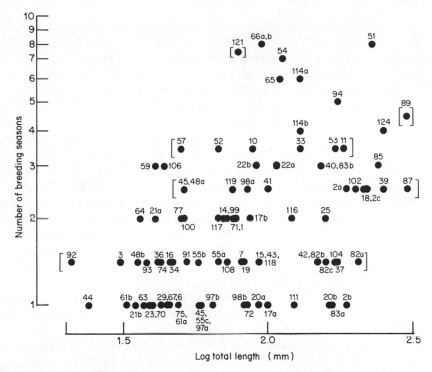

Fig. 7. Potential reproductive life (as number of breeding seasons) in relation to maximum total length for gobioid fishes; note that, on vertical axis, parentheses denote species whose reproductive life is probably greater than the number of breeding seasons (as value below) deduced from age at maturity and approximate life-span.

Species and sources as Figs 4–6, otherwise: 2: *Acanthogobius flavimanus* (a: Miyazaki, 1940; b, Brittan *et al.*, 1970; c: Baker, 1975); 6: *Aphia minuta* (Collett, 1878); 11: *Boleophthalmus chinensis* (Enami and Dotu, 1961); 15: *Chaenogobius isaza* (Takahashi, 1974; Nagoshi and Kojima, 1976); 16: *Ch. scrobiculatus* (Dotu, 1961b); 17: *Ch. urotaenia* (a: Takeuchi, 1971, b: Dotu, 1955c); 19: *Chaeturichthys sciistius* (Suzuki and Kimura, 1979); 20: *Chasmichthys dolichognathus* (Sasaki and Hattori, 1969); 20a: *Ch. gulosus* (Sasaki and Hattori, 1969); 22: *Coryphopterus nicholsii* (Wiley, 1973; a: male; b: female); 23: *Crytallogobius linearis* (Collett, 1878); 29: *Elacatinus oceanops* (Feddern, 1967; Colin, 1975); 33: *Eucyclogobius newberryi* (Carpelan, 1961); 37: *Gillichthys mirabilis* (Walker *et al.*, 1961); 39: *Glossogobius giuris* (Marquez, 1960); 45: *Gobiosoma bosci* (Dawson, 1966); 48: *G. robustum* (Springer and McErlean, 1961; a: male, b: female); 51: *Gobius cobitis* (Gibson, 1970); 52: *G. couchi* (Miller and El-Tawil, 1974); 53: *G. niger* (Miller, 1961 and unpub.); 55: *Gobiusculus flavescens* (a and b: Johnsen, 1945; c, Gwyther, unpubl.); 61: *Knipowitschia caucasica* (a: Koblitskaya, 1961; b: Baimov, 1963); 63: *Kn. panizzae* (Gandolif, 1972; Miller, 1972a); 66: *Lesueurigobius friesii* (a: Gibson and Ezzi, 1978; b: Nash, 1982); 70: *Luciogobius elongatus* (Shiogaki and Dotsu, 1972a); 72: *L. platycephalus* (Shiogaki and Dotsu, 1977); 77: *Microgobius thalassinus* (Schwartz, 1971); 82: *Neogobius fluviatilis* (a: Dmitrievna, 1966; b and c: Bilko, 1965); 83: *N. melanostomus* (Kostyuchenko, 1961; a: male, b: female); 85: *N. syrman* (Maiskii, 1963); 89: *Ophiocara aporos* (Herre, 1927); 97: *Pomatoschistus microps* (a: Pethon, 1975; b: Miller, 1963b, 1975); 98: *P. minutus* (a: Hesthagen, 1977, b: Lee, 1974); 100: *P. pictus* (Miller, 1972b); 102: *Pseudapocryptes lanceolatus* (Hora, 1936; Koumans, 1941); 104: *Pterogobius zacalles* (Shiogaki, 1981); 108: *Rhinogobius giuris* (Goshima *et al.*, 1978); 114: *Thorogobius ephippiatus* (a: Miller, 1969; b: Dunne, 1976); 118: *Tridentiger obscurus* (Goshima *et al.*, 1978); 121: *Typhlogobius californiensis* (Macginitie, 1939); 124: *Zosterisessor ophiocephalus* (Dolgii, 1962).

also reported in Japanese marine and freshwater gobies, including *Chaenogobius* (Dotu, 1954, 1955c, 1961b; Takeuchi, 1971; Takahashi, 1974; Nagoshi and Kojima, 1976) and *Rhinogobius* (Dotu, 1961a; Goshima *et al.*, 1978), the New World warm-temperate *Gobiosoma* species (Hildebrand and Cable, 1938; Springer and McErlean, 1961; Gunter and Hall, 1962; Dawson, 1966; Munroe and Lotspeich, 1979) and *Lophogobius cyprinoides* (Darcy, 1980), the small Antipodean sleepers *Hypseleotris* (Lake, 1967a,b; Mackay, 1973a) and *Gobiomorphus cotidianus* (Stephens, 1982), and numerous midwater feeders such as the semelparous aphyines (Collett, 1878; Pillay and Sarojini, 1950; Tamura and Honma, 1969; Liu and Walford, 1971; Miller, 1973a), *Parioglossus taeniatus* (Dotu, 1955e), *Pandaka lidwilli* (Dotu, 1957c) and *Gobiusculus flavescens* (Johnsen, 1945). In more southern populations of the warm-temperate *Gobiosoma* species, sexual maturity is achieved within five months (Dawson, 1966), perhaps in as little as two months for some individuals of *G. robustum* (Springer and McErlean, 1961). All the preceding gobies must live at great risk from predation (Lie, 1961; Rae, 1965; Dawson, 1966; Lake, 1967c). Other tiny gobies, such as *Eviota* and *Lythrypnus*, which take refuge in crevices but feed on plankton, have similar reproductive strategies (Dotsu *et al.*, 1965; Wiley, 1976), perhaps indicating the perils in midwater, noted by Lassig (1976, 1977) for displaced coral-dwelling *Paragobiodon*.

In some habitats frequented by gobies, there may be erratic environmental changes lethal to individuals regardless of cover and body size. Harmful extremes of irregular frequency are more likely to be encountered by species in higher latitudes, in estuaries and fresh waters (especially hill-streams), or living in unstable substrates. Such species would be expected to show similar reproductive traits to those developed among the highly predated forms. The sexual maturity at one year and short reproductive life found in members of the north-western Pacific *Luciogobius* (Dotu, 1957b,d; Dotu and Mito, 1958; Shiogaki and Dotsu, 1972a, 1977; Shiogaki *et al.*, 1974) may be associated with instability of intertidal gravel beds within which these elongate fishes burrow. Similar reproductive traits seen in *Clevelandia ios*, and contrasting with the later maturity and longer life of related species, could be attributed to the more variable conditions of the higher intertidal zone where *C. ios* frequents burrows (Brothers, 1975). Early maturation and all-year spawning of the tropical *Sicyopterus extraneus* (Manacop, 1953) would be advantageous if violent spates sometimes shifted the stones under which these fish feed and deposit eggs. However, *Sicyopterus japonicus*, of warm temperate Kyushu, does not mature until two years old, although duration of adult life is not known (Dotu and Mito, 1955b).

The components of reproductive strategy directed towards offspring survival fall into two categories. The first is related to predictable limits of food availability in the postlarval habitat and is expressed in magnitude of bestowal and the timing of breeding within a seasonally fluctuating environment. Less predictable circumstances influencing larval survival induce selection for particular traits in adult reproductive dynamics, when survival of the reproducer is more assured, for example in a relatively stable habitat within which predation is reduced by cover and somatic adaptations. Environmental situations, in which juvenile mortality may be subject to stochastic influences, seem to have been successfully overcome by gobioid fishes in both temperate and tropical ecosystems. In the former, the correlation between the timing of gobioid breeding seasons and annual productivity cycles has already been discussed. However, differences in amplitude of production from year to year may introduce quantity as a less predictable element than timing in the annual occurrence of postlarval food supply. Resulting variation in year-class success of juveniles should induce selection for extended adult life, to permit reproductive attempts over a number of years, each time within a more or less narrow breeding season. The physiological requirements for this are to minimize the burden of reproduction on reproducer viability by delay in sexual maturation and lowered reproductive effort, per spawning and in spawning frequency. Late maturation, permitting attainment of larger size before somatic growth is checked, will also enhance fecundity without necessarily increasing the proportion of body resources devoted to reproduction. The breeding pattern resulting from these selection pressures has protracted iteroparity, and is seen in three relatively large cryptobenthic gobies of the warm-temperate eastern Atlantic and Mediterranean, *Gobius cobitis* (Gibson, 1970), *G. paganellus* (Miller, 1961; Dunne, 1978) and *Thorogobius ephippiatus* (Miller, 1969; Dunne, 1976), which are intertidal or subtidal, living beneath stones and about crevices. To judge from the literature, they suffer little predation. Maturity is not attained until after at least the second winter of life but thereafter reproduction may continue for as long as 8 or 9 years, with overall longevity up to 11. Along the western British Isles, number of broods in each breeding season is probably not more than two, with moderate primary reproductive effort at each spawning. Bestowal is relatively high but the planktonic life of postlarvae may last three months. Other cryptobenthic gobiids resembling these forms in reproductive strategy include several eastern Pacific species (*Ilypnus gilberti*, *Lepidogobius lepidus*, *Quietula y-cauda*, *Typhlogobius californiensis*), burrowing or symbiotic with burrowing decapod crustaceans (MacGinitie, 1939; Brothers, 1975; Grossmann, 1979), and the Atlantic-Mediterranean *Lesueurigobius friesii*, which tunnels in mud (Gibson and Ezzi, 1978; Nash, 1982). Both *Lepidogobius lepidus* and *Lesueurigobius friesii* exhibit fluctuation in recruitment from year to year (Grossmann, 1979; Gibson and Ezzi, 1978). Two burrowing gobionellines, *Pseudapocryptes lanceolatus* and *Odontoamblyopus rubicundus*, also have a potential reproductive life of more than two years under seasonal conditions for offspring (Hora, 1936; Dotu, 1957e). A symbiotic or otherwise cryptobenthic life-style, with refuge in a burrow but epibenthic feeding, does not, however, exclude predation (Wiley, 1973; Brothers, 1975; Grossmann, 1979).

Another set of circumstances, presumed to affect juvenile survival in an unpredictable way, may operate on the many gobiid species belonging to the complex ecosystems of hermatypic coral reefs. Over these communities, primary production occurs throughout the year and probably with limited fluctuation between years. Nevertheless, a critical phase in late juvenile life may occur at metamorphosis and recruitment into the adult ecosystem, where, if population density is limiting, entry may depend on random occurrence of vacancies left by predation and senescence (Sale, 1980). Again, selection should favour increase in number of spawnings by adults, frequency being permitted by stable feeding conditions but requiring a minimal primary effort at each spawning to reduce deleterious effects on the reproducer. However, there is less need to prolong adult life over many years, and a definite advantage gained from early maturation. A balance between intensity of reproductive effort and duration of reproductive life (number of spawnings) is probably set by the predation risk for adults and correspondingly better scope for recruitment among juveniles. Unfortunately, life-history details are lacking for most coral-dwelling gobies, but relatively early maturation is known in *Paragobiodon*, at nine months (Lassig, 1976) and in *Elacatinus oceanops* (Feddern, 1967; Colin, 1975), and probably obtains for other small species. Repeat-spawning has been recorded for several such gobies.

The preceding account considers gobiid reproductive strategies in terms of stochastic models for life-history evolution. The features noted for *Pomatoschistus* and related genera contrast markedly with those displayed by the various cryptobenthic species examined (Miller, 1979b; Grossmann, 1979). These two extremes in reproductive dynamics could be just as easily postulated to result from, respectively, r and K selection, based in original concept on the magnitude of density-dependent environmental factors (Parry, 1981). The species of *Pomatoschistus* and the other small epibenthic and nektonic gobies, which are believed to experience heavy predation throughout life, fluctuate markedly in abundance during the year (Healey, 1971a, 1972b; Fonds, 1973; Lee, 1974; Hesthagen, 1977) and are unlikely to be resource-limited. Their reproductive strategies are those of opportunistic species, with great scope for repopulation after climatic instability (Jones and Miller, 1966; Fonds, 1973), colonization of new habitats, such as the Aral Sea (Markova, 1963) and, perhaps, extension of geographical range after marine transgression (Miller, 1972a).

Conversely, the long-lived cryptobenthic species, finding shelter beneath stones, in crevices, or in burrows, may well have populations at saturation size for stable habitats where space resources of this kind must be less abundant than sea-bed surface area or space in the water column. In *Amblyeleotris*, a genus of gobiids commensal with snapping shrimps, Yanagisawa (1982) has noted the presence of smaller individuals which apparently lack burrows. For gobies of such life-styles, expending less on reproduction should leave more energy and material to improve reproducer fitness by success in competitive interactions involving somatic attributes, territory, resource subdivision among size/age classes, etc. Territorial species of Californian lagoons (*Ilypnus gilberti*, *Quietula y-cauda*, and *Lepidogobius lepidus*) mature at two years with a potential adult life of at least three years, contrasting with the sympatric *Clevelandia ios*, which, except for guarding males, does not defend territory and lives usually for less than two years (Brothers, 1975; Grossmann, 1979).

At present, so little is known about the relative importance of all the factors of ecotope mentioned above that we may need to regard reproductive strategies in gobies as the products of multiple causation, and that causes — both stochastic and deterministic — vary across the wide range of gobioid ecotopes (Southwood, 1977; Stearns, 1977).

So far, the reproductive features seen among the gobioid fishes have been interpreted as primary targets for selection in relation to aspects of the external environment. In comparison of various life-history parameters in fishes, Beverton and Holt (1959) noted relationships between longevity, age and size at maturity, and maximum size. Thus, it may be proposed that length of reproductive life (as number of breeding seasons) is determined by growth pattern and maximum size. However, in Fig. 7, reproductive life may be seen to differ widely between species of comparable size, except for the smallest forms, although accurate age-determination, underlying such comparisons, has been done for relatively few species. The hypothesis may be further tested by comparing species, similar in size and distribution but differing in ecotope (Miller, 1979b). Two species occur on muddy sand and sand off the western British Isles, *Pomatoschistus minutus*, whose adult female averages 55 mm and maximum standard length is about 75 mm, and *Lesueurigobius friesii*, with females averaging 60 mm and not reported over 74 mm (Lee, 1974; Gibson and Ezzi, 1978; Nash, 1982). The former is epibenthic, and heavily predated, while the latter burrows. Although comparable in size, *P. minutus* matures after the first winter, spawns frequently, and few adults survive a second winter, while *L. friesii* does not mature until two, spawns probably twice per season, and has an adult life of up to nine years. These marked differences in reproductive strategy have already been attributed to differences in adult or year-class survival. A hint of environmental involvement in the former phase is suggested by results for a smaller species of *Pomatoschistus*, *P. norvegicus*, not exceeding 50 mm in average adult size (Gibson and Ezzi, 1981). This goby, which is more offshore in occurrence than *P. minutus*, and therefore fully sympatric with *L. friesii*, has a higher proportion of adults surviving into a second breeding season. As a small species with a relatively extended life history, *Lebetus scorpioides* does not reach the maximum size of several *Pomatoschistus* species, but is believed to be cryptobenthic, living among coralline nodules, and does not mature before two years (Miller, 1963a).

Conversely, the large Ponto-Caspian *Neogobius* species resembling in size-range the cryptobenthic *Gobius* and *Thorogobius* forms, are known to suffer predation in more open epibenthic habitats, where commercial fisheries also exploit them (Maiskii, 1963; Kostyuchenko, 1970; Moskalkova, 1967). In these species, age at maturity is earlier, from one year in *N. syrman* to three in male *N. melanostomus*, and reproductive life does not usually exceed three years (Kostyuchenko, 1961; Maiskii, 1963; Bilko, 1965; Dmitrievna, 1966). Multiple spawning occurs in *N. melanostomus*, the males of which do not survive beyond a single season. The reproductive capabilities of *Neogobius* species have been illustrated by the rapid spread of several forms introduced into the Aral Sea, *N. fluviatilis* having colonized almost as swiftly as the much smaller and earlier reproducer *Knipowitschia caucasica* (Markova, 1963). The Atlantic-Mediterranean *Gobius niger*, although somewhat larger than *G. paganellus* in maximum size is, however, epibenthic and may not exceed about five years in maximum longevity, although maturation in British waters is not achieved until after the second winter of life (Miller, 1961; Vaas *et al.*, 1975).

The conclusion is that age at maturity and duration of reproductive life is not an immediate corollary of body size and is, in its own right, the primary object for selection by extrinsic forces whose nature has been discussed earlier. Nevertheless, some gobioid species, presumably as a trophic adaptation, reach a body size which may serve to minimize predation risk even under epibenthic or nektonic conditions. With greater certainty of adult survival as an outcome of size, such species, at stable population size, appear to display a reproductive strategy based on a long life and limited energy commitment. This may be exemplified by such large gobies as *Eleotris pisonis* (Flower, 1925), *Glossogobius* species (Marquez, 1960; Bhowmick, 1965; Senta and Hoshino, 1970), *Acanthogobius flavimanus* (Miyazaki, 1940; Dotu and Mito, 1955a), and *Perccottus glehni* (Kirpichnikov, 1945). However, in the new environment of San Francisco Bay, *A. flavimanus*, accidentally transported from the western Pacific, has proved an effective colonist (Brittan *et al.*, 1970; Baker, 1975) in keeping with a substantial reproductive effort reported for this species by Miyazaki (1940).

Finally, in concluding this account of gobioid tokology, it must be stressed that, while much information has been accumulated, barely a tenth of the likely complement of species has been studied and that the relative importance of the different selective forces which may operate on their reproduction remains a problem of daunting magnitude. However, the great ecological diversity seen in the Gobioidei should serve to promote their value as material for research into life-history evolution.

ACKNOWLEDGEMENTS

The author is most grateful to Dr R. M. McDowall, for unpublished data concerning *Gobiomorphus huttoni*, and to Mr T. Wiedemann, for advice on etymology. Many thanks are also due to Dr T. D. Iles, for presenting the author with a tokological souvenir of the Conference, and to all who signed this object.

REFERENCES

Aiyar, R. G. (1935). *Zool. Anz. Leipzig* **111**, 83–92.
Anderson, J. R., Lake, J. S. and Mackay, N. J. (1971). *Austr. J. mar. Freshw. Res.* **22**, 139–145.
Arai, R. (1964). *Bull. nat. Sci. Mus. Tokyo* **7**, 295–306.
Auty, E. H. (1978). *Austr. J. mar. Freshw. Res.* **29**, 585–597.
Baimov, U. A. (1962). *Uzbek. biol. Zh.* **4**, 63–68.
Baimov, U. A. (1963). *Vest. Kav. Fil. Akad. Nauk. Uz. SSR.* **3**, 51–59.
Baird, R. C. (1966). *Publ. Inst. mar. Sci. Univ. Tex.* **10**, 1–8.
Baker, J. C. (1975). "A contribution to the life history of the yellowfin goby (*Acanthogobius flavimanus*) in the San Francisco Bay delta area". M.Sc. Thesis, California State University, Sacramento.
Ballard, W. W. (1969). *Pubbl. Staz. zool. Napoli* **37**, 1–17.
Belsare, D. K. (1975). *Zool. Pol.* **25**, 5–11.
Beverton, R. J. H. and Holt, S. J. (1959). *In* "The Lifespan of Animals" (G. E. W. Wolstenholme and M. O'Connor, eds), pp. 142–180. Churchill Livingstone, London.
Bhowmick, R. M. (1965). *Proc. Indo-Pacif. Fish. Coun.* **11**, 99–115.
Bilko, V. P. (1965). *Gidrobiol. Zh.* **1965**, 56–60.
Bilko, V. P. (1971). *Vop. Ikhtiol.* **11**, 650–663.
Blanco, G. J. (1947). *Phil. J. Sci.* **77**, 83–95.
Böhlke, J. E. and Robins, C. R. (1968). *Proc. Acad. nat. Sci. Philad.* **120**, 45–174.
Bonnin, J. P. (1975). *C.r. Soc. Biol. Bordeaux* **169**, 548–552.
Breder, C. M. (1943). *Bull. Bingham oceanogr. Coll.* **8** (3), 1–49.
Breder, C. M. and Rosen, D. E. (1966). "Modes of Reproduction in Fishes". Natural History Press, New York.
Brittan, M. R., Hopkirk, J. D., Conners, J. D. and Martin, M. (1970). *Proc. Calif. Acad. Sci.* **38**, 207–214.
Brock, J. (1878). *Morph. Jb.* **4**, 505–572.
Brothers, E. B. (1975). "The comparative ecology and behavior of three sympatric California gobies". Ph.D. Thesis, University of California at San Diego.
Calow, P. (1979). *Biol. Rev.* **54**, 23–40.
Carpelan, L. H. (1961). *Copeia* **1961** (1), 32–39.
Cole, L. C. (1954). *Q. Rev. Biol.* **29**, 103–137.
Colin, P. (1975). "The Neon Gobies". TFH Publications, Neptune City, NJ.
Collett, R. (1878). *Proc. zool. Soc. Lond.* **1878**, 318–339.
Colombo, L. and Burighal, P. (1974). *Cell Tissue Res.* **154**, 39–49.
Colombo, L., Lupo di Prisco, C. and Binder, G. (1970). *Gen. comp. Endocr.* **15**, 404–419.
Colombo, L., Colombo Belvedere, P. and Pilati, A. (1977). *Boll. Zool.* **44**, 131–134.
Coujard, R. (1941). *C.r. Séanc. Soc. Biol.* **135**, 570–574.
Creutzberg, F. and Fonds, M. (1971). *Thalassia jugosl.* **7**, 13–23.
Cushing, D. H. (1959). *Fish. Inv., Lond.* (2) **22** (6), 1–22.

Dahlberg, M. D. and Conyers, J. C. (1973). *Fish. Bull. U.S. natn. ocean. atmos. Admin.* **71**, 279–287.
Dandekar, S. V. (1965). *J. mar. biol. Ass. India* **7**, 212–214.
Darcy, G. H. (1980). NOAA Techn. Mem. NMFS-SEFC, **15**, 1–55.
Dawson, C. E. (1966). *Am. Midl. Nat.* **76**, 379–409.
de Vlaming, V. L. (1971). *Biol. Bull., Woods Hole* **141**, 458–471.
de Vlaming, V. L. (1972a). *J. Fish Biol.* **4**, 131–140.
de Vlaming, V. L. (1972b). *Copeia* **1972** (2), 278–291.
de Vlaming, V. L. (1972c). *Fish. Bull. U.S. natn. ocean. atmos. Admin.* **70**, 1137–1152.
de Vlaming, V. L. (1972d). *J. exp. mar. Biol. Ecol.* **9**, 155–163.
de Vlaming, V. L. (1972e). *Comp. Biochem. Physiol.* **41A**, 697–713.
de Vlaming, V. L. (1974). *In* "Control of Sex in Fishes" (C. B. Schreck, ed.), pp. 13–83. Virginia Polytechnic Institute and State University, Blacksburg, Va.
Dmitrievna, E. N. (1966). *Vop. Ikhtiol.* **6**, 685–695.
Doha, S. (1974). *Bangladesh J. Zool.* **2**, 95–106.
Dolgii, V. N. (1962). *Uchen. Zap. Kishinev. gos. Univ.* **62**, 129–135.
Donato, A., Contini, A. and Berdar, A. (1975). *Riv. Biol. Norm. Patol.* **1**, 77–93.
Dotsu, Y., Arima, S. and Mito, S. (1965). *Bull. Fac. Fish. Nagasaki Univ.* **18**, 41–50.
Dôtu, Y. (1954). *Jap. J. Ichthyol.* **3**, 133–138.
Dôtu, Y. (1955a). *Bull. biogeogr. Soc. Japan* **16–19**, 338–344.
Dôtu, Y. (1955b). *Sci. Bull. Fac. Agric. Kyushu Univ.* **15**, 77–86.
Dôtu, Y. (1955c). *Sci. Bull. Fac. Agric. Kyushu Univ.* **15**, 367–374.
Dôtu, Y. (1955d). *Sci. Bull. Fac. Agric. Kyushu Univ.* **15**, 483–487.
Dôtu, Y. (1955e). *Sci. Bull. Fac. Agric. Kyushu Univ.* **15**, 489–496.
Dôtu, Y. (1957a). *Jap. J. Ichthyol.* **6**, 97–104.
Dôtu, Y. (1957b). *J. Fac. Agric. Kyushu Univ.* **11**, 69–76.
Dôtu, Y. (1957c). *Sci. Bull. Fac. Agric. Kyushu Univ.* **16**, 85–92.
Dôtu, Y. (1957d). *Sci. Bull. Fac. Agric. Kyushu Univ.* **16**, 93–100.
Dôtu, Y. (1957e). *Sci. Bull. Fac. Agric. Kyushu Univ.* **16**, 101–110.
Dôtu, Y. (1957f). *Sci. Bull. Fac. Agric. Kyushu Univ.* **16**, 261–274.
Dôtu, Y. (1958a). *Sci. Bull. Fac. Agric. Kyushu Univ.* **16**, 359–370.
Dôtu, Y. (1958b). *Sci. Bull. Fac. Agric. Kyushu Univ.* **16**, 371–380.
Dôtu, Y. (1958c). *Sci. Bull. Fac. Agric. Kyushu Univ.* **16**, 343–358.
Dôtu, Y. (1958d). *Sci. Bull. Fac. Agric. Kyushu Univ.* **16**, 427–432.
Dôtu, Y. (1959). *Bull. Fac. Fish. Nagasaki Univ.* **8**, 196–201.
Dôtu, Y. (1961a). *Bull. Fac. Fish. Nagasaki Univ.* **10**, 120–125.
Dôtu, Y. (1961b). *Bull. Fac. Fish. Nagasaki Univ.* **10**, 127–131.
Dôtu, Y. (1961c). *Bull. Fac. Fish. Nagasaki Univ.* **10**, 133–139.
Dôtu, Y. and Fujita, S. (1959). *Bull. Fac. Fish. Nagasaki Univ.* **8**, 191–195.
Dôtu, Y. and Fujita, S. (1963). *Bull. Jap. Soc. scient. Fish.* **29**, 669–675.
Dôtu, Y. and Mito, S. (1955a). *Jap. J. Ichthyol.* **4**, 153–161.
Dôtu, Y. and Mito, S. (1955b). *Sci. Bull. Fac. Agric. Kyushu Univ.* **15**, 213–221.
Dôtu, Y. and Mito, S. (1958). *Sci. Bull. Fac. Agric. Kyushu Univ.* **16**, 419–426.
Dôtu, Y. and Mito, S. (1963). *Bull. Fac. Fish. Nagasaki Univ.* **15**, 1–3.
Dôtu, Y. and Tsukahara, H. (1964). *Bull. Jap. Soc. scient. Fish.* **30**, 335–342.
Dôtu, Y. and Tsutsumi, T. (1959). *Bull. Fac. Fish. Nagasaki Univ.* **8**, 186–190.
Dôtu, Y., Mito, S. and Ueno, M. (1955). *Sci. Bull. Fac. Agric. Kyushu Univ.* **15**, 359–365.
Duncker, G. (1928). *Tierwelt. N.-u. Ostsee* **12g**, 121–148.
Dunne, J. (1976). *Proc. R. Ir. Acad.* **76 (B)**, 121–132.
Dunne, J. (1978). *Proc. R. Ir. Acad.* **78 (B)**, 179–191.

Egami, N. (1960). *J. Fac. Sci. Tokyo Univ.* (Zool.) **9**, 67–100.

Eggert, B. (1931). *Z. wiss. zool.* **139**, 249–517.

Eggert, B. (1933). *Z. wiss. Zool.* **144**, 402–420.

Enami, S. and Dotu, Y. (1961). *Bull. Fac. Fish. Nagasaki Univ.* **10**, 141–147.

Feddern, H. A. (1967). *Bull. mar. Sci. Gulf Caribb.* **17**, 367–375.

Flower, S. S. (1925). *Proc. zool. Soc., Lond.* **1925**, 247–268.

Fonds, M. (1973). *Neth. J. Sea Res.* **6**, 417–478.

Fouda, M. M. (1979). *J. Zool. Lond.* **189**, 503–522.

Fouda, M. M. and Miller, P. J. (1981). *Estuar. cstl. shelf Sci.* **12**, 121–129.

Fritzsche, R. A. (1982). *In* "Synopsis and Classification of Living Organisms" (S. Parker, ed.), Vol. 2, pp. 934–935. McGraw-Hill, New York.

Gandolfi, G. (1972). *Boll. Zool.* **39**, 621–622.

Georghiev, J. M. (1966). *Izv. navchnoizsled. Inst. Ribno stop. Okeanogr. Varna* **7**, 159–228.

Gibson, R. N. (1970). *J. Fish Biol.* **2**, 281–288.

Gibson, R. N. and Ezzi, I. A. (1978). *J. Fish Biol.* **12**, 371–389.

Gibson, R. N. and Ezzi, I. A. (1981). *J. Fish Biol.* **19**, 697–714.

Gordina, A. D. (1973). *J. Ichthyol.* **13**, 152–155.

Goshima, S., Yamaoka, K., Nagano, M. and Enami, S. (1978). *Jap. J. Ecol.* **28**, 357–366.

Gould, S. J. (1977). "Ontogeny and Phylogeny". Harvard University Belknap Press, Cambridge, Mass.

Grossman, G. D. (1979). *Envir. Biol. Fish.* **4**, 207–218.

Guitel, F. (1891). *C.r. hebd. Séanc. Acad. Sci., Paris* **114**, 612–616.

Gunter, G. and Hall, G. E. (1962). *Gulf Res. Rep.* **1**, 189–307.

Harder, W. (1975). "Anatomy of Fishes" 2 vols. E. Schweizerbart-sche Verlagsbuch-handlung, Stuttgart.

Harms, J. W. (1935). *Z. wiss. Zool.* **146**, 417–462.

Healey, M. C. (1971a). *J. Zool. Lond.* **163**, 177–229.

Healey, M. C. (1971b). *Trans. Am. Fish. Soc.* **100**, 520–526.

Healey, M. C. (1972a). *J. nat. Hist.* **6**, 133–145.

Healey, M. C. (1972b). *J. Fish. Res. Bd Can.* **29**, 187–194.

Herre, A. W. C. T. (1927). *Monogr. Philipp. Bur. Sci.* **23**, 1–352.

Hesthagen, I. H. (1975). *Norw. J. Zool.* **23**, 235–242.

Hesthagen, I. H. (1977). *Sarsia* **63**, 17–26.

Hildebrand, S. F. and Cable, L. E. (1938). *Bull. Bur. Fish., Wash.* **48**, 505–642.

Hilge, V. (1975). *Berdt. wiss. kommn. Meeresforsch.* **24**, 172–183.

Hoese, D. F. (1971). "A revision of the Eastern Pacific species of the gobiid fish genus *Gobiosoma*, with a discussion of relationships of the genus". Ph.D. Thesis, University of California at San Diego.

Holt, E. W. L. (1890). *Ann. Mag. nat. Hist.* (6) **6**, 34–40.

Hora, S. L. (1936). *Int. Congr. Zool. 12 Lisbon* **1936**, 841–864.

Hudson, R. C. L. (1977). *Z. Tierpsychol.* **43**, 214–220.

Johnsen, S. (1945). *Bergens Mus. Årb.* **1944** (1), 1–129.

Jones, D. and Miller, P. J. (1966). *Hydrobiologia* **27**, 515–528.

Juszczyk, D. (1976). *Przegl. zool.* **20**, 338–342.

Kanabashira, Y., Sakai, H. and Yasuda, F. (1980). *Jap. J. Ichthyol.* **27**, 191–198.

Khryzhanovskii, S. G. and Ptchelina, Z. M. (1941). *Zool. Zh.* **20**, 446–455.

Kinzer, J. (1960). *Zool. Beitr.* **6**, 207–290.

Kirpichnikov, V. S. (1945). *Bull. Soc. Nat. Moscou (Biol.)* **50**, 14–27.

Kishi, Y. (1979). *Res. Popul. Ecol.* **20**, 211–215.
Kobayashi, T., Dotsu, Y. and Miura, N. (1972). *Bull. Fac. Fish. Nagasaki Univ.* **33**, 49–62.
Koblitskaya, A. F. (1961). *Vop. Ikhtiol.* **1**, 253–261.
Koefoed, J. H. (1979). *Fauna* **32**, 112–120.
Kostyuchenko, V. A. (1961). *Trudy azov. chernomorsk nauch. rybokhoz.* **19**, 45–60.
Kostyuchenko, V. A. (1970). *Trūdy vres. nauchno-issled. Inst. morsk. ryb. Khoz. Okeanogr.* **71**, 51–67.
Koumans, F. P. (1941). *Mem. Indian Mus.* **13**, 205–329.
Kovtun, I. F. (1977). *J. Ichthyol.* **17**, 566–573.
Kulikova, N. I. (1977). *In* "Metabolism and Biochemistry of Fishes" (G. S. Karzinkin, ed.), pp. 462–468. Indian National Scientific Documentation Centre, New Delhi.
Kulikova, N. I. and Fandeeva, V. N. (1975). *Trūdy vres. nauchno-issled. Inst. morsk. ryb. Khoz. Okeanogr.* **96**, 18–27.
Kulikova, N. I. and Fandeeva, V. N. (1976). *In* "Reproductive Physiology in the Black Sea Fishes" (M. I. Shatunivskij, V. S. Apekin, I. Kulikova and E. A. Kamenskaya, eds), pp. 70–81. Moscow.
Kuntz, A. (1916). *Bull. Bur. Fish., Wash.* **34**, 407–429.
Lachner, E. A. and Karnella, S. J. (1978). *Smithson. Contr. Zool.* **286**, 1–23.
Lake, J. S. (1967a). *Austr. J. mar. Freshw. Res.* **18**, 137–153.
Lake, J. S. (1967b). *Austr. J. mar. Freshw. Res.* **18**, 155–173.
Lake, J. S. (1967c). *N.S.W. Stat. Fish. Res. Bull.* **7**, 1–48.
Lassig, B. (1976). *Mar. Behav. Physiol.* **3**, 283–293.
Lassig, B. (1977). *Proc. Third int. Coral Reef Symp.* **1977**, 565–570.
Le Danois, E. (1913). *Annls. Inst. oceanogr. Monaco* **5** (5), 1–214.
Le Menn, F. (1979). *Comp. Biochem. Physiol.* **62A**, 495–500.
Lee, S.-C. (1974). "Biology of the sand goby, *Pomatoschistus minutus* (Pallas) (Teleostei: Gobioidei)". Ph.D. Thesis, University of Bristol.
Liddell, H. G. and Scott, R. (1940). "A Greek-English Lexicon" (9th edn, revised by H. Stuart Jones). Clarendon Press, Oxford.
Lie, U. (1961). *Sarsia* **3**, 1–36.
Liu, R. K. and Walford, R. L. (1970). *Expl. Geront.* **5**, 214–246.
MacGinitie, G. E. (1939). *Am. Midl. Nat.* **21**, 489–505.
Mackay, N. J. (1973a). *Aust. J. Zool.* **21**, 53–66.
Mackay, N. J. (1973b). *Aust. J. Zool.* **21**, 67–74.
Mackay, N. J. (1974). *Aust. J. Zool.* **22**, 449–456.
Maiskii, V. N. (1963). *Trūdy azov chernomorsk nauchmo-issled. Inst. morsk. ryb. Khoz.* **6**, 95–103.
Manacop. P. R. (1953). *Philipp. J. Fish.* **2**, 1–55.
Mancini, L. and Cavinato, P. G. (1969). *Boll. Pesca Piscic. Idrobiol.* **24**, 49–60.
Manna, G. K. and Prasad, R. (1974). *Cytologia* **39**, 609–618.
Markova, E. D. (1963). *In* "Acclimatization of Animals in the USSR" (A. I. Yanushevich, ed.), pp. 178–000. Israel Program for Scientific Translations, Jerusalem, 1966.
Marquez, J. R. S. (1960). *Philipp. J. Fish.* **8**, 71–99.
Mashiko, K. (1976a). *Jap. J. Ecol.* **26**, 91–100.
Mashiko, K. (1976b). *Jap. J. Ichthyol.* **23**, 69–78.
Mayer, F. (1929). *Aquatic Life, Baltimore* **13**, 167–168.
McDowall, R. M. (1965). *Trans. R. Soc. N.Z. Zool.* **5**, 177–196.
Miller, P. J. (1961). *J. mar. biol. Ass. U.K.* **41**, 737–769.
Miller, P. J. (1963a). *Bull. Br. Mus. nat. Hist.*, Ser. D. *Zool.* **10**, 205–256.

Miller, P. J. (1963b). "Studies on the biology and taxonomy of British gobiid fishes".
Ph.D. Thesis, University of Liverpool.
Miller, P. J. (1969). *J. mar. biol. Ass. U.K.* **49**, 831–855.
Miller, P. J. (1972a). *J. mar. biol. Ass. U.K.* **52**, 145–160.
Miller, P. J. (1972b). *Ann. Mus. civ. Stor. nat. Genova* **79**, 53–88.
Miller, P. J. (1973a). *J. Fish Biol.* **5**, 353–365.
Miller, P. J. (1973b). *J. Zool. Lond.* **171**, 397–434.
Miller, P. J. (1973c). *Proc. Challenger Soc.* **4**, 197–198.
Miller, P. J. (1975). *J. Zool. Lond.* **177**, 425–448.
Miller, P. J. (1979a). *Symp. zool. Soc. Lond.* **44**, 1–28.
Miller, P. J. (1979b). *Symp. zool. Soc. Lond.* **44**, 263–306.
Miller, P. J. (1982). *Senckenberg. biol.* **62**, 5–19.
Miller, P. J. and El-Tawil, M. Y. (1974). *J. Zool. Lond.* **174**, 539–574.
Miller, P. J., El-Tawil, M. Y., Thorpe, R. S. and Webb, C. J. (1980). *In* "Chemosystematics: Principles and Practice" (F. A. Bisby, J. G. Vaughan and C. A. Wright, eds), pp. 195–233. Academic Press, London.
Miyazaki, I. (1940). *Bull. Jap. Soc. sci. Fish.* **9**, 159–180.
Mizuno, N. (1960). *Mem. Coll. Sci. Kyoto Univ.* Ser. B, **27**, 97–115.
Moiseeva, E. B. (1970). *Dokl. Akad. Nauk. SSSR. Biol.* **194**, 561–564.
Moiseeva, E. B. (1971). *Dokl. Akad. Nauk. SSSR. Biol.* **198**, 467–470.
Moiseyeva, Y. B. (1972). *J. Ichthyol.* **12**, 802–806.
Moiseyeva, Y. B. and Ponomareva, V. P. (1973). *J. Ichthyol.* **13**, 368–381.
Moiseyeva, Y. B. and Rudenko, V. I. (1978). *J. Ichthyol.* **18**, 690–692.
Moskalkova, K. I. (1967). *Morf.-ecol. Anal. Razv. Ryb*, 48–75.
Munroe, T. A. and Lotspeich, R. A. (1979). *Estuaries* **2**, 22–27.
Mutsaddi, K. B. and Bal, D. V. (1970). *J. Univ. Bombay* **39**, 58–76.
Nair, G. S. (1961). *Bull. centr. Res. Inst. Univ. Kerala*, Ser. C, **8**, 38–54.
Nagoshi, M. and Kojima, T. (1976). *Physiol. Ecol. Japan* **17**, 297–301.
Nash, R. D. M. (1982). *J. Fish Biol.* **21**, 69–85.
Nelson, J. S. (1976). "Fishes of the World". Wiley, New York.
Nishikawa, S., Amaoka, K. and Nakanishi, K. (1974). *Jap. J. Ichthyol.* **21**, 61–71.
Nyman, K. J. (1953). *Acta Soc. Faun. Flor. fenn.* **69** (1), 1–11.
Okada, Y. and Suzuki, K. (1955). *Rep. Fac. Fish. prefect. Univ. Mie* **2**, 112–123.
Oppenheimer, J. (1954). *Pubbl. Sta. zool. Napoli* **25**, 18–25.
O'Toole, M. J. (1978). *Inv. Rep. Div. Sea Fish. S. Afr.* **116**, 1–28.
Padoa, E. (1953). *Monogr. Faun. Flor. Golf. Nap.* **38**, 648–678.
Parry, G. D. (1981). *Oecologia* **48**, 260–264.
Petersen, C. G. J. (1891). *Rep. Dan. biol. Stn.* **2**, 1–9.
Petersen, C. G. J. (1919). *Rep. Dan. biol. Stn.* **26**, 47–66.
Pethon, P. (1975). *Fauna* **28**, 23–30.
Pianka, E. R. (1976). *Am. Zoologist* **16**, 775–784.
Pilati, C. (1950). *Arch. zool., ital.* **35**, 171–183.
Pillay, T. V. R. and Sarojini, K. K. (1950). *Proc. natn. Inst. Sci. India* **16**, 181–187.
Prasad, R. R. (1959). *Proc. natn. Inst. Sci. India* **25B**, 12–20.
Qasim, S. Z. (1956). *J. Cons. perm. int. Explor. Mer* **21**, 144–155.
Rae, B. B. (1965). *J. Zool. Lond.* **146**, 114–122.
Rajalakshmi, M. (1966). *Gen. Comp. Endocr.* **6**, 378–385.
Reese, E. S. (1964). *Oceanogr. mar. Biol. Ann. Rev.* **2**, 455–488.
Riehl, R. (1978). *Helgoländer wiss-Meeresunters.* **31**, 314–332.
Robertson, D. R. and Justineu, G. (1982). *Env. Biol. Fish.* **7**, 137–142.
Ryan, M. (1828). *Lancet* **14**, 394–400.

Saksena, D. N. and Bhargava, H. N. (1972). *Zool. Jb. (Anat.)* **89**, 611–620.
Saksena, D. N. and Bhargava, H. N. (1975). *Zool. Jb. (Anat.)* **94**, 499–502.
Sale, P. F. (1980). *Oceanogr. mar. Biol. Ann. Rev.* **18**, 367–421.
Sasaki, T. and Hattori, J. (1969). *Jap. J. Ichthyol.* **15**, 143–155.
Schwartz, F. J. (1971). *Chesapeake Sci.* **12**, 156–166.
Senta, T. and Hoshino, N. (1970). *Jap. J. Ichthyol.* **17**, 1–6.
Shih, S. H. (1979). "Pituitary structure and cycles of the common goby, *Pomatoschistus microps* (Krøyer) (Teleostei: Gobiidae)". Ph.D. Thesis, University of Bristol.
Shiogaki, M. (1981). *Jap. J. Ichthyol.* **28**, 70–79.
Shiogaki, M. and Dotsu, Y. (1971). *Bull. Fac. Fish. Nagasaki Univ.* **32**, 17–25.
Shiogaki, M. and Dotsu, Y. (1972a). *Bull. Fac. Fish. Nagasaki Univ.* **34**, 9–18.
Shiogaki, M. and Dotsu, Y. (1972b). *Bull. Fac. Fish. Nagasaki Univ.* **34**, 19–27.
Shiogaki, M. and Dotsu, Y. (1974a). *Bull. Fac. Fish. Nagasaki Univ.* **37**, 1–8.
Shiogaki, M. and Dotsu, Y. (1974b). *Bull. Fac. Fish. Nagasaki Univ.* **38**, 65–70.
Shiogaki, M. and Dotsu, Y. (1977). *Jap. J. Ichthyol.* **24**, 43–48.
Shiogaki, M., Miura, N. and Dotsu, Y. (1974). *Bull. Fac. Fish. Nagasaki Univ.* **38**, 57–64.
Shulman, G. E. (1967). *Dokl. Akad. Nauk SSSR.* **175**, 710–713.
Sircar, A. K. and Har, S. P. (1975). *Symp. Pap. Pac. Sci. Assoc. Symp. mar. Sci.* **1975**, 63–64.
Skazkina, Y. P. and Kostyuchenko, V. A. (1968). *Vop. Ikhtiol.* **8**, 303–311.
Smith, C. L. and Tyler, J. C. (1972). *Bull. nat. Hist. Mus. Los Angeles* **14**, 125–170.
Sonoda, T. and Imai, S. (1971). *Mem. Fac. Fish. Kagoshima Univ.* **20**, 197–202.
Southwood, T. R. E. (1977). *J. anim. Ecol.* **46**, 337–365.
Springer, V. G. and McErlean, A. J. (1961). *Tulane Stud. Zool.* **9**, 87–98.
Sriramalu, V. and Rajalakshmi, M. (1966). *Z. mikrosk.-anat. Forsch.* **75**, 64–73.
Stanley, H., Chieffi, G. and Botte, V. (1965). *Z. Zellforsch. mikrosk. Anat.* **65**, 350–362.
Staples, D. J. (1975a). *J. Fish Biol.* **7**, 1–24.
Staples, D. J. (1975b). *J. Fish Biol.* **7**, 25–45.
Staples, D. J. (1975c). *J. Fish Biol.* **7**, 47–69.
Stearns, S. C. (1976). *Q. Rev. Biol.* **51**, 3–47.
Stearns, S. C. (1977). *Ann. Rev. Ecol. Syst.* **8**, 145–171.
Stephens, R. T. T. (1982). *J. Fish Biol.* **20**, 259–270.
Suzuki, K. and Kimura, S. (1979). *Jap. J. Ichthyol.* **26**, 203–208.
Swedmark, M. (1958). *Arch. Zool. exp. gén.* **95**, 32–51.
Takagi, K. (1966). *J. Tokyo Univ. Fish.* **52**, 83–127.
Takahashi, S. (1974). *Bull. Jap. Soc. scient. Fish.* **40**, 847–857.
Takahashi, S. (1978). *Zool. Mag. Tokyo* **87**, 216–220.
Takeuchi, N. (1971). *Misc. Rep. Res. Inst. nat. Sci.* **75**, 16–24.
Tamura, E. and Honma, Y. (1969). *Bull. Jap. Soc. scient. Fish.* **35**, 875–884.
Tamura, E. and Honma, Y. (1970a). *Jap. J. Ichthyol.* **17**, 29–36.
Tamura, E. and Honma, Y. (1970b). *Bull. Jap. Soc. scient. Fish.* **36**, 661–669.
Tan, O. K. K. and Lam, T. J. (1973). *Aquaculture* **2**, 411–423.
Tavolga, W. N. (1950). *J. Morph.* **87**, 467–492.
Tavolga, W. N. (1954). *Bull. Am. Mus. nat. Hist.* **104**, 427–460.
Tavolga, W. N. (1956). *Zoologica, N.Y.* **41**, 49–64.
Tavolga, W. N. (1958). *Physiol. Zool.* **31**, 259–271.
Te Winkel, L. E. (1935). *J. Morph.* **58**, 463–535.
Todd, E. S. (1975). *Copeia* **1975** (3), 564–568.
Vaas, K. F., Vlasblom, A. G. and de Koeijer, P. (1975). *Nethl. J. Sea Res.* **9**, 56–68.
Valenti, R. J. (1972). *Copeia* **1972** (3), 477–482.

Vestergaard, K. (1976). *Vidensk. Meddr dansk naturh. Foren.* **139**, 91–108.
Vijayaraghavan, P. (1973). *Indian J. Fish.* **20**, 523–532.
Vivien, J.-H. (1938a). *C.r. hebd. Séanc. Acad. Sci., Paris* **206**, 938–940.
Vivien, J.-H. (1938b). *C.r. hebd. Séanc. Acad. Sci., Paris* **207**, 1452–1455.
Vivien, J.-H. (1939a). *Trav. Sta. zool. Wimereux* **13**, 713–721.
Vivien, J.-H. (1939b). *C.r. hebd. Séanc. Acad. Sci., Paris* **208**, 948–949.
Vivien, J.-H. (1941). *Bull. biol. Fr. Belg.* **75**, 257–309.
Vladimirov, M. Z. and Kubrak, I. F. (1972). *J. Ichthyol.* **12**, 941–952.
Walker, B. W., Whitney, R. R. and Barlow, G. W. (1961). *Fish. Bull. Calif.* **113**, 77–91.
Webb, C. J. (1980). *Phil. Trans. R. Soc.* (B) **291**, 201–241.
Weisel, G. F. (1947). *Copeia* **1947** (2), 77–85.
Weisel, G. F. (1948). *Physiol. Zool.* **21**, 40–48.
Weisel, G. F. (1949). *Copeia* **1949** (2), 101–110.
Wickler, W. (1962). *Senckenberg. biol.* **43**, 201–205.
Wiley, J. W. (1973). *Trans. S. Diego Soc. nat. Hist.* **17**, 187–208.
Wiley, J. W. (1976). *Trans. S. Diego Soc. nat. Hist.* **18**, 169–184.
Williams, G. C. (1966). "Adaptation and Natural Selection". Princeton University Press, Princeton.
Winterbottom, R. and Emery, A. R. (1981). *Env. Biol. Fish.* **6**, 139–149.
Wootton, R. J. (1979). *Symp. zool. Soc. Lond.* **44**, 133–159.
Yamamoto, T.-O. (1969). *In* "Fish Physiology" (W. S. Hoar and D. J. Randall, eds), Vol. 3, pp. 117–175. Academic Press, New York.
Yanagisawa, Y. (1982). *Jap. J. Ichthyol.* **28**, 401–422.
Young, R. T. and Fox, D. L. (1937). *Proc. natn. Acad. Sci. U.S.A.* **23**, 461–467.

9. Reproduction in Estuarine Fish

P. R. DANDO

Marine Biological Association of the United Kingdom, Plymouth, U.K.

Abstract: Estuaries typically show rapidly fluctuating and microbial-rich conditions which are not ideal for egg and larval development. Many species inhabiting estuaries migrate into either fresh water or the sea to spawn. Only a few estuarine fish are true estuarine residents in that they both live and breed in estuaries. Some marine fish spawn in estuaries or the lower reaches of rivers. The majority of fish that breed in estuaries show some reproductive specialization.

Numerous marine species use the sheltered and nutrient-rich estuaries as nursery grounds. Post-larvae of marine spawners often enter the estuaries when only a few weeks old and concentrate, together with post-larvae from estuarine spawners, in narrow zones within the estuaries.

I. THE CLASSIFICATION OF ESTUARINE FISH

In this review I shall use Pritchard's (1955) definition of an estuary as "a semi-enclosed coastal body of water having a free connection with the open sea and within which sea-water is measurably diluted with fresh-water run-off". Estuaries may be classified or sub-divided in a variety of ways (Carriker, 1967) and similarly there have been several suggested classifications of their fish fauna (Pearcy and Richards, 1962; McHugh, 1967; Perkins, 1974; Day *et al.*, 1981). For the purpose of this study "estuarine" fish may be divided into six groups:

(1) The "passage migrants", anadromous and catadromous species such as many Salmonidae, Petromyzonidae and *Anguilla* spp.

(2) Freshwater species which, often seasonally, penetrate into low salinities for feeding. Many may be displaced into the estuary by river spates. Examples are *Carassius carassius* (carp), *Leuciscus leuciscus* (dace), *Thymallus thymallus* (grayling). Some of these, such as the dace, are known to form permanent populations in the tidal freshwater regions of long estuaries.

(3) Marine species which penetrate the mouth or lower reaches of an

FISH REPRODUCTION
ISBN: 0-12-563660-1

estuary as opportunist feeders. They frequently enter and leave with the tide. Examples from the Tamar estuary in S.W. England are monk fish, *Squatina squatina*; conger eel, *Conger conger*; and mackerel, *Scomber scombrus*.

(4) Estuarine fish, those that spend most or all of their lives in euryhaline conditions. The "true" estuarine fish are considered to be those that spend their entire life cycle in the estuary (McHugh, 1967). Examples of these are many gobies, such as the common goby, *Pomatoschistus microps*; the marsh killifish, *Fundulus confluentus*; and the feather blenny, *Hypsoblennius hentzi*. Other estuarine fish leave the estuaries for short periods, usually for breeding, e.g. the flounder, *Platichthys flesus*; the menhaden, *Brevoortia tyrannus*; and the white perch, *Morone americana*.

(5) Marine species which use estuaries as nursery grounds. As noted by McHugh (1967) these species are often the dominant members of Atlantic estuaries. They include members of many major groups such as the Clupeidae, *Clupea harengus*, *C. sprattus*, Serranidae, *Pogonias cromis*, *Dicentrarchus labrax*, and the Heterosomata *Solea solea* and *Paralichthys dentatus*.

(6) Freshwater and marine species which enter estuaries as adults to breed, for example *Galaxias* spp. and *Pseudopleuronectes americanus*.

Many of the marine species ascend into fresh water to spawn but their post-larvae or young juveniles have estuarine nursery grounds, for example shads, *Alosa* spp., and smelt, *Osmerus eperlanus*.

Classifications of this type are artificial and this one is no exception. Different individuals of a species may differ in habitat. Some adult inanga, *Galaxias maculatus*, are resident and spawn in New Zealand estuaries although most adults of the species are confined to fresh-water and only descend to the estuaries for breeding (McDowall, 1968). Some inanga have even been reported to spawn in fresh-water above tidal limits. The trout, *Salmo trutta*, may spend its entire life in fresh water as a "brown trout", migrate to sea as a "sea trout" or spend most of its adult life in the estuary as a "slob trout" (Kennedy, 1969). All these forms spawn in freshwater.

The classification can also vary with area. For example, the flounder, *Platichthys flesus*, is entirely estuarine in the Tamar outside the spawning season and the first six or seven weeks of its life. Hartley (1940) described it as the estuarine fish "par excellence". Further north in the Ythan estuary, on the east coast of Scotland, adult flounder regularly spend the summer at sea (Summers, 1979) whereas on the west coast, owing to the sharply descending rivers, the fish may be entirely marine.

This review will deal with aspects of reproduction in the last three groups since the problems of estuarine conditions affect them all at some stage in their early life history.

II. THE PROBLEMS OF ESTUARINE LIFE

Estuaries are well known to be highly variable environments where conditions such as salinity, temperature, turbidity and the oxygen concentration of the water can fluctuate rapidly, both temporally and spatially. This is particularly true of short, shallow estuaries. They also have greater temperature extremes than the adjacent coastal waters.

Both drought and flood conditions can greatly alter the character of the estuary. As well as the obvious effects on temperature and salinity, river spates can cause the displacement of sediment from the upper reaches and its deposition in the middle and lower reaches where the estuary broadens and the current slackens. At the same time fish and other fauna are displaced. Not infrequently juvenile flounder in the Tamar are washed out of the freshwater nursery grounds as a result of increased fresh-water run-off following heavy rain and are caught in Plymouth Sound 30 km down-estuary. Conversely low river run-off results in increased tidal scour and the sediment is transported back to the upper reaches. The mechanisms by which sediment is retained in estuaries have been reviewed by Postma (1967).

It is not surprising that mass mortalities of estuarine fish, especially juveniles, are not uncommon after sudden changes in conditions (Brongersma-Sanders, 1957). Abrupt decreases in temperature have been reported to cause larval and juvenile mortalities in many species and may result in the loss of a complete year-class (June and Chamberlain, 1959; Reintjes and Pacheo, 1966; Tabb, 1966; Joseph, 1972; Dey, 1981; Pihl and Rosenberg, 1982). Temperature is thought to be the major factor influencing year-class strength in both the striped bass, *Morone saxatilis* (Kernehan et al., 1981) and the winter flounder, *Pseudopleuronectes americanus* (Jefferies and Johnson, 1974). High summer temperatures have been reported to retard growth in young *Leiostomus xanthrus* (Weinstein and Walters, 1981).

Lillelund (1961) has demonstrated that fresh-water flow, combined with water temperature during egg development, can be used to predict year-class strength in the smelt, *Osmerus eperlanus*. Sudden salinity changes can have catastrophic consequences on estuarine young (Tabb, 1966). Dead eggs of *Anchoa mitchilli* are found in estuarine areas where the salinity is less than 15‰ (Wang and Kernehan, 1979).

Low oxygen levels are another major cause of heavy mortalities in eggs, larvae and juveniles (Kohler, 1981; Wang and Kernehan, 1979). This problem is frequently associated with high levels of suspended matter in the water and egg siltation. A less expected cause of egg mortality is stranding in high winds and subsequent desiccation (Mansueti, 1961a).

The eggs and larvae of many other estuarine fish are known to require a restricted range of temperature and salinity for hatching and for the development of normal larvae (McMynn and Hoar, 1953; Jones, 1962; Westerhagen, 1970; Popova, 1972; Hu and Liao, 1981; Morgan *et al.*, 1981). Salinity and temperature requirements are often interdependent (Alderdice and Forrester, 1968; Rogers, 1976; Morgan *et al.*, 1981). Dovel *et al.* (1969) suggest that light and temperature interact in the development of hogchoker, *Trinectes maculatus*, eggs.

The spawning grounds of the tomcod, *Microgadus tomcod*, may be limited by the loss of sperm activity at salinities greater than 20‰ (Hardy, 1978).

Another problem facing estuarine spawners is the deposition of silt on spawning grounds and on eggs (Mansueti, 1961a; Talbot, 1966; Wang and Kernehan, 1979). Eggs of the striped bass, *Morone saxatilis*, need to be kept suspended if many are to hatch (Talbot, 1966). Very few of the eggs hatch if they are left on silt (Bayliss, 1968). This may not be due solely to oxygen deficiency (Albrect, 1964). Growth of bacteria, fungi and protozoa on silt-covered demersal eggs is a common cause of egg mortality (Lillelund, 1961; Mansueti, 1964; Talbot, 1966).

Estuaries are some of the most productive regions in the world (Schelske and Odum, 1961) and in order to exploit these productive waters the estuarine fish have had to adapt to the frequently rapidly changing conditions.

III. REPRODUCTIVE TACTICS

A. Breeding outside the estuary

In discussing the breeding of estuarine species I shall follow Russell (1976) in using the term "larva" to refer to the yolk sac stage and "post-larva" for young fish between the larval and juvenile stages.

Since estuarine conditions are hostile to egg and larval development it is not surprising to find that many estuarine fish breed elsewhere. In the Tamar estuary, England, I believe that only six of the 76 recorded species spend their entire life-cycle in the estuary. This compares with a possible seven residents among 55 species in the Blackwood estuary, Western Australia (Lenanton, 1976); three among more than 29 species in the Ahuriri Estuary, New Zealand (Kilner and Akroyd, 1978); 12 among 58 species in South African Estuaries (Day *et al.*, 1981) and seven among 83 species in the York River Estuary system, eastern U.S.A. (McHugh, 1967). In contrast there are believed to be 17 residents among the 55 species recorded from the Mystic estuary, Connecticut (Pearcy and Richards, 1962) and no residents among the 17 species collected in the estuary of Walker Creek, California (Jones, 1962).

Some estuarine fish migrate into freshwater to spawn, e.g. the longnose gar, *Lepisosteus osseus*, (Hildebrand and Schroeder, 1927; Echelle and Riggs,

1972), the white perch, *Morone americana* (Mansuetti, 1961b, 1964) and the gizzard shad, *Dorosoma cepedianum* (Miller, 1960).

Many marine species which use estuaries as nursery grounds also ascend into freshwater to spawn, e.g. smelt, *Osmerus eperlanus* (Lillelund, 1961), shads, *Alosa* spp. (Kennedy, 1969; Dovel, 1971) and sturgeons, *Acipenser* spp. (Vladykov and Greeley, 1963). This enables the eggs to develop in clean well-oxygenated water. Typically these fish produce demersal, and frequently adhesive eggs and the larvae possess large yolk-sacs. During the larval period, and egg stage in shads (Mansueti, 1962), they are carried downstream and feeding commences in the productive oligohaline or mesohaline zones of the estuary (Dovel, 1971). One of the requirements of a spawning site is that it should be far enough upstream so that there is a sufficient transport distance to allow the eggs and larvae to develop before they are carried too far down the estuary. Post larvae of the white perch, *Morone americana*, will not survive salinities above 8‰ (Mansueti, 1964) and *Osmerus eperlanus* eggs and larvae will not survive salinities above 16‰ (Lillelund, 1961). It is significant that most species with non-buoyant passively transported eggs tend to have short hatching times of 2–3 days (Jones *et al.*, 1978; Wang and Kernehan, 1979).

However, the majority of estuarine fish undertaking spawning migrations breed at sea, e.g. mullet such as *Liza macrolepis* (Wallace, 1975a) and *Liza ramada* (Hickling, 1970; Demir, 1971) and flounder, *Platichthys flesus* (Hartley, 1940).

Wallace (1975b) in a study of estuarine fish from the east coast of South Africa noted that, apart from a few small species, nearly all the estuarine fish were marine spawners. Frequently these marine migrators are pelagic spawners which spawn inshore in bays in the vicinity of estuary mouths. This not only increases the chances of post-larvae or juveniles migrating into the estuarine nursery grounds (Wallace, 1975b) but gyres in the bays will help to prevent the dispersal of pelagic eggs and larvae. Some fish with demersal eggs are also known to migrate to the more constant salinity conditions in the region of estuary mouths to breed, e.g. the cottid, *Leptocottus armatus* (Jones, 1962), *Glossogobius giurius* of the Ganges delta (Hora, 1935), and the sand goby, *Pomatoschistus minutus* (Lebour, 1920; Lee, 1974) one of the most abundant species in the Tamar estuary.

Wallace (1975b) noted that the dominant species in the South African estuaries he studied had extended spawning seasons of up to eight months. This prolonged the period of post-larval and juvenile recruitment to the estuaries and gave a "buffering" effect against recruitment failure because of droughts or unseasonal floods.

Another advantage of marine spawners is that dispersal of some of the young stages and imperfect homing or long migrations by adults will result in the colonization of estuaries and gene-flow between populations. A mark/recapture study of 9000 flounder, *P. flesus*, in the Tamar showed that individual fish have narrow home-ranges within the estuary and return to these areas after being displaced by spates or when transplanted elsewhere (Dando, unpublished studies). Flounder usually spawn within 15 miles of the estuary mouth and females may spend less than two weeks at sea during the spawning season. The majority of fish return to their own home range in the estuary during the post-spawning period each year, but as many as 10% may migrate east along the English Channel. Marked fish have been recaptured in the post-spawning period 200 miles from the Tamar (Hartley, 1947). This explains the high degree of genetic uniformity observed within this sub-species, *Platichthys flesus flesus*, (Galleguillos and Ward, 1982).

Estuarine fish which spawn at sea, together with the numerous marine species which use estuaries as nursery grounds, have the problem of migrating into the estuary when very young. Wallace and van der Elst (1975) found that many large species entered Natal estuaries when less than 20 mm in length and that the most active recruitment was completed before a length of 50 mm was attained. Post-larvae frequently enter estuaries before metamorphosis. Flounder and sole, *Solea solea* enter the Tamar estuary when 9–12 mm total length, often before eye migration has started. Atlantic menhaden, *Brevoortia tyrannus* enter as small as 8 mm, although most are larger (June and Chamberlin, 1959).

How do these post-larval fish migrate inshore? Some species are positively buoyant until late in development and accumulate in the neuston. Riley *et al.* (1981) have shown that the numbers of O-Group turbot, *Scophthalmus maximus* along the coast are correlated with the frequency of on-shore winds. This species, like the brill, *S. rhombus* has an extended post-larval life and possesses a swimbladder until it metamorphoses (Russell, 1976). Popova (1972) has shown that the year-class strength of the Black Sea turbot, *Scopthalmus maeoticus* is related to wind force and direction. Offshore winds lead to a poor survival of the young.

Menhaden, *B. tyrannus*, post-larvae occur mainly in the upper 15 m of the water column and the spawning period coincides with the season of stronger onshore winds. Nelson *et al.* (1972) concluded that wind was the most significant factor affecting recruitment in this species. The distribution of five species of neustonic young fish off the south-eastern U.S.A. was studied by Powles (1981). Three of these were estuarine dependent species, two mullets, *Mugil cephalus* and *M. corema* and the blue fish *Pomatomus saltatrix*, while the other two were estuarine independent *Coryphaena* spp. The smallest post-larvae of the three estuarine dependent species were found near the 180 m contour at 35‰ salinity and larval lengths were inversely related to the distance from the coast. No such relationship was observed for the young of the *Coryphaena* spp. Powles (1981) looked for a relationship between wind direction and fish distribution. He concluded that the inshore migration of *M.*

cephalus post-larvae could be explained by wind-driven movement of the surface water (Ekman drift) but was unable to account for the transport of *M. corema* and *P. saltatrix* young since the winds were predominantly offshore during their migration.

Young fish can also utilize currents and tides for migrating. Flatfish (Heterosomata) start lying on their sides on touching the bottom at the start of metamorphosis. They use this behaviour when ascending estuaries, lying on the bottom during the ebb and swimming up into the water column on the flood. During April metamorphosing flounders, *P. flesus*, can be captured in townets in the lower reaches of the Tamar on the flood tide but not on the ebb. A net fished 10 cm off the bottom will only catch these fish on the first of the flood tide as they leave the bottom. These post-larvae rapidly ascend the estuary, to judge by the low densities in the lower and middle reaches, and finally settle in the first section of the estuary which contains freshwater. There they complete metamorphosis before moving further upstream. Metamorphosing stone flounder, *Kareius bicoloratus* ascend to the tidal limits of Japanese estuaries in a similar manner (Tsuruta, 1978).

The metamorphosing stages of plaice, *Pleuronectes platessa*, and dab, *Limanda limanda* are found just above the sea bed (Harding and Talbot, 1973). Creutzberg *et al.* (1978) studied the migration of plaice post-larvae from the North Sea towards the tidal inlets of the Wadden Sea and considered that the fish might be carried inshore by the residual bottom drift. They found that starvation induces pelagic swimming in the post-larvae and suggest that swimming activity is reduced when the fish can detect extracts of food organisms in the water. The young plaice would be more likely to remain on the bottom when water movement was away from the productive mud-flats of the Wadden Sea.

Elver, *Anguilla anguilla*, migration into the Wadden Sea has also been studied by Creutzberg (1961). The young eels were found high in the water on the flood tide and near the bottom on the ebb. In experimental tanks the elvers tended to cling to the bottom or burrow in the sand during a simulated ebb tide in which seawater was mixed with river water. This behaviour was not induced when the river water was replaced by either tap-water or by water which had been passed through a charcoal filter. Creutzberg (1961) proposed that passive pelagic transport by residual currents accounted for the movement of elvers into the tidal Wadden Sea.

The young of many other marine spawners migrate up-estuary to near the freshwater–saltwater interface (Mansueti, 1960; Jones, 1962; Reintjes and Pacheco, 1966; Dovel, 1971; Thomas and Smith, 1973). Most of these young fish probably utilize the net up-stream flow of the saline current along the estuary bottom. Pritchard (1951) has calculated that in Chesapeake Bay a migration rate of 6·5 miles/day could be attained by this means.

B. Breeding in the estuary

1. *Pelagic eggs.* In their study of fish larvae and post-larvae in the Mystic River estuary Pearcy and Richards (1962) observed that 97% had hatched from demersal eggs. With the exception of eggs of the bay anchovy, *Anchoa mitchilli*, and of labrid eggs, low catches of pelagic eggs were made and they were distributed near the mouth of the estuary, suggesting that they had been carried in by currents. A similar pattern was observed in upper Chesapeake Bay where most of the pelagic eggs derived from two species, *A. mitchilli* and the soleid, *Trinectes maculatus* (Dovel, 1971). Estuary spawning by species producing pelagic eggs is uncommon. This is not surprising since pelagic larvae can be rapidly flushed out of the estuary and dispersed by the net seaward transport of the surface layers. Larvae of the estuary-spawning whitebaits of Australasia are rapidly washed out to sea (Blackburn, 1950; McDowell, 1968, 1975). This is a problem for all estuarine larvae. Pearcy (1962) calculated that young larvae of winter flounder, *Pseudopleuronectes americanus*, despite being non-buoyant, were lost at the rate of 4%/day from the Mystic River estuary. He calculated that the loss rate for pelagic larvae would have been approximately 10%/day, assuming that the larvae were evenly distributed in the water column.

Both *A. mitchilli* and *T. maculatus* have partly overcome this problem of dispersion by spawning at midsummer when water temperatures, and hence development rates, are at a maximum (Dovel, 1971). Eggs of *A. mitchilli* hatch in 24 hours (Dovel, 1971) and those of *T. maculatus* in less than 36 hours (Hildebrand and Cable, 1938).

The larval phase of *T. maculatus* is complete in a further 48 hours. Despite the short hatching period of the latter species its eggs may be transported 11 km offshore (Hildebrand and Cable, 1938). However, the post-larvae rapidly ascend the estuary, possibly transported by the salt-wedge, to the nursery grounds at the saltwater–freshwater interface (Dovel et al., 1969). Newly hatched larvae of *A. mitchilli* are epibenthic for up to 24 h post-hatching (Wang and Kernehan, 1979) before becoming pelagic and, as with *T. maculatus* there is a rapid up-estuary migration to the low salinity nursery grounds.

2. *Demersal eggs.* The true estuarine residents, together with the few marine and freshwater species which enter estuaries to spawn, show various adaptations to spawning under estuarine conditions. Most deposit demersal eggs. Pearcy and Richards (1962) found that 15 of the 17 resident species in the estuary of the Mystic River, Connecticut, had demersal or non-buoyant eggs. In contrast the majority of larvae in the adjacent Long Island and Block Island Sounds hatched from pelagic eggs. In Maine estuaries and coastal waters Chenoweth (1973) found that 9 of 15 post-larval species originated from

demersal eggs or from ovoviviparous or oviparous fish and that these post-larvae accounted for 99·5% of the total catch.

Demersal eggs may, in part, be an adaptation to breeding in ice-covered northern estuaries and seas (Rass, 1959). They will certainly help to prevent losses in estuaries having a net seaward flow. Moiseev (1956) has suggested that demersal eggs were evolved by species living in areas with rapid currents. In silt-laden water demersal eggs suffer from the disadvantage that they may be buried and deprived of oxygen as well as being coated with bacteria, fungi and protozoa (Lillelund, 1961; Mansueti, 1964; Talbot, 1966).

Species such as the striped bass, *M. saxatilis*, produce eggs with a density slightly greater than that of the water and usually spawn upstream of the nursery grounds in an area where the current is sufficient to keep the eggs suspended. *M. saxatilis* spawns in fresh or almost fresh water, spawning in salinities greater than 5‰ leads to poor survival. The egg of *M. saxatilis* has a specific gravity of 1·0005 or less and is suspended at surface velocities of 18 cm/sec or more (Albrect, 1964). Mansueti (1961a) suggested that the large perivitelline space in the egg may act as a breathing chamber and be an adaptation to silt-laden waters. The eggs hatch in 2–3 days at 18°C and the post-larvae congregate in the area of greatest zooplankton abundance at the freshwater–saltwater interface (Mansueti, 1961a; Setzler-Hamilton *et al.*, 1981).

Another tactic to avoid silting of the eggs is to deposit the eggs out of the water. This approach is used by the freshwater estuary-spawning *Galaxias* spp. of New Zealand and also by several *Fundulus* spp. The inanga, *G. maculatus* spawns on the top of flooded grass flats after the highest high-water spring tide (McDowell, 1968). Spawning commences at high water and continues for approximately three-quarters of an hour. As the tide recedes the eggs are washed down to the bases of the grass clumps where the high humidity of the vegetation protects them from desiccation until the next spring tides a fortnight later (McDowell, 1975). Hatching normally occurs within two spring tides, the eggs hatch rapidly when immersed in water, but can be delayed for two months or more (McDowell, 1968). During delayed hatching the larvae feed on the yolk, which is so large that larvae hatching on the first spring tide after spawning will not feed for two weeks. It is not known how these freshwater fish synchronize their spawning migration to arrive in the estuary at the correct time of the tidal cycle (Burnet, 1965). *Galaxias* spp. are also unusual in that, although they may spawn in estuaries, the larvae are washed out to sea where the juveniles spend approximately six months before returning to fresh water.

Several *Fundulus* spp. show a similar spawning behaviour including *F. confluentus*, the marsh killifish (Harrington, 1959). This fish spawns on flooded salt marshes where the eggs are found among matted algae. The eggs are held by long chorion strands which are trapped between the algal filaments. The eggs develop while exposed to air and can remain viable for at least three months. Hatching usually occurs on the next flood when most larvae hatch within 30 minutes of being immersed (Harrington, 1959). The mummichog, *F. heteroclitus*, follows a similar spawning pattern (Pearcy and Richards, 1962; Taylor *et al.*, 1977). Eggs are deposited at Spring tides on *Spartina* leaves such that they are exposed to air at low tide. The eggs are ready for hatching in 7–8 days, but like the preceding species, hatching is delayed until the eggs are immersed in water when they emerge within 15–20 minutes (Taylor *et al.*, 1977). *F. parvipinnis*, the California killifish, also spawns on grass flats (Fritz, 1975). The eggs of this species also have a chorion which forms an adhesive thread. Hubbs (1965) has noted that if they are kept in the dark hatching is delayed. This may be an adaptation to prevent larvae hatching when the eggs are under sediment.

Some populations of *F. heteroclitus* spawn in empty shells of the intertidal mussel *Modiolus demissus* (Able and Castagna, 1975). This spawning behaviour was observed in an aquarium where the fish chose mussel shells as a spawning site in preference to algae. It was suggested that this behaviour was an adaptation against predation by other adults on the eggs and that the thickened chorion on these eggs would prevent desiccation at low tide (Able and Castagna, 1975). Wang and Kernehan (1979) have suggested that leaving the eggs exposed to air may be an adaptation to prevent egg predation by fish and other aquatic predators.

Many estuarine fish produce eggs of a straw or orange colour due to the presence of carotenoids. Carotenoids are known to be involved in providing an intracellular oxygen store in vertebrate and invertebrate tissues (Karnaukhov, 1971, 1973; Balon, Chap. 3, this volume). Nikolsky (1963) has suggested that there is a direct relationship between the concentration of carotenoids in the eggs of a species and the degree of oxygenation of the water at the spawning site.

Another tactic which prevents silting and poor oxygenation of demersal eggs is parental care (see also Potts, Chap. 13, this volume). Many gobies breed in estuaries, depositing their eggs in shells or on the underside of stones. Some use depressions in the ground or burrows in the sand or mud. The eggs are attached to the substratum by means of a special disc fringed by elongated filaments (Russell, 1976). The male guards the eggs and aerates them, using his pectoral fins, until they hatch (Hora, 1935; Jones, 1937; Ishikawa and Nakamura, 1940; Dôtu, 1955, 1957). *Gobiosoma bosci* and *G. ginsburgi* nest in areas where the tidal current is sufficient to restrict siltation and water stagnation at low tide (Dahlberg and Conyers, 1973). None of the nests were exposed at low-water spring tides. This choice of breeding area is common to most species as empty shells form favourite nesting sites and these would be filled with mud in areas of high siltation. Gobies appear to be particularly successful estuarine breeders since their larvae and post-larvae dominate the ichthyoplankton in many estuaries (Miller, Chap. 8, this volume). Larvae of *Gobiosoma bosci* accounted for 55% of all the fish post-larvae collected in upper Chesapeake Bay by Dovel (1971). In a salt marsh in California Leithiser (1981) found that four species of goby accounted for 83% of the post-larvae caught. Lenanton (1976) observed that gobiids and atherinids dominated the larval and post-larval collections in the Blackwood estuary, Australia. In the summer post-larvae of the gobies *Pomatoschistus microps* and *P. minutus* are the major species caught in the Tamar estuary.

Several other families of fish have breeding habits which allow them to survive under estuarine conditions. The oyster toadfish, *Opsanus tau* deposits large (6–7 mm) eggs on oyster shells. The eggs are held by an attachment disc on the chorion. After hatching the larvae also remain held by this disc for 4–27 days (Gray and Winn, 1961). The male guards the eggs and larvae and ventilates them with his pectorals. He also remains with the free-swimming post-larvae for 5–18 days after release. Blennies may also nest in estuaries. *Hypsoblennius hentzi* and *Chasmodes bosquianus* nest in oyster shells with the male attending the eggs (Hildebrand and Cable, 1938).

Some marine and estuarine sticklebacks, e.g. *Apeltes quadracus* and *Gasterosteus wheatlandi* nest in estuaries (Nichols and Breder, 1927; Wootton, 1976). The male ventilates and attends the eggs and larvae.

A few cichlids, e.g. *Etroplus suratensis* nest in estuaries (Panikkar, 1920). In this species the newly hatched larvae attach to the egg membrane by cement glands. The female picks them up by mouth and places them in a nursery pit constructed in the bottom by the male. The pits are fanned to remove debris and the larvae are transferred to a fresh pit at least once a day. The larvae use their cement glands to attach to sand particles in the bottom of the pit. Post-larvae leave the brood pits and are guarded by the male and herded by the female. The related *E. maculatus*, although inhabiting estuaries, migrates into freshwater to breed (Panikkar, 1920; Jones, 1937).

The sea catfish *Galeichthys felis* and *Bagre marinus* are known to both spawn and brood the young in estuaries (Gudger, 1916; Gunter, 1947). The male incubates the large eggs, up to 15 mm long, in its buccal cavity. As many as 55 eggs have been found in a single male. The young are retained until the post-larval stage.

Finally, pipefish (Syngnathidae) are well adapted for estuarine breeding. They are common among *Zostera* or algal beds. The eggs and larvae are brooded by the male in special brood flaps. On release the young may be demersal, as in *Syngnathus acus*, or be pelagic, as in *S. rostellatus* for a period (Russell, 1976). The post-larvae may be nourished from the epithelial layer of the brood pouch before emergence (Bigelow and Schroeder, 1953).

IV. THE ADAPTATION OF YOUNG FISH TO ESTUARINE LIFE

Larvae and post-larvae from species spawning in fresh water, the estuary and the sea come together in two main estuarine regions. The highest concentrations of post-larvae are normally found in the highly productive zone below the fresh water interface in the 1–15‰ salinity region of the estuary. Dovel (1971) reported that 95% of the post-larvae collected in his survey of upper Chesapeake Bay were caught in the 0–11‰ salinity region. This zone has been termed the "critical zone" by Massman (1963). The second region is the productive shallow areas of the estuary with marginal vegetation. Examples of these are salt marsh areas and the *Zostera* beds. These areas are favoured by mullet, some drums and many gobies (Munro, 1945; Wallace and van der Elst, 1975; Leithiser, 1981).

A major problem confronting these young fish is how to maintain station in these productive areas against the tidal currents and the seaward freshwater flow. Estuarine copepods and mysids have been shown to do this by adjusting their position both vertically and laterally to utilize different currents and maintain position (Wooldridge and Erasmus, 1980). In the middle of an estuarine channel there is a net outflow at the surface and a net inflow along the bottom whereas at the shallow margins currents are slacker and sometimes counter to that of the mainstream. Young fish can remain in their own region of the estuary by using these currents and by altering their position within them.

Pearcy (1962) has demonstrated that the winter flounder, *Pseudopleuron-ectes americanus*, reduces translocation losses by spawning demersal eggs in the upper estuary which hatch to give non-buoyant passive larvae having a specific gravity of 1·022. As the post-larvae develop and become more active the translocation loss becomes smaller. Newly hatched larvae of the weakfish, *Cynoscion regalis*, also sink to the bottom. The larvae are thought to be transported from the mouth of the Delaware estuary to the upper estuary nursery area by the sub-surface saline current (Thomas, 1971). Post-larvae of the naked goby, *Gobiosoma bosci* (Massman *et al.*, 1963), the Japanese bass, *Lateolabrax japonicus* (Matsumiya *et al.*, 1982) and the black drum, *Pogonias cromis* (Thomas and Smith, 1973) are thought to ascend the estuary on the flood tide and to move into the shallows on the ebb.

Post-larvae are able to move towards preferred water sources. Young *P. cromis* are seen to congregate around marsh outflows (Thomas and Smith, 1973). The southern flounder, *Paralichthys lethostigma* will withdraw, at the post-larval stage, from water of low oxygen content (Deubler and Posner, 1963). Post-larval flounder, *Platichthys flesus*, acquire a greater tolerance to fresh water as they develop. After metamorphosis they actively swim towards river water, as opposed to sea water, in Y-chamber experiments (S. Hutchinson, pers. comm.). Juvenile flounder removed from the fresh water nursery ground and kept in sea water for two weeks will swim toward river water inflows whereas fish of the same age reared entirely in sea water did not respond (Dando and Powles, unpublished results). The ability to detect chemical cues from the home area may be involved in the homing ability of this species.

Fish post-larvae can reach high concentrations on the nursery grounds. Pearcy and Richards (1962) obtained an average catch of $10/m^3$ in March in the Mystic estuary. Metamorphosing *Pseudopleuronectes americanus* attained densities of $2\cdot4/m^2$ on the bottom of the same estuary (Pearcy, 1962) and I have observed juvenile *Platichthys flesus* at densities of $3\cdot4/m^2$ in the upper reaches of the Tamar. Post-larval concentrations up to $18\cdot3/m^3$ have been reported in a Californian salt marsh (Leithiser, 1981). The post-larvae of the goby *Pomatoschistus microps* are observed at mean densities up to $75/m^3$ in the region of the freshwater–saltwater interface in the Tamar estuary (Dando, unpublished studies). These densities are much higher than those normally found in coastal marine waters. Houde (1977) has shown that post-larval *Anchoa mitchilli* can be reared at densities up to $32\,000/m^3$ provided that food is abundant.

As the young fish grow they usually descend to the middle and lower reaches of the estuary. Several studies have shown that competition between the different species in the juvenile stage is minimized by differences in temporal and spatial distribution as well as diet (Riley, 1975; Chao and Musick, 1977; Powell and Schwartz, 1977). Populations of fish living permanently in low salinity areas are able to genetically adapt to them (Dushkina, 1973; Solemedal, 1973). Frequently the juveniles and adults show similar salinity tolerances, for example some adult *Platichthys flesus* co-exist with the O-group on the freshwater nursery grounds.

In marine species the adults are mostly less tolerant of lower salinities than the young which are found to move progressively into more saline conditions as they grow (Gunter, 1938, 1945, 1957; Wallace and van der Elst, 1975). This difference in tolerance effectively prevents the adult fish from invading the nursery areas and preying upon the dense concentrations of larval and young fish.

REFERENCES

Able, K. W. and Castagna, M. (1975). *Chesapeake Sci.* **16**, 282–284.
Albrect, A. B. (1964). *Calif. Fish Game* **50**, 100–113.
Alderdice, D. F. and Forrester, C. R. (1968). *J. Fish. Res. Bd Can.* **25**, 495–591.
Bayliss, J. D. (1968). *Proc. Ann. Conf. Southeast. Assoc. Game Fish Comm.* **21**, 233–244.
Bigelow, H. B. and Schroeder, W. C. (1953). *Fish. Bull. Fish Wildl. Serv. U.S.* **53**, 1–577.
Blackburn, M. (1950). *Aust. J. mar. Freshwat. Res.* **1**, 155–198.
Brongersma-Sanders, M. (1957). *Mem. geol. Soc. Am.* **67**, 941–1010.
Burnet, A. M. R. (1965). *N.Z. J. Sci.* **8**, 79–87.
Carriker, M. R. (1967). *In* "Estuaries" (G. H. Lauff, ed.), pp. 442–487. American Association for the Advancement of Science, Washington.
Chao, L. N. and Musick, J. A. (1977). *Fishery Bull. natn. oceanic atmos. Adm. U.S.* **75**, 657–702.

Chenoweth, S. B. (1973). *Fishery Bull. natn. oceanic atmos. Adm. U.S.* **71**, 105–113.

Creutzberg, F. (1961). *Neth. J. Sea Res.* **1**, 257–338.

Creutzberg, F., Eltink, A. T. G. W. and van Noort, G. J. (1978). *In* "Physiology and Behaviour of Marine Organisms" (D. S. McLusky and A. J. Berry, eds), pp. 243–251. Pergamon Press, Oxford and New York.

Dahlberg, M. D. and Conyers, J. C. (1973). *Fishery Bull. natn. oceanic atmos. Adm. U.S.* **31**, 279–287.

Day, J. H., Blaber, S. J. M. and Wallace, J. H. (1981). *In* "Estuarine Ecology with Particular Reference to South Africa" (J. H. Day, ed.), pp. 197–221. A. A. Balkema, Rotterdam.

Demir, N. (1971). *J. mar. biol. Ass. U.K.* **51**, 235–246.

Deubler, E. E. and Posner, G. S. (1963). *Copeia* **1963**, 312–317.

Dey, W. P. (1981). *Trans. Am. Fish. Soc.* **110**, 151–157.

Dovel, W. L. (1971). *Spec. Rep. Nat. Resour. Inst. Univ. Md.* **4**.

Dovel, W. L., Mihursky, J. A. and McErlean, A. J. (1969). *Chesapeake Sci.* **10**, 104–119.

Dôtu, Y. (1955). *Bull. biogeogr. Soc. Japan* **16–19**, 338–344.

Dôtu, Y. (1957). *Sci. Bull. Fac. Agric. Kyushu Univ.* **16**, 93–100.

Dushkina, L. A. (1973). *Mar. Biol.* **19**, 210–223.

Echelle, A. A. and Riggs, C. D. (1972). *Trans. Am. Fish. Soc.* **101**, 106–112.

Fritz, E. S. (1975). *Fish. Bull. Calif.* **165**.

Galleguillos, R. A. and Ward, R. D. (1982). *Biol. J. Linn.* Soc. **17**, 395–408.

Gray, G. A. and Winn, H. E. (1961). *Ecology* **42**, 274–282.

Gudger, E. W. (1916). *Zoologica, N.Y.* **2**, 126–158.

Gunter, G. (1938). *Ecol. Monogr.* **8**, 313–346.

Gunter, G. (1945). *Publ. Inst. mar. Sci. Texas* **1**, 1–190.

Gunter, G. (1947). *Copeia* **1947**, 217–223.

Gunter, G. (1957). *Copeia* **1957**, 13–16.

Harding, G. and Talbot, J. W. (1973). *Rapp. P.v. Réun. Cons. int. Explor. Mer.* **164**, 261–269.

Hardy, J. D. (1978). "Development of Fishes of the mid-Atlantic Bight. Vol. II", U.S. Dept. Int., Fish and Wildlife Service.

Harrington, R. W. (1959). *Ecology* **40**, 430–437.

Hartley, P. H. T. (1940). *J. mar. biol. Ass. U.K.* **24**, 1–68.

Hartley, P. H. T. (1947). *J. mar. biol. Ass. U.K.* **27**, 53–64.

Hickling, C. F. (1970). *J. mar. biol. Ass. U.K.* **50**, 609–633.

Hildebrand, S. F. and Cable, L. E. (1938). *Bull. Bur. Fish., Wash.* **48**, 505–642.

Hildebrand, S. F. and Schroeder, W. C. (1927). *Bull. Bur. Fish., Wash.* **43**, 1–388.

Hora, S. L. (1935). *C.r. XIIᵉCongrès Internatnl. Zool. Lisbonne* **2**, section 5, 841–863.

Houde, E. D. (1977). *Mar. Biol.* **43**, 333–341.

Hu, F. and Liao, I-C. (1981). *Rapp. P.-v. Réun. Cons. int. Explor. Mer* **178**, 460–466.

Hubbs, C. (1965). *Calif. Fish Game* **51**, 113–122.

Ishikawa, M. and Nakamura, N. (1940). *Bull. Jap. Soc. scient. Fish.* **8**, 365–366.

Jefferies, H. P. and Johnson, W. C. (1974). *J. Fish. Res. Bd Can.* **31**, 1057–1066.

Jones, A. C. (1962). *Univ. Calif. Publs. Zool.* **67**, 321–368.

Jones, S. A. (1937). *Proc. Indian Acad. Sci., Bangalore* Sect. B **5**, 261–289.

Jones, P. W., Martin, F. D. and Hardy, J. D. (1978). "Development of Fishes of the Mid-Atlantic Bight, Vol. 1". U.S. Dept. Int., Fish and Wildlife Service.

Joseph, E. G. (1972). *Chesapeake Sci.* **13**, 87–100.

June, F. C. and Chamberlin, L. (1959). *Proc. Gulf Caribb. Fish. Inst.* **11**, 41–45.

Karnaukhov, V. N. (1971). *Expl. Cell Res.* **64**, 301–306.
Karnaukhov, V. N. (1973). *Expl. Cell Res.* **80**, 479–483.
Kennedy, M. (1969). "The Sea Angler's Fishes". Stanley Paul, London.
Kernehan, R. J., Headrick, M. R. and Smith, R. E. (1981). *Trans. Am. Fish Soc.* **110**, 137–150.
Kilner, A. R. and Akroyd, J. M. (1978). *Fish. tech. Rep. N.Z.* **153**.
Kohler, A. (1981). *Helgölander wiss Meeresunters* **34**, 263–285.
Lebour, M. V. (1920). *J. mar. biol. Ass. U.K.* **12**, 253–260.
Lee, S C. (1974). "Biology of the sand goby *Pomatoschistus minutus* (Pallas) (Teleostei Gobiodei) in the Plymouth area". Ph.D. Thesis, University of Bristol.
Leithiser, R. M. (1981). *Rapp. P.-v. Réun. Cons. int. Explor. Mer.* **178**, 174–175.
Lenanton, R. C. J. (1976). *Fish. Res. Bull. West. Aust.* **19**, 1–72.
Lillelund, K. (1961). *Arch. Fischwiss.* **12**, 1–128.
McDowall, R. M. (1968). *Fisheries Res. Bull. N.Z.* **2**.
McDowall, R. M. (1975). *Inf. Leaflet; Fish Div. N.Z.* **6**.
McHugh, J. L. (1967). *In* "Estuaries" (G. H. Lauff, ed.), pp. 581–620. American Association for the Advancement of Science, Washington, D.C.
McMynn, P. G. and Hoar, W. S. (1953). *Can. J. Zool.* **31**, 417–432.
Mansueti, R. J. (1960). *Chesapeake Sci.* **4**, 207–210.
Mansueti, R. J. (1961a). *Proc. Gulf Caribb. Fish. Inst.* **14**, 110–136.
Mansueti, R. J. (1961b). *Chesapeake Sci.* **2**, 142–205.
Mansueti, R. J. (1962). *Chesapeake Sci.* **3**, 173–205.
Mansueti, R. J. (1964). *Chesapeake Sci.* **5**, 3–45.
Massman, W. II. (1963). *Bull. Sport Fish. Inst.* **141**, 1–2.
Massman, W. H., Norcross, J. J. and Joseph, E. B. (1963). *Chesapeake Sci.* **4**, 120–125.
Matsuniya, Y., Mitani, T. and Tanaka, M. (1982). *Bull. Jap. Soc. scient. Fish.* **48**, 129–138.
Miller, R. R. (1960). *Fishery Bull. Fish Wildl. Serv. U.S.* **60**, 371–392.
Moiseev, P. (1956). *In* "Papers presented at the International Technical Conference on the Conservation of the Living Resources of the Sea. Rome 18th April–10th May (1955)", pp. 266–289. United Nations, New York.
Morgan, R. P., Rasin, V. J. and Copp, R. L. (1981). *Trans. Am. Fish. Soc.* **110**, 95–99.
Munro, I. S. R. (1945). *Mem. Qd. Mus.* **12**, 136–153.
Nelson, W. R., Ingham, M. C. and Schaaf, W. E. (1977). *Fishery Bull. natn. oceanic atmos. Adm. U.S.* **75**, 23–42.
Nichols, J. T. and Breder, C. M. (1927). *Zoologica, N.Y.* **9**, 1–192.
Nikolsky, G. V. (1963). "The Ecology of Fishes". Academic Press, London and New York.
Panikkar, N. P. (1920). *Madras Fish. Bull.* **12**, 156–166.
Pearcy, W. G. (1962). *Bull. Bingham Oceanogr. Coll.* **18**, 16–38.
Pearcy, W. G. and Richards, S. W. (1962). *Ecology* **43**, 248–259.
Perkins, E. J. (1974). "The Biology of Estuaries and Coastal Waters". Academic Press, London and New York.
Pihl, L. and Rosenberg, R. (1982). *J. exp. mar. Biol. Ecol.* **57**, 273–301.
Popova, V. P. (1972). *J. Ichthyol.* **12**, 961–967.
Postma, H. (1967). *In* "Estuaries" (G. H. Lauff, ed.), pp. 158–179. American Association for the Advancement of Science, Washington, D.C.
Powell, A. B. and Schwartz, P. J. (1977). *Chesapeake Sci.* **18**, 334–339.
Powles, H. (1981). *Rapp. P.-v. Réun. Cons. int. Explor. Mer.* **178**, 207–209.
Pritchard, D. W. (1951). *Trans. N. Am. Wildl. Conf.* **16**, 365–375.
Pritchard, D. W. (1955). *Proc. Am. Soc. civ. Engrs.* **81**, 1–12.

Rass, T. S. (1959). *J. Cons. perm. int. Explor. Mer.* **24**, 243–254.

Reintjes, J. W. and Pacheco, A. L. (1966). *Spec. Publs Am. Fish. Soc.* **3**, 50–58.

Riley, J. D. (1975). *In* "The Humber Estuary", Proceedings of a Joint Symposium organized by the University of Hull/Humber Advisory Group (N.V. Jones, ed.). The University of Hull, Hull.

Riley, J. D., Symonds, D. J. and Woolner, L. (1981). *Rapp. P.-v. Réun. Cons. int. Explor. Mer.* **178**, 223–228.

Rogers, C. A. (1976). *Fishery Bull. Fish Wildl. Serv. U.S.* **74**, 52–58.

Russell, F. S. (1976). "The Eggs and Planktonic Stages of British Marine Fishes". Academic Press, London and New York.

Setzler-Hamilton, E. M., Boynton, W. R., Polgar, T. T. and Mihursky, J. A. (1981). *Trans. Am. Fish. Soc.* **110**, 121–136.

Schelske, C. L. and Odum, E. P. (1961). *Proc. Gulf Caribb. Fish. Inst.* **14**, 75–80.

Solemedal, P. (1973). *Oikos* Suppl. **15**, 268–276.

Summers, R. W. (1979). *J. nat. Hist.* **13**, 703–723.

Tabb, D. C. (1966). *Spec. Publ. Am. Fish. Soc.* **3**, 59–67.

Talbot, G. B. (1966). *Spec. Publ. Am. Fish. Soc.* **3**, 37–49.

Taylor, M. H., Di Michele, L. and Leach, G. J. (1977). *Copeia* **1977**, 397–399.

Thomas, D. L. (1971). *Bull., Ichthyological Associates Inc.* **5**.

Thomas, D. L. and Smith, B. A. (1973). *Chesapeake Sci.* **14**, 124–130.

Tsuruta, Y. (1978). *Tohoku J. agric. Res.* **29**, 136–145.

Vladykov, V. D. and Greeley, J. R. (1963). *In* "Fishes of the Western North Atlantic" (Y. H. Olsen, ed.), Mem. 1, Part 3, pp. 24–60. Sears Foundation for Marine Research, New Haven.

Wallace, J. H. (1975a). *Investl. Rep. Oceanogr. Res. Inst., Durban* **40**, 1–72.

Wallace, J. H. (1975b). *Investl. Rep. Oceanogr. Res. Inst., Durban* **41**, 1–51.

Wallace, J. H. and van der Elst, R. P. (1975). *Investl. Rep. Oceanogr. Res. Inst., Durban* **42**, 1–63.

Wang, J. C. S. and Kernehan, R. J. (1979). "Fishes of the Delaware Estuaries. A Guide to the Early Life History Stages". E. A. Communications, Townson, Maryland.

Weinstein, M. P. and Walters, M. P. (1981). *Estuaries* **4**, 185–197.

Westerhagen, H. von. (1970). *Helgölander wiss Meeresunters* **21**, 21–102.

Wooldridge, T. and Erasmus, T. (1980). *Estuar. cstl. mar. Sci.* **11**, 107–114.

Wootton, R. J. (1976). "The Biology of Sticklebacks". Academic Press, London and New York.

10. Geographical Variation in the Life-History Tactics of Some Species of Freshwater Fish

R. H. K. MANN, C. A. MILLS AND D. T. CRISP*

Freshwater Biological Association, River Laboratory, Wareham, U.K.

Abstract: Most species of freshwater fish in Europe are widely-distributed and are relatively unspecialized in their food and habitat requirements. This plasticity may stem from an evolutionary experience of fluctuating conditions which has resulted in the genome of an individual fish being capable of a wide range of phenotypic expression. Thus there has been an evolution in many species towards maximum reproductive success over a wide range of environmental conditions. However, the adaptation of individual populations to local ecological conditions is likely to result in alterations in genetic frequencies.

This paper examines the life-history tactics of three species: the sculpin *Cottus gobio*, the loach *Noemacheilus barbatulus* and the gudgeon *Gobio gobio*. In the productive chalk streams of southern England these species are short-lived, they grow fast and mature early, and each female lays several batches of eggs each year. These tactics are contrasted with those of fish in more northerly populations, and with those described in other published reports. In unproductive moorland streams the life-span of *C. gobio* is seven to eight years (c.f. two to three years in chalk streams), maturation occurs later, growth is slower and each female produces only one batch of eggs each year. Similar effects are found in northern populations of *N. barbatulus* and *G. gobio*, although the fractional spawning tactic is retained. An exception is a population of *N. barbatulus* in Finland in which each female spawns only once each year.

The underlying nature of the variations in the reproductive tactics of *C. gobio* was investigated by the reciprocal transfer of fish between a southern productive and a northern unproductive stream. The results showed that the variation in the number of egg batches and in the differences in growth rate are both phenotypic characteristics.

I. INTRODUCTION

In 1963 Mayr observed that all the widespread species of animals and plants that had been studied carefully consisted of geographically distinct pop-

* F.B.A. Teesdale Unit, c/o Northumbrian Water Authority, Lartington Treatment Plant, Lartington, Barnard Castle, Co. Durham DL12 9DW, England.

FISH REPRODUCTION
ISBN: 0-12-563660-1

ulations that differed from one another in their ecology. Such isolated populations can be either genetically similar or genetically different. In the first case, through the evolutionary experience of living in fluctuating conditions, genomes have evolved that express sufficient phenotypic flexibility to allow individuals in local populations to respond to their contemporary environment in a manner which maximizes their reproductive fitness, that is, to maximize their ability to produce the largest number of mature progeny. Alternatively populations may have evolved unique genetic identities when two or more populations from the same gene pool have become physically separated from one another in different environments, and have been subject to different selection pressures. If the genotypes lack sufficient phenotypic flexibility to respond adaptively to the new environment, then some genetic assimilation of the adaptive phenotypic traits may occur through natural selection. This, of course, is the process which leads to geographic speciation. Although selection is the major factor involved in evolutionary change, chance variation in allele frequencies may also occur, although the success or failure of new genotypes will still depend upon the influence of natural selection.

Considerable efforts have been made to arrange the life-history tactics of groups of organisms along an r–K continuum (MacArthur and Wilson, 1967). By analogy to the logistic equation:

$$\frac{dN}{dt} = rN(1 - \frac{N}{K})$$

where N is population density, K is maximum equilibrium density and r is the intrinsic rate of natural increase.

K-selected life-histories develop in stable environments where numbers are controlled by density-dependent factors. Favoured traits include late maturity, low reproductive effort, fewer but larger offspring and multiple broods (iteroparity). Conversely, r-selected life-histories develop in populations in less predictable environments; here the characteristic traits include early maturity, high reproductive effort, high fecundity and single broods (semelparity).

Among freshwater fishes, there are many species that occupy a wide range of habitats and that show larger variations in the survival rates of the pre-adults than of the adults. Those few studies (marine and freshwater) that have compared the life-histories of a single fish species living in different aquatic environments, indicate that such an approach may provide some insight into the way life-histories are determined (Blaxter, 1958; Bagenal, 1966; Schaffer and Elson, 1975; Fox, 1978a,b; Mann and Mills, 1979). Consequently, in this paper, we examine the life-history tactics employed in a range of habitats by three species of European freshwater fish: the sculpin *Cottus gobio* L., the stone loach *Noemacheilus barbatulus* (L.) and the gudgeon *Gobio gobio* (L.).

These are small benthic species, rarely exceeding 15 cm in length, which occur in many lotic and lentic habitats throughout Europe and Scandinavia. Our study combines data from our own observations with data published by other workers. We also describe the effects of a reciprocal transfer of the sculpin *C. gobio* between two contrasting streams in the north and south of England, with special reference to its growth and reproduction.

II. VARIATION IN LIFE-HISTORY TACTICS

A. The sculpin *Cottus gobio* L., Cottidae

This sculpin species is the most widespread of the European freshwater Cottidae. Because of its spawning requirements it favours habitats with stone or gravel substrates, although it may be found occasionally on areas of sand or mud. The eggs are laid in batches (*ca.* 50–350 eggs per batch), usually on the undersurface of large stones where they are guarded and fanned by the male. Each "nest" may contain egg batches from different females, with the batches often being at different stages of development. The spawning behaviour of *C. gobio* is described by Morris (1954), and aspects of its biology including reproduction are described by Mann (1971) and Fox (1978a,b). Koli (1969) examined the range of variation in external morphology among *C. gobio* populations in northern Europe, but did not mention differences in life history.

Table I summarizes the growth and reproductive characteristics of *C. gobio* in a range of habitats; the data are not complete, but evidence of dissimilar life-history tactics is apparent. Growth rates are least in the less productive (northern) streams and consequently most fish mature at two years old, compared with one year in the faster-growing fish of the very productive chalkstreams in southern England. In the south, sculpins become sexually mature at the end of their first year of life only if they are 4·5 cm or more in length (Mann, 1971). A trade-off appears to exist between growth and longevity, although the data are not as convincing as for *N. barbatulus* (see later). Few sculpins live for more than three years in chalkstreams, whereas fish up to ten years old have been found in some of the Pennine moorland streams in northern England. But the most striking difference between the two types of population is that, in the low productivity streams, spawning is highly synchronized over a two to three week period, usually in April, when each female lays one batch of eggs. In the highly productive chalkstreams, spawning may occur from February to May and during this period each female may lay up to four batches of eggs (Fox, 1978a,b).

What factors might induce such differences? Fatio (1882) found that altitude (hence water temperature) influenced the commencement of spawn-

TABLE I. Some life-history characteristics of the sculpin C. gobio in various habitats.

Habitat	Source	Ca^{2+} mg l^{-1}	Productivity (approx.)	Length (cm) at one year	Oldest fish aged (yr)	No. of egg batches ♀$^{-1}$ year^{-1}	Absolute fecundity 5·0 cm	7·5 cm
Willow Brook	Morris (1963, 1965)	180	high	5·9	3	3–4(?)	–	–
Bere Stream	Mann (1971)	94	high	4·9	3	3–4	327	739
Malham Tarn	Smyly (1957)	54	moderate	5·0	4	1	95	–
Kamienny Potok	Witkowski (1972)	46	moderate	–	5	–	–	–
R. Tees	Crisp et al. (1974)	18	low	3·7	8	1	86	229
Maize Beck	Crisp et al. (1974)	16	low	4·3	8	1	74	–
Trout Beck	Crisp et al. (1975)	7	low	4·4	10	1	129	–
Windermere	Smyly (1957)	6	low	4·5	5	1	63	–
R. Brathay	Smyly (1957)	5	low	3·6	5	1	–	–
Afon Llafar	Morris (1963, 1965)	4	low	3·9	4	1(?)	–	–

ing of *C. gobio* in Switzerland. Close to sea level, spawning occurred in February but, with increasing altitude, this was delayed so that in streams and lakes at altitudes over 600 m, it took place in May or June. Unfortunately there is no mention of any change from single-batch to multiple spawning (or vice-versa).

Water temperature and food availability have been suggested as major influences in the more complex situation which exists in Windermere, a lake in northern England, and in the River Brathay, one of its main supply streams (Smyly, 1957). No somatic growth occurs in the river population between October and April, but in the lake the period of growth cessation is confined to January and February. Despite their longer growing season, the lake sculpins grow only slightly faster than those in the river. However, they lay more (Fig. 1) and larger eggs, they spawn a single batch, marginally earlier in the year, and 49% are sexually mature at 11 months old compared with 6% in the river.

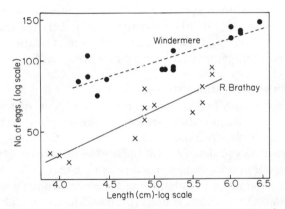

Fig. 1.   Relationships between length and fecundity (log:log scale) of *Cottus gobio* in Windermere and the River Brathay, based on data given by Smyly (1957).

Crisp *et al.* (in press) describe changes in a *C. gobio* population in the River Tees, northern England following the construction of a regulating reservoir at Cow Green. After construction of the dam there was a substantial reduction downstream in the diel water temperature changes, and delays in the autumn cooling and spring warming of the water. The very high (winter) and low (summer) water flows ceased; in particular there were no more sudden spates, which were characteristic of the pre-impoundment flow regime. Comparison with a *C. gobio* population in Maize Beck, an unregulated tributary downstream of the dam, showed that river regulation had not noticeably affected growth but that the fecundity of individual females and the mean age at first sexual maturity had been reduced. Under the more stable flow conditions more O group sculpins survived and, eventually, there were more adults per unit area of river; consequently population fecundity (number of eggs laid per square metre) increased even though there had been a decrease in the fecundity:length relationship for individual sculpins.

B. The stone loach *Noemacheilus barbatulus* (L.), Cobitidae

The stone loach has very similar habitat requirements to *C. gobio*, although it is absent from some of the more extreme and northerly habitats occupied by *C. gobio*, and it is more tolerant of mud and sand substrates. Welton *et al.* (in press) give an account of interactions between the two species in a chalkstream habitat.

The maximum recorded age in any fish population may be influenced by the length of the study period and the number of fish examined. In the case of the stone loach, in studies in which substantial numbers of fish have been aged (using otoliths), maximum ages range from three years to six years (Table II). There is a significant ($P<0.05$) inverse relationship between these values and the mean length at one year old (Fig. 2a), and a direct relationship ($P<0.01$) between the percentage of sexually mature loach at one year old and their mean length (Fig. 2b).

In most of the populations studied, *N. barbatulus* is a multiple spawner, each female depositing two or more groups of eggs in one season. Smyly (1955) noted that its breeding season in the English Lake District is protracted. In a Czechoslovakian river population, Libosvarsky (1957) found several size-frequency peaks of eggs at the start of the spawning period, with a progressive loss of intermediate peaks through the season. We have obtained similar results from loach populations in the River Frome, a southern chalk river, in Malham Tarn which is a small upland limestone lake in northern England, and in the River Leet, Scotland. Examples of the size-distribution of eggs in these habitats are shown in Fig. 3. Also included are data from a stone loach population in Lake Konevesi, central Finland (latitude 62°30′N). Our preliminary examination of ovaries collected in May 1982, shortly after the ice cover had melted, has revealed that most fish contain only one major peak of mature eggs (Fig. 3). Further, these eggs are considerably larger (mean 1·08 mm; Sterba, 1947) than the largest found in the multiple spawners (mean *ca.* 0·75 mm). The results from Lake Konnevesi support the observations by Sauvonsaari (1971) that *N. barbatulus* in two other Finnish lakes (Table II) did not spawn until they were two or three years old, and that spawning activity only lasted for a few days in late May or early June, the precise time being dependent on water temperature (spawning commences when the shore water warms to about 8°C).

TABLE II. Some life-history characteristics of the stone loach *N. barbatulus* in various habitats.

Habitat	Source	Ca^{2+} mg l^{-1}	No. of fish aged	Length (cm) at one year	Oldest fish aged (yr)	% mature at one year	Eggs g^{-1} 7·5 cm loach
Willow Brook	Morris (1963, 1965)	180	323	6·5	?	100	—
R. Frome	this paper	87	547	6·5	?	88	532 ($\geq$0·56 mm), 2766 ($\geq$0·24 mm)
R. Sirhowy	Williams and Harcup (1974)	61[a]	97	3·9[b]	4	0	211 (mature eggs)
Esthwaite	Smyly (1955)	6	219	5·7	3	20–25	—
Black Brows Beck	Smyly (1955)	6	405	5·5	5	20–25	—
Docken's Water	Mann (1971)	5	51	5·3	5	0	—
Afon Llafar	Morris (1963, 1965)	4	1180	4·5	4	7	—
Rivers in Czechoslovakia	Libosvarsky (1957)	—	—	5·5	5	>50	1895 (>0·2 mm)
R. Paimionjoki	Kännö (1969)	—	168	4·9	5	—	—
L. Päijänne	Sauvonsaari (1971)	—	449	4·6	6	0	533 (mature eggs)
L. Päilkänevesi	Sauvonsaari (1971)	—	169	4·6	5	0	533 (mature eggs)

[a] Polluted river, [b] September.

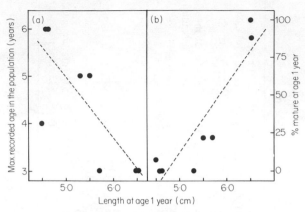

Fig. 2.   Relationships between (a) length at one year old and maximum recorded age, (b) length and % maturity at one year old for populations of *Noemacheilus barbatulus*.

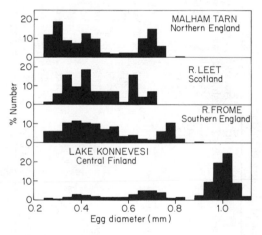

Fig. 3.   Characteristic size-frequency histograms for unshed, ripe eggs of *Noemacheilus barbatulus* from four different habitats. The length, weight, gonad weight and date of capture are given for each specimen sampled. *Malham Tarn;* 10·6 cm, 9·29 g, 1·13 g (22.10.81): *River Leet;* 10·0 cm, 14·40 g, 2·80 g (26.5.81): *River Frome;* 9·0 cm, 8·44 g, 1·92 g (10.5.82): *Lake Konnevesi;* 10·7 cm, 10·27 g, 2·57 g (20.5.82).

The trends that arise in the data parallel those for *C. gobio*; in productive, high conductivity waters stone loach grow rapidly, mature early and are short-lived but in unproductive waters the converse is true (Table II). Although, in Great Britain, streams with low productivity are found in the north where the climate is colder, low productivity streams also occur in the south. Comparison between *N. barbatulus* in such a stream with those in a chalkstream only 50 km away (Table II) shows that reproductive strategies can differ between populations which are relatively close together.

C. The gudgeon *Gobio gobio* (L.), Cyprinidae

The most southerly population of *G. gobio* recorded is in the River Jarama, central Spain (latitude 40°N) where it was introduced earlier this century (Dr J. Lobon-Cervia, pers. comm.). The populations in southern Finland (latitude 64°N) are probably the most northerly (A. Eloranta, pers. comm.). Details of life-history characteristics are given by Bernet (1960), Kennedy and Fitzmaurice (1972) and Mann (1980). These are set out in Table III, together with our own results and those from other publications.

In all populations, growth during the first year of life is small and, as a result, no sexually mature gudgeon younger than two years old have been recorded. The small size at one year old is probably associated with the relatively late spawning season. Reproductive activity is usually at a peak in May or June, but may be as late as August in Spain (Dr J. Lobon-Cervia, pers. comm.). In the River Nivelle, France, Bernet (1960) recorded spawning in September although peak activity was in June. No evidence of single-batch spawning was found in any of the populations studied.

We collected *G. gobio* from the River Don, near Aberdeen, Scotland where it was introduced some 50 or 60 years ago (Dr M. Young, pers. comm.). The growth and reproductive characteristics of this population were compared with an endemic population in the River Frome, a chalkstream in southern England (Mann, 1980). Although both sets of females were multiple spawners, the gonadosomatic index (GSI) in the River Don was less than that of the Frome gudgeon, at least up to a fish length of 13 cm (Fig. 4). This suggests that the reproductive output of female *G. gobio* is lower in the Don than in the Frome. However, GSI is only an approximate measure of reproductive effort (Calow, 1978) and the relative GSI values would change if different numbers of egg batches were laid by females in each population. At present we have no information on this point. Mann (1980) showed that Frome gudgeon are extremely variable in their annual recruitment, and the Don population has a similar characteristic (Table IV).

III. RECIPROCAL TRANSFER OF *COTTUS GOBIO* BETWEEN TWO CONTRASTING STREAM HABITATS

The observations made on sculpin populations in streams in the north and south of England (Section II.A) led to the obvious question, "Do the different reproductive strategies in this species arise from genetic (ultimate) differences

TABLE III. Some life-history characteristics of the gudgeon *G. gobio* in various habitats.

Habitat	Source	Productivity (approx.)	Length (cm) at		Oldest fish aged (yr)	Age at first maturity (yr)	Eggs g^{-1} age 3 yr
			one year	two years			
R. Frome	Mann (1980)	high	4·2	9·5	5	2	482
R. Jarama	Lobon-Cervia (pers. comm.)	high	3·4	6·0	4	2	426
R. Thames	Mann (1965), Mathews (1971)	high	(5·5)[a]	(8·6)[a]	8	3	332
R. Dunajec	Skora and Wlodek (1969)	moderate	–	7·3	7	2	205
R. Nivelle	Bernet (1969)	moderate	3·7	6·0	5	2	150
R. Allow	Kennedy and Fitzmaurice (1972)	low	3·3	7·4	7	2	–

[a]Converted from mean weights (Mann 1965) using length:weight relationships for R. Frome gudgeon.

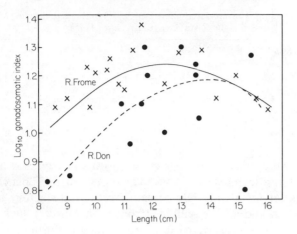

Fig. 4.   Relationship between the gonadosomatic index and fish length in samples of ripe female *Gobio gobio* in the River Frome, Dorset (X) and the River Don, Scotland (●).

TABLE IV.   The age-frequency distribution of *Gobio gobio* in the River Frome, Dorset and the River Don, Scotland.

Age (yr)	1	2	% No. of fish 3	4	5	6	No. of fish*
R. Frome (1975–76)	28·0	30·0	39·2	2·8	—	—	254
R. Don (June 1981)	17·0	10·6	4·3	31·9	29·7	3·9	47

or from environmental (proximate) influences?" An experiment, based upon the reciprocal transfer of one year old *C. gobio* between a northern and a southern stream, was designed. Fish were transferred in May 1979 and observations were made during the following twelve months on their growth and reproduction.

The sources of material were the Bere Stream, a chalkstream in Dorset (Mann, 1971) and Scur Beck, a low conductivity stream in Co. Durham approximately 440 km to the north. Table V gives the monthly mean temperatures from Bere Stream (Mann, 1971) and from the River Tees (Crisp *et al.*, 1975) of which Scur Beck is a tributary. Sculpins from both streams were stocked in separate artificial channels (10 m × 0·6 m) in a disused water-cress bed at Waterston, Dorset (Fox, 1978a,b). The northern site was a disused fish ladder at Hury Reservoir, only a few kilometres from Scur Beck. Here, wire mesh (0·65 mm) cages (1·2 m × 1·2 m × 0·6 m) were placed in the steps of the

TABLE V.   The monthly mean water temperatures (C) in the Bere Stream (Mann, 1971) and the River Tees (Crisp et al., 1975).

Month	J	F	M	A	M	J	J	A	S	O	N	D
Bere Stream	9·4	8·4	9·8	11·1	12·6	14·9	15·9	14·7	13·5	11·8	9·6	9·0
River Tees	1·5	0·9	1·6	4·7	9·3	12·0	13·7	13·6	10·9	8·0	2·8	2·0

ladder and were lined with stones from the nearby stream. At both experimental sites sculpins were stocked at about 5 m^{-2} (32 per channel, 8 per cage). Cages set up in the Bere Stream were unsatisfactory because they accumulated silt and all the sculpins (from both sources) died.

The channels and cages were examined frequently during the spring 1980; eggs were removed, counted and weighed and, at the end of May 1980 when no more eggs were being laid, the surviving C. gobio were measured, weighed and their sex determined by internal examination. No females were found with unspawned eggs. Summaries of growth and reproduction of sculpins from different sources kept at different sites are summarized in Tables VI and VII.

TABLE VI.   The survival, growth in length (cm) and instantaneous growth rates (May–May) of Cottus gobio stocked in artificial channels (area 6·0 m^2) and cages (area 1·44 m^2) at Waterston, Dorset and Hury Reservoir, Co. Durham, respectively.

Source of C. gobio	Scur Beck		Bere Stream	
	No. of fish	Mean length (cm)	No. of fish	Mean length (cm)
Waterston	2 channels		2 channels	
1979 25 May	64	3·88	64	4·87
9 Aug	13	5·71	40	6·19
1980 31 Jan	7	7·94	49	7·60
30 May	7	8·07	33	7·66
Inst. growth rate (length)		0·73		0·45
Hury	2 cages		3 cages	
1979 23 May	16	4·26	24	4·93
14 Aug	15	6·69	22	5·80
1980 4 March	4	6·25	14	6·26
27 May	6	6·43	10	6·95
Inst. growth rate (length)		0·41		0·34

TABLE VII. The reproduction of *Cottus gobio* in artificial channels (Waterston) and cages (Hury reservoir).

Source of *C. gobio*	Scur Beck	Bere Stream	Scur Beck	Bere Stream
Experimental site		Waterston		Hury
No. of ♀ *C. gobio*	5	19	0	8
Spawning period	26iii–23v	11iii–23v	–	18iv–27v
No. eggs ♀$^{-1}$	712	1110	–	91
No. batches ♀$^{-1}$	2·60	3·42	–	0·75
No. eggs batch^{-1}	297	357	–	121
No. eggs g^{-1} total weight	126	192	–	33
Mean dry weight per egg (g)	0·0013	0·0014	–	–

The Waterston channels supported a thick growth of water cress (*Rorippa*) in mid-summer which prevented all the sculpins being found during the August sampling. All the overwinter survivors of Scur Beck fish at Hury were males, but field data showed that female sculpins in Scur Beck itself were single-batch spawners.

The data in Table VII show that transferred *C. gobio* adopted the reproductive characteristics of the local population, but that the switch was not always complete. Scur Beck fish transferred to southern England laid, on average, fewer batches of eggs than the local, Bere Stream fish: mean number 2·60 compared with 3·42. In contrast their somatic growth (Table VI) was greater, although this may merely reflect their lower population density (Table VI). Fox (1978a) using the same Waterston channels, stocked with local *C. gobio*, found a strong correlation between population density and number of egg batches laid by each female. At a density of 5 m^{-2} each female laid three batches, at 80 m^{-2} only one batch was laid per female and at 500 m^{-2} no eggs were laid.

IV. DISCUSSION

In 1930, R. A. Fisher stated that a knowledge of the physiological processes which control the allocation of energy reserves to the gonads and the rest of the body would be most instructive, as also would an understanding of the life-history and environment circumstances which favour a larger (or smaller) share of the available resources going towards reproduction. During the last 50 years there have been many theoretical discussions on these problems, but there have been few successful attempts to demonstrate causal relationships — especially with regard to fishes. Even so, some broad principles have become generally accepted and in this discussion we examine these ideas, particularly in relation to the three European fishes described earlier.

Life-history characteristics can be considered as adaptive because the fitness of an individual organism depends strongly on such traits as fecundity, age at first sexual maturity and longevity. However, as Dobzhansky (1956) has emphasized, natural selection does not act on each life-history trait in isolation, but rather on the combined traits of the whole genotype (Stearns and Crandall, Chap. 2, this volume). Thus the modification of a particular trait, which might potentially improve the fitness of the organism, may only occur at the cost of an opposing decrease in fitness through changes in another trait. An example of this type of trade-off is seen in the sculpin *C. gobio* in which the benefits of multiple spawning (large numbers of offspring now) are balanced against an associated decrease in longevity (fewer offspring in the future). The optimal compromise between such conflicting traits varies in accordance with the prevailing environmental conditions. Calow (1979) could find no convincing evidence of such a trade-off (negative correlation) between life-span and reproductive output. Indeed, despite the very strong circumstantial evidence, a causal relationship is difficult to establish.

Thoday (1953) suggested that in heterogenous or relatively unstable environments, successful species are those selected for phenotypic flexibility, especially if they have a long period of reproductive life. In extremely stable habitats, neither genetic nor phenotypic plasticity are selected; instead species become closely adapted to their environment and often exhibit extremes of specialization. An ichthyological example is the development of mouth-brooding via nest-guarding among the Cichlidae in African lakes, which has enabled these species to dispense with spawning migrations into the various supply streams and rivers on which other groups (e.g. Cyprinidae) depend (Fryer and Iles, 1972; McKaye, Chap. 14, this volume). Such stability and specialization is unknown in Europe where geological history has been extremely varied, with marked variations in mean temperature and periodic Ice Ages.

In the range of life-history tactics of *C. gobio*, *N. barbatulus* and *G. gobio* there appears to be a general trend from single spawning, delayed maturity and prolonged generation times in low productivity streams to multiple spawning and a short period of reproductive life in high productivity streams. The major differences between these two types of habitat are that the low productivity streams are generally colder (most of them are in the north of England), and they are more subject to extremes of discharge than are the spring-fed southern chalkstreams. Thus there are compromises between rapid ageing on the one hand and the combination of fast growth and high reproductive output on the other. Such trade-offs could explain most, perhaps all, of the geographic variations described for these three species without invoking a genetic explanation. The data from the sculpin transfer experiment certainly supports the thesis of a strong environmental influence upon life-history tactics.

It is clear that the data are not in accordance with the predictions of *r* and K theory. Although the theory has been useful in providing the stimulus for much discussion, it is inflexible and an alternative must be sought. Stearns (1982) proposed the use of age-specific models that incorporate the costs of reproduction (Ware, Chap. 19, this volume). Although current electrophoretic studies are revealing differences in allele frequencies between neighbouring fish populations due to drift or selection, our tentative conclusion is that genetically determined differences in life-history tactics are overshadowed by the effects of productivity and temperature. Clearly there is a great need for more experimental studies on causal relationships, and for more precise methods of assessing reproductive effort.

ACKNOWLEDGEMENTS

The authors are most grateful to Dr J. Lobon-Cervia for information on gudgeon in the Jarama River, Spain, to Dr A. Witkowski for chemical data on Kamienny Potok, Poland and to Dr M. Young and Dr D. H. Mills for assistance in obtaining samples of gudgeon and stone loach from Scotland.

REFERENCES

Bagenal, T. B. (1966). *J. mar. biol. Ass. U.K.* **46**, 161–186.
Bernet, B. (1960). *Annls Stn. Cent. Hydrobiol. appl.* **8**, 127–180.
Blaxter, J. H. S. (1958). *Rapp. P.-v. Reun. Cons. perm. int. Explor. Mer* **143**, 10–19.
Calow, P. (1978). "Life Cycles, an Evolutionary Approach to the Physiology of Reproduction, Development and Ageing", pp. 164. Chapman and Hall, London.
Calow, P. (1979). *Biol. Rev.* **54**, 23–40.
Crisp. D. T., Mann, R. H. K. and McCormack, Jean C. (1974). *J. Appl. Ecol.* **11**, 969–996.
Crisp, D. T., Mann, R. H. K. and McCormack, Jean C. (1975). *J. Fish Biol.* **7**, 573–593.
Crisp, D. T., Mann, R. H. K. and Cubby, P. R. *J. Appl. Ecol* (in press).
Dobzhansky, Th. (1956). *Am. Nat.* **90**, 337–347.
Fatio, V. (1882). "Faunes des Vertebres de la Suisse 4, Poissons 1" Geneve et Bale.
Fisher, R. A. (1930). "The Genetical Theory of Natural Selection", 2nd ed., 1958. Dover, New York.
Fox, P. J. (1978a). "The population dynamics of the bullhead (*Cottus gobio* L., Pisces) with special reference to spawning, mortality of young fish and homeostatic mechanisms". Ph.D. Thesis, University of Reading.
Fox, P. J. (1978b). *J. Fish Biol.* **12**, 5–11.
Fryer, G. and Iles, T. D. (1972). "The Cichlid Fishes of the Great Lakes of Africa". Oliver and Boyd, Edinburgh.
Kanno, S. (1969). *Ann. Zool. Fennici* **6**, 87–93.
Kennedy, M. and Fitzmaurice, P. (1972). *J. Fish Biol.* **4**, 425–440.
Koli, L. (1969). *Ann. Zool. Fennici* **6**, 353–390.
Libosvarsky, J. (1957). *Zool. listy* **6**, 367–386.
MacArthur, R. H. and Wilson, E. O. (1967). "Theory of Island Biogeography". Princeton University Press, Princeton.

Mann, K. H. (1965). *J. Anim. Ecol.* **34**, 253–275.
Mann, R. H. K. (1971). *J. Anim. Ecol.* **40**, 155–190.
Mann, R. H. K. (1980). *J. Fish Biol.* **17**, 163–176.
Mann, R. H. K. and Mills, C. A. (1979). *In* "Fish Phenology: Anabolic Adaptiveness in Teleosts" (P. J. Miller, ed.), pp. 161–177. Academic Press, London.
Mathews, C. P. (1971). *J. Fish Biol.* **3**, 157–180.
Mayr, E. (1963). "Animal Species and Evolution". Oxford University Press, London.
Morris, D. (1954). *Behaviour* **7**, 1–32.
Morris, V. (1963). *Proc. 1st Brit. Coarse Fish Conf., Liverpool* 8–16.
Morris, V. (1965). "A comparison of the biology of minnow, loach and bullhead from hard and soft waters". Ph.D. Thesis, University of Liverpool.
Sauvonsaari, J. (1971). *Ann. Zool. Fennici* **8**, 187–193.
Schaffer, W. M. and Elson, P. F. (1975). *Ecology* **56**, 577–590.
Skora, S. and Wlodek, J. M. (1969). *Vest. csl. Spol. zool.* **33**, 351–368.
Smyly, W. J. P. (1955). *J. Anim. Ecol.* **24**, 167–186.
Smyly, W. J. P. (1957). *Proc. zool. Soc. Lond.* **128**, 431–453.
Stearns, S. C. (1982). *Env. Biol. Fish.* **7**, 187–191.
Sterba, G. (1947). *Z. mikrokosk.-anat. Forsch.* **63**, 581–588.
Thoday, J. M. (1953). *Symp. Soc. exp. Biol.* **7**, 96–113.
Welton, J. S., Mills, C. A. and Rendle, E. L. (1983). *Arch. Hydrobiol.* **97**, 434–454.
Williams, R. and Harcup, M. F. (1974). *J. Fish Biol.* **6**, 395–414.
Witkowski, A. (1972). *Pol. Arch. Hydrobiol.* **19**, 403–419.

11. The Role of Environmental Factors in the Timing of Reproductive Cycles

VICTOR J. BYE

Fisheries Laboratory, Ministry of Agriculture, Fisheries and Food, Lowestoft U.K.

Abstract: The majority of fish outside the tropics shows seasonal reproductive cycles with young produced when environmental conditions are conducive to survival. Endogenous circannual reproductive cycles are probably universal and are synchronized with the seasons by response to environmental conditions. Light and temperature are the most common cues initiating or controlling the rate of sexual development but other environmental, physiological and behavioural conditions are important in the immediate prespawning and spawning periods. The factors operating as cues or controls may be different for each phase of the reproductive cycle.

The evidence for endogenous circannual reproductive rhythms in fish and the influence of the environment on sexual cycles is reviewed with particular reference to salmonids, cyprinids, gasterosteids and marine flatfish.

Environmental and genetic methods for the artificial modification of seasonal sexual development are discussed.

I. INTRODUCTION

The majority of fish species exhibit an annual cycle of reproductive development which is maintained for as long as the animal is reproductively competent (Breder and Rosen, 1966; Woodhead, 1979). A few species, such as sturgeons (Nikolsky, 1963) and dolly varden (*Salvelinus malma*) (Armstrong and Morrow, 1980) reproduce at two to three year intervals while others, including Pacific salmon and many small fish (Miller, 1979) spawn only once in their lifetime.

Many tropical fish, in fresh waters and the sea, have extended spawning seasons with different individuals breeding at different times throughout the year. None the less there are still regularly recurring periods of intense spawning activity. Other species, including many around the equator, have predictable, restricted spawning periods (reviewed Lowe-McConnell, 1979).

FISH REPRODUCTION
ISBN: 0-12-563660-1

Even in the constant environment of the deep seas, where there is continuous darkness and no seasonal change in temperature, many fish species have well defined annual reproductive cycles (Mead *et al.*, 1964) which may be timed by seasonal variations in the availability of food (reviewed by Gordon, 1979). For fish inhabiting an environment with pronounced seasonal climatic variability the breeding season is almost invariably confined to a brief and specific period of the year. In temperate and polar species the timing of reproductive events can be precise. Cushing (1970) reviewed the extensive data (some covering over 70 years) on peak spawning times of Southern Bight plaice, Norwegian herring, Vestfjord cod and Fraser River salmon and showed that there was virtually no change in the mean date of peak spawning and the standard deviation about this date was no more than seven days. He proposed that, in an environment where the variability in the timing of the annual production cycle results from a combination of factors, a fixed spawning time on the same ground each year is most likely to ensure a match between larvae and food. In the anticyclones of the subtropics and tropics the production cycle is continuous and relatively constant so precisely timed spawning is not as important and breeding occurs throughout much of the year (Cushing, 1975).

A. Environmental timing

For each species or stock occupying a particular niche the timing of annual spawning has evolved to ensure that the young hatch and commence feeding at the season most conducive to their survival. There will be strong selection pressure on accurate reproductive control, for should individuals breed at any time of the year other than the ideal they will pass on few, if any, genes to the next generation. As Scott (1979) has pointed out this thesis is undoubtedly an oversimplification since the relationship between endogenous and exogenous rhythms is subtle and "the timing of a species' reproductive cycle is certainly a compromise involving many environmental considerations".

Although the spawning period in seasonal breeders is relatively brief, varying from one to two days in salmonids up to eight weeks in many highly fecund marine species, the annual cycle of gametogenesis is much more extended. Frequently it needs to start well in advance of the spawning season, usually when environmental conditions are entirely inappropriate for survival of the young. Although prevailing conditions of temperature, light, nutrients and hence food availability ultimately determine the survival of the young the cues which initiate gonadal development must anticipate the season suitable for spawning as much as eight months in advance (Scott *et al.*, 1983). The cues which coordinate reproductive and environmental cycles are obviously those which are most reliable as calendars and most appropriate to the animal in its own niche. Daylength, temperature and food availability predominate in temperate and polar regions but with the exception of the latter these are of limited value in the tropics. In environments where primary productivity and spawning are not inhibited by temperature and light, it is probable that seasonality is imposed by nutrient deficiencies in the food web, direct climatic effects on fish larvae (turbulence, salinity etc.), or biotic pressures such as competition for spawning sites, living space or food (McKaye, Chap. 14, this volume). In these conditions the later phases of gametogenesis may be initiated or synchronized by environmental changes such as monsoons, flooding, salinity change or upwelling in the sea and in freshwaters. The rapid increase in nutrient levels associated with such events is followed by a burst of productivity and increased food availability. Even in tropical conditions there is a finite time required for full gametogenesis and in order to permit the young to take full advantage of the abundant food it is necessary for gametogenesis to commence before the environmental changes. It has not yet been established whether the subtle climatic variations in pressure, temperature and wind which precede monsoons and upwelling conditions are perceived by the fish, or if an endogenous rhythm takes them to the final stage of maturity which is then maintained until spawning is triggered by sudden environmental fluctuation (Schwassmann, 1971, 1978).

Dry, cold and calm conditions or lunar cycles have also been shown to impose a reproductive seasonality on some tropical species (Lowe-McConnell, 1979). Even in an aseasonal environment where climate and food do not restrict breeding there are advantages to annual reproduction. Synchronized spawning with spatial aggregation ensures that the sexes mature simultaneously and maintain a wide genetic mix in the population.

In the exceptionally stable environment characterized by the tropical coral reef the availability of living and spawning space is the main limitation on population size. Since vacancies arise by random mortality there is an overriding selection pressure for extended spawning and individual fish produce young throughout the year. Lowe-McConnell (1979) has argued that communities in aseasonal environments are stable but fragile, whereas communities in which the species show seasonal sexual rhythms may have extreme fluctuations yet are ultimately resilient.

II. ENDOGENOUS CONTROL

From this brief introduction and the cited reviews it is apparent that fish have adopted a considerable variety of tactics to guarantee accurate timing of their sexual cycles and hence ensure reproductive success. Common to all seasonal breeders is the possession of an internal clock indicating when the reproductive season is imminent (Follett and Follett, 1981).

A. Seasonal cycles in constant conditions

Endogenous control of reproductive development ensures that even under constant environmental conditions an animal will exhibit an approximately annual rhythm of gonadal maturation. Normally this cycle is synchronized with seasonal changes in the environment by the response of the animal to a variety of cues. Although it is probably impossible to entirely exclude environmental influences (Palmer, 1976) there are strong indications of internally driven circannual reproductive cycles in higher vertebrates (Follett and Follett, 1981). The evidence for endogenous control of fish reproduction is limited but it is probable that in a great many, if not most, species an endogenous cycle is the foundation of the annual rhythm of sexual maturation. There is reliable evidence for such cycles in only a few species where fish were maintained for at least 12 months in a constant environment but still matured at approximately the same time as the controls maintained under natural conditions. The most comprehensive study was that conducted for three years on female catfish *Heteropneustes fossilis* (Sundararaj et al., 1973; Sundararaj and Vasal, 1976). The annual cycle of changing ovarian weight persisted for three years when the fish were maintained in a constant temperature ($25 \pm 1°C$) and either continuous light or continuous darkness. The amplitude of the cycle was slightly reduced and it was just out of phase with the controls indicating a free-running circannual endogenous cycle with a duration not exactly equal to 12 months.

Brook trout, *Salvelinus fontinalis*, were reared for three years from the age of five months at constant $8·3°C$ and in continuous light, continuous darkness or simulated natural photoperiod (Pyle, 1969; Poston and Livingston, 1971). The fish matured for the first time at two years of age when spawning of the females in the three environments was virtually simultaneous while the males in continuous light spermiated eight weeks earlier than the other two groups.

At second maturation the females in simulated natural photoperiods spawned at the same time as fish in natural conditions. The fish under continuous illumination commenced spawning four weeks later and those in constant darkness eight weeks later. The males in continuous illumination spermiated 14 weeks earlier than the simulated light controls and those in constant darkness six weeks later. The duration of spermiation was shorter (81 days) in 24L:0D than in simulated photoperiod controls (131 days) or 0L:24D (145 days). The consequence was that at the second maturation in continuous light the production of gametes by the two sexes did not overlap.

These results indicate the existence of an endogenous reproductive rhythm and suggest that it is of different duration in males and females. In experiments of this type it is probably impossible to establish a neutral photoperiodic influence on the two sexes. Maturation may have been better synchronized if a continuous 12L:12D illumination had been used. The correct experimental procedure for investigating endogenous cycles has yet to be established (see Baggerman, 1980).

Htun Han (1975) kept a temperate marine flatfish, the dab (*Limanda limanda*), at constant temperature ($11 \pm 1°C$) and in a variety of photoperiods for at least 18 months. The females in constant 12L:12D and in a simulated natural light cycle showed a sequence of changing gonad weight and oogenesis which was similar to that of fish taken from the sea.

In a similar way female rainbow trout (*Salmo gairdnerii*) were reared only for a year at constant temperature (9°C) and on constant 12L:12D. They matured and spawned at the same time as the controls, and oestradiol and vitellogenin cycles in the two groups were also synchronized (Whitehead *et al.*, 1978).

It seems probable that these species, at least, are able to maintain a seasonal cycle of sexual maturation with a period of approximately one year without initiation or synchronization by external stimuli.

An observation, which may be related to the endogenous cycle, is that fish maintained in constant long photoperiods (18L:6D) for a year or more mature at approximately six monthly intervals. This has been recorded in brook trout (Henderson, 1963), the dab (Htun Han, 1975), the stickleback (Baggerman, 1980) and the rainbow trout (Scott and Sumpter, 1983) (Fig. 1) and cannot be explained by current hypotheses. It is possible that in these conditions two gametogenic cycles are running concurrently and out of phase.

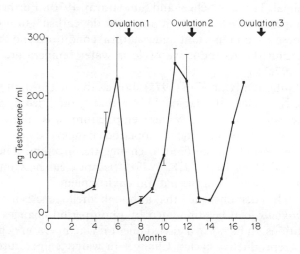

Fig. 1.   Ovulation frequency and plasma testosterone cycles in rainbow trout maintained in constant 18L:6D photoperiod. (Mean ± 2 s.e.m.). Scott and Sumpter (1983).

III. ENVIRONMENTAL CONTROL

A. Caveat

Accepting that in many fish there is an endogenous circannual rhythm providing the primary drive for the seasonal cycle of reproductive development it is clear that the environment still exerts a profound influence on the timing of the system. Although the evidence for environmental regulation of sexual maturation is extensive (see reviews of de Vlaming, 1972, 1974; Jalabert, 1976; Sundararaj and Vasal, 1976; Billard and Breton, 1978; Peter and Hontela, 1978; Peter and Crim, 1979; Scott, 1979; Baggerman, 1980; Crim, 1982) it must be interpreted with great caution. A considerable number of the studies have been poorly planned and inadequately controlled making it impossible to assess the relative importance of the endogenous and exogenous factors. In addition most research has examined the influence of a single environmental factor in isolation without taking account of possible synergistic or confounding effects or even of the physiological condition of the experimental animals and their previous environmental history. This is understandable since it facilitates the design and analysis of experiments but as Scott (1979) has emphasized this can give a false impression of the natural response of the animal although demonstrating its physiological potential. This difficulty is illustrated by research of the Asian catfish at the laboratory of Sundararaj over the past 12 years. The original experiments using constant temperature and varying photoperiod supported the thesis that the catfish reproductive cycle was primarily timed by photoperiodic responses (Sundararaj and Sehgal, 1970a,b; Sehgal and Sundararaj, 1970). Further work with changing temperatures showed that although the catfish can use photoperiodic cues, these are unimportant under natural conditions and that the main factor regulating the reproductive cycle is water temperature (Vasal and Sundararaj, 1976).

Similarly, although Htun Han (1975) showed that in constant temperature the reproductive cycle of the dab could be radically modified by photoperiod the response was lost if the water temperature was allowed to cycle (6·9–15·7°C) out of phase with the photoperiod changes (Scott et al., 1980). So although photoperiod can be used to change the breeding time of farmed flatfish (Bye and Htun Han, 1978, 1979) it is not clear how important the photoperiodic response is in the natural environment.

Scott (1979) has demonstrated that although vitellogenesis in the minnow, Phoxinus phoxinus, can be stimulated by photoperiod changes under controlled conditions, in its normal environment it is temperature change which synchronizes reproductive cycles. Changes in water temperature produce a behavioural response which places the minnow in photoperiodic conditions which stimulate reproductive development.

These studies indicate that laboratory experiments can demonstrate an influence of photoperiod on reproductive cycles which is out of proportion to the effect it has under natural conditions and should promote caution in the design and interpretation of experiments. It may also indicate that the overwhelming importance of photoperiod in the control of fish reproductive cycles may be more an experimental artifact than a biological reality (Scott, 1979).

Most of the investigations of environmental influences on reproductive events in fish have concentrated on fresh water and diadromous species from the Northern temperate zone. Since there are about 8000 fresh water species, 12 000 in the sea and 120 which regularly move between the two environments, and at least 70% of the species are tropical (Cohen, 1970) it is clearly premature to propose any unifying hypothesis. In addition there are many cases where species of a family or even different races of the same species occupy an extended geographical range and thus encounter very varied environmental conditions. In these circumstances the different stocks have evolved individual responses to those environmental conditions which are most suitable as controllers in their own habitat. For example different strains of rainbow trout vary in their reproductive response to the same photoperiodic stimuli (Busack and Gall, 1980; Scott et al., 1983).

B. Recommendation

Clearly what is required are comprehensive, multidisciplinary studies of a few "simple" fish which will allow an evaluation of the relative importance of endogenous and exogenous controls and provide the basis for some generalizations.

The economic importance of salmonids and cyprinids has made them the subjects of extensive research on reproduction and its control and this is likely to continue. Similarly the potential value of flatfish in mariculture will ensure a continuing research programme, although information on this group is limited at present. The suitability of minnows and sticklebacks as experimental animals and their sensitivity to environmental manipulations make them ideal fish for this research. Finally, the extensive data on the reproductive process and its environmental control in the Asian catfish requires its inclusion as a model for subtropical species.

The remainder of this review will summarize the present state of knowledge on the environmental timing of reproductive cycles in some of these "model" groups and point to practical applications.

C. Salmonids

Environmental influences on salmonid reproduction have been well reviewed (de Vlaming, 1974; Htun Han, 1977; Billard *et al.*, 1978; Billard and Breton, 1978, 1981; Poston, 1978; Dodd and Sumpter, 1983; Scott and Sumpter, 1983) and the consensus is that the predominant environmental cue is photoperiod.

The season of peak spawning varies considerably both between and within species. Brown and brook trout, Pacific and Atlantic salmon tend to spawn in late Autumn, *Coregonus* in January, and the original steelhead and Mount Shasta-McCloud River strains of rainbow trout in early spring. Arctic charr spawn from September to March in different geographical locations with an Icelandic variety breeding in July. However, the pressure from fish farmers to extend the natural spawning season has resulted in strains of rainbow trout which produce eggs in every month of the year (Buss, 1982; Bromage, 1982) and even a Japanese stock which spawns twice each year (Purdom, pers. comm.). The dramatic alteration in breeding season which has been achieved in less than a century mainly results from deliberate or unconscious selection. This is mostly undocumented but some data are available from North America (Millenbach, 1973; Busack and Gall, 1980) and records from the Nikko Trout Hatchery in Japan demonstrate a progressive advance in peak spawning time from late March in the 1910s to early December 50 years later (Kato, 1973).

Genetic modification requires relatively long-term programmes and considerable facilities if broodstocks spawning throughout the year are to be produced. The process is also uncertain. Progeny from August spawning rainbow trout broodstock spawned from July to at least November and autumn spawning trout restocked in the wild eventually reverted to spring spawning (Buss, 1982). In addition other salmonid species are, for a variety of reasons, less amenable to selection (Buss, 1980, 1982). Because of these difficulties environmental control of spawning time has been examined as an alternative to selection and photoperiod has been the preferred variable.

1. *Photoperiod.* The earliest recorded experiments by Hoover and Hubbard (1937) showed that subjecting brook trout to increasing day-length early in the year followed by rapidly decreasing day-length advanced spawning by three months in second time spawners. Similar compressed or enhanced cycles of changing daylength have accelerated maturation and advanced spawning time in brook trout (Hazard and Eddy, 1951; Corson, 1955; Nomura, 1962; Henderson, 1963), rainbow trout (Nomura, 1962; Goryczko, 1972; Kunesh *et al.*, 1974; Breton and Billard, 1977; Billard and Breton, 1977; Whitehead *et al.*, 1978, 1979, 1980; Buss, 1980; Eriksson and Lundqvist, 1980), coho salmon (MacQuarrie *et al.*, 1978) and pink salmon (MacQuarrie *et al.*, 1979).

A logical extension of the compressed cycle procedure was to eliminate the periods of gradually changing daylength and instead change abruptly between those photoperiods thought to be most stimulatory. This was tested in part by Breton and Billard (1977) with rainbow trout. The fish were transferred in

February directly to a 16 h daylength which was then gradually decreased to 8 h, eliciting a 3 month advance in maturation. In a series of studies Whitehead and colleagues (Whitehead et al., 1980; Bromage et al., 1982) showed that constant periods of long daylength and short daylength, with abrupt changes between, were as effective in advancing spawning of rainbow trout as were gradually changing photoperiods. However, maturation in precocious male Atlantic salmon from the Baltic is accelerated more effectively by gradually decreasing daylength than by a sudden change even if the decrease from 17 h to 7 h photoperiods is accomplished in ten steps at daily intervals (Eriksson and Lundqvist, 1980). This result indicates that photoperiod stimulation is a differential rather than a proportional effect (Aschoff, 1960) although whether this also applies to other species, strains or even females of the same strain is open to question. This aspect of photoperiodism requires further testing since the differential effect appears important in other aspects of salmonid physiology, including growth and smoltification (reviewed by Poston, 1978).

Delayed spawning has been achieved using photoperiod manipulations of a similar kind to those which successfully accelerate maturation and also by maintaining fish in continuous light or darkness. In these conditions spawning was delayed by one to two months in brook trout (Shiraishi and Fukuda, 1966; Poston and Livingston, 1971), rainbow trout (Shiraishi and Fukuda, 1966; Billard et al., 1978) and sockeye salmon (Combs et al., 1959; Shiraishi and Fukuda, 1966). It is not clear if continuous light or darkness provides information on photoperiod or merely allows expression of an endogenous reproductive rhythm. Photoperiod cycles extended from 12 to 15 or 18 months delayed spawning by 8–20 weeks in rainbow trout (Bromage, 1982) and in coho and pink salmon (MacQuarrie et al., 1978, 1979).

Constant short or long daylengths imposed at times when the natural photoperiod is the opposite induced spawning delays of up to 24 weeks in brook trout (Allison, 1951; Hazard and Eddy, 1951; Henderson, 1963; Shiraishi and Fukuda, 1966), rainbow trout (Shiraishi and Fukuda, 1966; Billard et al., 1978; Bromage, 1982; Bromage et al., 1982) and male Atlantic salmon (Eriksson and Lundqvist, 1980).

The coincidence of elevated sex steroids and recrudescing gonads with the decreasing photoperiods following the summer solstice, and the stimulatory effect of constant short days on gametogenesis led to the hypothesis that in natural conditions decreasing photoperiods trigger gonad maturation in salmonids (Whitehead et al., 1978; Billard et al., 1978). More sensitive indicators of the onset of gonad development, such as elevated plasma levels of gonadotrophin, sex steroids and vitellogenin, show that gametogenesis commences in the spring when daylength is increasing (reviewed by Scott et al., 1983). When considered together with the observations that spawning is delayed by short days applied and maintained before gametogenesis but advanced by long days imposed at the same time, it appears that an alternative interpretation is more valid. It seems probable that the increasing photoperiods following the winter solstice initiate gametogenesis and the shortening daylengths from midsummer promote the later stages of maturation. Response to a specific daylength cycle will vary throughout the year depending on the physiological condition of the animal (Scott *et al.*, 1983). No matter what photoperiod conditions are imposed they will not permanently prevent spawning; the endogenous cycle ensures that it occurs eventually, even if delayed by six months or more.

Additional variability in response may be introduced by sex, age, reproductive history and genetic strain (reviewed by Scott and Sumpter, 1983). For example autumn and winter spawning strains of rainbow trout commence gametogenesis at different times although subjected to the same conditions (Fig. 2) (Scott *et al.*, 1983). When exposed to continuous 18 h daylength from March, spawning of the autumn strain was delayed and that of the winter strain advanced (A. P. Scott, unpublished).

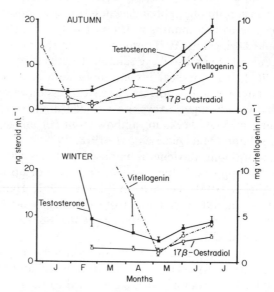

Fig. 2.   Steroid and vitellogenin cycles in autumn and winter spawning strains of rainbow trout maintained under identical conditions. (Mean ± 2 s.e.m.). Scott *et al.* (1983).

2. *Spectrum and intensity.*   There is little information on the spectral quality and intensity of illumination required to achieve photoperiodic modification of spawning time although both incandescent and fluorescent light sources have been used successfully. Royce (1951) reported that spawning in lake trout was advanced following a consistently cloudy summer, but since

temperature was also reduced it is not possible to directly implicate reduced light intensity.

3. *Temperature*. The influence of temperature on gametogenesis in salmonids appears insignificant as long as it remains within physiological limits although there have been few substantial investigations. Henderson (1963) reported that long days promoted gametogenesis in female brook trout at 16°C but not at 8°C, and higher temperatures enhanced the response to decreasing photoperiod in rainbow trout (Billard and Breton, 1977). Genetically similar broodstocks maintained under identical natural illumination spawned at different times when maintained in either constant or fluctuating water temperature (Buss, 1982).

Temperature may play a greater part in the final stages of maturation, ovulation and egg release. There are several reports of abnormally low water temperatures inhibiting ovulation in salmonids (see Goryczko, 1972). Evidence for the importance of other factors in spermiation, ovulation and oviposition is limited. Monosex populations of rainbow and brown trout become fully mature suggesting that pheromones and behavioural stimulation from the opposite sex are not essential for ovulation and spermiation. Oviposition by feral rainbow trout in Europe is rare (Frost, 1974) suggesting that an essential environmental trigger is missing.

D. Cyprinids

Sexual development and spawning in cyprinids is modulated both by temperature and photoperiod although temperature is the predominant influence in most species. Gametogenesis is initiated at different seasons in cyprinids (Billard and Breton, 1981). Carp spawn in spring and summer; the next gametogenic cycle commences immediately in the spent fish and may be completed as early as October. Development is then suspended until the environment is warm enough for final maturation and ovulation. In the tench, gametogenesis is not initiated until the spring and there is a long period of gonadal quiescence following summer spawning (Billard *et al.*, 1978). Elevated temperatures advance maturation and prolong spawning in the tench but ovarian development is blocked at temperatures below 10°C (Breton *et al.*, 1980a,b). High temperatures also enhance sexual maturation and promote the final stages of gametogenesis in goldfish (Gillet and Billard, 1981) and chub (Ahsan, 1966).

In some species low temperature appears to be important for stimulating early stages of gametogenesis (Ahsan, 1966; Gillet *et al.*, 1977a,b; Breton *et al.*, 1980b; Gillet and Billard, 1981) and since in many late spring and summer spawners gametogenesis is initiated during the winter this may be more important than has been realized.

Carp require warm water for reproduction and at 20–22°C there is virtually continuous gametogenesis with several waves of spermatogenesis in the males (Billard *et al.*, 1978). However, there is evidence that a seasonal rhythm of temperature is required to maintain a normal reproductive cycle in some cyprinids since constant temperatures inhibit spermatogenesis (de Vlaming, 1975; de Vlaming and Paquette, 1977; Gillet *et al.*, 1977a,b; Lofts *et al.*, 1968). Excessively high temperatures can inhibit ovulation and induce gonadal regression.

Photoperiodic influences in cyprinids are subtle tending to enhance or diminish responses which are more directly controlled by temperature. The increasing daylength following the winter solstice accelerates gonadal development in goldfish (Gillet and Billard, 1981). The stimulatory influence of daylength on sexual development in the lake chub is only detectable at low temperatures (Ahsan, 1966). Although in female carp several warm days are followed by a rapid rise in plasma gonadotrophin this does not inevitably lead to ovulation if the environment is not appropriate. Temperature and photoperiod interact with the endogenous reproductive cycle to ensure that the gonads are mature at the appropriate season but ovulation, spermiation and gamete release require other stimuli (Stacey, Chap. 12, this volume). A variety of environmental factors may facilitate or inhibit these climactic stages of the reproductive cycle. Physical and chemical properties of the water, including current velocity, pH, dissolved oxygen content and salinity have all been shown to exert an effect (reviewed by Billard *et al.*, 1981). Biological factors are also important. These may include population crowding under natural or farming conditions, stress induced by handling or pollution, and pheromones which may inhibit or enhance reproduction (Solomon, 1977; Billard *et al.*, 1981; Honda, 1982). The presence of appropriate vegetation or other suitable cover has been shown to be important in several species (Scott, 1979; Stacey *et al.*, 1979a).

The timing of gamete release can be controlled by circadian cycles of light or temperature or by interaction between the two rhythms (Stacey *et al.*, 1979a,b) or even by lunar cycles (see Gibson, 1978; Lowe-McConnell, 1979; Scott, 1979; Dodd and Sumpter, 1983).

E. Pleuronectiformes

Although flatfish have many advantages for mariculture there is little published information on environmental control of their reproductive cycles.

Pronounced changes in the time of spawning of dab, turbot and sole were achieved by photoperiod manipulation at constant temperatures (Htun Han, 1975, 1977; Bye and Htun Han, 1978, 1979). Even with a cycling temperature which was approximately in phase with the photoperiod rhythm an advance in spawning was achieved with the turbot, as well as with sea bass and sea bream

(Girin and Devauchelle, 1978). Temperature cycles which are out of phase with the photoperiod change may have prevented significant changes in the rate of gonad development in the dab (Scott *et al.*, 1980).

In all the species examined it was possible to advance spawning by subjecting the fish to an annual light cycle compressed to 6–10 months. Dab maintained on a six month cycle at constant $11 \pm 1°C$ spawned six months early although only a few fish were used (Htun Han, 1975). Alternating periods of long and short daylengths have been used to advance or delay spawning with specific conditions designed for the species under test. For turbot which spawn in June and July, eight weeks of short daylength immediately after spawning followed by continuous long days advanced spawning by several months. A similar system has also been effective with sole. With turbot when the long days which naturally occur at spawning were extended artificially for two months followed by an annual photoperiod cycle two months out of phase, spawning was two months later than normal (O'Connel, unpublished; Bye, unpublished). It appears that those Pleuronectiformes which spawn in late spring and summer have a reproductive cycle which is initiated by short winter days and accelerated by the increasing daylengths following the winter solstice. Evidence for the influence of daylength on winter spawning species is inadequate but it is likely that gametogenesis is initiated by long days and subsequent development promoted by short days. Spawning in the dab occurred at six month intervals in fish maintained continuously on alternating periods of 8L:4D, a phenomenon for which no convincing explanation has yet been offered (Htun Han, 1975).

In commercial farms and research establishments systems have been developed to ensure continuous egg production from four or five broodstocks with peak spawning at three month intervals. The most usual method is to advance spawning to the required time by one or more series of compressed photoperiod cycle and then maintain the broodstock on a 12 month cycle which is out of phase with the natural rhythm. However, our understanding of the environmental control of reproduction in this group of fish is poor and more research is needed.

F. Gasterosteids

Photoperiod appears to be the primary environmental condition synchronizing the endogenous reproductive cycle in this group. The studies of Baggerman on *Gasterosteus aculeatus* (reviewed by Baggerman, 1980) demonstrate a circannual gonadal cycle which is maintained in a constant, permissive environment for at least three cycles but which can be modified by photoperiod. Gasterosteids spawn in late spring and early summer, with gametogenesis starting the previous autumn. Spermatogenesis and the previtellogenic growth of oocytes takes place relatively independently of photoperiod and temperature, but fish kept under constant conditions of short photoperiod show no further sexual maturation. Long photoperiods can stimulate the development of full sexual maturity if imposed any time between autumn and late spring. In males, activity of the Leydig cells and androgen secretion is stimulated whilst in females vitellogenesis takes place. Short photoperiods become increasingly effective at inducing sexual maturation as the time of normal spawning approaches. The rate at which sexual maturation is achieved increases with temperature. The termination of summer spawning appears to be mainly under endogenous control since it occurs under constant conditions, but it is advanced by short days.

G. Other models

There is considerable information available on the endocrine and environmental control of reproduction in the minnow (Cyprinidae) (reviewed by Scott, 1979) and the Asian catfish (Saccobranchidae) (Sundararaj *et al.*, 1978). Both appear to be suitable experimental animals for the detailed, multidisciplinary studies, encompassing physiology, ecology and ethology, required to establish the manner in which fish normally time their reproductive cycles.

IV. PRACTICAL APPLICATIONS

The majority of fish species used in aquaculture are seasonal breeders with spawning confined to a brief, fixed period of the year. This places unwelcome constraints on fish farming practices (Bye and Htun Han, 1978, 1979) and considerable effort has been devoted to extending the spawning period of farmed fish. For example in rainbow trout farming in the U.K., 20% of the egg supplies are imported from the U.S.A. and Denmark, mainly to cover those periods of the year when there are no home produced eggs available (Scott, 1981).

   The time of spawning is genetically determined and as already described, the period of egg availability in rainbow trout has been extended by selection to cover ten months of the year (Busack and Gall, 1980). However this is a slow and expensive procedure and a variety of environmental manipulations, usually involving photoperiod, have been employed to achieve a quicker result. Nevertheless, in the long run genetic selection will be the most satisfactory method for extending the egg season since the broodstocks do not require controlled environments. These need to be carefully constructed and maintained (Buss, 1980) and are difficult to apply to species reared in extensive or cage culture conditions.

   Corson (1955), Girin and Devauchelle (1978), Bye and Htun Han (1978,

1979), Buss (1980, 1982), MacQuarrie *et al.* (1981) and Bromage (1982) have described current practices for photoperiod modification of spawning times in salmonids, sea bass, sea bream and flatfish. The most commonly used method is to advance spawning by subjecting the fish to an annual cycle of changing daylength compressed to a period ranging from six to ten months. This is then maintained to further advance spawning in each subsequent year or alternatively the fish are then reared in a simulated 12 month cycle of changing daylength which is out of phase with the natural cycle. Problems may be encountered if a too radical compression of the cycle is attempted since a parallel acceleration of maturation is not always achieved. For example in rainbow trout maintained on a six month cycle spawning is advanced only by three months so that for at least two months before spawning daylengths are increasing and not decreasing as they would do under natural conditions (Whitehead *et al.*, 1978). It is possible that there is a minimum period required for full ovarian development in fish which may be around five to seven months in salmonids and flatfish. This may be related to the considerable energy investment in the ovary which may ultimately comprise 25–35% of the total weight of the fish.

Recently, egg availability has been increased by delaying spawning, either by extending the seasonal daylength cycle to 15 or 18 months or by maintaining fish on constant short daylength (Bromage, 1982; W. O'Connell unpublished).

Commercial operators are also achieving out of season maturation by subjecting their broodstocks to alternating periods of constant long or short daylengths designed to advance or retard maturation. The change between long and short daylengths is abrupt but there are some indications that a gradual change over 10–20 days is more effective (Eriksson and Lundqvist, 1980; W. O'Connell unpublished). This aspect of photoperiod manipulation requires further investigation. Recent work has shown that in some strains of rainbow trout constant long daylengths induce spawning at six month intervals (A. P. Scott, unpublished). However, with fish under constant conditions effectively free running on an endogenous cycle there is a risk that spawning in the broodstock will become extended, making practical operations difficult. In addition maturation in males and females may be desynchronized so that there is no overlap in gamete availability. Therefore this approach must be attempted with caution.

It is recommended that photoperiod manipulated broodstock should be maintained in environments where the temperature is constant or has a limited range since if temperature and photoperiod cycles are out of phase gametogenesis may be inhibited. For species where temperature is the primary controller an appropriate cycle of temperature change must be achieved.

Although there have been suggestions that the quality and quantity of eggs is influenced by photoperiod manipulation the evidence is limited and other husbandry conditions are likely to exert a greater effect. Eggs from first time spawners are often of inferior quality and it is recommended that manipulation of female broodstock does not start until after their first spawning.

V. CONCLUSIONS

Although it is clear that most fish outside the tropics have seasonal cycles of reproduction which are controlled by an endogenous rhythm and synchronized with the environment by response to physical variables, far too few species have been examined in sufficient detail to allow generalization. Although photoperiod and temperature appear to be the predominant factors modulating all, but the final stages of reproduction, this may be a misinterpretation resulting from the fact that they are the most obvious and most easily controlled conditions in experimental investigations. As Scott (1979) has stressed, any recurring environmental variable within the sensory competence of the organism can act as a timing cue.

The relative importance of endogenous and environmental control is difficult to evaluate since most studies have examined only one factor and have changed it at a time or to an extent that would never occur under natural conditions. Although environmental changes can radically modify reproductive cycles under experimental conditions the extent to which they do under natural conditions remains to be established. Further detailed, multidisciplinary investigations on a few "model" species employing natural, interacting environmental changes are required to provide an answer.

Attempts have been made to use family groups as the basis for a classification of environmental influences but these are premature and in fact a classification related to environment and life style seems more valid. Obviously each species, strain or local stock has evolved a unique life cycle which utilizes as controllers those variables which are most appropriate to its own environment.

Nevertheless, even with our limited understanding, artificial environmental manipulations can be used to control reproduction in fish and these will increasingly be used for research and aquacultural purposes.

REFERENCES

Ahsan, S. N. (1966). *Can. J. Zool.* **44**, 161–171.
Allison, L. N. (1951). *Progve Fish Cult.* **13**, 111–116.
Armstrong, R. H. and Morrow, J. E. (1980). *In* "Charrs" (E. K. Balon, ed.), pp. 99–140. Dr W. Junk bv Publishers, The Hague.
Aschoff, J. (1960). *Cold Spring Harb. Symp. quant. Biol.* **25**, 11–28.

Baggerman, B. (1980). *In* "Environmental Physiology of Fishes" (M. A. Ali, ed.), pp. 533–567. Plenum Press, New York and London.

Billard, R. and Breton, B. (1977). *Cah. Lab. Montereau* **5**, 5–24.

Billard, R. and Breton, B. (1978). *In* "Rhythmic Activity of Fishes" (J. E. Thorpe, ed.), pp. 31–53. Academic Press, London and New York.

Billard, R. and Breton, B. (1981). *Cah. Lab. Montereau* **12**, 43–56.

Billard, R., Breton, B., Fostier, A., Jalabert, B. and Weil, C. (1978). *In* "Comparative Endocrinology" (P. J. Gaillard and H. H. Boer, eds), pp. 37–48. Elsevier/North-Holland Biomedical Press, Amsterdam.

Billard, R., Bry, C. and Gillet, C. (1981). *In* "Stress and Fish" (A. D. Pickering, ed.), pp. 185–208. Academic Press, London and New York.

Breder, C. M. and Rosen, D. E. (1966). "Modes of Reproduction in Fishes." Natural History Press, New York.

Breton, B. and Billard, R. (1977). *Ann. Biol. anim. Biochim. Biophys.* **17**, 331–340.

Breton, B., Horoszewicz, L., Billard, R. and Bieniarz, K. (1980a). *Reprod. Nutr. Develop.* **20**, 105–118.

Breton, B., Horoszewicz, L., Bieniarz, K. and Epler, P. (1980b). *Reprod. Nutr. Develop.* **20**, 1011–1024.

Bromage, N. R. (1982). *In* "Proc. Commercial trout farming Symp. IFM", pp. 165–172. Janssen, Chislehurst.

Bromage, N. R., Whitehead, C. and Elliot, J. (1982). *Gen. Comp. Endocr.* **46**, 391 (abstract).

Busack, C. A. and Gall, G. A. E. (1980). *Calif. Fish Game* **66**, 17–24.

Buss, K. W. (1980). *Aquaculture Magazine* **6**, 45–48.

Buss, K. W. (1982). *In* "Proc. Commercial trout farming Symp. IFM", pp. 116–126. Janssen, Chislehurst.

Bye, V. J. and Htun Han, M. (1978). *Fish Farmer* **1** (4), 10–11.

Bye, V. J. and Htun Han, M. (1979). *Fish Farmer* **2** (5), 27–28.

Cohen, D. M. (1970). *Proc. Calif. Acad. Sci.* **38**, 341–345.

Combs, B. D., Burrows, R. E. and Bigej, R. G. (1959). *Progve Fish. Cult.* **21**, 63–69.

Corson, B. W. (1955). *Progve Fish. Cult.* **17**, 99–102.

Crim, L. W. (1982). *Can. J. Fish. aquat. Sci.* **39**, 17–21.

Cushing, D. H. (1970). *J. Cons. int. Explor. Mer.* **33**, 81–97.

Cushing, D. H. (1975). "Marine Ecology and Fisheries." Cambridge University Press, Cambridge.

de Vlaming, V. L. (1972). *J. Fish Biol.* **4**, 131–140.

de Vlaming, V. L. (1974). *In* "Control of Sex in Fishes" (C. B. Schreck, ed.), pp. 13–83. Virginia Polytechnic Institute and State University, Blacksburg, Virginia.

de Vlaming, V. L. (1975). *Biol. Bull.*, Woods Hole **148**, 402–415.

de Vlaming, V. L. and Paquette, G. (1977). *Copeia* **1977**, 793–797.

Dodd, J. M. and Sumpter, J. P. (1983). *In* "Marshall's Physiology of Reproduction" (G. E. Lamming, ed.), 4th edn, Chap. 1. Churchill Livingstone, London (in press).

Eriksson, L.-O. and Lundqvist, H. (1980). *Naturwissenschaften* **67**, 202–203.

Follett, B. K. and Follett, D. E. (eds) (1981). "Biological Clocks in Seasonal Reproductive Cycles." Wright, Bristol.

Frost, W. E. (1974). A survey of the rainbow trout (*Salmo gairdneri*) in Britain and Ireland. Publication by London, Salmon & Trout Association. 36 pp.

Gibson, R. N. (1978). *In* "Rhythmic Activity of Fishes" (J. E. Thorpe, ed.), pp. 201–213. Academic Press, London and New York.

Gillet, C. and Billard, R. (1981). *Cah. Lab. Montereau* **11**, 41–48.

Gillet, C., Billard, R. and Breton, B. (1977a). *Can. J. Zool.* **55**, 242–245.

Gillet, C., Billard, R. and Breton, B. (1977b). *Cah. Lab. Montereau* **5**, 25–42.

Girin, M. and Devauchelle, N. (1978). *Ann. Biol. anim. Bioch. Biophys.* **18**, 1059–1065.
Gordon, J. D. M. (1979). *Symp. zool. Soc. Lond.* **44**, 327–359.
Goryczko, K. (1972). *Rocz. Nauk rol.* **94**, H, 57–68.
Hazard, T. P. and Eddy, R. E. (1951). *Trans. Amer. Fish. Soc.* **80**, 158–162.
Henderson, N. E. (1963). *J. Fish. Res. Bd Can.* **20**, 859–897.
Honda, H. (1982). *Bull. Jap. Soc. scient. Fish.* **48**, 47–49.
Hoover, E. E. and Hubbard, H. E. (1937). *Copeia* **1937**, 206–210.
Htun Han, M. (1975). "The effects of photoperiod on maturation in the dab, *Limanda limanda* (L)." Ph.D. Thesis. University of East Anglia, Norwich, U.K. 107 pp.
Htun Han, M. (1977). Libr. Inf. Leafl. Fish. Lab., Lowestoft. No. 6, 30 pp.
Jalabert, B. (1976). *Oceanis, Paris* **2**, 141–150.
Kato, T. (1973). *Bull. Freshwat. Fish. Res. Lab., Tokyo* **23**, 33–43.
Kunesh, W. H., Freshman, W. J., Hoehm, M. and Nordin, N. G. (1974). *Progve Fish. Cult.* **36**, 225–226.
Lofts, B., Pickford, G. E. and Atz, J. W. (1968). *Biol. Bull.* **134**, 74–86.
Lowe-McConnell, R. H. (1979). *Symp. zool. Soc. Lond.* **44**, 219–241.
MacQuarrie, D. W., Markert, J. R. and Vanstone, W. E. (1978). *Ann. Biol. anim. Bioch. Biophys.* **18**, 1051–1058.
MacQuarrie, D. W., Vanstone, W. E. and Markert, J. R. (1979). *Aquaculture* **18**, 289–302.
MacQuarrie, D. W., Markert, J. R. and Vanstone, W. E. (1981). *In* "Salmonid Broodstock Maturation" (T. Nosho, ed.), pp. 41–42. University Washington Press, Seattle.
Mead, G. W., Bertelsen, E. and Cohen, D. M. (1964). *Deep Sea Res.* **11**, 569–596.
Millenbach, C. (1973). *In* "Proc. Internat. Symp. Atlantic Salmon" (M. W. Smith and W. M. Carter, eds), pp. 254–257. Internat. Atlantic Salmon Foundation, New York.
Miller, P. J. (1979). *Symp. zool. Soc. Lond.* **44**, 263–306.
Nikolsky, G. V. (1963). "The Ecology of Fishes." Academic Press, New York and London.
Nomura, M. (1962). *Bull. Jap. Soc. scient. Fish.* **28**, 1070–1076.
Palmer, J. D. (1976). "An Introduction to Biological Rhythms." Academic Press, New York and London.
Peter, R. E. and Crim, L. W. (1979). *Ann. Rev. Physiol.* **41**, 323–335.
Peter, R. E. and Hontela, A. (1978). *In* "Environmental Endocrinology" (I. Assenmacher and D. S. Farner, eds), pp. 20–25. Springer Verlag, Berlin.
Poston, H. A. (1978). Technical Paper. *U.S. Fish. Wildlife Serv.* **96**, 1–14.
Poston, H. A. and Livingston, D. L. (1971). *Fish. Res. Bull. N.Y.* **33**, 25–29.
Pyle, E. A. (1969). *Fish. Res. Bull. N.Y.* **31**, 13–19.
Royce, W. F. (1951). *U.S. Fish Wildlife Serv. Fish. Bull.* **52**, 59–76.
Schwassmann, H. O. (1971). *In* "Fish Physiology" (W. S. Hoar and D. J. Randall, eds), pp. 371–428. Academic Press, New York and London.
Schwassmann, H. O. (1978). *In* "Rhythmic Activity of Fishes" (J. E. Thorpe, ed.), pp. 187–200. Academic Press, London and New York.
Scott, A. P. (1981). *Fish Farmer* **4** (2), 28–29.
Scott, A. P. and Sumpter, J. P. (1983). *In* "Control Processes in Fish Physiology" (J. C. Rankin, R. T. Duggan and T. J. Pitcher, eds). Praeger, Eastbourne.
Scott, A. P., Htun Han, M., Bye, V. J., Springate, J. R. C. and Baynes, S. M. (1980). *Gen. comp. Endocr.* **40**, 336 (abstract).
Scott, A. P., Sumpter, J. P. and Hardiman, P. A. (1983). *Gen. comp. Endocr.* (in press).
Scott, D. B. C. (1979). *Symp. zool. Soc. Lond.* **44**, 105–132.
Sehgal, A. and Sundararaj, B. I. (1970). *Biol. Reprod.* **2**, 425–434.

Shiraishi, Y. and Fukuda, Y. (1966). *Bull. Freshwat. Fish. Res. Lab., Tokyo* **16**, 103–111.

Solomon, D. J. (1977). *J. Fish. Biol.* **11**, 369–376.

Stacey, N. E., Cook, A. F. and Peter, R. E. (1979a). *J. Fish Biol.* **15**, 349–361.

Stacey, N. E., Cook, A. F. and Peter, R. E. (1979b). *Gen. comp. Endocr.* **37**, 246–249.

Sundararaj, B. I. and Sehgal, A. (1970a). *Biol. Reprod.* **2**, 413–424.

Sundararaj, B. I. and Sehgal, A. (1970b). *Biol. Reprod.* **2**, 435–443.

Sundararaj, B. I. and Vasal, S. (1976). *J. Fish. Res. Bd Can.* **33**, 959–973.

Sundararaj, B. I., Vasal, S. and Halberg, F. (1973). *Int. J. Chronobiol.* **1**, 362–363.

Sundararaj, B. I., Nath, P. and Jeet, V. (1978). *In* "Comparative Endocrinology" (P. J. Gaillard and H. H. Boer, eds), pp. 137–144. Elsevier/North Holland Biomedical Press, Amsterdam.

Vasal, S. and Sundararaj, B. I. (1976). *J. exp. Zool.* **197**, 247–263.

Whitehead, C., Bromage, N. R., Forster, J. R. M. and Matty, A. J. (1978). *Ann. Biol. anim. Bioch. Biophys.* **18**, 1035–1043.

Whitehead, C., Bromage, N. R., Breton, B. and Matty, A. J. (1979). *J. Endocrinol.* **81**, 139–140 (abstract).

Whitehead, C., Bromage, N. R., Harbin, R. and Matty, A. J. (1980). *Gen. comp. Endocr.* **40**, 329–330 (abstract).

Woodhead, A. D. (1979). *Symp. zool. Soc. Lond.* **44**, 179–205.

12. Control of the Timing of Ovulation by Exogenous and Endogenous Factors

N. E. STACEY

Department of Zoology, University of Alberta, Alberta, Canada

Abstract: Ovulation in teleosts is regulated both by endogenous factors which initiate and mediate preovulatory changes in the oocyte and follicle, and by exogenous factors which determine when the endogenous factors will become functional. Endogenous factors include hypothalamic gonadotropin-releasing hormone (GnRH), preoptic area gonadotropin release-inhibiting factor (GRIF), pituitary gonadotropin (GtH), and local ovarian mediators of GtH action (steroids and prostaglandins). Elevation of blood GtH prior to spontaneous ovulation has been demonstrated in several species, and studies of GtH-induced ovulation in many teleosts indicate increased blood GtH is a common prerequisite for spontaneous ovulation. Mammalian LHRH and LHRH analogues stimulate GtH release in several teleosts; however, whether endogenous GnRH stimulates preovulatory GtH release is not known. In goldfish, preovulatory GtH release may be due at least in part to temporary withdrawal of a GRIF which normally inhibits GtH release; other possible mechanisms for preovulatory GtH release are increased pituitary sensitivity to GnRH and reduction of an oestrogen negative feedback on GtH release associated with completion of vitellogenesis. Preovulatory levels of GtH trigger two distinct ovarian processes which can be dissociated experimentally—final maturation of the oocyte, which appears to be stimulated by 17α-hydroxy-20β-dihydroprogesterone of follicular origin, and follicular rupture, which evidently is stimulated by prostaglandin. In contrast to the research effort concerned with the endogenous regulation of teleost ovulation, the roles of exogenous ovulatory factors have received relatively little attention. In many species, ovulation is not simply the consequence of completed vitellogenesis but is a rapid response to specific factors such as temperature change, pheromones or spawning substrate. For example, the incidence of spontaneous ovulation in goldfish is greatly increased if females are exposed to aquatic vegetation, the natural substrate for oviposition. In goldfish which ovulate spontaneously at 20°C on a 16L:8D photoperiod, blood GtH increases dramatically during the latter half of the photophase, peaks during the latter half of scotophase, at which time follicular rupture occurs, and returns to preovulatory levels at the onset of photophase, when spawning begins. In many other teleosts, diel spawning, which may provide benefits such as reduction of predation and synchronization of spawners during the brief postovulatory period in which oocyte viability is maximal, also may be timed indirectly by photoperiodically

FISH REPRODUCTION
ISBN: 0-12-563660-1

synchronized ovulation. However, in salmonids, where oocytes in the body cavity can retain maximal viability for a week or more after ovulation, the timing of ovulation appears to be determined not by environmental factors prevailing in the immediate preovulatory period, but rather by the completion of vitellogenesis. Whereas endogenous regulation of ovulation appears to vary little among the teleosts which have been examined, it is likely that both the nature and function of exogenous ovulatory factors will be found to vary considerably in accordance with the environmental and social conditions determining the reproductive success of each species.

I. INTRODUCTION

The timing of reproduction in female teleosts may be viewed as the product of numerous biotic and abiotic stimuli which exert both long-term effects on ovarian growth and short-term effects on final maturation and ovulation of the oocytes (see Bye, Chap. 11, this volume). A temporally appropriate reproductive response to these exogenous cues maximizes reproductive success by achieving an optimal balance between survival of spawning adults and their progeny. Obviously, the cost of a temporally inappropriate reproductive attempt varies greatly with reproductive strategy, being greatest in those species (e.g. Pacific salmon, *Oncorhynchus*) which ovulate only once, and considerably less in the partial spawners which ovulate many times over an extended breeding season. Nevertheless, it can be assumed that the considerable metabolic cost inherent in any form of teleost reproduction has resulted in selection for physiological mechanisms which effectively regulate the timing of ovulation, an event which irreversibly commits reproductive investment.

In the great majority of teleosts — those which reproduce by external fertilization — the ovulatory process marks a distinct and critical transition in female reproduction. In the preovulatory period, high energy yolk stores (vitellogenin) are accumulated by growing oocytes to provide nutrients for future larvae. Following completion of vitellogenesis, oocytes are then maintained within the ovary for a variable period until a series of endocrine events stimulates their *final maturation* (migration and breakdown of the nucleus or germinal vesicle, accompanied by completion of meiosis) and *ovulation* (detachment and release from the follicle) (Jalabert, 1976). At this point, ovulated oocytes within the peritoneal cavity (gymnovarian species) or ovarian lumen (cystovarian species) must be oviposited and fertilized within a relatively brief period (usually several hours to several days, depending on the species) if maximal viability of the oocytes and larvae is to be achieved.

This review will consider the regulation of teleost ovulation both in terms of the exogenous factors which may affect the occurrence of ovulation and in terms of the endogenous neuroendocrine and endocrine changes which mediate these effects. The endocrinology of ovulation in teleosts has received considerable attention in recent years, not least because of the economic incentives for controlled reproduction of food fishes. In contrast, relatively little is known of the role of exogenous factors in regulating teleost ovulation.

II. ENDOGENOUS FACTORS

A. Gonadotropin releasing and inhibiting factors

Evidence for a gonadotropin-releasing hormone (GnRH) in the teleost brain comes from a variety of studies which have employed bioassay of brain extracts (Breton et al., 1975b; Crim and Evans, 1980) and immunocytochemistry (Dubois et al., 1979; Schreibman et al., 1979; Nozaki and Kobayashi, 1979; Munz et al., 1981). The structure of teleost GnRH is not known. It appears to be very similar, if not identical, to GnRH from reptiles and birds, to be different from GnRH of amphibia and mammals, and to have biological activity in a mammalian bioassay system roughly equivalent to that of the GnRHs from other vertebrate groups (King and Millar, 1979, 1980; Barnett et al., 1980; Idler and Crim, 1982).

Brain lesions have been used in several teleosts to identify sites which may be involved in GnRH production. As it is not yet possible to directly monitor changes in GnRH production, the effects of these lesions are measured indirectly, either by radioimmunoassay for gonadotropin (GtH), or by determining changes in gonadosomatic index (GSI). Lesions in the hypothalamic nucleus lateralis tuberis (NLT) consistently decreased GSI in male and female goldfish (Peter, 1970; Peter and Crim, 1978; Peter and Paulencu, 1980) and in male *Fundulus heteroclitus* (Pickford et al., 1981) and Atlantic salmon parr (Dodd et al., 1978). With the exception of large lesions of the nucleus preopticus (NPO) in goldfish, which are discussed below, lesions in areas other than the NLT have not consistently affected GSI in these species. Surprisingly, NLT lesions which decreased GSI in goldfish did not result in decreased blood GtH levels (Peter and Crim, 1978; Peter and Paulencu, 1980); however, Peter (1982) finds that NLT lesions do abolish the daily cycle of GtH in goldfish (Hontela and Peter, 1978), which may be necessary for ovarian recrudescence. The use of L-glutamate, which destroyed neuronal perikarya in select brain regions of goldfish, has provided further evidence that the NLT is involved in GnRH regulation (Peter et al., 1980). In support of these lesion studies, immunocytochemical investigations have identified LHRH-positive cell bodies in the NLT of the platyfish, *Xiphophorus maculatus* (Schreibman et al., 1979), and goldfish (Kah et al., 1982).

In addition to providing evidence for a GnRH in teleosts, lesioning studies also have shown that, at least in goldfish, the brain produces a gonadotropin release-inhibiting factor (GRIF). Lesions in the anterior preoptic area, the hypothesized source of GRIF, caused dramatic increases in blood GtH which often caused ovulation; similar effects were caused by lesions along a path running from the anterior preoptic area, through the lateral anterior hypothalamus to the pituitary stalk (Peter and Paulencu, 1980). These results suggest that damage to the pituitary stalk was probably the cause for the earlier, apparently paradoxical, findings (Peter et al., 1978) that large NLT lesions increased GtH. Subsequent work strongly indicates that dopamine may function as a GRIF in goldfish. Blood GtH levels in female goldfish were elevated following injection of either 6-hydroxydopamine, a catecholaminergic neurotoxin, several drugs which reduce synthesis of dopamine, or pimozide, a dopamine antagonist; furthermore, injection of dopamine or the dopamine agonist, apomorphine, both reduced GtH levels in normal female goldfish and blocked the large increase in blood GtH following either preoptic lesion or injection of a superactive LHRH analogue (Chang et al., 1983; J. P. Chang and R. E. Peter, unpublished results). These findings in goldfish are consistent with a preliminary report that dopamine inhibits in vitro GtH release from rainbow trout pituitaries (Crim, 1982). The foregoing results suggest that a GRIF of brain origin, possibly dopamine released from the type B aminergic fibres that directly innervate GtH cells in goldfish (Kaul and Vollrath, 1974) and other teleosts (review by Peter, 1983), acts directly on GtH cells to inhibit both spontaneous and GnRH-stimulated GtH release.

It is not clear how the apparent dual regulation of GtH release by GnRH and GRIF might normally participate in the control of teleost ovulation. Induction of ovulation by injection of LHRH and LHRH analogues in a variety of species (Lam, 1982; Peter, 1983) indicates that the pituitary is able to respond to GnRH without apparent modification in GRIF activity. However, the recent finding (J. P. Chang and R. E. Peter, unpublished results) that combined treatment with LHRH analogue and the dopamine antagonist, pimozide, is more effective in inducing GtH release and ovulation in goldfish than is either treatment alone, suggests that release of preovulatory levels of GtH may involve both stimulation by GnRH and abatement of GRIF activity. Alternatively, the possibility cannot be ruled out that in some species (e.g. salmonids) preovulatory GtH release is not triggered by altered neuroendocrine activity, but is a pituitary response to some other factor, such as changing steroid levels.

B. Preovulatory gonadotropin

Teleosts evidently have two types of gonadotropin, a low carbohydrate content ("Con A-1") GtH capable of stimulating both vitellogenin uptake into oocytes and, in some species, steroidogenesis, and a relatively high carbohydrate content ("Con A-2") GtH capable of stimulating steroidogenesis, oocyte maturation, ovulation and spermiation (Idler et al., 1975; Idler and Ng, 1979; Ng and Idler, 1979). Presently, only Con A-2 GtH can be measured by radioimmunoassay.

The demonstration that, in a great number of teleost species, mature females can be induced to ovulate by injection of a variety of GtH preparations strongly implicates a preovulatory increase in blood GtH in the normal ovulatory process (review by Donaldson and Hunter, 1983). Indeed, in the few species examined this has proved to be the case. Ovulation in goldfish is preceded by a dramatic increase in blood GtH which is terminated several hours after follicular rupture (Stacey et al., 1979a). A periovulatory increase in GtH also is seen in the carp, Cyprinus carpio (Fish Reproductive Physiology Research Group and Peptide Hormone Group, 1978). Also in a number of salmonids, blood GtH has been shown to increase in the periovulatory period (Crim et al., 1973, 1975; Jalabert et al., 1978; Fostier et al., 1978, 1981; Jalabert and Breton, 1980; Stuart-Kregor et al., 1981; Breton et al., 1983). At least in rainbow trout (Jalabert and Breton, 1980; Fostier et al., 1981) and brown trout, Salmo trutta (Fostier et al., 1981), postovulatory blood GtH levels greatly exceed those in the immediate preovulatory period, and may remain elevated for several weeks. The functional significance of the difference in postovulatory GtH profiles of salmonids and cyprinids is not known, but may be related to the extended period of postovulatory oocyte viability in salmonids (Jalabert and Breton, 1980).

C. Ovarian ovulatory response to GtH

Considerable research effort has focused on the mechanisms of GtH-stimulated oocyte final maturation and ovulation in teleosts, as an understanding of these processes may lead to techniques of induced ovulation which do not require the use of GtH or LHRH. Both steroids and prostaglandins have been demonstrated to mediate the ovulatory action of GtH.

1. *Steroids.*   Studies in a variety of teleosts showing that GtH induces final maturation of the oocyte indirectly, by stimulating follicular steroidogenesis (Hirose, 1976; Jalabert, 1976), have led to investigations of the nature of the steroid(s) mediating these effects of GtH. In rainbow trout, goldfish, and northern pike, Esox lucius (Jalabert, 1976), yellow perch, Perca flavescens (Goetz and Theofan, 1979), brook trout, Salvelinus fontinalis (Duffey and Goetz, 1980), and amago salmon, Oncorhynchus rhodurus (Nagahama et al., 1980), the steroid most potent in inducing oocyte final maturation is 17α-hydroxy-20β-dihydroxyprogesterone (17α-20β-OHP). In support of these findings, 17α-20β-OHP has been shown to increase in the blood just prior to spontaneous ovulation in rainbow trout (Fostier et al., 1981), and to be synthesized in vitro by GtH-stimulated ovaries of ayu, Plecoglossus altivelis (Suzuki et al., 1981). However, in zebrafish, Brachydanio rerio, deoxycorti-

costerone is more effective than 17α-20β-OHP in inducing maturation (Van Ree *et al.*, 1977), and in other species, notably the catfish, *Heteropneustes fossilis*, there is evidence that GtH induces ovulation by stimulating synthesis of interrenal corticosteroids which in turn act on the ovary (Sundararaj and Goswami, 1977; Truscott *et al.*, 1978).

Although in some species (*Heteropneustes fossilis*, Goswami and Sundararaj, 1971; *Perca flavescens*, Goetz and Theofan, 1979) ovulation normally follows *in vitro* steroid-stimulated final maturation, in most cases *in vitro* steroid treatment induces ovulation only infrequently (rainbow trout, goldfish, northern pike; Jalabert, 1976: brook trout; Goetz and Bergman, 1978: *Fundulus heteroclitus*; Wallace and Selman, 1978). Considerable evidence (review by Stacey and Goetz, 1982) indicates that ovulation (expulsion of the oocyte from the follicle) in teleosts is stimulated by prostaglandin. Whether species differences in the *in vitro* ovulatory response to steroids represent significant variation in the regulation of ovulation, or simply the result of differing tendencies for *in vitro* prostaglandin synthesis is not known.

In addition to their demonstrated role as local ovarian mediators of the ovulatory action of GtH, ovarian steroids also may act at the level of the brain or pituitary to regulate preovulatory GtH release. Autoradiography has been used to demonstrate steroid binding in the pituitary and in several brain regions including the NLT (suggested GnRH centre) and preoptic area (suggested GRIF centre) (Morell *et al.*, 1975; Kim *et al.*, 1978). Gonadectomy and steroid injection experiments have demonstrated inhibitory effects on blood GtH levels (Billard, 1978; Bommelaer *et al.*, 1981) and stimulatory effects on pituitary GtH content (Crim and Peter, 1978; Crim *et al.*, 1981). In addition, antioestrogens (clomiphene, tamoxifen) have been effective in increasing blood GtH levels and inducing ovulation in a variety of teleosts (Pandey *et al.*, 1973; Breton *et al.*, 1975a; Ueda and Takahashi, 1977; Billard and Peter, 1977; Donaldson *et al.*, 1981/1982). Although it is clear that experimental steroid manipulations can modify GtH levels and induce ovulation, the relevance of these findings to the normal regulation of teleost ovulation is not understood. Changes in preovulatory steroid levels might conceivably exert a variety of effects on neuroendocrine mechanisms of GtH release. However, as discussed in more detail below, considerable evidence that the occurrence of ovulation in many teleosts is not simply an inevitable finale to oocyte growth, but rather a rapid and well regulated response to specific exogenous factors, indicates that fluctuations in blood steroids are unlikely to be of widespread importance in regulating preovulatory GtH release.

2. *Prostaglandins.* As has been demonstrated in a variety of mammalian species (review by Espey, 1980), prostaglandins evidently play a critical role in stimulating the final stages of teleost ovulation, rupture of the follicle and

expulsion of the mature oocyte (reviews by Stacey and Goetz, 1982; Goetz, 1983). The prostaglandin synthesis inhibitor, indomethacin, completely blocked *in vivo* follicular rupture in goldfish injected with human chorionic gonadotropin (hCG) (Stacey and Pandey, 1975) and *in vitro* follicular rupture of yellow perch oocytes matured with 17α-20β-OHP (Goetz and Theofan, 1979); in both studies several prostaglandins were effective in restoring indomethacin-blocked follicular rupture. Additional demonstrations that prostaglandins can stimulate *in vitro* ovulation in teleosts come from studies of rainbow trout (Jalabert and Szollosi, 1975), brook trout (Goetz and Smith, 1980), and goldfish (Kagawa and Nagahama, 1981).

Consistent with these effects of prostaglandins and indomethacin, ovarian prostaglandin F levels have been shown to increase around the time of follicular rupture in hCG-treated loach, *Misgurnus anguillicaudatus* (Ogata *et al.*, 1979), and in spontaneously ovulating brook trout (Cetta and Goetz, 1983). Prostaglandin F levels were found to be high in ovarian fluid from ovulated fish and to increase in the blood following follicular rupture both in hCG-treated goldfish (Bouffard, pers. comm.) and in spontaneously ovulating brook trout (Cetta and Goetz, 1983). Although these postovulatory increases in blood levels of prostaglandin F support the hypothesis (reviews by Stacey, 1981; Stacey and Goetz, 1982) that prostaglandin plays a hormonal role in female sexual behaviour of some externally fertilizing teleosts, there is at present no indication that prostaglandins play any role in teleost ovulation other than as local ovarian mediators of the ovulatory action of GtH.

III. EXOGENOUS FACTORS

An extremely common finding in studies of teleost reproduction is that although vitellogenesis usually is completed in captivity, ovulation does not readily occur. As GtH treatment generally induces rapid ovulation, absence of spontaneous ovulation can reasonably be assumed to result from absence of the normal preovulatory GtH release. Why this might be so is obvious considering the nature of external fertilization. Ovulation marks the commitment of considerable metabolic investment and can lead to successful reproduction only if critical external factors (presence of a male and spawning substrate, low level of predation, etc.) are appropriate. Furthermore, as ovulated oocytes may have only a brief period of viability within the ovary or body cavity (Chen *et al.*, 1969; Hogendoorn and Vismans, 1980), an effective ovulatory mechanism should "assess" the state of external factors necessary for successful spawning prior to initiating events leading to ovulation. Surprisingly little is known of how exogenous factors regulate the occurrence of ovulation in teleosts.

A. Photoperiod

Ovulation in several teleosts has been shown to be well synchronized with photoperiod. In goldfish maintained at 20°C on 16L:8D photoperiod, ovulation is induced by a surge of blood GtH which begins during the latter half of photophase, peaks during the latter half of scotophase, at which time follicular rupture occurs, and terminates shortly after the onset of the following photophase, at which time spawning commences (Stacey et al., 1979a); entrainment of ovulation time to a reversed LD cycle occurs within two weeks (Stacey et al., 1979b). In medaka, Oryzias latipes, ovulation occurs during the latter portion of scotophase almost every day during the breeding season, spawning commencing soon after the onset of light (Robinson and Rugh, 1943; Egami, 1954). This diel pattern of ovulation and oviposition, evidently triggered by a photoperiodically synchronized release of ovulatory GtH levels (Iwamatsu, 1978), rapidly entrains to altered photoperiods and becomes irregular in constant light or dark (Robinson and Rugh, 1943; Egami, 1954; Egami and Nambu, 1961). In Menidia audens (Hubbs, 1976) and Brachydanio rerio (Eaton and Farley, 1974) there is evidence that diel spawning activity results from photoperiodically synchronized ovulation. Chen and Martinich (1975), however, find that ovulation and spawning in Brachydanio can occur at any time of day.

Diel spawning behaviour has been reported in many marine (Simpson, 1971; Meyer, 1977; Lobel, 1978; Johannes, 1978; Ferraro, 1980) and freshwater fish (Marshall, 1967; Chien and Salmon, 1972; Brown and Marshall, 1978; Breder and Rosen, 1966) for which the time of ovulation apparently is not known. Photoperiodic cues may act directly on neural mechanisms to determine the time of spawning in these species, but the close temporal association between ovulation and spawning in many teleosts, suggested to result from the behavioural response to postovulatory increase in prostaglandin (Stacey, 1981; Stacey and Goetz, 1982), argues that photoperiodically synchronized ovulation, followed rapidly by spawning, may be a phenomenon widespread among teleosts.

B. Temperature

Temperature influences many functions of the teleost reproductive system including the rate of secretion and clearance of GtH (Cook and Peter, 1980a), pituitary responsiveness to GnRH (Weil et al., 1975), gonadal binding of GtH (Cook and Peter, 1980b), daily cycles of GtH (Hontela and Peter, 1978), synthesis and catabolism of steroids (Kime, 1980; Kime and Saksena, 1980), and the latency from GtH stimulation to follicular rupture (Horvath, 1978; Stacey et al., 1979b). However, while there also is evidence that acute temperature change can trigger spawning behaviour (Lasker, 1974), there are few experimental demonstrations that temperature directly stimulates endocrine events leading to ovulation.

Yamamoto *et al.* (1966) reported that, whereas goldfish maintained on natural photoperiod and cold ($<14°C$) water develop vitellogenic ovaries but do not ovulate, increasing water temperature to $20°C$ at any time of year can induce ovulation within a day. Subsequently, this technique has been verified in many studies which required goldfish in a preovulatory condition (Peter *et al.*, 1978; Peter and Paulencu, 1980; citations in Stacey *et al.*, 1979b). Stacey *et al.* (1979b), however, have shown that goldfish ovulate spontaneously even in cold water if they are exposed to aquatic vegetation, the normal spawning substrate. Furthermore, although warming alone is sufficient to trigger ovulation in some females, the proportion responding increases significantly if warming is combined with exposure to vegetation. Significantly, the time of ovulation was similar for females held in cold or warm water, suggesting that the time of preovulatory GtH release may shift with temperature to synchronize ovulation with photoperiod.

In the tench, *Tinca tinca*, Breton *et al.* (1980) demonstrated that increased water temperature in outdoor ponds stimulated vitellogenesis and advanced the onset of spawning. The first ovulation of the season occurred at a fairly constant number of degree-days above $10°C$, a critical minimum temperature required for initiation of vitellogenesis, and successive ovulations occurred as long as the mean daily temperature exceeded $20°C$. The holding ponds used in this study presumably contained the aquatic vegetation which tench use as a spawning substrate (Breder and Rosen, 1966). If vegetation serves as a trigger for ovulation in tench, as it does in goldfish (Stacey *et al.*, 1979b), then in tench increased temperature may play only an indirect role in stimulating ovulation, shortening the time required for completion of vitellogenesis and thus advancing the time at which fish become responsive to the presence of vegetation.

C. Spawning substrate

The importance of spawning substrate in the regulation of ovulation is likely to be influenced by specificity of substrate requirements, spatio-temporal distribution of the substrate, and the length of time ovulated oocytes remain viable in the ovarian or body cavity. For example, ovulation in pelagophils, which simply release eggs into the water (Balon, 1975), might be expected to occur regardless of substrate conditions. Indeed marine pelagophils such as the red snapper, *Lutjanus campechanus* (Arnold *et al.*, 1978), and the gilthead seabream, *Sparus auratus* (Zohar and Gordin, 1979), ovulate spontaneously in apparently bare aquaria. Even in salmonids, lithophils with rather strict substrate requirements, ovulation of captive fish occurs spontaneously in the absence of gravel spawning substrate; presumably presence of spawning substrate is not a prerequisite for salmonid ovulation because migration to traditional spawning areas, combined with an extended postovulatory period of oocyte viability (Escaffre *et al.*, 1977; Bry, 1981), serves as an effective means for synchronizing ovulation with potential substrate availability.

In some other teleosts with specific substrate requirements, there is evidence that absence of appropriate substrate inhibits ovulation, whereas exposure to substrate can rapidly induce ovulation. As discussed above, exposure to aquatic vegetation induces ovulation in goldfish (Stacey *et al.*, 1979b), a species in which reproductive success is increased if the adhesive eggs are attached to vegetation during incubation. If the postovulatory period of oocyte viability in goldfish is similar to the brief period reported for a number of cyprinids (Chen *et al.*, 1969; citations in Horvath, 1978), it is not surprising that ovulation should be inhibited in the absence of vegetation. Although experimental demonstrations that vegetation induces ovulation in other phytophils appear to be lacking, there are considerable indications that this is the case. In the African catfish, *Clarias gariepinus*, the latency to spawning from rainfall and/or inundation is equivalent to that following GtH injection (Bruton, 1979), indicating a direct effect on preovulatory GtH release. However, as is the case with this and many other field observations that spawning rapidly follows rainfall and flooding (Lowe-McConnell, 1975; Schwassmann, 1978; Sundararaj, 1981), it is not clear whether rainfall acts by increasing availability of spawning substrate, or by altering any one of a number of parameters of water quality. In support of the latter possibility, Lake (1967) has suggested that spawning in a number of species may be stimulated by petrichor, a mixture of organic compounds released by inundation of previously dry ground.

D. Social factors: visual and chemical

Although it is clear that visual and chemical stimuli from conspecifics can increase spawning frequency in females of some species, for the most part these factors appear to act by stimulating ovarian development and not by triggering ovulation directly (reviews by Liley, 1980, 1982). Stimuli from males might be expected to affect the occurrence of ovulation in species where male territoriality leads to separation of the sexes during the breeding season. Kramer (1972) found that in the blue gourami, *Trichogaster trichopterus*, ovulation is rapidly induced by brief exposure to a nest-building male, although the nature of the stimulus involved was not investigated. However, in *Brachydanio rerio*, a species where males and females might be expected to remain together throughout the breeding season, brief exposure to a male can induce ovulation the following day (Eaton and Farley, 1974). Stimulation of ovulation by water from males and inhibition of ovulation by water from crowded aquaria indicates that the mechanism regulating spontaneous ovulation in *Brachydanio* responds both to stimulatory pheromones and inhibitory metabolites (Chen and Martinich, 1975).

E. Ovulation in the apparent absence of specific exogenous cues

The fact that females of many teleost species complete vitellogenesis yet fail to ovulate in captivity indicates that activation of the ovulatory mechanism requires exogenous stimuli which are both distinct from those required for ovarian recrudescence, and lacking in the artificial environment. In several species, however, ovulation apparently occurs simply as a consequence of gonadal maturation and evidently without direct influence by environmental factors. In many salmonids, for example, ovulation occurs spontaneously in aquaria without gravel substrate normally used in nest-digging and oviposition. Although the timing of the single annual ovulation can be considerably advanced or delayed by manipulating photoperiod (Bye, Chap. 11, this volume; Bromage, pers. comm.), the data suggest these effects on ovulation are mediated indirectly by accelerated or decelerated ovarian rescrudescence. As suggested above, such apparent insensitivity of the salmonid ovulatory mechanism to exogenous factors of immediate relevance to spawning may be related to both the reproductive migratory behaviour and lengthy postovulatory oocyte viability characteristic of this group.

While it is not clear whether a salmonid type of ovulatory mechanism, apparently regulated indirectly by the action of photoperiod (or other factors) on ovarian recrudescence, is common among teleosts, such control of ovulation would not be inconsistent with several reproductive strategies. Species which display lunar periodicity in spawning (Johannes, 1978; May et al., 1979; Taylor and Di Michelle, 1980) presumably increase reproductive success by synchronizing ovulation with factors such as periodically available spawning substrates, or specific tidal currents which may aid in offshore dispersal of pelagic eggs. Because the availability of these factors associated with the lunar cycle is likely to be highly predictable, ovulation in these species may occur as a consequence of cyclic recrudescence, rather than as a direct response to specific exogenous cues, although this possibility appears not to have been investigated experimentally. Schooling pelagophils, requiring no spawning substrate, also might be expected to regulate ovulation in this way; however, some pelagophils such as *Lutjanus* ovulate in captivity (Arnold et al., 1978), whereas others such as *Mugil cephalus* do not (Kuo and Nash, 1975). It is difficult to evaluate the significance of the presence or absence of spontaneous ovulation in captive fish. Failure of captive *Mugil* to ovulate spontaneously may be due to absence of gyral currents reported in areas of natural spawning (see Johannes, 1978), or simply a result of stressful holding conditions. On the other hand, Pacific herring, *Clupea harengus pallasi*, a phytolithophyllic species displaying considerable substrate selection, can ovulate at the normal time following a year in bare aquaria under natural photoperiod (Stacey and Hourston, 1982); while these findings might suggest the regulation of ovulation is similar in herring and salmonids, it is possible that the smooth aquarium walls, which herring will use as a spawning substrate, are sufficient stimulus for ovulation.

IV. CONCLUSION

Although the regulation of ovulation has been studied extensively in only a few species, several trends have emerged which are applicable to the majority of teleosts. Studies of spontaneous and GtH-induced ovulation in many species suggest a common endogenous ovulatory process in which a preovulatory elevation of blood GtH, possibly generated in response to altered GnRH and/or GRIF activity, stimulates synthesis of ovarian steroids involved in oocyte final maturation and prostaglandin involved in follicular rupture. At present, it appears that initiation of this endogenous process is accomplished in either of two fundamentally different ways. In the first, exemplified by the salmonids, ovulation evidently occurs as a consequence of completed ovarian development. This type of ovulatory system appears analogous to that of spontaneously ovulating mammals in which pre-ovulatory GtH release is regulated by ovarian steroids. In the second type of ovulatory system, seen in many teleost groups, ovulation occurs rapidly in response to specific exogenous factors relevant to reproductive success. Here, regulation of ovulation might be compared to that of mammalian reflex ovulators which complete follicular development but do not ovulate in the absence of coitus-related stimuli.

The common failure of female teleosts to ovulate spontaneously in captivity obviously has been a major factor stimulating research on hormonal induction of ovulation. Ironically, the evident applicability of hormonal intervention to the control of ovulation in many species has tended to discourage investigation of the presumed reason for ovulatory failure in captive fish — the absence of specific exogenous cues triggering preovulatory GtH release. Whether identifying the nature of these external factors will yield economically viable alternatives to hormonal intervention obviously will depend on a host of considerations unique to the problems of culture in each species. However, such knowledge undoubtedly will increase our appreciation of the role of ovulatory control mechanisms in reproductive strategies of teleosts.

ACKNOWLEDGEMENTS

This work was funded by grant U0007 from the Natural Sciences and Engineering Research Council of Canada. The author is grateful to J. P. Chang and R. E. Peter for allowing reference to their unpublished findings, and to A. L. Kyle and R. E. Peter for their useful comments on the manuscript.

REFERENCES

Arnold, C. R., Wakeman, J. M., Williams, T. D. and Treece, G. D. (1978). *Aquaculture* **15**, 301–302.

Balon, E. K. (1975). *J. Fish. Res. Bd Can.* **32**, 821–864.

Barnett, F. H., Sohn, J., Reichlin, S. and Jackson, I. M. D. (1980). *Biochem. Biophys. Res. Comm.* **105**, 209–216.

Billard, R. (1978). *Ann. Biol. anim. Biochem. Biophys.* **18**, 813–818.

Billard, R. and Peter, R. E. (1977). *Gen. Comp. Endocrinol.* **32**, 213–220.

Bommelaer, M.-C., Billard, R. and Breton, B. (1981). *Reprod. Nutr. Develop.* **21**, 989–997.

Breder, C. M. and Rosen, D. E. (1966). "Modes of Reproduction in Fishes". Natural History Press, Garden City, New York.

Breton, B., Jalabert, B. and Fostier, A. (1975a). *Gen. Comp. Endocrinol.* **25**, 400–404.

Breton, B., Jalabert, B. and Weil, C. (1975b). *Gen. Comp. Endocrinol.* **25**, 405–415.

Breton, B., Horoszewicz, L., Bieniarz, K. and Epler, P. (1980). *Reprod. Nutr. Develop.* **20**, 1011–1024.

Breton, B., Fostier, A., Zohar, Y., Le Bail, P. Y. and Billard, R. (1983). *Gen. Comp. Endocrinol.* **49**, 220–231.

Brown, D. H. and Marshall, J. A. (1978). *Behaviour* **67**, 299–321.

Bruton, M. N. (1979). *Trans. zool. Soc. Lond.* **35**, 1–45.

Bry, C. (1981). *Aquaculture* **24**, 153–160.

Cetta, F. and Goetz, F. W. (1982). *Biol. Reprod.* **27**, 1216–1221.

Chang, J. P., Cook, A. F. and Peter, R. E. (1983). *Gen. Comp. Endocrinol.* **49**, 22–31.

Chen, F. Y., Chow, M. and Sin, B. K. (1969). *Malay. Agric. J.* **47**, 24–38.

Chen, L.-C. and Martinich, R. L. (1975). *Fish. Bull.* **73**, 889–894.

Chien, A. K. and Salmon, M. (1972). *Forma et Functio* **5**, 45–74.

Cook, A. F. and Peter, R. E. (1980a). *Gen. Comp. Endocrinol.* **42**, 76–90.

Cook, A. F. and Peter, R. E. (1980b). *Gen. Comp. Endocrinol.* **42**, 91–100.

Crim, L. W. (1982). *In* "Neurosecretion" (K. Lederis and D. S. Farner, eds), p. 446. Plenum Press, New York.

Crim, L. W. and Peter, R. E. (1978). *Ann. Biol. anim. Biochem. Biophys.* **18**, 689–694.

Crim, L. W. and Evans, D. M. (1980). *Gen. Comp. Endocrinol.* **40**, 283–290.

Crim, L. W., Meyer, R. K. and Donaldson, E. M. (1973). *Gen. Comp. Endocrinol.* **21**, 69–76.

Crim, L. W., Watts, E. G. and Evans, D. M. (1975). *Gen. Comp. Endocrinol.* **27**, 62–70.

Crim, L. W., Peter, R. E. and Billard, R. (1981). *Gen. Comp. Endocrinol.* **44**, 374–381.

Dodd, J. M., Stuart-Kregor, P. A. C., Sumpter, J. P., Crim, L. W. and Peter, R. E. (1978). *In* "Comparative Endocrinology" (P. J. Gaillard and H. H. Boer, eds), pp. 101–104. Elsevier-North Holland, Amsterdam.

Donaldson, E. M. and Hunter, G. A. (1983). *In* "Fish Physiology" (W. S. Hoar and D. J. Randall, eds), Vol. IX. Academic Press, New York (in press).

Donaldson, E. M., Hunter, G. A. and Dye, H. M. (1981–1982). *Aquaculture* **16**, 143–154.

Dubois, M. P., Billard, R., Breton, B. and Peter, R. E. (1979). *Gen. Comp. Endocrinol.* **37**, 220–232.

Duffey, R. J. and Goetz, F. W. (1980). *Gen. comp. Endocrinol.* **41**, 563–565.

Eaton, R. C. and Farley, R. D. (1974). *Copeia* **1974**, 195–204.

Egami, N. (1954). *Annot. Zool. Japon.* **27**, 57–62.

Egami, N. and Nambu, M. (1961). *J. Fac. Sci., Univ. Tokyo*, IV, **9**, 263–278.

Escaffre, A.-M., Petit, J. and Billard, R. (1977). *Bull. Fr. Piscic.* **265**, 134–142.

Espey, L. L. (1980). *Biol. Reprod.* **22**, 73–106.

Ferraro, S. P. (1980). *Fish. Bull.* **78**, 455–464.

Fish Reproductive Physiology Research Group and Peptide Hormone Group. (1978). *Acta Biochim. Biophys. Sinica* **10**, 399–407.

Fostier, A., Weil, C., Terqui, M., Breton, B. and Jalabert, B. (1978). *Ann. Biol. anim. Biochem. Biophys.* **18**, 929–936.

Fostier, A., Breton, B., Jalabert, B. and Marcuzzi, O. (1981). *C. R. Acad. Sci. Paris* **293D**, 817–820.

Goetz, F. W. (1983). *In* "Fish Physiology" (W. S. Hoar and D. J. Randall, eds), Vol. IX. Academic Press, New York (in press).

Goetz, F. W. and Bergman, H. L. (1978). *Biol. Reprod.* **18**, 293–298.

Goetz, F. W. and Smith, D. G. (1980). *Biol. Reprod. Suppl.* **1**, 114A.

Goetz, F. W. and Theofan, G. (1979). *Gen. Comp. Endocrinol.* **37**, 273–285.

Goswami, S. V. and Sundararaj, B. I. (1971). *J. exp. Zool.* **178**, 457–466.

Hirose, K. (1976). *J. Fish. Res. Bd Can.* **33**, 989–994.

Hogendoorn, H. and Vismans, M. M. (1980). *Aquaculture* **21**, 39–53.

Hontela, A. and Peter, R. E. (1978). *Can. J. Zool.* **56**, 2430–2442.

Horvath, L. (1978). *Aquacultura Hungarica* **1**, 58–65.

Hubbs, C. (1976). *Copeia* **1976**, 387–388.

Idler, D. R. and Ng, T. B. (1979). *Gen. Comp. Endocrinol.* **38**, 421–440.

Idler, D. R. and Crim, L. W. (1982). *In* "Proceedings of the Ninth International Symposium on Comparative Endocrinology" (B. Lofts, ed.). University of Hong Kong Press (in press).

Idler, D. R., Bazar, L. S. and Hwang, S. J. (1975). *Endocr. Res. Comm.* **2**, 237–249.

Iwamatsu, T. (1978). *J. exp. Zool.* **206**, 355–364.

Jalabert, B. (1976). *J. Fish. Res. Bd Can.* **33**, 974–988.

Jalabert, B. and Breton, B. (1980). *C. R. Acad. Sci. Paris* **290D**, 799–801.

Jalabert, B. and Szollosi, D. (1975). *Prostaglandins* **9**, 765–778.

Jalabert, B., Goetz, F. W., Breton, B., Fostier, A. and Donaldson, E. M. (1978). *J. Fish. Res. Bd Can.* **35**, 1423–1429.

Johannes, R. E. (1978). *Env. Biol. Fish* **3**, 65–84.

Kagawa, H. and Nagahama, Y. (1981). *Bull. Jap. Soc. scient. Fish.* **47**, 1119–1121.

Kah, O., Chambolle, P., Dubourg, P. and Dubois, M. P. (1982). International Symposium on Reproductive Physiology of Fish, Wageningen, Netherlands, August, 1982 (in press).

Kaul, S. and Vollrath, L. (1974). *Cell Tiss. Res.* **154**, 231–249.

Kim, Y.-S., Stumpf, W. E., Sar, M. and Martinez-Vargas, M. C. (1978). *Am. Zool.* **18**, 425–433.

Kime, D. E. (1980). *Gen. Comp. Endocrinol.* **41**, 164–172.

Kime, D. E. and Saksena, D. N. (1980). *Gen. Comp. Endocrinol.* **42**, 228–234.

King, J. A. and Millar, R. P. (1979). *Science N.Y.* **206**, 67–69.

King, J. A. and Millar, R. P. (1980). *Endocrinology* **106**, 707–717.

Kramer, D. L. (1972). *Anim. Behav.* **20**, 798–807.

Kuo, C.-M. and Nash, C. E. (1975). *Aquaculture* **5**, 19–29.

Lake, J. S. (1967). *Aust. J. mar. Freshwat. Res.* **18**, 137–153.

Lam, T. J. (1982). *Can. J. Fish. aquat. Sci.* **39**, 111–137.

Lasker, R. (1974). *In* "Proceedings of the Fifth Annual Meeting, World Mariculture Society", pp. 313–318. Louisiana State University, Baton Rouge, Louisiana.

Liley, N. R. (1980). *In* "Fish Behavior and its Role in the Capture and Culture of Fish" (J. E. Bardach, J. J. Magnuson, R. C. May and J. M. Reinhart, eds), pp. 210–246. ICLARM Conference Proceedings 5, Manila.

Liley, N. R. (1982). *Can. J. Fish. aquat. Sci.* **39**, 22–35.

Lobel, P. S. (1978). *Pacific Sci.* **32**, 193–207.

Lowe-McConnell, R. H. (1975). "Fish Communities in Tropical Freshwaters: Their Distribution, Ecology and Evolution". Longman, London.

Marshall, J. A. (1967). *Anim. Behav.* **15**, 510–513.

May, R. C., Akiyama, G. S. and Santerre, M. T. (1979). *Fish. Bull.* **76**, 300–304.

Meyer, K. Λ. (1977). *Jap. J. Ichthyol.* **24**, 101 112.

Morell, J. I., Kelley, D. B. and Pfaff, D. W. (1975). *In* "Brain-endocrine Interaction. II. The Ventricular System in Neuroendocrine Mechanisms" (K. M. Knigge, D. E. Scott, H. Kobayashi and S. Ishii, eds), pp. 230–256. Karger, Basel.

Munz, H., Stumpf, W. E. and Jennes, L. (1981). *Brain Res.* **221**, 1–13.

Nagahama, Y., Kagawa, H. and Tashiro, F. (1980). *Bull. Jap. Soc. scient. Fish.* **46**, 1097–1102.

Ng, T. B. and Idler, D. R. (1979). *Gen. Comp. Endocrinol.* **38**, 410–420.

Nozaki, M. and Kobayashi, H. (1979). *Arch. Histol. Japon.* **42**, 201–219.

Ogata, H., Nomura, T. and Hata, H. (1979). *Bull. Jap. Soc. scient. Fish.* **45**, 929–931.

Pandey, S., Stacey, N. E. and Hoar, W. S. (1973). *Can. J. Zool.* **51**, 1315–1316.

Peter, R. E. (1970). *Gen. Comp. Endocrinol.* **14**, 334–356.

Peter, R. E. (1982). *Can. J. Fish. aquat. Sci.* **39**, 48–55.

Peter, R. E. (1983). *In* "Fish Physiology" (W. S. Hoar and D. J. Randall, eds), Vol. IX. Academic Press, New York (in press).

Peter, R. E. and Crim, L. W. (1978). *Ann. Biol. anim. Biochem. Biophys.* **18**, 819–823.

Peter, R. E. and Paulencu, C. R. (1980). *Neuroendocrinology* **31**, 133–141.

Peter, R. E., Crim, L. W., Goos, H. J. Th. and Crim, J. W. (1978). *Gen. Comp. Endocrinol.* **35**, 391–401.

Peter, R. E., Kah, O., Paulencu, C. R., Cook, H. and Kyle, A. L. (1980). *Cell Tiss. Res.* **212**, 429–442.

Pickford, G. E., Knight, W. R., Knight, J. N., Gallardo, R. and Baker, B. I. (1981). *J. exp. Zool.* **217**, 341–351.

Robinson, E. J. and Rugh, R. (1943). *Biol. Bull., Woods Hole* **84**, 115–125.

Schreibman, M. P., Halpern, L. R., Goos, H. J. Th. and Margolis-Kazan, H. (1979). *J. exp. Zool.* **210**, 153–159.

Schwassmann, H. O. (1978). *In* "Rhythmic Activity of Fishes" (J. E. Thorpe, ed.), pp. 187–200. Academic Press, New York.

Simpson, A. C. (1971). *J. Cons. int. Explor. Mer* **34**, 58–64.

Stacey, N. E. (1981). *Am. Zool.* **21**, 305–316.

Stacey, N. E. and Goetz, F. W. (1982). *Can. J. Fish. aquat. Sci.* **39**, 92–98.

Stacey, N. E. and Hourtson, A. S. (1982). *Can. J. Fish. aquat. Sci.* **39**, 489–498.

Stacey, N. E. and Pandey, S. (1975). *Prostaglandins* **9**, 597–607.

Stacey, N. E., Cook, A. F. and Peter, R. E. (1979a). *Gen. Comp. Endocrinol.* **37**, 246–249.

Stacey, N. E., Cook, A. F. and Peter, R. E. (1979b). *J. Fish Biol.* **15**, 349–361.

Stuart-Kregor, P. A. C., Sumpter, J. P. and Dodd, J. M. (1981). *J. Fish Biol.* **18**, 59–72.

Sundararaj, B. I. (1981). Food and Agriculture Organization of the United Nations — Aquaculture Development and Coordination Program **16**, 1–82.

Sundararaj, B. I. and Goswami, S. V. (1977). *Gen. Comp. Endocrinol.* **32**, 17–28.

Suzuki, K., Tamaoki, B. and Hirose, K. (1981). *Gen. Comp. Endocrinol.* **45**, 473–481.

Taylor, M. H. and Di Michelle, L. (1980). *Copeia* **1980**, 118–125.

Truscott, B., Idler, D. R., Sundararaj, B. I. and Goswami, S. V. (1978). *Gen. Comp. Endocrinol.* **34**, 149–157.

Ueda, H. and Takahashi, H. (1977). *Bull. Fac. Fish., Hokkaido Univ.* **28**, 106–117.

Van Ree, G. E., Lok, D. and Bosman, G. (1977). *Proc. Kon. Ned. Akad. Wetensch. C* **80**, 353–371.

Wallace, R. A. and Selman, K. (1978). *Devel. Biol.* **62**, 354–359.

Weil, C., Breton, B. and Reinaud, P. (1975). *C. R. Acad. Sci. Paris* **280D**, 2469–2472.

Yamamoto, Nagahama, Y. and Yamazaki, F. (1966). *Bull. Jap. Soc. scient. Fish.* **32**, 977–983.

Zohar, Y. and Gordin, H. (1979). *J. Fish Biol.* **15**, 665–670.

13. Parental Behaviour in Temperate Marine Teleosts with Special Reference to the Development of Nest Structures

GEOFFREY W. POTTS

Marine Biological Association U.K., Plymouth, U.K.

Abstract: Parental care among teleosts is widespread and has evolved independently in many marine and freshwater families. It consists of a series of often quite complex behavioural patterns that take place both before and after the gametes are fertilized and which serve to increase the chances of survival of the eggs or young that the parent fish has produced. Before fertilization it may be difficult to assess the significance of the adult fish's behaviour (courtship, territoriality and nest building) in terms that can be clearly identified as a parental investment. However, activities such as nest building do have a clear relationship to parental care and would be of little or no significance to the adult fish alone. An examination of the environmental pressures upon inshore fish gives clues about why certain types of behaviour have evolved, their adaptive significance and the controlling mechanisms. Examples of parental care are discussed and especially the role of nest building in the inshore environment.

I. INTRODUCTION

There have been a number of important reference works and reviews on the reproduction of marine fish (Reese, 1964; Breder and Rosen, 1966; Gibson, 1969, 1982; Wootton, 1976; Johannes, 1978; Keenleyside, 1979) and several that have made specific reference to the role of parental care (Ridley, 1978; Perrone and Zaret, 1979; Blumer, 1979; Werren *et al.*, 1980; Barlow, 1962, 1981; Baylis, 1978, 1981; Keenleyside, 1981). These works clearly show that parental care in fish is widespread and may be found in both fresh water and marine environments, in tropical or temperate waters at many depths and associated with many different habitat types. So many cases of convergent evolution (Marshall, 1971) provide a rich comparative field for the evolutionary biologist (Barlow, 1962; Balon, 1975) who can draw parallels from different habitats or from dissimilar taxonomic groups. More recently discussions are emerging on the evolutionary significance of reproductive

FISH REPRODUCTION
ISBN: 0–12–563660–1

behaviour initiated by the ideas on parental investment and sexual selection (Trivers, 1972; Williams, 1975) and developed into evolutionary models by Maynard Smith (1977), Stearns (1980) and others. Important as these reviews are in providing a better understanding of the underlying mechanisms and principles involved, there is a tendency to minimize or oversimplify the role of the environment. There is also the basic assumption that individual species are inflexible in their *modus operandi* and that once a strategy is adopted minor changes in the environment will seriously threaten their survival. In reality it is more usual to find that the tactical elements within a single strategy are such that they provide a degree of behavioural flexibility and give the individual the ability to respond effectively to environmental change.

The temperate inshore environment is subjected to dramatic variation, not only due to seasonal and climatic changes, but also to short term tidal factors (Lewis, 1964). The resulting habitat can change from calm conditions with a good underwater visibility to turbulent seas in which the underwater visibility is reduced to zero within a few hours. Under such conditions it is important that inshore fishes are able to respond quickly and that their reproductive tactics give them the flexibility to respond appropriately (Gibson, 1969; Frank and Leggett, 1981). It is also probable that the high proportion of demersal eggs among inshore temperate fish (Russell, 1976) is related to the selective pressures of a turbulent environment in which floating eggs are vulnerable to being cast ashore (Marshall, 1965). The decision as to whether a fish can afford to adopt an inflexible reproductive strategy in a changeable environment, or whether it is prudent to go for an opportunistic strategy, will be examined with special reference to the significance of nest building among inshore fish.

II. CLASSIFICATION AND REPRODUCTION

There have been several attempts to classify the modes of reproduction of teleost fishes and in all cases much of the data is obtained from that important descriptive review by Breder and Rosen (1966) using the systematic classification of Greenwood et al. (1966). Breder and Rosen divide the fish taxa into seven main divisions based upon a number of anatomical, developmental and behavioural characters. Any such classification is bound to have its shortcomings and of the estimated 20 000 known species (Cohen, 1970) Breder and Rosen (1966) have described details for only about 300 species. Balon (1975) uses this information to create his own ecological classification of 32 "guilds" or descriptive categories designed to encompass all known fish. Such classifications are helpful in relating species to their environment, but do not easily cope with behavioural change or intraspecific variability.

Balon (1975) indicates that there are two main environmental factors responsible for determining the course of reproductive and parental behaviour as well as the subsequent development of the larvae: these are the presence of predators and the availability of oxygen. The importance of these factors can clearly be seen in the adoption of territorial behaviour, nest building and the subsequent nest care, but there are other factors as important in controlling the parental behaviour and these will be discussed.

III. PELAGIC FISH AND DEMERSAL EGGS

Examination of the marine fishes of the N.E. Atlantic region (Wheeler, 1969) shows that of the 68 most common families of teleosts present only 15 (22%)* show parental care and 31 (45%) produce free floating eggs and exhibit no parental care. This latter group are in the main pelagic species which produce eggs in very large numbers (*Mola mola* the Atlantic sunfish is reported to produce 300 million eggs). Most of these families are represented by fish that themselves swim in mid water with the most notable exception being the flat fish. The large numbers of eggs produced and their rapid dispersal makes it impossible for the adults to show any form of parental care and such territoriality as may be present is often a temporary phenomenon of short duration and designed to increase the chance of a fish successfully fertilizing eggs in the presence of competition.

The production of demersal eggs is a fundamental step in the evolution of parental care in fish and it is interesting to examine some examples where such eggs are produced, but where parental care is reduced or absent. Demersal eggs are mostly larger and produced in smaller numbers than pelagic eggs (Williams, 1959) and unless protected in some way are vulnerable to predation and other environmental hazards. The herring is an exception, being a pelagic species in which each race has its own spawning ground where demersal eggs are produced. As is customary with pelagic species the eggs are produced in very large numbers and while it is known they attract predators (i.e. haddock) it is possible the quantity of eggs satiates the predators rapidly so reducing the total effect of predation.

The Ammodytidae have demersal eggs which are buried in sandy substrates in the winter months (Reay, 1973; Winslade, 1974), but usually particulate substrates, because of their mobility and the risks of smothering and abrasion, are unsuitable for raising eggs. Eggs left on the sea floor for even a short time are exposed to predation and without some form of parental care are better sited where these threats are minimized. The Belonidae, Osmeridae and some species of the Exocoetidae have overcome this problem by attaching eggs to weeds, sticks, rocks and other prominent topographic features to keep them

* These figures may be compared with those given by Blumer (1979) who showed that 84 families (20%) of the 422 families of teleosts listed in the classification of Greenwood et al. (1966) showed parental care.

off the bottom and in a site of good water movement (Gudger, 1937). In these and many other marine teleosts with demersal eggs the eggs are relatively large (Williams, 1959) and provided with an adhesive coat or fine filamentous hairs to aid attachment to the substrate (Russell, 1976).

IV. REPRODUCTIVE BEHAVIOUR IN INSHORE FISH

Where inshore teleosts show parental care it is performed predominantly by the male fish (Baylis, 1978, 1981; Loiselle, 1978; Ridley, 1978; Blumer, 1979; Keenseyside, 1979, 1981) and the female after spawning has little or no additional role in looking after the developing eggs with a few exceptions (Gudger, 1927; Daniels, 1979). The role played by the male fish varies considerably between different species and even within a single species males of different age or type may have very different behaviours (Dipper *et al.*, 1977; Dipper and Pullin, 1979; Gross and Charnov, 1980; Gross, Chap. 4, this volume). Taking Blumer's (1979) (see also Keenseyside, 1981) definition of parental care to include not only behaviour designed to increase the survival of the zygote, but also non-gametic contributions, it is convenient to start by identifying some of those behaviours that constitute parental care. Blumer lists a series of behaviours that may be regarded as parental care and identifies which sex is responsible for each within the families reviewed. Several of his categories are more conveniently joined when considering inshore fish.

A. Spawning site selection

Demersal eggs of inshore fish are not deposited at random, but put at preselected sites within the fishes' range that may afford some protection for them. The mechanism of site selection is almost completely unknown in fish although some details have been identified (Colgan and Ealey, 1973; Keenleyside and Prince, 1976). However, there may be parallels with the selection of nesting sites and preferred habitats in other taxa and which has been examined by Hinde and Steel (1966), Partridge (1978) and others. Certainly synchronizing the reproductive states of male and female fish is of great importance and especially in an environment as turbulent and variable as the temperate coastal zone (Gibson, 1969; Keenleyside, 1979).

B. Territorial behaviour

Once a spawning site is selected then inshore fish normally show an increase in territorial aggression. Initially the defended area may have significance to the adult fish as a defended food resource, but it will also provide an "exclusion zone" around the spawning site where the territorial aggression reaches its greatest intensity (Assem, 1967). The significance of this territoriality is to increase the probability of a male fish fertilizing any particular clutch of eggs (Perrone and Zaret, 1979) and to afford protection for the developing eggs (Murray, 1981).

C. Nest building

Having chosen a spawning site the next decisions by the fish are how much protection does the unmodified site provide and what is needed to augment this? These decisions are related and tackled in different ways by different species of fish. If the site is optimal (Baylis, 1981) it will need no modification and parental care is not necessary. Thus at its simplest the eggs are laid onto the substrate and little or no additional protection is provided. By contrast the most elaborate nest structures are always produced by fish that show extended parental care presumably in response to suboptimal conditions. These sites vary in complexity from burrows, depressions and mounds in particulate substrates to the use of shells, stones, algae and complex nests in which materials are arranged into highly organized structures.

D. Courtship and spawning

The courtship and spawning behaviours of inshore fish are strikingly different between species. In pelagic species sexual dimorphism and dichromism are reduced or absent just as are most forms of parental care, but fish with demersal eggs show an increasing dimorphism as the nature of the parental role differs with each sex. In most inshore fish it is the male fish that builds the nest and guards the eggs and is often larger and more brightly coloured than the female (Ridley, 1978; Blumer, 1979; Keenleyside, 1979).

E. Parental care and parental investment

Each of Blumer's (1979) behavioural categories has a direct bearing upon the survival of the eggs despite some being performed before the eggs are laid, and must be considered part of the total parental investment. Trivers (1972) defines the parental investment of an adult animal as that investment made by the parent that will increase the chances of survival of an individual offspring at the cost of the parent investing in other offspring. Thus, parental investment covers many activities shown by the parent before the gametes are fertilized as well as those designed specifically to increase the survival of the zygotes. Blumer (1979) uses a modified definition of parental care to cover "non-gametic contributions that directly or indirectly contribute to the survival and reproductive success of the offspring". This definition is wider in scope than that of Trivers (1972) and offers the chance to consider the significance of environmental variability on reproductive behaviour.

The most common expressions of parental care among inshore fish consist of nest building, territoriality, nest cleaning, removal of dead eggs and decaying matter from the nest (mouth manipulation) and fanning behaviour. Fanning itself may occur at a nest in the absence of eggs which suggests the fish is in a state of physiological readiness waiting only for the appropriate external stimulus, namely the eggs to initiate the full parental fanning cycle (van Iersel, 1953). Many of our present ideas on the reproductive behaviour of fish stem from studies on the mutal inhibition between the sexual and parental drives (van Iersel, 1953; Sevenster, 1961 and others) and the extensive body of work on the three spined stickleback *Gasterosteus aculeatus* (literature reviewed in Wootton, 1976).

V. NEST BUILDING AND PARENTAL CARE IN INSHORE FISH

Inshore fish are well adapted to the turbulence of the littoral zone as may be shown by such morphological adaptations as, small body size, compressed or anguilliform bodies, modified fins, reduced swimbladders and physiological and behavioural adaptations (Gibson, 1969, 1982; Miller, 1979b). Among these adaptations are the development of parental care and the use of sheltered spawning sites and nests to help egg survival. The present section examines the development of nest structures in relation to environmental pressures.

A. Unguarded egg masses

Fine particulate substrates such as mud, sand or coarse sands are relatively mobile in shallow inshore waters and fish that live on or in association with such areas normally have pelagic eggs (flatfish, Callionymidae, Triglidae and Trachiuridae), thereby preventing the risk of them being abraded or smothered by moving particles. In deeper water where conditions are less turbulent there is less risk of smothering and eggs may be deposited on the bottom in ribbons (Lophiidae). While no parental care or territoriality is known among the Lophiidae it may be speculated that the egg ribbons themselves are unpalatable so avoiding predation and light enough to drift over the substrate thus preventing them being smothered.

B. Crevice spawning sites

Where a particulate substrate is compacted with occasional outcrops of rock, stones and shells there may be found a mixture of both particulate spawning gobies and those families normally associated with rocky substrates such as the Cottidae, (Thomopoulos and Bauchot, 1957), Scorpaenidae, Cyclopteridae (Demartini, 1978; Witman, 1978), Pholidae (Gudger, 1927; Qasim, 1956, 1957a; Sawyer, 1967), and Blenniidae (Qasim, 1957b; Wickler, 1957;

Gibson, 1969) Tripterygiidae (Wirtz, 1978). In these families the demersal eggs are deposited in clumps or in flat layers attached to the substrate and often associated with crevices (Fig. 1b). In several families one or both parents remain with the eggs driving away would-be predators and providing limited parental care (e.g. *Centronotus gunnellus* (Gudger, 1927).

The Cottidae and Scorpaenidae are anatomically very similar and most live

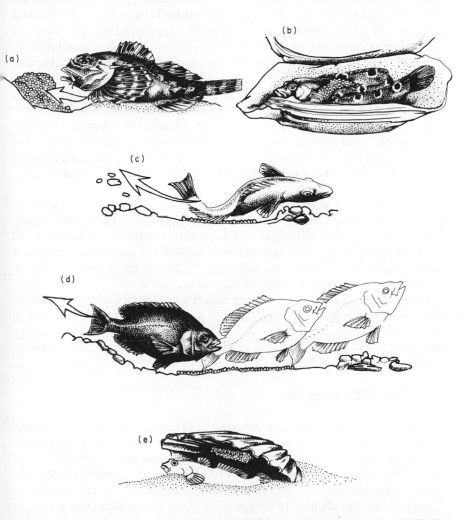

Fig. 1.   The spawning sites of some common inshore fishes: (a) Open site (Cottidae); (b) Simple crevice (Pholidae); (c) Shallow depression (*Labrus mixtus*, Labridae); (d) Shallow depression (*Spondyliosoma cantharus*, Sparidae); (e) Sheltered crevice site involving some excavation (Gobiidae). Figs (c) and (d) indicate the way each fish excavates the spawning depression. The arrows show the direction of water movement created by the fishes' fanning and nest clearing activities.

in deep water and little is known about their reproductive behaviour except for the littoral *Taurulus bubalis*. In this species the fish become mature in spring (April, May) when the males court the females with a series of head nods, and raising of the unpaired fins. If receptive the female seeks out a suitable spawning site where the eggs are fertilized by the male. The eggs are often laid in association with a crevice, but may be deposited in exposed sites (Fig. 1a). The male and/or female may remain at the egg site for several hours and the male has been recorded by Le Danois (1913) and Thomopoulos and Bauchot (1957) as guarding and fanning the eggs although this does not always occur (personal observation). [See conflicting reports mentioned by Ridley (1978).] It has been suggested that during courtship the males may engulf the head of the female, but this does not often occur as the male fish is mostly smaller than the female. The larger females dominate the behaviour and one female may have one or several males attempting to court her at the same time, although it is not known if more than one male attempts to fertilize her eggs. No territorial behaviour has been identified in the marine species, but it is fully developed in the fresh water *Cottus gobio* where the male is larger than the female, is territorial and has a fully developed fanning cycle (Morris, 1954).

Other inshore fish with demersal eggs and similar anatomical features to the Cottids may have similar behaviour, the Liparidae (Demartini, 1978), Agonidae and Gobiesocidae may all have similar modes of reproduction. All are known to have demersal eggs that may be found in gelatinous clumps and some form of limited parental care may be shown by laying the eggs in crevices, egg fanning and guarding behaviour.

The Blennidae like the Cottidae are best known from a freshwater example *Blennius fluviatilis* (Wickler, 1957). In this species the male drives the female away after spawning and looks after the eggs by fanning, rubbing and the removal of dead eggs. The review of Gibson (1969) should be consulted for further details of this family.

C. Excavated spawning sites

In deeper water below the main influence of the waves the coarse particulate sands and shell gravels are relatively stable and the risk of smothering is less except during violent storms. Here a single species of British sparid *Spondyliosoma cantharus* and the labrid *Labrus mixtus* spawn. In both cases the male fish undergo striking colour changes; the black bream (*S. cantharus*) changing from silvery grey to conspicuous black with a white bar, while the cuckoo wrasse (*L. mixtus*) undergoes two phases of colour change, firstly the natural blue and yellow colours of the body intensify and take on an iridescent hue and during courtship and spawning the top of the head becomes white (Wilson, 1958). *L. mixtus* also shows dichromism and the female is brown with conspicuous black and white blotches on the top of the caudal peduncle.

The nest of these species consists of a shallow depression prepared by the male beating its tail to clear gravel and by pushing and spitting gravel with the mouth. The black bream remains upright when beating the nest, moving across the nest and gradually turning its head upwards so that the main thrust of the tail is downwards and into the nest depression (Fig. 1d) a movement very similar to that seen in the freshwater Centrarchid *Lepomis* (Keenleyside, 1979). By contrast the cuckoo wrasse provides its main digging thrust by turning its flank into the nest depression and vigorously beating the tail (Fig. 1c) (Wilson, 1958). In addition the wrasse may use its open mouth to push gravel clear of the spawning site. In both the cuckoo wrasse and black bream the male remains at the nest depression guarding the area and chasing away other fish. Females are courted with vibration displays and will eventually spawn in the nest depression producing a single layer of eggs adhering to the nest floor. Several females may spawn in each nest. After spawning the black bream chases away the female and defends the nest and adjacent area from other fish or even decapod crustacea. As the nest is an open depression and eggs deposited as a single layer it might be supposed that oxygen deficiency is never a serious threat, but even so the male fish has been observed by Wilson (1958) slowly swimming above the eggs "wriggling his body and fanning vigorously with tail and fins". The purpose of this behaviour must be primarily to prevent silt from smothering the eggs. The behaviour of the male *L. mixtus* is very similar.

Details of the reproduction and parental care of the ballan wrasse, *L. bergylta* are not well known. The older literature (Mathews, 1887) described them as constructing an algal nest, but this is now known to be incorrect as they have been seen producing nest depressions similar to *L. mixtus* in aquaria (Sjolander *et al.*, 1972, and personal observation). It is expected that they will use similar behavioural tactics to *L. mixtus*, but more observations are needed. The role of parental investment and parental care is particularly interesting in *L. bergylta* and *L. mixtus* as both have been shown to undergo sex reversal, where the mature and functional females change sex and become functional males (Dipper *et al.*, 1977). The factors controlling sex change in these labrids are not yet known, but may involve social suppression of the kind found in tropical anthiids (Shapiro, 1981a,b, Chap. 7, this volume) and labrids (Robertson, 1972).

D. Crevices, burrows and parental building

One of the most successful families occupying the inshore and estuarine region are the gobies (Miller, 1961, 1979a; Reese, 1964; Gibson, 1969; Ridley, 1978 and others). Small bodied fish with pelvic fins modified into a ventral sucker they are well adapted to survive in shallow marine areas (Miller, Chap. 8, this volume). One of the most common is the genus *Pomatoschistus* which lives on sand and estuarine muds. The male fish provides protection for the eggs by selecting a sheltered spawning site beneath stones or shells and guarding it against other males (Vestergaard, 1976). The crevice may be deepened by burrowing activities of the adult until there is an adequate space beneath for the eggs and also the male and female fish (Fig. 1e). Sargent and Gebler (1980) and Sargent (1982) have shown that sticklebacks have higher reproductive success when their eggs are protected in crevice nests making them less vulnerable to predators, and reducing the risk of interference by conspecifics during courtship and of nest intrusions. The same advantages probably also apply to gobies which may achieve considerable densities over inshore sands. In such areas the conspicuous behaviour of the courting and territorial male increases their own vulnerability to larger predators and it is probable that on such occasions the spawning crevice serves to protect the adult fish as well as the eggs. This is certainly true of gobies living in or in association with burrows.

Several females spawn in each nest and the male remains with the eggs guarding them from predators and preventing silting of the nest crevice. Nyman [quoted by Keenleyside (1979)] discusses the excavation techniques in *P. microps* and which include mouth digging, pushing, fin digging, tail digging and egg fanning. The risk of silting is always present in inshore waters where turbulent conditions move very considerable quantities of particulate organic and inorganic material and it is probable that this has been a major factor in the evolution of nest fanning and other types of parental care.

With the use of burrows and crevices by marine gobies the situation arose where they would at times use burrows excavated by other marine organisms. Provided these organisms did not prey upon the goby or eggs the way was open to evolve some form of symbiotic dependency and this has occurred with many goby/shrimp (Luther, 1958; Karplus *et al.*, 1972, 1979; Preston, 1978) and goby/anemone (Abel, 1960) associations. In these associations not only do the symbionts derive benefit from the extra protection and warning of other predators, but they may also both participate in digging the burrow and keeping the entrance clear.

E. Nests

At its simplest the spawning crevice needs very little modification by the adult fish, but once the eggs are laid a high level of attendance by the adult fish is needed to protect and care for them. In species that have prolonged periods of parental care either owing to slow egg development or the need to look after several clutches of eggs the energetic demands can be significant and the fish will need to feed during this period. For some species the area adjacent to the nest can provide an adequate supply of food, but other species must forage over wide areas leaving the eggs unattended for relatively long periods of time.

In such situations the fish are often found to build nests in which the eggs are covered. In the Gasterosteidae the algal nest is bound together with mucoprotein strands produced by the kidney of the male (Fig. 2a). Enclosed within this nest the eggs are protected from sudden predation so that the male fish can leave the nest for territorial or feeding forays. The actual survival value of this added protection will depend upon balancing the risk of leaving such a nest unattended against the extra effort of building and maintaining it. One of the main risks comes from conspecific males in the area of a nest and which make attempts to pilfer eggs (Semler, 1971), although this is not always so (Wootton, 1971). The extra protection afforded by a covered or closely woven nest reduces external predation but at the same time increases the risk

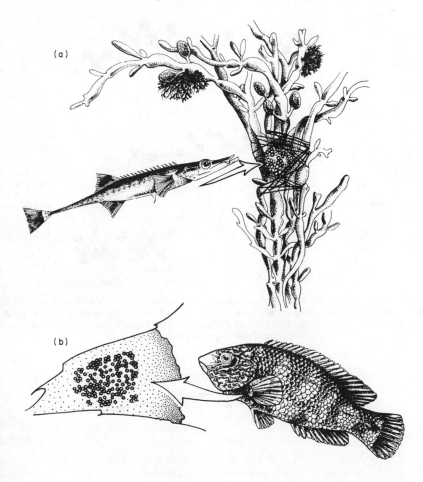

Fig. 2. The nests of (a) *Spinachia spinachia* (Gasterosteidae) and (b) *Crenilabrus melops* (Labridae). The arrows indicate the direction of water movement created by the fanning activities of the fish. The nests are shown diagrammatically in section to show the position of the eggs.

of silting and so fanning, pushing, boring and mouthing become an important part of parental care. The role of fanning has been examined in the sea stickleback (Sevenster, 1951), the fresh water three-spine stickleback (van Iersel, 1953; Sevenster, 1961), the ten-spine stickleback (Morris, 1958) and the river Bullhead (Morris, 1954). Studies by the author on the marine sea stickleback, *Spinachia spinachia* have shown that this species may also spend a considerable part of the post spawning period in fanning (Fig. 3) and that this activity will increase if silt is placed on the nest, the carbon dioxide level is increased or if the oxygen levels at the nest are reduced (Fig. 4).

The covered nest also provides the opportunity for the adult to rear several

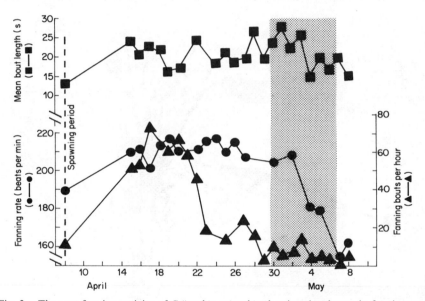

Fig. 3. The nest fanning activity of *Spinachia spinachia* showing the change in fanning rate (●———●), fanning bout length (■———■) and number of fanning bouts per hour (▲———▲) during parental care. The spawning period is indicated and the stippled area represents the period during which the eggs are hatched.

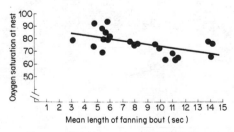

Fig. 4. The effect of environmental oxygen on the mean length of each fanning bout of *Spinachia spinachia*.

clutches of eggs as may be exemplified by the labrid *Crenilabrus melops* (Potts, 1974, 1985) which has one of the most elaborate nest structures so far recorded in marine teleosts. The nest building of *C. melops* will be dealt with in some detail.

In the second and third year the male *C. melops* becomes mature, but it is not until the fourth year that they show striking sexual dimorphism and build a nest. The fourth year male shows a darkening of the body pigmentation and the development of irridescent blue markings on the opercular covers (Potts, 1974). These males become territorial in spring driving away other fish and begin to build algal nests in suitable crevices (Fig. 2b). The algal composition of the nest depends upon the situation of the crevice and the species of algae available (Potts, 1985). Fiedler (1964) only recorded a relatively simple nest structure from Banyuls, France, but the present author has found far more complex nests in the Western Channel. Further within one region sublittoral sites may have a different algae composition to littoral sites. Sublittoral nests contain more Coralline algae than those built in the littoral zone which have a lower proportion of *Corallina* and a higher quantity of *Gigartina*, *Polyides* and other species of algae. Table I shows the difference in the algae composition of representative nests collected from the midlittoral region and from the shallow sublittoral region. Further analysis of the nest also indicates that it has a definite structure such that different algae are incorporated at different sites

TABLE I. The algal composition of two nests of *Crenilabrus melops*, one taken from the midlittoral zone, the other from the sublittoral zone.

Alga	Midlittoral nest Wet weight (g)	(%)	Sublittoral nest Wet weight (g)	(%)
Corallina officinalis L.	336·9	32·0	1276·4	72·7
Gigartina stellata (Stack h. in With)	422·1	40·1	248·0	14·1
Calliblepharis ciliata (Huds.)	67·8	6·4	—	—
Polysiphonia lanosa (L.)	165·0	15·7	0·4	0·1
Polyides rotundus (Huds.)	12·4	1·2	4·8	0·3
Ahnfeltia plicata (Huds.)	8·2	0·8	4·2	0·2
Cystoseira tamariscifolia (Huds.)	0·8	0·1	—	—
Gigartina pistillata (S.G. Gmel.)	10·6	1·0	—	—
Lomentaria articulata (Huds.)	8·4	0·8	—	—
Ascophyllum nodosum (L.)	0·9	0·1	—	—
Laurencia pinnatifida (Huds.)	0·4	0·1	1·3	0·1
Plocamium cartilagineum (L.)	—	—	80·5	4·6
Gelidium sp.	7·4	0·7	136·9	7·8
Ulva sp.	3·9	0·4	—	'
Fucus sp.	0·3	0·1		
Enteromorpha sp.	0·4	0·1		
Unidentified	8·0	0·8	2·5	0·1
Total	1053·5		1755·0	

within the nest (Fig. 5). If the nest is divided into four fractions from the back of the crevice towards the front, it is found that the deepest part of the nest contains a higher percentage of the algae *Gigartina* and *Polyides* which constitutes the egg laying substrate where the eggs are deposited at spawning. Towards the outer face of the nest there is an increase in the percentage of *Corallina* whose function is to provide a protective outer layer to the nest. Its functional significance as a protective layer can be seen by the fact the broken ends form adhesive terminals which stick to themselves or other algae and which cause the *Corallina* face to form a cohesive network holding the nest

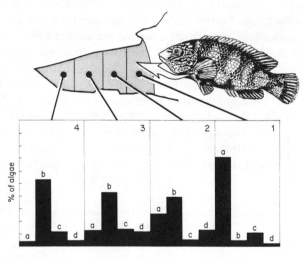

Fig. 5. Histogram of the relative proportions of the most abundant algae found in different fractions of a representative nest of *Crenilabrus melops*. Fraction 1 being the front face, fraction 4 the part deepest in the nesting crevice. a: *Corallina*; b: *Gigartina*; c: *Polysiphonia*; d: *Polyides*.

together in the crevice and protecting the eggs. While the proportion of *Corallina* is highest in sublittoral nests where it is most abundant, it is also an important component of littoral nests where it is collected from rock pools and sites of standing water by the male fish. Examination of the nest suggests that the fish builds from the back of the crevice towards the front gradually changing from algae suitable for an egg laying substrate to the protective cover of *Corallina*. Such a system would closely match that found in birds (Hinde and Steel, 1962, 1966). However, direct underwater observations have shown that the nesting male builds the nest along crevices rather than from back to front, and puts the different algae as they are collected in the appropriate parts of the nest (Fig. 2b). This would suggest that the control of nest building is not governed by changes in blood hormones as has been shown in birds, but is controlled by direct environmental feedback once the fish reaches maturity and is in spawning condition (see Bye, Chap. 11, this volume and Stacey, Chap. 12, this volume) for discussion of the hormonal control of reproductive behaviour]. By building along a crevice the male can spawn with more than one female as well as reducing the exposed spawning surface of the nest to predators or nest intruders.

A further aspect of the parental behaviour of *C. melops* should be noted at this stage. During the early part of nest building the male is aggressive to both male and female conspecifics and other fish that approach the nest. Once the nest structure is well formed aggressive attacks of the male on the mature females are modified to form courtship displays which eventually attracts the female to the nest where they spawn (Potts, 1974). Immediately after spawning the male becomes aggressive towards the female again and chases her away from the nest where he proceeds to cover the exposed eggs with algae. When the eggs are covered the male is again ready to court and spawn with another female. It is suggested that the male is aggressive when exposed eggs are present in the nest and also that their presence induces the male to start a bout of nest building until the eggs are covered. Once they are covered the male is then ready to spawn again and in this way protection is provided for several clutches of eggs during the season. The explanation of this behaviour would again suggest that once the fish is physiologically primed the external environment (the presence of exposed eggs at the nest) acts as a trigger in controlling the behaviour of the adult male. Eventually the male covers the remaining nest with *Corallina* and proceeds to fan and guard the nest until the eggs hatch between 11 and 16 days later, depending upon the number of clutches present and the water temperature.

The protective function of the nest is important from several points of view. That it protects the developing eggs is obvious, but equally important is that by being covered it allows the male to leave the nest for periods of time when gathering more nesting material or when foraging for food. This takes on special significance when it is recognized that some *C. melops* nests are built in the littoral region during high water. Under these conditions the male is forced to leave the nest unattended as the tide drops, when the males form non-aggressive feeding aggregations in the immediate sublittoral region. When the tide rises the males return to their same nest and once more show territorial aggression and nest orientated behaviour depending upon the state of development of the nest.

The exposed mid-littoral nest is vulnerable to desiccation, temperature fluctuations and predation by littoral predators, but the bulk of the structure, its tight-knit surface and the crevice situation guarantee that the developing eggs remain moist, at a suitable temperature and well protected. The environmental stability of the inner part of the nest was clearly seen by records of nest temperatures taken in mid-summer. Inner regions of the nest containing eggs remained at the same temperature as inshore sea water and were at times several degrees lower than adjacent rock pools and could be 10–15°C cooler than the air temperature. The vulnerability of fish eggs to desiccation and significance of algae in controlling this have also been shown by Marliave (1981) for *Clinocottus* sp.

Thus it would appear that the control of reproductive behaviour in *C. melops* is similar to that found in sticklebacks (Baggerman, 1968) combined with the effect of temperature on the overall metabolic rate and rate of gonad maturation (Hoar, 1969; Schneider, 1969). Once the male fish are mature they retain hormonal levels constant throughout the spawning season and rely upon environmental feedback mechanisms to control events. The value of this system becomes clear when considering the changeability of the environment in which temperate marine fish live. It enables fish to remain responsive to reproductive opportunities throughout turbulent conditions so that during periods of suitable calm the fish can at once continue reproductive activities and parental care. It is only after the young hatch and are released from the nest that the male shows an overall decline in its parental behaviour although *C. melops* has been shown to be capable of building several nests in one season (Potts, 1974).

F. Brood pouches

Of the temperate marine species only members of the Syngnathidae possess a brood pouch. The pouch is only present in male fish and is best developed in the sea horses where it contains the developing eggs which are deposited by the female. In the pipefish the eggs are uncovered carried attached to depressions in the ventral surface of the male fish. The brood pouches of the Syngnathidae enable them to provide parental care without the need for a nest or permanent site attachment. Such a system is important to a group which are mostly sedentary in habit and weak swimmers (Fiedler, 1955; Ridley, 1978).

VI. NEST INTRUSIONS

While discussing the functional significance of the nests of inshore fishes the phenomenon of nest intrusion should be mentioned. From the evidence available it is clear that apart from primary nesting males there may be secondary males without nests which intrude upon the spawning act of the nesting male in an attempt to fertilize eggs. Most data relates to the fresh water sticklebacks (Assem, 1967; Wootton, 1971; Li and Owings, 1978) where it has been shown that nest intrusion is one of the commonest causes of brood failure (Black, 1971). Recently Sargent and Gebler (1980) and Sargent (1982) have indicated that an adequate nest structure reduces the impact of nest intrusions. Nest intrusion in the sunfish *Lepomis* was recorded by Keenleyside

(1972) and in a recent study by Gross and Charnov (1980). This genus was shown to have two alternative mating strategies: nest intrusion (cuckoldry) (Gross, Chap. 4, this volume) or parental care. A similar system might also be operating in some British labridae where males that resort to nest intrusion are female mimics (Dipper, 1981).

VII. DISCUSSION

Inshore fish have evolved many behavioural, anatomical and physiological adaptations that suit them for an environment that is both unpredictable and changeable (Lewis, 1964; Gibson, 1969, 1982; Thompson and Lehner, 1976). These adaptations are clearly shown by examining the behavioural tactics of inshore fishes and in particular their parental care (Breder and Rose, 1966; Ridley, 1978; Blumer, 1979; Keenleyside, 1979).

In the inshore environment pelagic eggs are vulnerable to being cast ashore or damaged by abrasion and it is not therefore surprising to find that most inshore fish produce demersal eggs which have some means of attachment. A few species lay demersal eggs attached to rocks or algae and the parent fish exhibits no parental care, but while such eggs may be in exposed sites and well oxygenated, they are also vulnerable to predators. It is possible these eggs are unpalatable in some way which affords some protection and enables them to survive unguarded by the adult fish. Unattended eggs are almost always laid in the sublittoral region away from the risk of desiccation and extremes of temperature and salinity (Marliave, 1981) and other environmental variables.

The first stages in the adoption of crevice spawning sites may have originated from the adult's preference for such a site during spawning. Crevice sites are abundant in shallow coastal regions, involve no constructional work on the part of the parent fish and yet they offer protection from physical dislodging for both eggs and adult fish during turbulent conditions. Crevices are also more easily defended (Sargent, 1982) and permit effective single parent defence against egg predators (which are usually smaller in size than the parent fish). The normal defensive reaction of inshore gobies entails hiding in crevices and burrows and it is not surprising that they should evolve the use of these crevices in providing sites for egg protection. It is probable that the crevice nesting sites of several of the smaller species of inshore fish serve to protect both eggs and adult fish.

The more sheltered the spawning site the easier it is to provide protection from predators, but at the same time there is an increase in the risk of the eggs being smothered in silt and the consequent build up in bacteria, protozoa and fungal infections (Arora, 1948; Masneti, 1964; Talbot, 1966). These will not only compete for available eggs, but may also structurally harm the developing eggs.

Examination of the parental care of fish shows that they have many behavioural adaptations that cope with these problems. The choice of nesting site will have some influence (Kynard, 1978) and must play an important part in the subsequent need for parental care by the adult fish. Other adaptations include the attaching of eggs to the upperside of the crevice, the deposition of a single layer of eggs, the shape of the eggs (Miller, Chap. 8, this volume) as well as behavioural patterns such as fanning, mouthing, pushing and other ways of clearing the spawning site of unwanted organic and inorganic debris.

Baylis (1981) suggests that the evolution of structural nest sites results from a limited number of "optimal sites" in relation to the spawning population of adult fish. Under these conditions it is necessary for a proportion of adults to defend the limited resource and for the remaining adults to accept suboptimal sites that may need to be modified in some way to bring them to the necessary condition for a spawning site. This may explain the presence of littoral nests in a population of *C. melops* (Potts, 1974) where the main offshore population dominates the available space in the sublittoral region and subordinate males or late developers must adopt suboptimal sites in the littoral zone. Baylis (1981) also proposes that the accumulation of silt will render a nest suboptimal and will result in some kind of parental care to restore optimal conditions. Certainly in the highly developed nest structures of the Gasterosteidae and Labridae the risk of silting is considerable and in these families nest fanning, pushing and boring are particularly well developed and may occupy a high proportion of the parents time.

Table II identifies some of the main functions performed by the spawning

TABLE II. The main functions of the spawning sites and nests of inshore fish.

1. Provides the focal point of home range and territorial activity
2. Site attraction for mate
3. Spawning site
4. Provides physical containment of the eggs
5. Protects the eggs from nest intruders (spawners)
6. Increases the probability of paternity (male parental care)
7. Facilitates multiple spawning
8. Facilitates parental care
9. Protects the eggs from predators
10. Protects the parents from predators
11. Protects the eggs in absence of parent(s)
12. Protects the eggs from environmental stress (turbulence, dislodgement, silting, temperature extremes, oxygen deficit, carbon dioxide, etc.)
13. Protects the eggs against infection (bacterial, fungal, protozoan, etc.)

sites and nest structures of inshore fish. The functional significance of each nest will vary from species to species and reflects the complex relationship between the behavioural tactics adopted by the fish and the nature of the environmental pressures acting upon the developing eggs.

The parental care of inshore fish is mostly performed by the male fish (Ridley, 1978; Loiselle, 1978; Blumer, 1979; Perrone and Zaret, 1979; Baylis, 1981; Keenleyside, 1979, 1981). Full discussions on the evolution of paternal care are given by Ridley (1978) who considers that the external mode of fertilization, the need for territoriality, the importance of female choice of the mate and/or spawning site and the opportunity to increase female fecundity are the most important factors involved. Similar conclusions are reached by Baylis (1981) and Blumer (1979) who emphasizes that much of the behaviour and apparent evolution of such behaviour patterns offers the opportunity for the male fish to obtain a "relatively high probability of genetic relatedness to the zygotes". Thus not only must the spawning site serve to protect the developing eggs from environmental hazards, but it must also ensure a site where the gametes of the parent fish have a greater probability of success than those of rival adults.

As most inshore fish exhibit external fertilization the female after laying the eggs has the opportunity to desert them after spawning and before the male fertilises the eggs. Thus if the eggs are to be provided with protection it is most likely that the male will take on this role. Conversely the internal fertilization found in most terrestrial mammals favours female parental care and permits male desertion (Dawkins and Carlisle, 1976). This hypothesis may be true in some cases, but it should be pointed out that female care is not uncommon in some groups of fish indicating other controlling factors in the evolution of parental care (Blumer, 1979).

The demersal eggs of inshore fish when first laid are exposed to fertilization by the nearest mature male. Thus to improve chances of paternity a male may need to drive away other fish from the spawning female. This has been shown to be most successful if spawning can occur in some form of crevice or nesting site (Sargent, 1982). As the protection of such a site is almost as effectively achieved by a single adult there is no advantage in both parents expending energy in territorial behaviour. When the male takes on sole parental care he also enables other females to spawn within his territory and so maximises his genetic contribution to the population. Having established a territory it must be expected that the male will remain and guard his investment. To leave the nest and to spawn elsewhere would not only leave the zygotes vulnerable to predation, but would necessitate the male reestablishing another territory in competition with other males. This would be costly in terms of time and energy and have considerable disadvantages in temperate climates where spawning seasons are of limited duration.

An important and often understated fact relates to the role that the female plays in selecting both the site where she lays her eggs and the "quality" of the male that will fertilize them (Ridley, 1978). Thus if she selects a dominant territorial male she is not only assessing the male's potential, but is also selecting for behavioural characters in the male that will provide protection for her eggs. The use of territorial males by transient females permits polygamy and multiclutch spawnings and it is significant that Ridley and Rechten (1981) have found that female sticklebacks as well as favouring mature nesting males also prefer to lay eggs in nests already containing eggs.

Many different families of inshore fish have independently evolved some form of parental care to provide protection for their demersal eggs. In most cases it is the male fish which exhibits territorial behaviour and provides or constructs a site where the female can spawn. The parental investment in constructing suitable nesting sites reflects upon the environmental and biological pressures that threaten the eggs. Careful examination of the more common types of spawning sites or nest construction indicate that they may serve many different protective functions both in the protection of the developing zygotes, and also for the parent fish. Within the constraints of a fixed spawning site and a limited behavioural repertoire fish have the ability to remain responsive to environmental cues throughout much of the reproductive season. This sensitivity to external triggers provides coastal fish with the ability to respond in the most flexible and appropriate way to the unpredictable inshore environment.

REFERENCES

Abel, E. F. (1960). *Vie et Milieu* 11, 518–531.
Arora, H. L. (1948). *Copeia* 1948, 89–93.
Assem, J. van den (1967). *Behaviour* (Suppl.) 16, 1–164.
Baggerman, B. (1968). *In* "Perspectives in Endocrinology: Hormones in the Lives of Lower Vertebrates" (E. J. W. Barrington and C. Barker Jørgensen, eds), pp. 351–404. Academic Press, London.
Balon, E. K. (1975). *J. Fish. Res. Bd Can.* 32, 821–864.
Barlow, G. W. (1962). *Amer. Zool.* 2, 504.
Barlow, G. W. (1981). *Envir. Biol. Fish.* 6, 65–85.
Baylis, J. R. (1978). *Nature, Lond.* 276, 738.
Baylis, J. R. (1981). *Envir. Biol. Fish.* 6, 223–251.
Black, R. (1971). *Anim. Behav.* 19, 532–541.
Blumer, L. S. (1979). *Q. Rev. Biol.* 54, 149–161.
Breder, C. M. and Rosen, D. E. (1966). "Modes of Reproduction in Fishes". Natural History Press, Garden City.
Cohen, D. M. (1970). *Proc. Calif. Acad. Sci.* Ser. 4, 38, 341–346.
Colgan, P. and Ealey, D. (1973). *J. Fish. Res. Bd Can.* 30, 853–856.
Daniels, R. A. (1979). *Science, N.Y.* 205, 831–833.
Danois, E. Le (1913). *Annls. Inst. oceanogr. Monaco* 10 (5), 1–214.
Dawkins, R. and Carlisle, T. R. (1976). *Nature, Lond.* 262, 131–133.

Demartini, E. E. (1978). *Copeia* **1978**, 537–539.
Dipper, F. (1981). *New Scient.* **90**, 444–445.
Dipper, F. A. and Pullin, R. S. V. (1979). *J. Zool.* **187**, 97–112.
Dipper, F. A., Bridges, C. R. and Menz, A. (1977). *J. Fish Biol.* **11**, 105–120.
Fielder, K. (1955). *Z. Tierpsychol.* **11**, 358–416.
Fielder, K. (1964). *Z. Tierpsychol.* **21**, 521–591.
Frank, K. T. and Leggett, W. C. (1981). *Can. J. Fish. aquat. Sci.* **38**, 215–223.
Gibson, R. N. (1969). *Oceanogr. mar. Biol. Ann. Rev.* **7**, 367–410.
Gibson, R. N. (1982). *Oceanogr. mar. Biol. Ann. Rev.* **20**, 363–414.
Greenwood, P. H., Rosen, D. E., Weitzman, S. H. and Myers, G. S. (1966). *Bull. Am. Mus. Nat. Hist.* **131**, 339–456.
Gross, M. R. and Charnov, E. L. (1980). *Proc. Natn. Acad. Sci. U.S.A.* **77** (No. 11), 6937–6940.
Gudger, E. W. (1927). *Nat. Hist.*, New York **27**, 65–71.
Gudger, E. W. (1937). *Amer. Nat.* **71**, 363–381.
Hinde, R. A. and Steel, E. A. (1962). *Anim. Behav.* **10**, 67–75.
Hinde, R. A. and Steel, E. A. (1966). *Symp. Soc. exp. Biol.* **20**, 401–426.
Hoar, W. S. (1969). *In* "Fish Physiology" (W. S. Hoar and D. J. Randall, eds), Vol. 3, pp. 1–72. Academic Press, London and New York.
Iersel, J. van (1953). *Behaviour*, (Suppl.) **3**, 1–159.
Johannes, R. E. (1978). *Envir. Biol. Fish.* **3**, 65–84.
Karplus, I., Szlep, R. and Tsurnamal, M. (1972). *Mar. Biol.* **15**, 95–104.
Karplus, I., Tsurnamal, M., Szlep, R. and Algom, D. (1979). *Z. Tierpsychol.* **49**, 337–351.
Keenleyside, M. H. A. (1972). *Copeia* **1972**, 272–278.
Keenleyside, M. H. A. (1979). "Diversity and Adaptation in Fish Behaviour". Springer Verlag, Berlin.
Keenleyside, M. H. A. (1981). *Amer. Nat.* **117**, 1019–1022.
Keenleyside, M. H. A. and Prince, C. E. (1976). *Can. J. Zool.* **54**, 2135–2139.
Kynard, B. E. (1978). *Behaviour* **67**, 178–207.
Lewis, J. R. (1964). "The Ecology of Rocky Shores". English University Press, London.
Li, S. K. and Owings, D. H. (1978). *Behaviour* **64**, 298–304.
Loiselle, P. V. (1978). *Nature, Lond.* **276**, 98.
Luther, W. (1958). *Z. Tierpsychol.* **15**, 175–177.
Mansueti, R. J. (1964). *Chesapeake Sci.* **5**, 3–45.
Marliave, J. B. (1981). *Can. J. Zool.* **59**, 1122–1125.
Marshall, N. B. (1965). "The Life of Fishes". Weidenfeld and Nicholson, London.
Marshall, N. B. (1971). "Explorations in the Life of Fishes". Harvard University Press, Cambridge, Massachusetts.
Matthews, J. D. (1887). *5th Ann. Rep. Fish. Board Scot.* **1887**, 245–247.
Maynard-Smith, J. (1977). *Anim. Behav.* **25**, 1–9.
Miller, P. J. (1961). *J. mar. biol. Assoc. U.K.* **41**, 737–769.
Miller, P. J. (1979a). *Symp. zool. Soc. Lond.* **44**, 1–28.
Miller, P. J. (1979b). *Symp. zool. Soc. Lond.* **44**, 263–306.
Morris, D. (1954). *Behaviour* **7**, 1–31.
Morris, D. (1958). *Behaviour* (Suppl.) **61**, 1–154.
Murray, B. G. Jr (1981). *Biol. Rev.* **56**, 1–22.
Partridge, L. (1978). *In* "Behavioural Ecology, an Evolutionary Approach" (J. R. Krebs and N. B. Davies, eds), pp. 351–376. Blackwell, Oxford and London.
Perrone, M. and Zaret, T. M. (1979). *Am. Nat.* **113**, 351–361.

Potts, G. W. (1974). *J. mar. biol. Ass. U.K.* **54**, 925–938.
Potts, G. W. (1985). *J. mar. biol. Ass. U.K.* **65**, 531–546.
Preston, J. L. (1978). *Anim. Behav.* **26**, 791–802.
Qasim, S. Z. (1956). *J. Cons. Int. Explor. Mer.* **21**, 144–155.
Qasim, S. Z. (1957a). *J. Anim. Ecol.* **26**, 389–401.
Qasim, S. Z. (1957b). *Proc. Zool. Soc. Lond.* **128**, 161–208.
Reay, P. J. (1973). *J. mar. biol. Ass. U.K.* **53**, 325–346.
Reese, E. (1964). *Oceanogr. Mar. Biol. Ann. Rev.* **1964**, 455–488.
Ridley, M. (1978). *Anim. Behav.* **26**, 904–932.
Ridley, M. and Rechten, C. (1981). *Behaviour* **76**, 152–161.
Robertson, D. R. (1972). *Science, N.Y.* **177**, 1007–1009.
Russell, F. S. (1976). "The Eggs and Planktonic Stages of British Marine Fishes". Academic Press, London.
Sargent, R. C. (1982). *Anim. Behav.* **30**, 364–374.
Sargent, R. C. and Gebler, J. B. (1980). *Behav. Ecol. Sociobiol.* **7**, 137–142.
Sawyer, P. J. (1967). *Copeia* **1967**, 55–61.
Schneider, L. (1969). *Oecologia* **3**, 249–265.
Semler, D. E. (1971). *J. Zool. Lond.* **165**, 291–302.
Sevenster, P. (1951). *Discovery* **12**, 52–56.
Sevenster, P. (1961). *Behaviour* (Suppl.) **9**, 1–170.
Shapiro, D. Y. (1981a). *J. Zool. Lond.* **193**, 105–128.
Shapiro, D. Y. (1981b). *Anim. Behav.* **29**, 1199–1212.
Sjolander, S., Larson, H. O. and Engstrom, J. (1972). *Rev. Comp. Animal* **6**, 43–51.
Stearns, S. C. (1980). *Oikos* **35**, 266–281.
Talbot, G. B. (1966). *Spec. Publ. Am. Fish. Soc.* **3**, 37–49.
Thomopoulos, A. and Bauchot, R. (1957). *Bull. Soc. zool. Fr.* **82**, 120–126.
Thompson, D. A. and Lehner, C. E. (1976). *J. exp. mar. Biol. Ecol.* **22**, 1–29.
Trivers, R. L. (1972). "Sexual Selection and the Descent of Man" (B. Campbell, ed.), pp. 36–179. Aldine, Chicago.
Vestergaard, K. (1976). *Vidensk. Meddr. dansk naturh. Foren.* **139**, 91–108.
Werren, J. H., Gross, M. R. and Shine, R. (1980). *J. theor. Biol.* **82** (4), 619–631.
Wheeler, A. C. (1969). "The Fishes of the British Isles and Northwest Europe". Macmillan, London.
Wickler, W. (1957). *Z. Tierpsychol.* **14**, 393–428.
Williams, G. C. (1959). *Copeia* **1959**, 18–24.
Williams, G. C. (1975). "Sex and Evolution". Princeton University Press, Princeton, N.J.
Wilson, D. P. (1958). *J. mar. biol. Ass. U.K.* **37**, 299–307.
Winslade, P. R. (1974). *J. Fish Biol.* **6**, 587–599.
Wirtz, P. (1978). *Z. Tierpsychol.* **48**, 142–174.
Witman, J. (1978). *Sea Front* **24**, 302–306.
Wootton, R. J. (1971). *Can. J. Zool.* **49**, 960–962.
Wootton, R. J. (1976). "The Biology of the Sticklebacks". Academic Press, London.

14. Behavioural Aspects of Cichlid Reproductive Strategies: Patterns of Territoriality and Brood Defence in Central American Substratum Spawners and African Mouth Brooders

KENNETH R. McKAYE

Duke University Marine Laboratory, Beaufort, U.S.A.

Abstract: Comparisons will be made on how predation pressure affects reproductive behaviour and community structure in New and Old World cichlids. Deep water predators appear to influence the location of territories of both substratum spawning and mouthbrooding cichlids. In Lake Jiloá, Nicaragua, substratum spawning cichlids are crowded into the shallows apparently to avoid the fry predator, *Gobiomorus dormitor*. In Lake Malawi, over 50 000 *Cyrtocara eucinostomus* congregate on a 4 km long breeding arena at depths between 3 and 9 m. It appears that this shallow depth distribution is influenced by the presence of large-deep dwelling catfish that move into shallow water to feed on adult cichlids.

Other similarities are also apparent between the New and Old World cichlids. Alternation of territories between species in Lake Jiloá and on a multispecific breeding arena in Lake Malawi both appear to be due to cooperative defence of eggs or fry from predators, and competition between conspecifics for territories and mates. On the multispecific arena there are at least six species of cichlids present which are specialized to prey on cichlid eggs. Three of these species, *C. labifer*, *C. insignis* and *C. ovatus* dart into nests and attempt to eat the eggs before a female can get them into her mouth. The latter two species hold territories up in the water column. Three other species. *C. orthognathus*, *C. liemi* and an undescribed species ram females in the water column and extract eggs and fry from their mouths. The multispecific arena is thought to exist as an anti-predator response to these egg-eaters. Where egg eaters do not occur, the arenas tend to be monospecific. The nearest neighbouring nest on the multispecific arena is significantly less likely to be a conspecific than that of another species. Therefore, a male courting a female is less likely to be interfered with by a conspecific male. But, the males of other species attack nest darters and reduce the probability that the eggs laid in the courting male's nest will be eaten.

Other mutualistic interactions in the defence of the young and eggs are found in both Lake Jiloá and Lake Malawi. Cichlids in both lakes adopt young of other species into

FISH REPRODUCTION
ISBN: 0–12–563660–1

their broods. About 50% of the broods in Lake Malawi are multispecific. Again, this mutualistic phenomenon is thought to be a response to fry predation. The addition of foreign fry reduces the probability of the fish's own young being taken by a predator.

I. BACKGROUND ON CICHLID FISHES

Cichlids have been the focus of considerable ecological, evolutionary, and behavioural research. Their explosive speciation, their unique feeding specializations, their diverse mating systems, and their great importance as a protein source in tropical countries have all been factors stimulating this work (Fryer and Iles, 1972). These fishes occur primarily in Africa and South and Central America. The family is the most species rich of all freshwater percoid fishes. The cichlids of the rift valley lakes of Africa represent the most spectacular examples of speciation and adaptive radiation within a single vertebrate family. The exact number of species in each rift valley lake is still unknown, as many undescribed species are being discovered and described from newly explored areas (Eccles and Lewis, 1977, 1978; van Oijen et al., 1979; Witte, 1981; Witte and Witte-Maas, 1981; McKaye and Mackenzie, 1982). In Lake Malawi, it is thought that over 500 species are present (consensus of ichthyologists working in Malawi). The radiation of cichlids in Central America since the late Pliocene has also been impressive as close to 100 species have arisen, most of whom belong to the genus *Cichlasoma* (Barlow, 1974).

The manner by which so many species evolved and the mechanisms by which they coexist are central questions of both evolutionary and ecological biology (Lowe-McConnell, 1975). The organization and evolution of these highly complex cichlid communities are intimately linked to their reproductive systems (Fryer and Iles, 1972; Lowe-McConnell, 1975). Knowledge of mate selection and of intrinsic and extrinsic isolating mechanisms in these fishes is crucial to understanding the process of their speciation (Greenwood, 1964, 1974; Kosswig, 1947, 1963; Barlow, 1974; Holzberg, 1978; Fryer, 1977; McKaye, 1980; McKaye et al., 1982). Data on the biological and physical factors controlling the temporal sequencing and spatial patterning of cichlid reproduction are critical to determining the processes which allow such high diversity systems to exist (Lowe-McConnell, 1975, 1979). The biological processes of competition and predation may be the driving forces behind the patterns observed. The study of cichlid community structure and cichlid reproductive behaviour must of necessity go hand in hand.

Cichlid reproductive behaviour is probably the best studied aspect of cichlid biology (Fryer and Iles, 1972; Barlow, 1974; Keenleyside, 1979). Considerable attention has been focused upon cichlid reproduction since: (1) they are easy to breed under laboratory conditions (Barlow, 1974); (2) they show a wide range of breeding behaviour, ranging from biparental care of offspring to both maternal or paternal (uniparental) mouthbrooding (Fryer and Iles, 1972); (3) they are territorial and good subjects for studies on aggression (FitzGerald and Keenleyside, 1978); (4) they engage in mutualistic cooperative care of young and adopt or kidnap young not their own (McKaye, 1981a); (5) their reproductive success is a component of their management as important food stocks (Lowe, 1952).

The earliest field studies of cichlid reproductive behaviour are the classical works of Lowe-McConnell (1956, 1959) and Fryer (1959). Within the last decade and a half considerably more information concerning the breeding biology *in situ* has become available on: Asian (Ward and Wyman 1975, 1977; Ward and Samarakoon, 1981), neotropical (Lowe-McConnell, 1969; Barlow, 1974, 1976; Keenleyside and Bietz, 1981) and African (Fernald and Hirata, 1977; Holzberg, 1978; Eccles and Lewis, 1981; Marsh et al., 1981; Ribbink et al., 1981) cichlids. The accumulation of both laboratory and field data now makes it possible: (1) to compare and contrast the behaviour and ecology of cichlids in diverse habitats, and (2) to examine the underlying processes which determine the observed reproductive patterns.

I have been fortunate to study two very different communities of cichlid fishes: the nine substratum-spawning cichlids of Lake Jiloá, Nicaragua, and the approximately 100 species of sand-dwelling cichlids in southern Lake Malawi. Here, I present several current hypotheses that underlie my present field work and experiments in Lake Malawi, along with some of the data on which they are based. I have taken this opportunity to use a comparative approach in the analysis of the reproductive behaviour of cichlid fishes in these two communities. Hopefully, this exercise will provide new insights and pinpoint key hypotheses for the processes which determine the patterns of reproductive behaviour seen in such widely divergent social systems, the monogamous pairs of Lake Jiloá versus the polygamous cichlids of Lake Malawi.

II. BACKGROUND INFORMATION ON TWO LAKES

A. Lake Jiloá

Lake Jiloá is a small neotropical crater lake immediately adjacent to Lake Managua in the Great Lakes Basin on the Pacific side of Nicaragua. It has an area of approximately 380 hectares and a maximum depth of approximately 92 m (Riedel, 1964; see Barlow, 1976, for map of region). The bottom profile of Lake Jiloá is transitional between that of the two shallow Great Lakes and that of the steep-sided crater lakes (Barlow, 1976). The water chemistry of these lakes is discussed by Barlow et al. (1976). The southeast shore is closest to Lake Managua and consequently similar to it. There the bottom consists mostly of silt and sand and slopes gently toward the depths. The rock area commences to the west along the southern shore. This rocky area, with large jumbled boulders and rock formations descending rapidly to the depths, is typical of Nicaraguan crater lakes (McKaye, 1977a).

There are nine cichlid species which live in this lake and they are all substratum spawners. Three species live primarily in sandy habitats, but migrate into rocks to breed: *Cichlasoma nicaraguense*, *C. rostratum*, and *C. longimanus*. Five species live and breed primarily in the rocks: *C. nigrofasciatum*, *Neetroplus nematopus*, *C. citrinellum*, *C. managuense* and *C. dovii*. Finally, the ninth species, *C. centrarchus*, was never observed breeding in the lake during the period I was there. Details of the reproductive behaviour and basic biology of the fishes in this lake are available (Barlow, 1974, 1976; Lim *et al.*, 1976; McKaye, 1977a,b, 1979, 1980; McKaye and Barlow, 1976; McKaye and McKaye, 1977; McKaye *et al.*, 1979a,b).

B. Lake Malawi

Lake Malawi, the southern most of the rift valley lakes of East Africa, is the world's ninth largest lake (560 km long, 70 km wide and 695 m maximum depth). The lake is a mosaic of habitats, with alternating rocky, sandy and weedy environments which serve to isolate fish populations along the shore. Detailed descriptions of the lake can be found in Jackson *et al.* (1963), Fryer and Iles (1972), Eccles (1974) and Lowe-McConnell (1975).

Since 1978, I have been studying the community ecology of the endemic mouthbrooding cichlids which occur over sand in the Cape Maclear region in the southern end of the lake. The breeding biology of *Cyrtocara eucinostomus*, the most common cichlid observed breeding in the area, has been analysed in detail (McKaye, 1983). Furthermore, I have examined the interactions of *C. eucinostomus* with *C. pleurotaenia*, *Lethrinops lituris*, *L. variabilis* and *L. aurita* on a multispecific breeding arena in a sandy area surrounded by rocks at Otter Point, Cape Maclear (see McKaye, 1981, Fig. 1: Otter Point is the point farthest west on the mainland in that figure). The interrelationship of these five species with paedophagous cichlids that take young from the mouths of brooding females is discussed in McKaye and Kocher (1983).

III. CICHLID REPRODUCTIVE BEHAVIOUR

A. Substratum spawners of Lake Jiloá

Basic information concerning the breeding biology of Central American cichlids is reviewed by Barlow (1974) and Keenleyside (1979). Here, I shall summarize the relevant characteristics of the reproductive biology and social

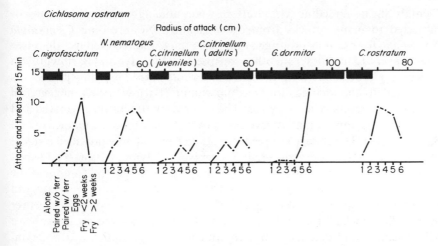

Fig. 1.   Mean number of attacks and threats per 15 minute by *Cichlasoma rostratum* directed against other cichlids and *Gobiomorus dormitor*. 1 = alone; 2 = paired without territory; 3 = paired with territory; 4 = with eggs; 5 = with fry less than 2 weeks old, and 6 = with fry greater than 2 weeks old.

system of the substratum spawning cichlids which inhabit Lake Jiloá. All the methods used to acquire both published and previously unpublished data are presented in McKaye (1977a,b) and McKaye and Barlow (1976).

1. *Timing of breeding and location of territories.*   The substratum-spawning cichlids had a bimodal temporal pattern in breeding, with peaks in both April and August (McKaye, 1977a). Territory establishment was rapid. An eight-fold increase in established cichlid pairs was observed from July to August, and a similar, eight-fold decrease occurred from April to May (McKaye, 1977a). Some species, such as *Neetroplus nematopus*, bred year round, but their numbers fluctuated greatly throughout the year. The other species in the lake appeared to have confined breeding seasons which lasted three to six months. The majority of all territories were in water shallower than 9 m depth in both wet and dry seasons (McKaye 1977a). Competition for space in shallow waters was high during the peak of the breeding season and territorial loss was great (McKaye, 1977a). I hypothesized that these cichlids were crowded into shallow water in order to reduce predation by the deep-dwelling eleotrid fish, *Gobiomorus dormitor* (McKaye, 1977a; McKaye *et al.*, 1979a).

2. *Pair formation and aggression.*   All of the cichlids in this community assumed a distinct breeding colour and formed pairs before attempting to take a territory (Barlow, 1974; McKaye and Barlow, 1976; McKaye, 1977a).

Cichlids in nonbreeding colouration were nonaggressive and were not subjected to many attacks from other cichlids. Nonbreeding *Cichlasoma citrinellum*, for example, averaged only one attack and received less than two attacks every 15 minutes from other conspecifics (McKaye and Barlow, 1976). However, *C. citrinellum* with the black and white barred breeding pattern, as contrasted to the spotted nonbreeding colour (Barlow, 1974), engaged in many more aggressive interactions. The number of attacks they received and gave increased approximately seven-fold over the nonbreeders (McKaye and Barlow, 1976). The change to breeding colouration not only provided a signal to possible mates, but triggered aggressive behaviour from established territorial fish.

3. *Territory formation.* Males and females formed pairs and swam together over shallow rocky areas while attempting to establish a territory. Together a pair occupied and defended an area with an average radius of 0·5–2·0 m, depending on the species. Pairs either established themselves in previously unoccupied areas or they aggressively evicted another pair (McKaye, 1977a). The only territorial modification made by a pair was the clearing of the substrate where the eggs were then laid.

4. *Length of time on territory.* Only 10% of the territory holders that I followed continuously were successful. Ninety per cent of the time either all of the young were consumed by predators or the pair was unable to withstand the challenge of other cichlid pairs attempting to take their territory. Those that were successful in rearing young held territories between 6–12 weeks (McKaye, 1977a).

5. *Parental defence of young and territory.* In the field I made 15 minute observations of territorial fishes and recorded all attacks and threats made by a pair (see McKaye and Barlow, 1976, for methods). At least 16 sets of observations of individuals or pairs were made in each of six reproductive states: (1) alone; (2) paired without territory; (3) paired with territory; (4) with eggs; (5) with fry less than two weeks old; and (6) with fry greater than two weeks old (see Figs 1 and 2). For this review, I have summarized these behavioural data for two species: *N. nematopus*, the most common species living over the rocks, and *C. rostratum*, a species which lives and feeds over the sand but moves into the rocks to breed (McKaye, 1977a).

Single individuals of both of these species, as well as of the other seven species, were relatively nonaggressive and averaged only one or two attacks against conspecifics in a 15 minute period (Figs 1 and 2; McKaye and Barlow, 1976). *Cichlasoma rostratum* became significantly more aggressive after pairing (Mann Whitney U, $P<0·01$) and averaged approximately ten attacks and threats per 15 minutes (Fig. 1). Comparable data for paired *N. nematopus*

Neetroplus nematopus

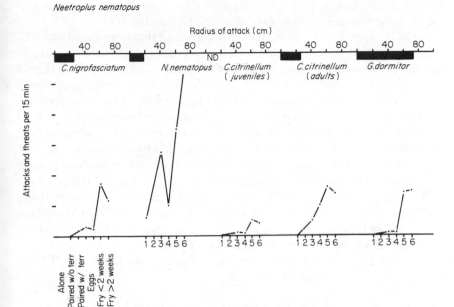

Fig. 2.   Mean number of attacks and threats per 15 minute by *Neetroplus nematopus* directed against other cichlids and *Gobiomorus dormitor*. 1 = alone; 2 = paired without territory; 3 = paired with territory; 4 = with eggs; 5 = with fry less than 2 weeks old, and 6 = with fry greater than 2 weeks old.

without territories are not available as this class of *N. nematopus* was rarely seen. For both species, once a territory was established, aggressive interactions continued to increase and became primarily directed against conspecifics (Figs 1 and 2).

For *C. rostratum*, the level of aggression increased greatly once the eggs were laid in the open. The number of attacks against *C. nigrofasciatum* and *N. nematopus*, the primary opportunistic egg predators in Lake Jiloá, increased. The defending *C. rostratum* parents averaged approximately one attack or threat every 30 sec; whereas *N. nematopus*, which hid their eggs in holes (McKaye, 1977a) only attacked at 1/3 that rate.

Once the fry emerged, both species attacked at the same average rate of once every 20 sec. For *N. nematopus* parents this represents an almost five-fold increase in rate of attack against both possible predators on their fry and challengers to their territory. *Neetroplus nematopus* attacks against conspecifics rose dramatically during this period (Fig. 2). Conspecifics pose a dual threat: (1) they cannibalize the defending parents' young and (2) they are possible usurpers of the territory. *Cichlasoma rostratum* also displayed an increase in aggression, particularly against *C. nigrofasciatum, N. nematopus* and *G. dormitor*, the primary predators on the smallest fry.

As the fry grew larger, the pattern of attacks and threats changed. Both *C. rostratum* and *N. nematopus* dramatically decreased aggression against *C. nigrofasciatum*, which was not capable of consuming the larger young (Figs 1 and 2). Both increased attacks against the eleotrid, *G. dormitor*, the primary predator on large fry and juvenile cichlids (Figs 1 and 2). The eleotrid predator only comprised 1–4% of the population at the depths where these species bred (McKaye, 1977a,b; McKaye *et al.*, 1979a). Nevertheless, *C. rostratum* with two week, or older, fry directed over 50% of its attacks against these sit-and-wait predators. *Neetroplus nematopus*, which occurred in shallower water where fewer of the eleotrids occurred (McKaye, 1977a: Fig. 5; McKaye *et al.*, 1979a: Fig. 3), directed approximately 20% of their attacks against them. Furthermore, whereas most cichlids were allowed to within 0·5 m of the broods before they were attacked (Fig. 1), *C. rostratum* attacked the eleotrids at a distance of over 1 m from the brood. The smaller *N. nematopus* also attacked the eleotrid at a greater average distance from the brood (0·75 m) than it attacked most cichlids (Fig. 2).

6. *Number, survivorship and dispersal of young.*   There was a wide range in sizes of territorial cichlids (McKaye, 1977a: Fig. 1), from the smallest *C. nigrofasciatum*, with a mean female SL of 34 mm and 3 g weight, to that of *C. dovii*, with a mean female SL of 220 mm and 440 g weight. Based on the mean weight of females and the mean number of eggs or first day, free-swimming fry observed *in situ*, there was a correlation between the number of offspring and the size of the females of each species (Fig. 3). Small *C. nigrofasciatum* females averaged approximately 70 young, while the largest cichlid, *C. dovii*, averaged over 2000 young.

Predation upon the young was great. The highest four week survival rate was for *C. dovii* fry; approximately 15% of the fry remained. The species was unusual; the successful broods had another cichlid, *C. nicaraguense*, aiding them in tending the brood (McKaye, 1977b). Survivorship of *C. citrinellum, C. nicaraguense* and *C. longimanus* fry was less than 10% after two weeks, and the smaller species, *C. nigrofasciatum* and *N. nematopus*, had an average of 20% of their brood remaining at the end of three weeks (Fig. 4). These data represent survival from date of emergence and include individual broods that entirely disappeared; thus, the data present an accurate estimate of the survival probability of an individual from birth. This evidence of high mortality within broods is consistent with the surveys of brood size of each species at various ages (Fig. 5). Except for *C. dovii*, surviving broods between 3–5 weeks averaged less than 40 individuals and, in most cases, were less than 20 (Fig. 5). After broods were three weeks old all species, except *C. nigrofasciatum* and *C. dovii*, began to include some young that were not their own in the brood (McKaye and McKaye, 1977).

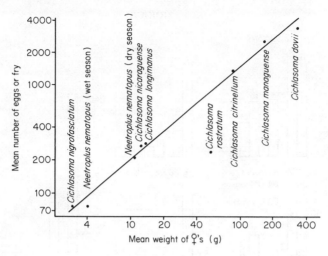

Fig. 3. Mean number of eggs laid or fry emerging on the first day free swimming versus mean weight of paired cichlid females. Lower number of eggs for *Cichlasoma rostratum* may reflect predation which already occurred on eggs which are laid in the open in Lake Jiloá, Nicaragua.

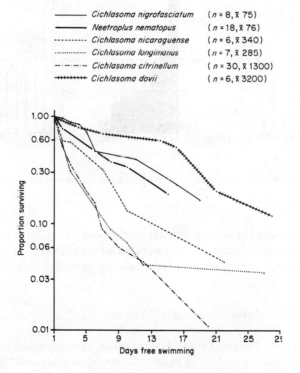

Fig. 4. Survivorship rate of cichlid fry in Lake Jiloá, Nicaragua.

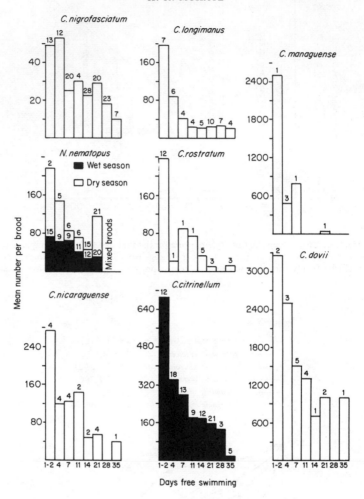

Fig. 5.   Mean number of young in cichlid broods of each age class in Lake Jiloá, Nicaragua.

After 4–10 weeks the young cichlids moved out of the parental territory; they began to forage in the water column and on the rocks in the near vicinity. They, nevertheless, remained near the breeding grounds, and often tried to feed on eggs or small fry.

B. Endemic mouthbrooders of Lake Malawi

The work of Fryer, Iles and Lowe-McConnell are classic studies and excellent reviews of the breeding biology of many of Lake Malawi's cichlid fishes (Fryer and Iles, 1972; Lowe-McConnell, 1975). All the endemic cichlids in Lake Malawi have a female mouthbrooding reproductive system. The females immediately take the fertilized eggs into their mouths and brood the young alone. Data on the reproductive behaviour of the sand-dwelling cichlids of Lake Malawi, especially those in which the males form breeding arenas are summarized in McKaye (1983). In that paper it is concluded that the cichlid breeding arena is analogous to a bird lek, as suggested by Fryer and Iles (1972).

1. *Timing of breeding and location of territories.*   Bimodal peaks in cichlid breeding seasons occur within the Cape Maclear region of southern Lake Malawi. Since August, 1981 nests have been counted at six different areas equally spaced along the 4 km beach at Cape Maclear, using five 400 m^2 transects at five depth intervals between 0–15 m. In August, the average number of nests at each site was 500 per 2000 m^2, but by November the average had dropped to 100. In March 1982, the average had increased to 300, but by April it dropped again, to an average of 50 nests (Fig. 6). *Cyrtocara eucinostomus* breeds year round (McKaye, 1982) as does *Lethrinops lituris*, but most of the species have confined breeding seasons ranging from between 1·5–4 months.

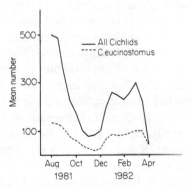

Fig. 6.   Mean number of *Cyrtocara eucinostomus* and mean number of all breeding cichlids at six sampling sites between 0–15 m along 4 km beach at Cape Maclear, Lake Malawi, Africa (per 2000 m^2).

The majority of the cichlid species observed bred in water less than 12 m deep. *Cyrtocara eucinostomus*, for example, has bred consistently in a narrow band along this beach (Fig. 7; McKaye, 1983). I have hypothesized that the shallow breeding distribution of *C. eucinostomus* is due to higher predation by larger fish in deeper water (McKaye, 1983). The evidence on which this

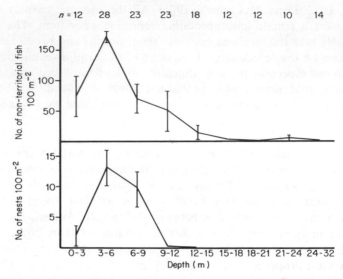

Fig. 7.   Depth distribution of *Cyrtocara eucinostomus* based on 100 m² transects, 0·5 m above substrate. Vertical lines equal two standard errors. *n* = number of 100 m² transects. (McKaye, 1983.)

hypothesis is based, briefly stated, is as follows. (1) Of 349 *Bagrus meridonalis* predators caught in trammel nets set on or near the arena, 120 had food in their stomachs. Of the 47 stomachs in which the contents could be identified to species unambiguously, all contained adult cichlids and 37 (79%) contained *C. eucinostomus*. There were a total of 63 individual *C. eucinostomus* in these 37 stomachs. An additional 73 catfish had cichlid remains in their stomachs which could not be identified to species; however, of these remains, 95% were most likely *C. eucinostomus*, given gill raker counts and other characteristics of the remains. Consequently, cichlids, and *C. eucinostomus* in particular, are utilized as prey by the bagrid, *B. meridonalis*. (2) When parallel nets were set at two depths, the deeper always had higher numbers of catfish. Two 90 m trammel nets were placed at 8–10 m in the arena and at 20–22 m for 11 nights in July–August, 1980. The deeper net at 21 m caught significantly more catfish ($\bar{x}=3\cdot7$, s.d. $=1\cdot40$) than the net at 9 m ($\bar{x}=1\cdot5$, s.d. $=0\cdot7$; Wilcoxon, $P<0\cdot01$). Thus, predation pressure by *B. meridonalis* on cichlids is greater in deeper portions of the shore depth gradient. (3) Finally, captures from 180 m trammel nets set overnight throughout the Cape Maclear region at depths down to 60 m substantiate that there are significantly more catfish in deep water than in shallow water (Fig. 8; McKaye, 1983). These observations suggest that the nocturnal catfish act as significant predators upon cichlids, and that their movement up from deeper depths tends to compress prey cichlid distributions into shallow water.

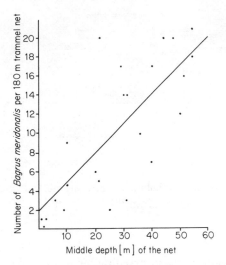

Fig. 8. Number of *Bagrus meridonalis* caught in trammel nets vs the depth of the net. There is a significant correlation between the number of catfish caught and increasing depth. (*Bagrus meridonalis* caught/180 net = 1·57 + 0·31 (depth (m); $r = 0·49$, $P < 0·05$.) (McKaye, 1983.)

2. *Pair formation and aggression.* Only the male assumes breeding colouration in the mouth-brooding species. Males assume their breeding colour prior to taking a nest territory; the breeding colour is blue for most Lake Malawi cichlids. No permanent pairs are formed. Sand-dwelling, non-territorial cichlids are not distinctively coloured and display little or no aggression to others while feeding (McKaye, pers. observ.). I have never observed an intruding, breeding-coloured male evict the territorial resident, although I have seen several territorial challenges which lasted about a minute. These fights involved carouseling and mouthlocking 3–5 m up in the water column above the nest territory. Territorial loss must occur from aggressive interactions from other males, but it is a rapid process which is difficult to observe.

3. *Territory formation.* Only males establish territories. The females school above these territories. The establishment of a permanent territory over sand always involves some substrate modification. Either a mound is built (Fig. 9) or a depression is dug into the sand. Nest form is species specific; thus, the observer can determine the species holding a territory even when the male is not immediately present. Some species, such as *Cyrtocara moori* (Kocher and McKaye, 1983), do not build permanent nest territories. *C. moori* males, for example, follow other larger fish such as *Lethrinops praeorbitalis*, which plunge into the sand to feed on benthic larvae, and *C. moori* then feed amid the

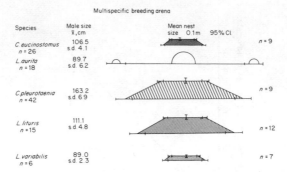

Fig. 9. Size of males and nests at multispecific breeding arena at Otter Point, Lake Malawi, Africa.

stirred up particles. The *C. moori* males then court females on the open sand. The phenomenon of a transient breeding territory, where males and females move together some distance while the female lays eggs, has also been observed for an unidentified *Lethrinops* species. These two species are the only ones of which I am aware that do not form permanent breeding territories; over 70 sand dwelling species have been documented to build nests (Fryer and Iles, 1972).

4. *Length of time on territory.* The amount of time a male spends on a territory in the Cape Maclear region varies greatly from species to species as well as within a species, depending on the location and composition of the breeding arena (McKaye, 1983). Of 120 *C. eucinostomus* males tagged on a large monospecific breeding arena, where males leave nests in the afternoon to feed, none were observed on the same nest the following day (McKaye, 1983). However, on another arena that is multispecific and where the males do not leave the arena in the afternoon (at Otter Point), tagging results indicate that the average residence time for successful males of *C. pleurotaenia*, *C. eucinostomus*, and *L. lituris* is approximately 10–14 days.

5. *Parental defence*

(a) Male defence of eggs. Initially one might assume that in female-mouthbrooding species the male plays no role in the defence of young (Peronne and Zaret, 1979). This view is not correct for the Malawi cichlids, where male aggressive behaviour and territorial defence may play a major role. The males keep egg predators away from the eggs during deposition and fertilization before the female picks them up and begins brooding them in her mouth. The intensity of egg predation varies considerably in different areas (Fryer and Iles, 1972; McKaye, pers. observ.). Conspecifics darting in from the side are the main source of egg predation on some breeding arenas (McKaye, 1982). On other arenas egg predators with specialized behaviour evolved to exploit this food resource are present. Much of the territorial male effort is then directed towards fending off these egg predators.

(b) Multispecific breeding arena with specialized egg predators.   At Otter Point in the multispecific breeding arena five species breed between June–August: *Cyrtocara eucinostomus, C. pleurotaenia, Lethrinops lituris, L. aurita* and *L. variabilis*. Between June–August 1980 this arena was studied in detail and the data presented here are from that period (McKaye and Kocher, 1983). A $\frac{1}{2}$-hectare study grid was established; all of the nests of the different cichlid species were counted every 10–14 days. Also, 15 minute sets of behavioural observations were made on all breeding species and on egg predator species. The egg predators were chased into block nets, measured (SL), and tagged with Dennison T-tags. Subsequently, the egg predators' movements were followed and mapped over the marked study grid.

(c) Nest synchrony.   On June 25, 1980 there were about 300 territorial males on the $\frac{1}{2}$-hectare study grid; by August 6 this had increased to almost 2000 (Fig. 10). The densities of all five breeding species increased in synchrony (Fig. 10).

(d) Egg predators.   Above the multispecific arena there were six species of cichlids which preyed upon the eggs of these mouthbrooding cichlids (Table I). Three of these species are designated as "nest darters": *Cyrtocara labifer, C.*

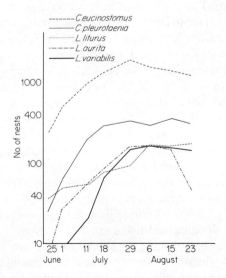

Fig. 10.   Number of nests (log scale) of five species on the multispecific arena at Otter Point (0·5 hectares) from June to August, 1980.

TABLE I. Specialized egg predators present at Cape Maclear, Lake Malawi.

Species	Standard length (cm) $\bar{x}$ and s.d.	Description
NEST DARTERS		
C. labifer	124·9	non-territorial — high vagility
n = 14	14·3	
C. insignis	100·9	both territorial and non-
n = 27	10·8	territorial, most abundant egg predator
C. ovatus	107·5	territorial — occurs
n = 6	14.9	primarily at rock-sand interface
MOUTH RAMMERS		
C. orthognathus	113·8	attacks from below and behind,
n = 7	10·3	mimics-C. eucinostomus-silvery with no stripe, and C. pleurotaenia-stripe present
C. liemi	107·9	attacks straight from below, no
n = 4	14·9	changes in coloration apparent
Undescribed	150·0	attacks from above, mimics C. pleurotaenia-stripe present

ovatus and C. insignis. These species all hover about 3 m above a nest territory. As a breeding male started to circle with a female, these species slowly dropped down in the water column (termed an "approach"). When the female laid her eggs, these egg predators, if they had not been driven off by an attacking male, darted into the nest and snatched the eggs before the female could circle and get them into her mouth (Table II). These egg predators often followed above specific females which were being courted and were laying eggs, and awaited their entering a male's nest where 2–8 eggs were laid per circle. The nest darter type egg predators "approached" a nest with a male and female courting approximately every three minutes (Table II). Over 95% of the time they were attacked and driven off by the resident male or one of the neighbouring males before they could dart into the nest to take the eggs. These nest-darter egg predators were successful at taking eggs every one to two hours (Table II). Of the 30 stomachs of C. labifer, C. insignis and C. ovatus that were examined during this period, all contained fish eggs.

Besides the three nest-darting egg predators there are three species designated as paedophages, C. orthognathus, C. liemi and an undescribed cichlid, since they fed on eggs and embryos ejected from the brooding mother's mouth. These fishes have been observed to ram brooding females in

TABLE II. Behavioural acts per hour by specialized egg predators. n = number of 15 min observations.

Nest darters				Mouth rammers	
	Approach	Dart	Successful		Attack
C. labifer	17·8	0·8	0·7	C. orthognathus	11·7
$n=26$				$n=22$	
C. insignis	16·4	1·4	0·5	C. liemi	7·0
$n=29$				$n=8$	
C. ovatus	21·8	3·2	1·4		
$n=24$					

the head to jolt the young out of their mouths (see McKaye and Kocher, 1983).

Both the nest darters and paedophagous cichlid predators were subjected to numerous attacks by territorial males (Table III). The greatest number of attacks were by *C. eucinostomus*, the most common territorial cichlid on the arena. A nest darter was attacked on the average almost once every two minutes, and the paedophages were attacked approximately once every minute.

Interestingly, two of the nest darters, *C. ovatus* and *C. insignis*, established permanent territories 3 m above the breeding arena. They attacked and chased out all other intruding egg predators, but concentrated their attacks on the two territorial nest darting species, *C. insignis* and *C. ovatus*. The third nest

TABLE III. Average number of attacks and threats received by egg predators per hour at Otter Point, Lake Malawi.

	Attacked by				
	E	A	P	L	V
NEST DARTERS					
C. labifer	27·8	0·2	15·3	2·8	3·0
$n=26$					
C. insignis	23·9	0·9	2·9	0·5	0·1
$n=29$					
C. ovatus	21·6	0·6	1·3	0·3	0·9
$n=24$					
MOUTH RAMMERS					
C. orthognathus	83·7	1·7	24·3	2·5	0·0
$n=22$					
C. liemi	39·0	5·2	0·5	0·0	3·8
$n=8$					

n = number of 15 min observations; E = *C. eucinostomus*; A = *L. aurita*; P = *C. pleurotaenia*; L = *L. lituris*; V = *L. variabilis*.

darter, *C. labifer*, did not form a territory, but rather swam continually over the breeding arena, sometimes as far as 200 m in 15 min. This species was much less aggressive and usually only attacked the rare conspecifics that it encountered while swimming about (Table IV).

(e) Distribution of breeding male territories. At 16 uniformly spaced locations on the grid, I mapped all of the nests at two week intervals during the June–August study period. The changes for one month at one such point are shown in Fig. 11. From such maps, the spatial relationship between nests of different species and the pattern of nest replacement over time was determined. Interestingly, the nests were not randomly distributed on any date. For example, except for the largest species, *C. pleurotaenia*, the nearest neighbour at the height of the breeding season (30 July, 1980) was more likely to be a heterospecific than would be predicted if the nests were distributed randomly (Table V). The area in which over 80% of *C. pleurotaenia* occurred was in the deeper, SW corner. In this region there were not territorial nest darters (Fig. 12).

(f) Attacks on cichlids by territorial males.   During the morning courtship hours, *C. eucinostomus* averaged 22 attacks per 15 minutes against cichlids, both on the multispecific arena at Otter Point and on the monospecific arena at the 4 km Cape Maclear beach (Table VI; McKaye, 1983). The ratio of attacks by *C. eucinostomus* against conspecifics to attacks against heterospecifics differed between arenas. On the monospecific arena, which was dominated by *C. eucinostomus*, 77% of the attacks were directed against heterospecific cichlids (McKaye, 1983). On the multispecific arena, where other cichlid species were more common, only 41% of the attacks were directed against heterospecifics (Table VI; Mann Whitney U, $P < 0.01$).

(g) Female defence of brood.   Females with mouthfuls of young usually leave the arena and brood the young for an unknown period of time. It is

TABLE IV.   Average number of attacks directed against nest darters by other nest darters.

	Attacked by C. labifer	C. insignis	C. ovatus
C. labifer n = 26	1·4	0·0	0·3
C. insignis n = 29	0·1	9·7	1·1
C. ovatus n = 24	0·2	6·8	0·7

n = number of 15 min observations.

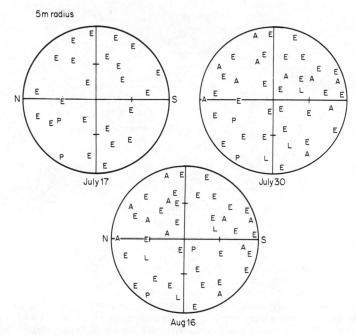

Fig. 11. Distribution of nests through time at one location at Otter Point, Lake Malawi from July 17–August 16, 1980. E = *Cyrtocara eucinostomus*; P = *C. pleurotaenia*; A = *Lethrinops aurita*; L = *L. lituris*.

TABLE V. Nearest neighbour on 30 July, 1980, at Otter Point multispecific breeding arena.

		1st nearest neighbour					
		E	A	P	L	V	
E	Observed	270	79	47	12	33	$\chi^2 = 61\cdot4$
	Expected	318·8	37·0	51·2	12·3	21·7	$P < 0\cdot01$
A	Observed	48	1	1	0	1	$\chi^2 = 12\cdot7$
	Expected	36·9	5·9	1·4	4·3	2·5	$P < 0\cdot02$
P	Observed	39	4	24	1	3	$\chi^2 = 38\cdot2$
	Expected	51·3	6·0	8·3	8·3	3·5	$P < 0\cdot01$
L	Observed	15	2	0	0	0	$\chi^2 = 3\cdot3$
	Expected	12·3	1·9	0·5	1·4	0·8	$P > 0\cdot1$
V	Observed	27	0	3	0	0	$\chi^2 = 6\cdot2$
	Expected	21·7	2·5	3·5	0·8	1·5	$P < 0\cdot1$

E = *C. eucinostomus*; A = *L. aurita*; P = *C. pleurotaenia*; L = *L. lituris*; V = *L. variabilis*.

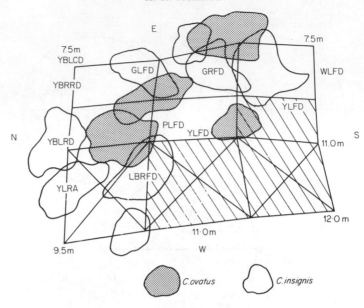

Fig. 12.   Territories of "nest darters" *C. ovatus* and *C. insignis* at 0·5 hectare study grid at Otter Point, Lake Malawi. Letters indicate colour code of tagged fish, for example YRRD = yellow-right rear dorsal. Where a territory is drawn a territorial fish was observed at least 5 times and followed over a 2 month period. These fish were always observed within the enclosed areas. Nonenclosed letters are sightings of tagged fish, but they were not followed at least 5 times. Fish which were territorial and could be individually recognized without tagging are represented by boundaries with no letters. Hatched lines in SW corner indicate where over 80% of *Cyrtocara pleurotaenia* occur. This area is the deepest portion of the arena.

TABLE VI.   Average number of attacks and threats per 15 min given by territorial *C. eucinostomus* on monospecific and multispecific breeding arenas.

		Attacks against:
	Conspecific	Heterospecific cichlids
Males in monospecific	5·0	16·8
arena $n = 34$	(0·9)	(3·3)
Males in multispecific	12·9	9·0
arena $n = 20$	(1·8)	(2·0)

n = number of 15 min observations. (   ) = standard error.

suspected that the females of the five species I have been discussing deposit their young into nursery grounds (Fryer and Iles, 1972; McKaye, pers. observ.) where millions of cichlid fry occur. Other species, especially those occurring over rocks, release fry to forage on zooplankton and will defend the area where the young occur. If the female is incapable of driving off possible predators on her young, she takes them into her mouth and moves to another area.

6. *Number, survivorship, and dispersal of young.* Unlike Lake Jiloá, where an observer can follow individual broods on a daily basis and estimate survival rate, an estimate of fry survival is not possible with most mouth brooders in the field. Even under these constraints a few patterns do emerge. First, the mouthbrooders lay fewer, but larger, eggs than do the substratum spawners (Fryer and Iles, 1972). *Cyrtocara eucinostomus* females, which are comparable in size to *Cichlasoma longimanus* females, lay an average of 45 eggs (McKaye, 1983) vs 250 smaller eggs for *C. longimanus. Cichlasoma nigrofasciatum* females, which are comparable in size to the mouthbrooding *Pseudotropheus livingstoni* of Lake Malawi (McKaye, 1978), average 70 small eggs vs seven large eggs for *P. livingstoni.* Furthermore, numerous mixed broods of fry, with females taking care of young of other species, are often observed in Malawi (Ribbink, 1977; Ribbink *et al.*, 1980, 1981; Lewis, 1980; McKaye, 1981a). These interspecific broods are not confined to cichlid–cichlid adoptions; bagrid catfish have also been observed to adopt and defend cichlid fry (McKaye and Oliver, 1980).

For most of the species I have been studying, the young are dispersed away from the breeding grounds. I have rarely seen small fry in these sandy areas. Over rocks the situation differs. Given the shelter that holes provide from predators, many of the rock-dwelling cichlids release their fry in this region (Fryer and Iles, 1972). Not surprisingly, most of the interspecific broods are seen over rocks (Ribbink *et al.*, 1980; Lewis, 1980; McKaye, 1981).

A nursery ground with significant numbers of cichlid young was found in September, 1981, in front of a stream outlet near the middle of the 4 km beach at Cape Maclear. Millions of fry of several species were present in this region. Unlike the coarse sand which predominates along the beach, this is an area of soft flocculent material, which is probably deposited by the stream's rainy season run-off. Either females "deposit" their young in this region or the young migrate to this area. Data are being gathered to distinguish between these two hypotheses.

C. Comparisons of the reproductive systems

Cichlid reproductive behaviour in Lake Jiloá and Lake Malawi contains both strikingly similar and contrasting facets (Table VII). The convergence of certain aspects of the reproductive patterns between independently evolved communities suggests that general processes may be responsible for some of the patterns observed. Competition for space, predation and mutualistic cooperation between species in defence of young play important roles in structuring both communities. The comparisons and hypotheses which follow

TABLE VII. Some comparisons between the reproductive behaviour of the substratum spawning cichlids of Lake Jiloá, Nicaragua, and the mouthbrooding cichlids of Lake Malawi, Africa.

SIMILARITIES

1. Breeding synchrony with two breeding peaks — one in the dry season and another in the wet season
2. Most species have restricted breeding season
3. A few species breed year round, but the number of territories fluctuates seasonally in these species
4. Most territories are crowded into shallow water and there is intense competition for space during a limited period
5. Territories are concentrated in certain preferred regions of the lake and in these high density areas territories alternate between species. Less likely to have a conspecific as nearest neighbor than would be predicted if randomly disperse within these areas
6. Parents engage in communal care and the adoption of foreign fry

DIFFERENCES

		Lake Jiloá	*Lake Malawi*
1.	Breeding colour	both male and female assume similar breeding pattern	only male assumes breeding colour — greater colour dimorphism
2.	Pair formation	male and female form pair away from territory; egg laying occurs several days after establishment of territory	male establishes nest alone; male displays briefly to female above nest; female lays eggs shortly after entering nest
3.	Mate fidelity	Monogamous for period necessary to raise a single brood	both polyandrous and polygynous
4.	Nest building	no nest building (except *C. citrinellum* over sand (McKaye, 1977a))	nest is built by male
5.	Length of time on territory	may be several months	usually less than two weeks
6.	Parental defence	both parents	male defends eggs in nest; all other defence by female
7.	Eggs produced	numerous small eggs	few large eggs
8.	Cannibalism of own young	never seen	male sometimes eats eggs laid in nest
9.	Specialized egg predators	none	six species
10.	Dispersal of young	from territory	female disperse young away from territory
11.	Location of breeding areas	sand dwelling species move into rocks to breed	sand dwelling species breed over sand

will hopefully stimulate both experimental field tests and comparative studies of other communities.

1. *Similarities.*   The crowding of territorial fish into the shallowest 12 m and the distinct breeding seasonality in both communities are two of the most striking features of the reproductive behaviour of these fishes. Competition for space in shallow water can be intense in both communities. Territory turnover in Lake Jiloá was high (McKaye, 1977a), as pairs up in the water column continually challenged territory holders (McKaye and Barlow, 1976). In Lake Malawi, when a territorial male was removed from its nest, another male occupied and defended the territory immediately (McKaye, 1983). Such observations suggest that space is also limited in these areas in Lake Malawi. In deeper water open space in which to breed was available in both communities. Furthermore, at some times of the year unoccupied space in shallow water was abundant. Why, then, do not the majority of species or individuals in a species simply establish territories deeper or breed later in the season when competition for space is less? The answer will probably involve the interplay of food availability and predation.

Synchrony of territorial establishment is dramatic in both communities. The six-fold increase in territory density within one month in Lake Jiloá and Lake Malawi is striking (McKaye, 1977a; Fig. 6). Such cichlid breeding synchrony is also evident in Lake Victoria (Witte, 1981) and in Sri Lanka (Ward and Samarakoon, 1981). In all of these communities, nevertheless, some species appear to breed year round at low levels. Perrone and Zaret (1979) have suggested that these tropical lakes are aseasonal and that cichlid breeding is continuous within them. Unfortunately, it is not quite that simple in the systems I have studied. In Lake Malawi, and in Lake Victoria, seasonality in plankton production has been documented (McKaye, 1983; Akiyama *et al.*, 1977). The seasonality in physical factors, such as rainfall, wind and nutrient influx into tropical lakes, affects plankton production which, in turn, must affect cichlid dynamics since it is an important food for both cichlid fry and many cichlid adults (Barlow, 1974; McKaye, 1977a, 1983; Lowe-McConnell, 1979; Ward and Samarakoon, 1981).

A change in food availability is the most likely explanation for the initiation of territory formation. Nevertheless, even though variation in food availability for adults may explain the triggering of the breeding season, such variation, by itself, does not satisfactorily explain a limited breeding season and "tolerance" of intense competition over a short period of time. An alternative strategy would be to build up fat reserves during periods of high food availability and wait until competition for space decreased before reproducing.

The evidence suggests that both the synchrony of breeding and the choice of shallow sites in Lake Jiloá is probably a response to predation pressure on the fry, especially by the deep-dwelling eleotrid fish, *Gobiomorus dormitor* (McKaye, 1977a,b; McKaye *et al.*, 1979a). Similarly, it may be hypothesized that predation pressure in Lake Malawi is significant in determining the patterns observed. It is probable that male cichlids in Lake Malawi establish their territories in shallow water to avoid predation by deep dwelling, nocturnal predators, such as *Bagrus meridonalis* (McKaye, 1983). Interestingly, the peak of breeding for both the eleotrid (McKaye, 1977a) and the bagrid follow cichlid peak breeding periods (Jackson *et al.*, 1963; McKaye and Oliver, 1980).

Anticipation of food availability for fry could be a reason for the synchrony in breeding. The limited data available suggests that zooplankton densities in Lake Malawi are lowest in September–November when the fry are dispersing (McKaye, 1982). More data on fluctuations in plankton densities and other food resources need to be gathered to test this hypothesis adequately.

The information presently available, suggests that by concentrating breeding in a limited time predators can be swamped (Elton, 1924; Janzen, 1971). By breeding in synchrony and dispersing young during a limited time period, the probability of either the adults or the fry being taken is reduced. There is safety in numbers (Hamilton, 1971). In Lake Malawi mouthbrooders, I hypothesize that females are, also, imposing the breeding synchrony upon the males. Once the females have built up enough energy to breed, it would be advantageous for them to breed simultaneously and release their young together. It is of little concern to the female what difficulties an individual male has in holding a territory. In fact, her choice among males is improved if the males are forced to compete. Females which lag and release their young later in the season might increase their young's vulnerability to predators.

In Lake Jiloá, both the female and male have to take and hold a territory. I have hypothesized that, for those that breed out of synchrony, predation upon their brood would be greater and defence of young more difficult (McKaye, 1977a). By having several species breed simultaneously and by alternating territories, predators can be swamped and driven away from the young (McKaye, 1977a). In Lake Malawi, the multispecific arena at Otter Point might be analogous and serve the same purpose. The males in this community may be acting mutualistically in attacking specialized egg predators. The data suggest that the synchrony of breeding and the reduction of attacks on heterospecifics, resulting in an alternation of territories, may be due to the presence of these territorial egg predators over the arena. The aggressive behaviour of the males is clearly important in reducing predation upon the eggs. It might be advantageous to have males of other species nearby attacking these egg predators, but not competing for the same females as would a nearby conspecific.

Furthermore, by breeding in synchrony the parents can assist in the defence of each other's young. The reasons why it appears that these adoptions are adaptive to the parents and mutualistic in nature are dealt with elsewhere (McKaye and Hallacher, 1973; McKaye and McKaye, 1977; McKaye, 1981a). Briefly stated here, it is adaptive for a parent to adopt unrelated young as a peripheral part of its own brood because when a predator strikes the probability of its own young being taken is reduced. In Lake Jiloá, the parents appeared to force unrelated young to the periphery of the brood. This phenomenon of adopted young being on the outside of the brood was observed unequivocally in Lake Malawi. Here, *Bagrus meridonalis* catfish guard cichlid young and force them to the outside of their brood (McKaye and Oliver, 1980).

If food resources for the parents are the only criteria for timing of breeding, then such timing should make little difference to the success of the fry. Food resources for the fry or predation, however, could make a major difference in survivorship, depending on availability or intensity. For example, if predators are reinforcing tight seasonality, the individuals that breed near the end of the season or at periods of low densities should be less successful in rearing young. I would expect less seasonality in breeding in communities where predation pressure is reduced either because predators are rare or because structure in the habitat (rocks, for example) provides a refuge from predators. Further comparative studies of the reproductive success of individuals of species which breed year round would test the predation hypothesis and further our understanding of the processes which mould the patterns seen.

2. *Differences.* The most striking difference between the two reproductive systems is that the male of the mouthbrooding species alone assumes breeding colour, builds a nest, establishes a territory, and engages in defence of this territory. The mouthbrooding females, on the other hand, "choose" several males with whom to lay their eggs and then move off to brood and defend the young alone. This social system is both polyandrous and polygynous. The substratum spawners, however, have a continuous division of labour in which the monogomous pairs defend their broods together. The length of time a successful pair holds a territory is six times longer than that of a male defending a territory in a Lake Malawi breeding arena. The average territory of substratum spawners is larger than that of a mouthbrooder. The physical presence of young requires, at a minimum, an area for them to forage. Thus more mouthbrooding species, theoretically, can be packed into a space-limited community. They do not require as large a territory nor do they remain on a territory for as long a period of time. Some mouthbrooding species, such as *Lethrinops furcicauda/furcifer*, establish territories for only four to six weeks in the year, whereas substratum spawners require at least 12 weeks to initiate breeding and successful raising of a brood. Although mouthbrooding has generally been thought to evolve as a response to predation (Fryer and Iles, 1972; Lowe-McConnell, 1975), the reduction in

both territory size and time on a territory could also be a response to competition and might be the primary aspect reinforcing the evolution of mouthbrooding.

With mouthbrooding females becoming totally responsible for the fry, the interests of the parents are less tightly linked. This is evident by the fact that territorial males cannibalize eggs, their own possible offspring (McKaye, 1983). Such energy acquisition, at the female's expense, may allow the male to stay on the arena longer, allowing him to increase his total number of eggs fertilized. A male substratum spawner would not increase his fitness by such behaviour.

Mouthbrooding also allows for a greater flexibility, since a territory is not absolutely required. The male and female can move about and still breed. Fry do not have to be defended in restricted areas for an extended period of time. Substratum spawners in Lake Jiloá, however, are restricted to breeding in rocky habitats. Defence of young is easier in an area where there is some structural heterogeneity. A complex environment provides places to hide eggs, gives the young a place to swim into, or at the very least reduces the number of possible predator attack angles. The presence of a boulder often provided "one side" of the territory (McKaye, 1977a). Over sand predators can attack easily from all directions.

Mouthbrooding has led to the evolution of a group of fishes which are specialized egg predators and paedophages (Greenwood, 1974; Wilhem, 1980; McKaye and Kocher, 1983). The large size of the eggs of mouthbrooders, the exposed nature of the nest where eggs are laid, and the vulnerability of a large number of females with a mouthful of young has made this feeding guild possible. Such specialized predators have been reported for Lake Victoria which is dominated by mouthbrooding cichlids (Greenwood, 1974). Such specializations are unknown for substratum cichlid communities. Substratum spawner eggs are much smaller and therefore contain less energy per unit (Fryer and Iles, 1972). Also, these eggs are usually concealed. The opportunistic egg eaters in Lake Jiloá are the smallest species or are juveniles less than 50 mm SL. For larger individuals the energy payoff probably does not make such small eggs an economic food source to exploit.

Much remains to be learned concerning the reproductive strategies of these fishes. Because of their wide range of breeding modes cichlids are ideal for testing various theories concerning reproductive behaviour and parental defence (Fryer and Iles, 1972; Barlow, 1974; Keenleyside, 1979; Perrone and Zaret, 1979). But to understand such behaviour we also must know more about the dynamics of the community in which the given species live. Seemingly anomalous behaviour which might seem maladaptive, such as the care of young of another species, will make sense when taken into the context of the community (McKaye, 1977b). A knowledge of cichlid mating systems and territoriality will aid in our understanding of the general processes which mould vertebrate reproductive behaviour and community dynamics. Hopefully, more field studies of this unique family of fishes will be initiated to test the generality of the observations and the hypotheses presented here and to examine the role of reproductive behaviour in the explosive radiation of this rapidly evolving group.

ACKNOWLEDGEMENTS

I especially wish to thank George Barlow who is responsible for generating my interest and enthusiasm for learning more about these remarkable fishes. Without his initial support none of these studies would have been made. Also the intellectual stimulation and help that I received from Geoffrey Fryer. Karel Liem and Rosemary Lowe-McConnell have guided much of the African studies. Their pioneering studies on the behaviour and ecology of Malawi cichlids are magnificent. Numerous individuals have worked with me in both Central America and Africa and I thank them collectively. My greatest appreciation goes to Svata Louda who has worked with me in Africa and has had to sit through long discussions on cichlid breeding behaviour. Her help with this manuscript was invaluable and her patience remarkable.

The help and support of both the Nicaraguan and Malawian Fisheries Departments are gratefully acknowledged. Without such support none of this work, of course, would have been possible. Financial support for both the Central American and African work came primarily from NSF.

REFERENCES

Akiyama, T., Kajumulo, A. A. and Olsen, S. (1977). *Bull. Freshwat. Fish Res. Lab., Tokyo* **27**, 49–61.
Barlow, G. W. (1974). *Am. Zool.* **14**, 9–34.
Barlow, G. W. (1976). *In* "Investigations of the Ichthyofauna of Nicaraguan Lakes" (T. B. Thorson, ed.), pp. 333–358. University of Nebraska, Lincoln.
Barlow, G. W., Baylis, J. R. and Roberts, D. A. (1976). *In* "Investigations of the Ichthyofauna of Nicaraguan Lakes" (T. B. Thorson, ed.), pp. 17–20. University of Nebraska, Lincoln.
Eccles, D. H. (1974). *Limnol. Oceanogr.* **19**, 730–742.
Eccles, D. H. and Lewis, D. S. C. (1977). *Ichthyol. Bull. Rhodes Univ.* **36**, 1–12.
Eccles, D. H. and Lewis, D. S. C. (1978). *Ichthyol. Bull. Rhodes Univ.* **37**, 1–11.
Eccles, D. H. and Lewis, D. S. C. (1981). *Envir. Biol. Fish.* **6**, 201–202.
Elton, C. S. (1924). *J. exp. Biol.* **2**, 119–163.
Fernald, R. D. and Hirata, N. R. (1977). *Anim. Behav.* **25**, 964–975.
FitzGerald, G. J. and Keenleyside, M. H. A. (1978). *Can. J. Zool.* **56**, 1367–1371.
Fryer, G. (1959). *Proc. zool. Soc. Lond.* **132**, 153–281.
Fryer, G. (1977). *Z. zool. syst. Evolutionsforsch.* **15**, 141–165.

Fryer, G. and Iles, T. D. (1972). "The Cichlid Fishes of the Great Lakes of Africa: Their Biology and Evolution". Oliver and Boyd, London.

Greenwood, P. H. (1964). *Proc. R. Instn. Gt Br.* **40**, 256–269.

Greenwood, P. H. (1974). *Bull. Br. Mus. (nat. Hist.)* **35**, 265–322.

Hamilton, W. D. (1971). *J. theor. Biol.* **31**, 295–311.

Holzberg, S. (1978). *Z. zool. syst. Evolutionsforsch.* **16**, 171–187.

Jackson, P. B. N., Iles, T. D., Harding, D. and Fryer, G. (1963). "Report on the Survey of Northern Lake Nyasa, 1954–1955". Government Printer, Zomba.

Janzen, D. H. (1971). *Ann. Rev. Ecol. Syst.* **2**, 465–492.

Keenleyside, M. H. A. (1979). "Diversity and Adaptation in Fish Behaviour". Springer Verlag, New York.

Keenleyside, M. H. A. and Bietz, B. F. (1981). *Envir. Biol. Fish.* **6**, 87–94.

Kocher, T. and McKaye, K. R. (1983). *Copeia* **1983**, 544–547.

Kosswig, C. (1947). *Nature, Lond.* **159**, 604–605.

Kosswig, C. (1963). *Copeia* **1963**, 238–244.

Lewis, D. S. C. (1980). *Copeia* **1980**, 874–875.

Lim, T. M., McKaye, K. R. and Weiland, D. J. (1976). *In* "Investigations of the Ichthyofauna of Nicaraguan Lakes" (T. B. Thorson, ed.). University of Nebraska, Lincoln.

Lowe, R. H. (1952). *Colon. Off. Fish Publ., Lond.* **1**, 1–122.

Lowe-McConnell, R. H. (1956). *Behaviour* **9**, 140–163.

Lowe-McConnell, R. H. (1959). *Proc. zool. Soc. Lond.* **132**, 1–30.

Lowe-McConnell, R. H. (1969). *Zool. J. Linn. Soc.* **48**, 255–302.

Lowe-McConnell, R. H. (1975). "Fish Communities in Tropical Freshwaters". Longman, London.

Lowe-McConnell, R. H. (1979). *Symp. zool. Soc. Lond.* **44**, 219–241.

Marsh, A. C., Ribbink, A. J. and Marsh, B. A. (1981). *Zool. J. Linn. Soc.* **71**, 253–264.

McKaye, K. R. (1977a). *Ecology* **58**, 291–302.

McKaye, K. R. (1977b). *Am. Nat.* **111**, 301–315.

McKaye, K. R. (1978). *Discovery, Lond.* **13**, 24–29.

McKaye, K. R. (1979). *Am. Nat.* **114**, 595–601.

McKaye, K. R. (1980). *Envir. Biol. Fish.* **5**, 75–78.

McKaye, K. R. (1981). *In* "Natural Selection of Social Behaviour" (R. Alexander and D. Tinkle, eds), pp. 173–183. Chiron, New York.

McKaye, K. R. (1983). *Envir. Biol. Fish.* **8**, 81–96.

McKaye, K. R. and Barlow, G. W. (1976). *In* "Investigations of the Ichthyofauna of Nicaraguan Lakes" (T. B. Thorson, ed.), pp. 311–319. University of Nebraska, Lincoln.

McKaye, K. R. and Hallacher, L. E. (1973). *Pac. Discovery* **26**, 1–8.

McKaye, K. R. and Kocher, T. (1983). *Anim. Behav.* **31**, 206–210.

McKaye, K. R. and Mackenzie, C. (1982). *Proc. biol. Soc. Wash.* **95**, 398–402.

McKaye, K. R. and McKaye, N. M. (1977). *Evolution* **31**, 674–681.

McKaye, K. R. and Oliver, M. K. (1980). *Anim. Behav.* **28**, 1287.

McKaye, K. R., Weiland, D. J. and Lim, T. M. (1979a). *Rev. Can. Biol.* **38**, 27–36.

McKaye, K. R., Weiland, D. J. and Lim, T. M. (1979b). *Copeia* **1979**, 542–544.

McKaye, K. R., Kocher, T., Reinthal, P. and Kornfield, I. (1982). *Zool. J. Linn. Soc.* **76**, 91–96.

van Oijen, M. J. P., Witte, F. and Witte-Maas, E. M. (1979). "Interim-report 1977–1979 from the Haplochromis Ecology Survey Team (HEST) operating in the Mwanza Area of Lake Victoria". Morphology Dept. University of Leiden, The Netherlands.

Perrone, M. and Zaret, T. M. (1979). *Am. Nat.* **113**, 351–361.
Ribbink, A. J. (1977). *Nature, Lond.* **267**, 243–244.
Ribbink, A. J., Marsh, A. C., Marsh, B. and Sharp, B. J. (1980). *S. Afr. J. Zool.* **15**, 1–6.
Ribbink, A. J., Marsh, A. C. and Marsh, B. A. (1981). *Envir. Biol. Fish.* **6**, 219–222.
Riedel, D. (1964). *FAO Inf. Pesca* **1885**, 1–46.
Ward, J. A. and Samarakoon, J. I. (1981). *Envir. Biol. Fish.* **6**, 219–222.
Ward, J. A. and Wyman, R. L. (1975). *Oceans* **8**, 42–47.
Ward, J. A. and Wyman, R. L. (1977). *Envir. Biol. Fish.* **2**, 137–145.
Wilhem, W. (1980). *Behaviour* **74**, 310–323.
Witte, F. (1981). *Neth. J. Zool.* **31**, 175–202.
Witte, F. and Witte-Maas, E. M. (1981). *Neth. J. Zool.* **31**, 203–231.

15. Implications of Parental Care of Offspring for the Anti-Predator Behaviour of Adult Male and Female Three-spined Sticklebacks, *Gasterosteus aculeatus* L.

N. GILES

School of Life Sciences, The University of Buckingham, U.K.

Abstract: This paper describes experiments performed upon fish from seven Scottish three-spined stickleback *Gasterosteus aculeatus* populations which are subject to a wide range of predation risks. Five of the populations consist of normally spined *Leiurus* morph, the other two of the rare spine-deficient morph. Stickleback adults and fry are known to be at risk from a wide variety of invertebrate, fish and bird predators. The anti-predator behaviour of adult male and female sticklebacks was measured during exposure to a live hunting pike (pike tests), and subsequent to the sudden presentation of a frightening overhead predator model (heron tests). Nineteen categories of behaviour were recorded during the pike tests, 13 in the heron tests. Twelve male and 12 female fish from each population were tested in each type of experiment. The resulting data were subjected to Principal Components Analysis (P.C.A.) with a Varimax rotation of axes. P.C.A. Factor 1 scores provided economical compound descriptors of the organization of the anti-predator behaviour of the tested fish.

In pike tests, before the stickleback became aware of the presence of the pike, male *Gasterosteus* exhibited more exploratory behaviour than females. When faced by a stalking pike female sticklebacks from all seven populations were significantly more cautious than males. In the heron tests also, adult females were, in general more cautious than males, taking longer to recover from the frightening overhead stimulus.

Parental care in *Gasterosteus* is undertaken exclusively by the male. Eggs and fry are at risk both from predators and from nest-raiding rival male sticklebacks which commonly steal eggs. Female *Gasterosteus*, playing no part in parental care must produce and spawn as many batches of eggs as possible. Both sexes must evade predators. It is proposed that the basis of the difference between sexes in anti-predator behaviour lies in the necessity of nest-tending and territorial defence by the male.

FISH REPRODUCTION
ISBN: 0–12–563660–1

Females apparently lose nothing by being very cautious in the presence of predators whilst males may lose the entire contents of their nest if they take too long to recover from an encounter with a predator.

I. INTRODUCTION

In freshwater habitats three-spined sticklebacks, *Gasterosteus aculeatus* become sexually mature during the early spring. Males develop a characteristic blue eye and red throat colouration and begin to defend reproductive territories within which they construct a nest. The siting of nests varies between water depths of less than 10 cm to greater than 100 cm from the shallow littoral to sheltered weed beds. A nest consists of a shallow depression in the substrate which is covered by a loose mat of aquatic vegetation glued together by the male fish with kidney secretions. When the nest is complete the male fish attracts and courts gravid females. Several clutches of eggs are collected within the nest and the resulting ova and fry are defended until they are self-sufficient. During the period of parental care the male periodically fans a current of water through the nest with his pectoral fins thus irrigating the developing eggs. Female *G. aculeatus* are capable of maturing several batches of eggs during the summer breeding season (Wootton, 1974) and may choose several different males to fertilize their eggs and to care for their developing fry. Females play no part in the parental care of offspring. Wootton (1976) gives a detailed review of the reproductive behaviour of male *Gasterosteus*.

The successive cycles of courtship and subsequent nest-guarding which progress through the breeding season involve the male in long periods of activity, often in open water where the risk of predation is likely to be high. The conspicuous male zig-zag courtship dance coupled with the bright nuptial colouration of the male stickleback make the fish readily visible to the human observer and probably also to any fish and bird predators. During this period the female fish are reported to spend much of their time in the cover of weed beds (Giles, 1981) or as part of a mixed shoal of female and juvenile fish (Wootton, 1976).

Male sticklebacks with developing eggs and small fry in their territories defend their nest contents not only from vertebrate and invertebrate egg predators, but also from nest-raiding sticklebacks which are capable of completely destroying a nest and causing total loss of its contents (Kynard, 1972). Egg stealing by adjacent *Gasterosteus* males is a common and widespread phenomenon (Wootton, 1971; Semler, 1971; Moodie, 1972; Kynard, 1972). Territorial defence against conspecific rivals is therefore an important activity for male sticklebacks which are subject to losses in reproductive output through cannibalism and through predation of offspring during later stages of their life cycle.

The anti-predator behaviour of *G. aculeatus* and the ten-spined stickleback, *Pungitius pungitius* was first described by Hoogland *et al.* (1957) who found that both species raise their dorsal and ventral spines upon the close approach of a small hunting pike or perch. The relatively larger spines of *Gasterosteus* were found to afford better protection than the smaller, more numerous spines of *Pungitius*. Benzie (1965) analysed the separate components of the anti-predator behavioural responses of both species in detail. During a predator encounter, *G. aculeatus* abruptly stops its normal bouts of slow pectoral swimming to either "leap" away in alarm, or freeze and remain motionless with spines raised in vegetation, or at the bottom of the tank. When sticklebacks are hiding from a predator all fin and bodily movements are suppressed and the fish rely upon their mottled brown cryptic colouration for protection. Considerable variation in the tendency to be bold when faced by a hunting pike, and in the degree of territorial aggression shown toward rival males occurs between male *Gasterosteus*. Huntingford (1976) has shown that males which exhibit boldness toward a predator also tend to be highly aggressive towards conspecific males. Timid males show extreme caution toward the pike coupled with a lower tendency to defend their nests.

The data used in this paper resulted from a study of seven Scottish *G. aculeatus* populations. Experiments were conducted to measure the responses of adult male and female sticklebacks from all seven populations to a frightening overhead stimulus (heron tests) and to a small live pike (pike tests). During the interpopulation comparisons of behaviour (Giles and Huntingford, in prep.) differences in adult male and female *Gasterosteus* antipredator behaviour emerged, these differences are the subject of this paper.

II. MATERIALS AND METHODS

The study sites included four on the Scottish mainland; Loch Lomond, a large mesotrophic loch; the Mar burn, a small shallow fast-running stream; the River Luggie, a eutrophic suburban river; and Lennox Castle reservoir, a small storage reservoir; and three on the Isle of North Uist (Outer Hebrides) — Loch Fada, Loch a Bharpa and Loch an Daimh, all of which are peaty, oligotrophic waters. These sites represent a wide range of potential predation risk categories. The Loch Lomond and Loch Fada *Gasterosteus* populations are at high risk from pike, perch (Lomond) and trout (Fada) whereas Lennox Castle has no fish predators and the Luggie very few. The Mar burn is adjacent to a large heronry, and gulls are known to predate sticklebacks at Lennox Castle.

Gasterosteus from the Lomond, Luggie, Lennox, Mar and Daimh populations used during the present study belonged to the *Leiurus* morph with low numbers of lateral plates (Wootton, 1976). Fish from the Fada and Bharpa populations are very unusual in having no lateral plates, reduced or absent dorsal spines, and a reduced or absent pelvic girdle with no ventral spines, such fish belong to the spine-deficient morph (Fig. 1). Adult sticklebacks were caught by sweeping a 40 cm diameter handnet through any available weed beds within reach of the shore or within wading depth. Samples of 12 adult males and 12 adult females were taken from each population, transported back to the laboratory, and housed in 30 L aquaria at a density of 12 fish per tank. All fish were fed daily on either Tubificid worms or *Daphnia*, a constant aeration and filtration system was employed. Cover was provided in the tanks by clumps of *Sphagnum* moss, a light regime of 16L,8D was used. Great care was taken to ensure that communal holding tanks and experimental tanks were at a similar temperature and under equivalent light intensities so that fish transferred between tanks experienced minimal stress.

The anti-predator behaviour of 12 adult male and 12 adult female sticklebacks from each of the seven study sites was measured by performing pike and heron tests, separate batches of fish were used for each type of test

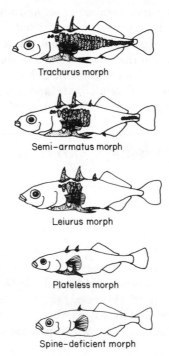

Trachurus morph

Semi–armatus morph

Leiurus morph

Plateless morph

Spine-deficient morph

Fig. 1.   Phenotypic variability in the morphs of *Gasterosteus aculeatus* from the study area.

(i.e. a total of 24 males and 24 females from each population). The test tanks used during the pike and heron tests are represented below (Fig. 2). During pike tests the stickleback was introduced into a releasing box and allowed to settle down for 5 min. The trap door of the box was then lowered allowing the stickleback to swim out into the open water of the experimental tank containing the pike, a 10 min vocal recording of the subsequent behaviour of

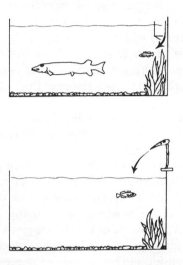

Fig. 2. Test tanks used during the pike and heron tests.

the fish began at this point. The time when the stickleback made its first obvious response to the pike was termed the "predator contact point". During the heron tests the stickleback was introduced into the test tank and allowed 5 min to settle down, the vocal commentary beginning at this point. For 5 min a recording of the behaviour of the stickleback was made (the pre-predator contact period), the model of the heron's head was then suddenly lowered over the tank so that the tip of the bill splashed on to the water surface; and raised back to a vertical position. The sudden presentation of the heron model overhead was also termed the "predator contact point". A 5 min post-predator contact period of stickleback behaviour was then recorded.

In the pike tests all behaviours relating to the presence and position of the pike were tape-recorded subsequent to the predator contact point. Each experiment was split into a pre-predator contact and a post-predator contact period and the frequency of occurrence and total duration of each of the recorded behaviours was calculated for each of these periods. The frequency of performance of each behaviour pattern was then converted to a rate per minute value for the two periods for each fish tested, and the duration of each behaviour was converted to an average proportion of each minute spent performing that behaviour during each period. This procedure was necessary because the timing of first predator contact was very variable in the pike tests and therefore the frequency of performance and duration of each behaviour needed to be related to the length of the pre- and post-predator contact periods in a given test.

The data from the pre-contact pike test periods represents the exploratory behaviour of the fish in a novel environment, the post-contact data representing the anti-fish predator behaviour of the sticklebacks. The pre-contact data from the heron tests is omitted from discussion as it also represents exploratory behaviour, but the post-contact data from these experiments is a measure of the anti-aerial predator behaviour of *G. aculeatus* and is included.

In order to analyse the data obtained from the pike and heron tests economically Principal Components Analyses (P.C.A.) (B.M.D. program, Dixon, 1973) were run on the data matrices (average frequencies and durations of behaviours per minute). Variables which were composed largely of zero scores were omitted. The P.C.A. calculates a Pearson product-moment correlation matrix for the behaviour scores and on the basis of these correlations it constructs a new set of mutually uncorrelated axes or components. Concise explanations of P.C.A. are given by Hope (1968), Child (1970), Davies (1971) and Maxwell (1977), the works of Huntingford (1976) and Aspey and Blankenship (1977) provide examples of the application of P.C.A. to ethological data. The use of P.C.A. allows the simplification of complex heterogeneous data matrices by grouping numbers of the original variables into compound components. The first component to emerge from the analysis accounts for the largest proportion of total variance within the data matrix (i.e. differences between individual sticklebacks). The second component (orthogonal to the first) accounts for the next largest proportion, and so on until a complete set of components (equal in number to the original number of variables) is produced. A component produced by a P.C.A. on the data used in this paper is composed of a group of highly correlated behaviours which are opposed to a second group of behaviours which differed maximally from them along a given axis. The degree to which a behaviour contributes towards a component is termed its loading. This can vary between the values $+1$ to -1, the initial sign is assigned arbitrarily, the relative signs and loadings of the subsequent behaviours are thus of importance.

In each of the P.C.A.'s described in the following section a "Varimax rotation" has been performed upon the components; this procedure seeks to maximize both the variance of the loadings of different acts on the same component and also the loadings of the same acts on different components. This process gives rise to either relatively large or relatively small values when compared with the original component loading (Maxwell, 1977). Multivariate analyses are particularly suitable for behavioural work since animals often perform behaviours in sequences and groups which can be readily identified and quantified with these statistical techniques. P.C.A. identifies groups of correlated behaviours, and if the original correlations are the result of internal factors, the analysis helps the identification of motivational systems.

In the following section the scores for the tested fish on the first rotated component to emerge from each P.C.A. (the factor 1 scores) are used as an economic description of the behaviour of the adult male and female sticklebacks.

III. RESULTS

The first factor to emerge from the P.C.A. of the pre-contact pike test data accounted for 25% of the total variance in the data matrix, the most important behaviours (i.e. those with the highest or lowest loadings) comprising this factor are presented in Fig. 3. The magnitude of the loadings for "duration in weed", "duration still" and "duration at bottom" is less than would normally be considered a significant contribution to the factor structure (loadings of >0.5 and < -0.5 were used in this study) these behaviours are included to illustrate those aspects of stickleback behaviour most closely associated with a late predator contact point in a pike test. Factor 1 from this P.C.A. can be interpreted as a measure of exploratory (positively loaded) behaviours versus timid (negatively loaded) behaviours. Mean factor 1 scores for 12 adult males and 12 adult females from each population are presented in Table I. These data were subjected to a two-way analysis of variance with replication (Sokal

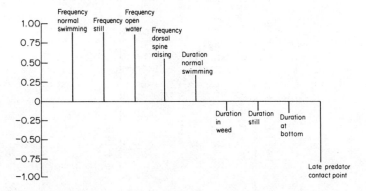

Fig. 3.   Factor 1 (rotated first component) behaviour loadings, pre-predator contact data: pike tests.

TABLE I. Factor 1 scores from Principal Component Analysis of pike test data before contact with predator.

	Daimh		Lomond		Luggie		Mar		Bharpa		Lennox		Fada	
	m	f	m	f	m	f	m	f	m	f	m	f	m	f
$\bar{x}$	−0·04	0·43	0·24	−0·37	0·19	−0·34	0·21	−0·53	0·35	0·047	−0·05	−0·24	0·07	0·028
s.d.	1·11	1·97	0·9	0·72	0·55	1·02	0·52	0·45	0·98	0·67	1·2	0·96	0·79	0·99

m: male; f: female.

and Rohlf, 1973) with the sexes and populations as factors. No significant sexual or population differences were found, but in general, male sticklebacks exhibited more exploratory behaviour in the novel environment of the pike test tank than adult females. The difference held true for all populations except Loch an Daimh where females behaved less timidly than males.

The first factor to emerge from the P.C.A. of the post-contact pike test data accounted for 27% of the total variance within the original data matrix. The most important behaviours comprising this factor, together with their factor loadings are given in Fig. 4. This factor served to separate fish which spent long periods still, hiding at the bottom (negative loadings) from fish which spent much of the time performing bouts of normal swimming in open water whilst encountering a stalking pike. Mean factor 1 scores for the 12 males and 12 females from each population are presented in Table II. A two-way anova with replication arranged as above gives for population effects: $F = 52.4$, d.f. $= 6,154$, $P < 0.001$ and for sex effects $F = 11.4$, d.f. $= 1,154$, $P < 0.001$ interaction effects are non-significant, i.e. highly significant behavioural differences for both factors. For all seven populations adult females were more cautious when faced with a stalking pike than adult males.

The heron test data were analysed in a similar way and factor 1 from the P.C.A. accounted for 27% of the total variance. Figure 5 illustrates the structure of the factor and gives the loadings for each behaviour. Fish which scored positively on this factor performed a lot of post-predator contact bouts of open water swimming, pausing frequently to feed, and recovered quickly from the frightening overhead stimulus. Fish which scored negatively on factor 1 took a long time to recover (resume normal swimming) after the frightening overhead stimulus presentation, remaining still for long periods either at the bottom or in the weed, i.e. they exhibited a more marked fright

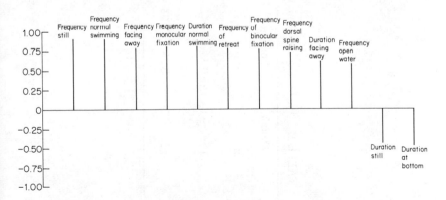

Fig. 4.   Factor 1 (rotated first component) behaviour loadings, post-predator contact data: pike tests.

TABLE II. Factor 1 scores from Principal Component Analysis of pike test data after contact with predator.

	Daimh		Lomond		Luggie		Mar		Bharpa		Lennox		Fada	
	m	f	m	f	m	f	m	f	m	f	m	f	m	f
$\bar{x}$	−0·5	−0·64	−0·33	−0·62	0·93	0·49	0·017	−0·29	−0·45	−0·6	1·89	1·89	−0·43	−0·7
s.d.	0·32	0·41	0·25	0·28	0·7	0·64	0·46	0·19	0·33	0·34	1·45	1·45	0·86	0·19

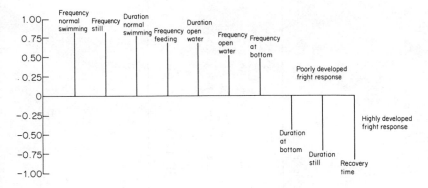

Fig. 5.   Factor 1 (rotated first component) behaviour loadings: heron tests.

response than positively scoring fish. Mean factor 1 scores for the heron tested fish are given in Table III. A two-way anova with replication gave for populations: $F=8·14$, d.f. $=6,154$, $P<0·001$, for sexes $F=7·4$, d.f. $=1,154$, $P<0·01$ interactions were also significant ($P<0·001$). Females exhibited more extreme fright responses than males in all populations except Loch an Daimh and Lennox Castle reservoir, the difference being most marked in the River Luggie population.

IV. DISCUSSION

Throughout the series of experiments described above there is a consistent trend for breeding male *Gasterosteus* to be less cautious in a novel environment and during predator–prey interactions than adult female *Gasterosteus*. This paper proposes that the basis for this sexual difference in behaviour lies in the parental care of offspring and territorial nest protection of the male. Males defend egg filled nests against predators of all types and against conspecific egg raiders, and endeavour to attract as many gravid females as possible to the nest to spawn their eggs and complete the multiple clutch. Females have only to shed their eggs in the nest of the fittest available male and then resume feeding to mature another egg batch; both sexes must avoid being predated. This differential demand upon the males' time may have led to the reduction in caution exhibited by breeding males which risk the loss of many eggs and/or fry by remaining in hiding for too long after predator encounters. The major discrepancy in the trend described above lies with the Loch an Daimh population where in the (pre-contact) pike tests the females were more exploratory than the males, and in the heron tests where the

TABLE III. Factor 1 scores from Principal Components Analysis of heron test data.

	Daimh			Lomond			Luggie			Mar			Bharpa			Lennox			Fada		
	m	f	fry	m	f	fry	m	f	fry	m	f	fry	m	f	fry	m	f	fry	m	f	fry
$\bar{x}$	−0·07	0·49	0·01	−0·5	−0·75	−0·54	1·7	−0·68	0·53	−0·8	−0·9	−0·3	0·3	0·06	0·5	−0·42	−0·05	0·07	0·3	−0·17	0·54
s.d.	1·14	0·9	0·9	1·15	0·64	0·55	1·4	0·82	1·07	0·42	0·51	0·94	0·7	0·59	0·42	1·01	0·39	0·96	0·67	0·79	0·7

(different) females tested were again bolder than the males. A possible explanation lies in the facts that Loch an Daimh is for the most part much more heavily weeded than the other study sites and also that nine-spined sticklebacks occur abundantly in the lake. These two facts may have led to a need for *Gasterosteus* females to advertize their presence to nesting males in a habitat where visibility is restricted and many of the female sticklebacks encountered will be of the wrong species. No information is available on the sex ratios at the study sites but if males are scarce at Loch an Daimh then female competition for males may occur in place of the normally envisaged male competition for females amongst breeding sticklebacks.

A second anomaly in the data is the boldness of the Lennox Castle females in the heron tests. The rapid recovery of these fish from the frightening overhead stimulus and resumption of normal swimming and feeding in open water may be explained by the fact that all 12 females were found to be heavily parasitized by plerocercoides of the pseudophyllidean cestode *Schistocephalus solidus*. Only three of the 12 heron-tested male Lennox Castle fish harboured the parasite. *Schistocephalus* is known to affect *Gasterosteus* behaviour (Lester, 1971), and in particular to suppress the overhead fright response.

A. The relationship between boldness and reproductive success

If the argument thus far is correct a positive relationship would be predicted between breeding male boldness toward egg, larval and adult predators of the species and reproductive success in species with paternal care. The interplay between boldness and caution will result in a trade-off at a point determined by local predator abundance and the degree of cover afforded by the habitat.

In the Bullhead, *Cottus gobio* paternal care involves the guarding of multiple clutches of eggs stuck to the underside of flat stones. This species has excellent cryptic camouflage and is largely inactive during the day (Smyly, 1957), defending exclusive small reproductive territories beneath individual stones. Conspicuousness is minimized in two ways, first by having no reproductive display save for a rapid head-bite administered by the male (Morris, 1954), and secondly by ritualizing territorial disputes into sequences of head darkening, opercular raising, fin spreading and head-nodding (grunting) displays. Smyly notes that males are markedly more active than females in the breeding season, *C. gobio* therefore minimizes predation risk from birds such as Kingfishers, *Alcedo athis* by remaining out of sight. The nine-spined stickleback also nests in sheltered sites, in this instance weed-beds and, like *G. aculeatus* has evolved a stereotyped "head-down" threat posture. Both *P. pungitius* and *G. aculeatus* are known to fight over territorial boundaries early in the breeding season, it appears, however, that once demarcation is achieved overt aggression may be much reduced. Wootton's

(1972) study of the River Wear *G. aculeatus* population revealed that nesting male sticklebacks spent only 20–30 secs per 20 min observation period in aggressive territorial defence.

Male *Gasterosteus* will minimize the risk of being predated by choosing nest sites in sheltered or otherwise concealed positions, a "safe" nest site would allow a quick return to nest guarding and territorial defence after a predator encounter. Sargent and Gebler (1980) have shown that under semi-natural conditions *Gasterosteus* males that nested in concealed sites (clay flower pots) spawned earlier, and more often, had a higher hatching success, suffered fewer stolen fertilizations, and fewer nest-raids and territorial encounters than males which nested in open positions. Kynard (1979) has discovered that under natural conditions in three separate *Gasterosteus* populations males of differing lateral plate phenotype prefer to nest in differing locations, with 14 plated individuals (total right hand side and left hand side) out-competing 16 plated individuals for preferred sites in vegetation at depths of greater than 45 cm. Moodie (1972) has also demonstrated significant differences in the distance from shelter that territorial *Gasterosteus* males choose to nest. An account of nest site selection of males from the present study is described elsewhere (Giles, 1981; Giles and Huntingford, in press), in general territorial sticklebacks at all seven sites chose sheltered nest positions and spread themselves out within the suitable nesting areas. Kynard (1972) presented nesting male *Gasterosteus* with tethered live Rainbow Trout *Salmo gairdneri* and found that those caring for fry were both bolder toward the trout and more aggressive toward a conspecific male than other males tested. Pressley (1981) has studied nest-defence behaviour in two natural *Gasterosteus* populations. Males with larger numbers of eggs or older eggs in their nests than other males remained in their territorial areas and attacked a dummy predator (prickly sculpin, *Cottus asper*) rather than desert the nest. Males with few eggs or eggs at an early developmental stage never attacked the dummy and deserted the nest site upon the presentation of the dummy (a predator of adult sticklebacks and their eggs). Pressley interprets these results as a demonstration of increased parental effort (risk of being predated) with increasing value of the present offspring in relation to the reproductive value of the parent. During the present study *Gasterosteus* were found to have a life span of *ca.* 18 months, surviving for a single breeding season; under these conditions it would be reasonable to predict that males would take greater risks in order to maximize their reproductive output than males from populations known to have a longer average lifespan. It is not known whether sticklebacks (of both sexes) which survive for more than one breeding season spawn successfully each year.

ACKNOWLEDGEMENTS

This research was funded by an S.R.C. grant and undertaken at the Department of Zoology, University of Glasgow. Drs F. A. Huntingford and R. Tippett supervised the work. Prof. A. J. Brook and Dr F. A. Huntingford criticized the original draft of the paper.

REFERENCES

Aspey, W. P. and Blankenship, J. E. (1977). *In* "Quantitative Methods in the Study of Animal Behaviour" (B. A. Hallett, ed.), pp. 75–120. Academic Press, New York.

Benzie, V. L. (1965). "Some aspects of the anti-predator behaviour of two species of stickleback." Ph.D. Thesis University of Oxford.

Child, D. (1970). "The Essentials of Factor Analysis." Holt, Rinehart and Winston, New York.

Davies, R. G. (1971). "Computer Programming in Quantitative Biology." Academic Press, New York.

Dixon, W. J. (ed.) (1973). "B.M.D. Biomedical Computer Programs." University of California Press, Berkeley.

Giles, N. (1981). "Predation effects upon the behaviour and ecology of Scottish *Gasterosteus aculeatus* L. populations." Ph.D. thesis, Department of Zoology, University of Glasgow.

Giles, N. and Huntingford, F. A. (1983). *Anim. Behav.* (in press).

Hoogland, R., Morris, D. and Tinbergen, N. (1957). *Behaviour* **10**, 205 237.

Hope, K. (1968). "Methods of Multivariate Analysis." University of London Press, London.

Huntingford, F. A. (1976). *Anim. Behav.* **24**, 485–497.

Kynard, B. E. (1972). "Male breeding behaviour and lateral plate phenotype in the three-spine stickleback (*Gasterosteus aculeatus*)." Ph.D. thesis, University of Washington.

Kynard, B. E. (1979). *Copeia* **1979**, 525–528.

Lester, R. J. G. (1971). *Can. J. Zool.* **49**, 361–366.

Maxwell, A. E. (1977). "Multivariate Analysis in Behavioural Research." Chapman and Hall, London.

Moodie, G. E. E. (1972). *Can. J. Zool.* **50**, 721–732.

Morris, D. J. (1954). *Behaviour* **7**, 1–32.

Pressley, P. H. (1981). *Evolution* **35**, 282–295.

Sargent, R. C. and Gebler, J. B. (1980). *Behav. Ecol. Sociobiol.* **7**, 137–142.

Semler, D. E. (1971). *J. Zool. Lond.* **165**, 291–302.

Smyly, W. J. P. (1957). *Proc. Zool. Soc. Lond.* **128**, 431–453.

Sokal, R. R. and Rohlf, F. J. (1973). "Introduction to Biostatistics." W. H. Freeman, San Francisco.

Wootton, R. J. (1971). *Can. J. Zool.* **49**, 960–962.

Wootton, R. J. (1974). *J. Zool. Lond.* **172**, 331–342.

Wootton, R. J. (1976). "The Biology of the Sticklebacks." Academic Press, London.

16. Reproductive Tactics: A Non-event in Aquaculture?

P. J. REAY

Department of Biological Sciences, Plymouth Polytechnic, Plymouth, U.K.

Abstract: Associated with the recent increase in aquaculture production research and development are three trends which are relevant in the present context: (1) the increase in the number of species being cultured or being investigated as potential candidates; (2) the increase in the use of hatcheries (involving captive broodstock) for seed production; and (3) the increase in the understanding of environmental and genetic influences on reproduction and the corresponding sophistication of manipulative techniques.

Reproductive tactics potentially affect: (1) the supply of seed, either from wild stocks or hatcheries; (2) production during the growing-on stage (as a result of early maturity); (3) the type of aquaculture practised and the technique used; and therefore, (4) the selection of species (or other taxa).

The selection of species may involve deciding between broad groups (such as salmonids or cichlids), but selection normally occurs at the level of species, or increasingly, at the sub-specific level. Marketing rather than biological criteria probably have the major influence on selection, and among the biological criteria, those associated with reproduction may not be the most important. It should also be noted that both the traditional and recent selection of species for culture, almost always derives from their status in relation to capture fisheries. However, there are instances where a reproductive tactic may impose a constraint to the use of a species, either in absolute terms or when tempered by economic reality.

I. INTRODUCTION

Pillay's (1979) data, and their subsequent modification and extrapolation, suggest that the annual production of teleosts from aquaculture is currently of the order of 4 million t. This compares with about 60 million t from capture fisheries. The bulk of the latter comes from marine temperate waters whereas aquaculture is concentrated in the fresh waters of low latitude areas. Capture fisheries exploit natural populations and communities, whereas in aquacul-

FISH REPRODUCTION
ISBN: 0–12–563660–1

ture the "population" often consists of a single species, a single cohort, and even a single sex, and suffers a sudden and almost total mortality before sexual maturity is reached.

Although Jhingran and Gopalakrishnan (1974) listed 314 species of teleost which were being utilized to some degree in aquaculture throughout the world, it is clear that only about one tenth of these are of much importance in terms of production level. Nevertheless eight orders are well represented: Acipenseriformes (e.g. *Acipenser*); Anguilliformes (e.g. *Anguilla*); Gonorhynchiformes (*Chanos*); Salmoniformes (e.g. *Oncorhynchus*); Cypriniformes (e.g. *Ctenopharyngodon*); Siluriformes (e.g. *Ictalurus*); Perciformes (e.g. *Sarotherodon, Mugil*); and Pleuronectiformes (e.g. *Scophthalmus*).

Of more significance in the present context, however, is reproductive variation, and Balon's (1975) scheme of reproductive guilds provides a useful framework. This is given in outline in Table I with aquacultural examples for each major guild type. Most aquaculture species (and most fish in general) are non-guarding open-substrate spawners. In contrast, internal bearers are not well represented, but it is probably the small size of most of these, rather than their reproductive characteristics, which limit their use in aquaculture food production; it is for example likely that *Sarotherodon* species would be just as valuable if they were internal rather than external bearers. The guarders, like the bearers, tend to be warm-water species and include species like *Trichogaster pectoralis* which accounts for 76% of the 17 000 t paddy field production in Thailand (Lam, 1982b).

Sexuality is not considered in the Balon scheme, but it is worth noting that although most species used in aquaculture are gonochorists there are examples of both protandrous (e.g. *Sparus auratus*) and protogynous (*Epinephelus tauvina*) hermaphrodites. There are also semelparous (e.g. *Oncorh-*

TABLE I.   Balon's (1975) major reproductive guilds with some examples from aquaculture.

A.	Non-guarders	
	A.1 Open substratum spawners	*Mugil* (pelagophil)
		Cyprinus (phytophil)
	A.2 Brood-hiders	*Salmo*
B.	Guarders	
	B.1 Substratum choosers	*Ophicephalus*
	B.2 Nest-spawners	*Trichogaster*
C.	Bearers	
	C.1 External	*Sarotherodon*
	C.2 Internal	*Gambusia*

ynchus) as well as iteroparous species. In other words, a superficial survey of the species used in aquaculture indicates that a wide range of tactics is represented, and it is suggested that there is no *a priori* reason to suppose that any tactic is completely incompatible with the objectives and practices of aquaculture.

To some extent this is because aquaculture itself consists of a wide range of practices, and is often divided into extensive and intensive systems. These terms are not rigidly defined but in an extensive system there is relatively little manipulation and the farmer would typically adapt to any reproductive peculiarities of his species. In a more intensive system the reproductive processes would tend to be manipulated in order to bypass any potential difficulties, or improve efficiency. A more useful classification for present purposes is shown in Table II where the two alternative sources of "seed" (fry, juveniles, fingerlings etc.) are indicated. Many substantial aquaculture industries still rely on wild populations for seed supply (e.g. *Anguilla*, *Chanos*, *Seriola* and *Mugil*). Japan produces 100 000 t yr^{-1} of *Seriola quinqueradiata* from wild seed, and The Philippines, Indonesia and Taiwan together produce 300 000 t yr^{-1} of *Chanos chanos*: in The Philippines alone $1·35 \times 10^9$ seed are harvested annually to supply the industry with its needs (Smith *et al.*, 1979). Many other, smaller industries also rely on wild seed harvesting: examples include *Oxyeleotris*, *Channa* and *Epinephelus* in S.E. Asia (Davy and Chouinard, 1981; Lam, 1982b). Although most of the species mentioned above have bred or have been induced to breed in captivity on a small scale, mass propagation has been achieved for relatively few groups: these include

TABLE II. The major types of aquaculture.

	Seed supply	Growing-on	
1.	Wild	in captivity	*Open culture* e.g.: *Chanos chanos, Mugil cephalus, Anguilla anguilla, Ophicephalus striatus*
2.	In captivity (hatcheries)	in captivity	*Closed culture* e.g.: *Ctenopharyngodon idella, Cyprinus carpio, Salmo gairdneri, Scophthalmus maximus*
3.	In captivity (hatcheries)	wild	*Ranching/stocking* e.g.: *Oncorhynchus keta, Sparus major, Gadus morhua*

the salmonids (*Salmo*, *Oncorhynchus*, *Salvelinus*, *Coregonus*), the carps (*Cyprinus*, *Carassius*), the chinese carps (*Ctenopharyngodon* etc.), the Indian carps (*Labeo* etc.), catfish (*Ictalurus* and some *Clarias* species) and a small number of marine species whose culture is still at an early stage (*Sparus*, *Lates*, *Dicentrarchus*, *Solea*, *Scophthalmus*). Virtually all Chinese carps in China are now produced in captivity by induced spawning techniques: this amounts to 20×10^9 seed each year. In India, 260×10^6 seed are produced in the same way from Indian carps, but ten times this amount are still being harvested from the wild populations in the rivers (Davy and Chouinard, 1981).

The inability either to obtain adequate supplies of seed from the wild, or to establish mass propagation from hatcheries, is commonly regarded as a major constraint to the initiation or expansion of aquaculture. It is an almost universal objective of research and development to achieve controlled seed production in hatcheries, although even where this has been achieved (e.g. in Chinese carps) some use may still be made of wild fish as a source of new genetic material, and Smith *et al.* (1979) has cautioned against the rapid development of hatcheries for *Chanos* in the Philipines, on the grounds that the wild seed collection industry could supply all needs.

The objectives of this paper are: (1) to identify which components of fish reproductive tactics could be important in aquaculture; (2) to indicate how any particular constraints may be overcome by manipulations of stock and environment; and (3) to assess the real impact of reproductive tactics in the development and operation of aquaculture industries.

II. REPRODUCTIVE TACTICS

If the universal reproductive strategy is to maximize the production of surviving progeny in relation to available energy and parental life expectancy, there are clearly many tactics (or sets of co-adapted traits according to Stearns 1976). An (incomplete) tactic may be, for example, to spawn 10 000 pelagic eggs at daily intervals from mid-May to mid-June in the first breeding season (the second year of life). There are five components or operations here: fecundity, spawning habitat, spawning frequency, spawning season and age at maturity. A more comprehensive, but still inevitably incomplete, list is given in Table III. It is from such a list that an overall tactic can be built-up. The main component headings will now be considered in relation to aquaculture.

A. Gonad production

Occasionally the gonad is the marketable product (as in caviar production from the Acipenseriformes) or at least has some market value (*Oncorhynchus* species). Normally, however, no gonad development is required during on-

TABLE III.   Reproductive components.

---

1. GONAD PRODUCTION
    1.1   annual[b]
    1.2   lifetime[b]

2. BEHAVIOURAL MECHANISMS (including associated morphological and physiological changes)
    2.1   pre-spawning behaviour
    2.2   spawning behaviour
    2.3   post-spawning behaviour[a]

3. SPATIAL and TEMPORAL PATTERNS
    3.1   spawning areas
    3.2   spawning (oviposition) sites[a]
    3.3   spawning seasons (annual cycle)
    3.4   spawning frequency and times (lunar, tidal and dict cycles within seasons)[b]

4. SEX
    4.1   sex ratios
    4.2   hermaphroditism and sex changes
    4.3   sexual dimorphism

5. PROGENY
    5.1   state of release from female and/or parental care[a]
    5.2   size at release
    5.3   numbers per female (fecundity and fertility)[b]
    5.4   requirements/adaptations of newly released progeny

6. REGULATORY MECHANISMS[b]
    6.1   egg production as a function of adult food supply
    6.2   atresia
    6.3   density independent survival of progeny
    6.4   density dependent survival of progeny as a function of juvenile food
    6.5   density dependent survival of progeny as a function of predation (including cannibalism)

---

[a] Incorporated into Balon's Guilds (1975).
[b] Incorporated into the "r" and "k" scheme.

growing. This is because it may divert energy and other resources away from somatic growth, and ripe fish are likely to have poor quality flesh and thus fetch a lower price than those which are sexually immature. In most aquaculture systems this is not a problem since harvesting typically occurs before sexual maturity is reached. However, grilsification, or precocious maturity, in male salmonids (Gardner, 1976; Nosho, 1981) and in tilapia where not only gonad maturation but also spawning can occur at an early age (Balarin and Hatton, 1979), are major difficulties whose control has received much attention. Grilse are worth only about half as much as older salmon, so that early maturation does have direct economic implications. In some cases sexual maturity may only temporarily depress growth as Lincoln (1981) has demonstrated in comparisons between normal and sterile flatfish.

In contrast to the on-growing situation, gonad development is obviously required in the broodstock and there would appear to be additional advantages in early maturity, batch-spawning, high gonad production (egg numbers, total egg volume) and prolonged iteroparity. Batch-spawning can result in much higher gonad production than would be indicated by the gonado-somatic index at any one point in time. Thus a 5 kg turbot (*Scophthalmus maximus*) spawned 7·5 kg of eggs in a single season at the SFIA Marine Farming Unit at Ardtoe in Scotland (Gillespie, pers. comm.). Zohar and Gordin (1979) noted that once spawning had been induced in the seabream *Sparus auratus* it continued to spawn every 24 h for between 4 and 100 days, all the ovulated oocytes in the ovary being released at each spawning.

B. Behavioural mechanisms

Once again these will be either undesirable or irrelevant in on-growing, but most will be an inevitable consequence of the natural spawning (as opposed to artificial stripping and fertilization) of broodstock. In some groups, notably catfish and tilapia, aggressive pre-spawning behaviour in confined conditions can lead to damage and even death of valuable female broodstock (e.g. El-Ibiary et al., 1977).

Migratory behaviour, essential in the wild for optimising distribution of progeny, is inhibited in captivity, and does not appear to be an essential prerequisite for successful spawning (e.g. in *Salmo salar*, *Pleuronectes platessa*). A simulation of environmental changes experienced during migration, such as a lowering of water temperature in tropical marine species, may be important in induced spawning. Anadromous migratory behaviour is of course specifically exploited in the ranching of salmonids. More attention to spawning behaviour, including both environmental requirements and social interactions, are likely to pay dividends in helping to induce more species to spawn in captivity. The general teleost characteristics of external fertilization greatly facilitates the artificial fertilization of stripped gametes. This enables natural spawning difficulties to be bypassed, and also has other advantages, for example in making hybridization between unrelated species more feasible than if natural mating had to be relied upon.

Most post-spawning behaviour is concerned with parental care of progeny. In the wild, this undoubtedly confers a survival advantage on the progeny but in captive conditions survival is likely to be high anyway and parental involvement may be considered disadvantageous: for example it may increase the inter-brood interval. If so, broods can be successfully removed from nests (e.g. *Osphronemus*) and buccal cavities (*Sarotherodon*), and reared separately.

C. Spatial patterns

When seed are harvested from the wild, the spawning areas and seasons will broadly determine when and where seed can be collected, although active and passive movements of the young fish will modify the pattern. For example, the fry of *Seriola quinqueradiata* with a body length of 15 mm begin to gather under floating *Sargassum* weed near the Japanese coasts of southern Honshu, Shikoku and Kyushu from March to July. They are harvested by fishermen, preferably when greater than 40 mm in length, using small purse-seines and dip-nets (Mitani, 1978). Differences in the spawning seasons of closely related species of grey mullet (Mugilidae) along the Israeli coast can be utilized to harvest the juveniles of only the most valuable species (*Mugil cephalus* and *Liza ramada*) according to Sarig (1981).

If eggs, as opposed to later developmental stages, are required, attention will also have to be paid to oviposition sites and spawning times. Eggs are in fact rarely collected, but they are still gathered from Indian major carp (e.g. *Labeo*) in the River Halda in Bangladesh. Here collection is made at the time of new and full moons between April and July (Davy and Chouinard, 1981). Spawning times and spawning seasons may also influence the timing of spawning in captivity; both can be manipulated (Zohar and Gordin, 1979; Bye, Chap. 11, this volume), but the geographical variation of spawning season in *Salmo gairdneri* can also be utilized to obtain year-round supplies of eyed ova by importing them from different parts of the world.

Provision of an appropriate spawning substrate can be critical to successful spawning in captivity and may in fact be a stimulus to spawning, at least in some species such as *Carassius auratus* (Stacey *et al.*, 1979). For pelagophils an appropriate chemical and physical environment rather than a spawning substrate is presumably required, though little seems to be known of such requirements. Several marine species will spawn spontaneously in captivity, and in the recent success with *Chanos chanos* in net cages off Guimeras Island in The Philippines it seemed that lack of stress rather than the provision of any specific physico-chemical characteristics was the critical factor (Lacanilao and Marte, 1981).

D. Sex

Secondary sexual characters may lead to one sex being more valued in culture, the most obvious example being the faster growth of male tilapia and female salmonids.

Most natural populations of fish have a sex-ratio of 1:1 but this may become inadvertently modified under culture conditions. For example, Liao (1981) has reported a preponderance of females in the culture of *Mugil* species.

Where one of the sexes has a particular advantage, there is clearly an advantage in producing monosex stock.

Both sexes are required among the broodstock, but a sex-ratio in favour of females may enable stock and facilities to be used with maximum efficiency (Sarig, 1981). Where natural spawning takes place, there may be an optimum sex ratio for the production of fertilized eggs depending on the social behaviour of the species involved. Three examples illustrate some of the variation: *Sparus major, Ictalurus punctatus* (1:1), group and single pair respectively); *Cyprinus carpio* (1♀:2–3♂♂); and *Osphronemus gourami* (2♀♀:1♂). Ling, 1977; Davy and Chouinard, 1981).

Where protandrous hermaphroditism occurs (as in several sparids and serranids for example) it can be used in conjunction with the cryopreservation of sperm to produce pure lines in three to four generations by self-fertilization (Purdom, 1979).

E. Progeny

The numbers, distribution, variability and size of wild seed are related to, and influenced by, the reproductive tactics of the parental populations. In captivity, high fecundity means that fewer broodstock need to be maintained (or that more seed can be produced), but larger progeny are assumed to be more viable and easy to rear. Generally this appears to be true and Gall's (1975) data on *Salmo gairdneri* clearly demonstrate a beneficial egg size effect within a single species. Interspecifically, larger eggs also produce larger larvae which tend to be easier to rear, but an exception is the halibut *Hippoglossus hippoglossus* which produces 4 mm eggs and 9 mm larvae, much larger than other flatfish, but apparently very sensitive and difficult to rear. High fecundity and large progeny are incompatible, but fecundity is more accessible to manipulation. It also has genetic advantages (Wilkins, 1981); many siblings can be raised from outstanding crosses, selection can be very intensive and therefore effective even if heritability is low, and gynogenesis becomes feasible.

Adaptations and requirements of the progeny will not be considered in detail, but they do give rise to the major problem of hatchery production which is rearing larvae to metamorphosis rather than producing eggs from broodstock (Pullin and Kuo, 1981). Differences between species mean that technology developed for one species cannot directly be transferred to another. An example of such differences is given by Kentouri and Divanach's (1982) work on sparids.

F. Regulatory mechanisms

The visible result of these mechanisms at the population level is a change of numbers in response to environmental parameters, and involving both density dependent and density independent interactions. As such, fluctuations in the supply of wild seed can be seen either in relation to density independent environmental factors or to density dependent interactions between stock and recruitment. The behaviour of tilapia populations in ponds (Balarin and Hatton, 1979) can also be examined against a similar background.

The effect of food supply on female egg production, and of density on the survival of progeny are examples of regulatory interactions which could have considerable bearing on the success of hatchery operations.

III. MANIPULATING TACTICS

From the above discussion, six potential problem areas associated with reproduction can be identified and grouped into three pairs. They are problems in the sense that they could prevent or delay the establishment of an aquaculture industry or significantly reduce its profitability. Four major sets of techniques for manipulating the system to overcome these problems are environmental, nutritional, hormonal and genetic. The relevance of each of these to the identified problem areas is indicated in Table IV and amplified below.

TABLE IV. Techniques available for overcoming problems associated with reproduction in aquaculture.

| | Manipulative techniques | | | | |
Problem area	Environmental (abiotic)	Nutritional	Hormonal	Genetic	Other
1. No spawning in captivity	+	+	+		social behaviour
2. Spawning occurs, but season too short or at an inconvenient time	+		+	+	gamete preservation
3. Egg production and quality from broodstock low		+		+	
4. Egg/larval size too small		+?		+?	
5. Growing stock matures/reproduces	+		+	+	includes production of monosex stock
6. Monosex stock required			+	+	

A. Induction of spawning

This includes both the induction of spawning of species which do not spawn spontaneously in captivity and changing the timing of spawning of species which do. Genetic manipulation does not play an important role here. Purdom (1979) has indicated that for *Salmo gairdneri* five generations of selection may be needed to shift the spawning season by two months, but this would seem to have no clear advantages over more direct environmental manipulations.

It is increasingly being acknowledged (e.g. Davy and Chouinard, 1981; Pullin and Kuo, 1981) that the nutritional status of the broodstock is of great importance in determining (a) whether spawning successfully takes place, and (b) whether the eggs are viable. Very little appears to be known about the nutritional requirements of broodstock, but the Chinese put much emphasis on nutritionally priming their carp broodstock before inducing spawning with hormone injections (Lin, 1982). It is perhaps unlikely that nutritional manipulation will by itself induce spawning, but without some attention being paid to the quantity and quality of broodstock food the success of spawning will remain elusive and unpredictable for many species.

Different sets of environmental factors are responsible for the maturation (vitellogenesis and spermatogenesis) and spawning of gametes. In captivity, maturation is less of a problem than spawning, or more precisely ovulation, and environmental manipulations here are used mainly to advance, retard or extend the spawning season. The main environmental factor involved is photoperiod, and photoperiod manipulation is becoming an increasingly common technique for a wide variety of fish species. Bye (Chap. 11, this volume) has reviewed some of the main aspects, and Nash and Shehadeh (1980) have provided a good example of the technique for *Mugil cephalus*. Such manipulations may have repercussions on other aspects of reproductive tactics, however, and McQuarrie's (1981) data on *Oncorhynchus kisutch* demonstrate an effect of photoperiod advance and retardation on fecundity and early mortality (Table V). Environmental factors such as the presence of

TABLE V. Photoperiod-induced off-season spawning of coho salmon (from Macquarrie, 1981).

Group	Time of sexual maturity	Mean egg fecundity	Mortality to swim-up stage (%)
1	normal	792	8·5
2	78–90 days early	645	16·0
3	148 days late	803	52·0

an appropriate spawning substrate, or a change in water flow or temperature to simulate monsoonal flooding or a spawning migration can stimulate spawning. Thus Stacey *et al.* (1979) found that the presence of macrophytic vegetation was an important factor in the spawning of *Carassius auratus*. For *Clarias batrachus* the spawning pits (650 ha^{-1}) are linear trenches 3 m wide and 1·5 m deep at the bottom of the ponds. The trenches are filled with water and mature fish are stocked so that one pair can utilize each pit, and spawning occurs when the water level is raised to fill the whole pond area. A similar response to flooding of ponds is found in both Chinese and Indian carps, and spawning will also occur if fish in the small net cages known as hapas are showered with fresh water (Davy and Chouinard, 1981).

If more were known about the environmental requirements of fish at spawning, then more use could be made of these and similar manipulations to achieve successful spawning in captivity. As it is, the main research impetus is on the use of endocrine manipulations which bypass the environmental triggers. This involves injecting hormones and has been very successful on a large scale for Chinese carps (Lin, 1982) and on a pilot scale for *Mugil cephalus* (Nash and Shehadeh, 1980) and several other species. In fact a very large number of species have been induced to spawn in this way and the literature is extensive. The subject will not be discussed further here because (a) it is covered by several papers at this Symposium; (b) there have been several recent reviews (e.g. Lam, 1981a; Pullin and Kuo, 1981); and (c) as an overall conclusion it appears that these hypophysation techniques (perhaps using steroids, clomiphere or LH-RH rather than the traditional but expensive pituitary extracts) will soon enable the ripe adults of any species to spawn in captivity at any time (Stacey, Chap. 12, this volume).

At the present time, however, the success of hypophysation is often variable and unpredictable. Its effectiveness depends on environmental factors such as temperature, the stage of oocyte maturation, the general conditions of both donor and recipient fish, and circadian/lunar/tidal rhythms.

Whether the final stages of gamete maturation are reached through environmental or endocrinological manipulation, the final act of gamete release and fertilization may be either natural or artificial. The latter involves stripping of gametes from ripe parents followed by artificial fertilization and has some advantages in the collection of fertilized eggs and the selection of parents. *Solea solea* have to be stripped because they will apparently not spawn spontaneously in captivity, and this raises intriguing questions on how such a characteristic which manifests itself in captivity relates to adaptive reproductive tactics in the wild.

B. Increasing egg production and quality

Egg production has two components: the number of eggs and their viability.

The latter may chiefly be a reflection of the chemical composition of the yolk and this in turn is known to depend on the nutritional status and condition of the females [e.g. Nosho (1981) for in *Oncorhynchus* species]. The weight of the individual eggs is also probably important, and Gall (1975) has demonstrated higher egg and fry weights in three-year-old, compared to two-year-old, broodstock. Although there is some intraspecific variation in egg size, this is generally small and probably offers little basis for selection. However, hybridization may confer from one species to another, any advantages of large egg size. This has been attempted with *Scophthalmus maximus* and *S. rhombus*. The latter has larger eggs and larvae (see Table VI), but the former has most other commercial advantages. Crosses between the two species do result in larger eggs and larvae which show better survival to metamorphosis than *Scophthalmus maximus* itself: unfortunately performance *after* metamorphosis is worse and trials have discontinued as a result (Bye, pers. comm.). Great variation in percentage hatching and surviving between batches of *S. maximus* eggs at the S.F.I.A. Marine Farm at Ardtoe in Scotland, probably reflects variations in the condition of the broodstock (Gillespie, pers. comm.), and attention to broodstock husbandry rather than selection for egg size is most likely to improve this aspect of egg production.

The numbers of eggs can be increased by increasing the number of broodstock, but this would tend to increase broodstock maintenance costs and there would appear to be advantages in increasing egg production per individual fish. This has already been shown above to be very high for batch spawners, and in addition, any factor which increases the size and growth-rate of the broodstock will tend to increase egg production. Gall's (1975) work on *Salmo gairdneri* suggested that an improvement in reproductive performance could be achieved by selecting for egg volume (the total volume of eggs spawned per female), and that the major genetic effects influencing egg number are additive. It is clear that an increase in egg number is of little value if egg viability is low, and since most species already have high intrinsic fecundities, attention is best directed to increasing viability, especially through improved broodstock management.

C. Prevention of maturation and production of monosex stock

It has already been noted that this is primarily a problem with salmonids and tilapia, and it is in these groups that most work has been carried out. For salmonids, and possibly tilapia, one of the most effective techniques is to produce monosex stock by steroid treatment of the homogametic sex to produce (in the case of salmonids) sperm-producing genetic females which are then crossed with unchanged females to produce all female stock. This overcomes the problem of early maturation which is usually associated with males. The same technique applied to tilapia does not necessarily prevent

TABLE VI. Evaluation of marine flatfish (Pleuronectiformes) for culture potential in the U.K. (adapted from Jones, 1972).

	Fecundity, no. eggs (kg^{-1})	Mean egg diameter (mm)	Mean length of newly hatched larvae (mm)	Production (kg m^{-2} yr^{-1})	Market price 1969–70 p kg^{-1}	Estimated net return in culture after 1 year p m^{-2}
Dover Sole (*Solea solea*)	728 000	1·30	3·1	3·0	58	+92
Plaice (*Pleuronectes platessa*)	150 000	1·93	6·1	1·7	14	−261
Halibut (*Hippoglossus hippoglossus*)	41 000	3·80	9·0	5·0	38	−18
Turbot (*Scophthalmus maximus*)	1 078 000	1·02	2·8	6·1	40	+202
Brill (*S. rhombus*)	465 000	1·30	3·8	3·6	26	−129

maturation, but it does prevent reproduction, and it enables only males, the faster growing sex, to be cultured.

One problem with feminization in *Salmo salar* is that direct feminization can reduce the proportion of fish which smolt at the end of one year (S_1) and since these are favoured in culture, treatment must be kept to the minimum period conducive to successful sex reversal.

Genetic manipulation of the age at maturity in salmonids is possible. Experiments on *Salmo gairdneri* by Moller *et al.* (1979) have demonstrated considerable variation in the proportion of mature to immature individuals in different sib-groups and indicated that non-additive genetic factors are likely to be the most important.

IV. THE REAL IMPACT OF REPRODUCTIVE TACTICS IN AQUACULTURE

This will be assessed in relation to five questions: (1) Have reproductive tactics been responsible for the late emergence of aquaculture compared to agriculture? (2) Do fish reproductive tactics hold any advantages over those of mammals and birds? (3) To what extent is the supply of seed constrained by the reproductive tactics of the parent fish? (4) Do reproductive tactics significantly affect the design and operation of aquaculture systems? (5) Are reproductive tactics an important consideration in the selection of species for aquaculture?

A. The late emergence of aquaculture

Agriculture is generally considered to be about 10 000 years old whereas the earliest record of aquaculture is of carp culture in China in 2000 B.C. Further, whereas almost all terrestrial production is now from agriculture, 90% of aquatic production is still from hunting and gathering.

The reproductive tactics of fish are sufficiently different from those of mammalian and avian livestock to require a different set of husbandry skills, and they are of course also quite different from man's own tactics. It is presumably no coincidence therefore that the earliest species to be cultured, *Cyprinus carpio*, spawns spontaneously in captivity as long as the water temperature is suitable and a spawning substrate is provided. *Chanos chanos* has a history of culture stretching back several hundred years but in this case spawning in captivity is avoided by harvesting seed from the wild. The earliest hatcheries were concerned with salmonids whose large eggs and fry (alevins) are easy to hatch and rear compared with those of most other fish species. The most difficult fish at the present time are those marine species which produce very small eggs hatching into small larvae (< 2 mm long in *Epinephelus* for example) whose feeding and other requirements are poorly understood.

Thus it can be argued that reproductive tactics have been associated with the delay in the development of aquaculture for some species, and possibly for aquaculture as a whole. In this context it is interesting to reflect on the fact that elasmobranch fish have received no attention as candidates for aquaculture, yet their reproductive tactics are in some ways more similar to mammalian and avian livestock than are teleosts. Clearly factors other than reproduction are important and these have probably been, and still are, the main reason for the delay in aquaculture development, and why potentially favourable species may be ignored. These other factors include the survival and growth of seed and "adults" in captivity, the availability of suitable food, conversion efficiency, the availability of suitable sites and water supply, the marketability of the product, overall economic viability and human investment. The last three non-biological factors are likely to be the most important overall and Nash (1979) has contrasted countries such as Israel, Japan and Taiwan with others which ... "while paying lip service to the anticipated importance and benefits of aquaculture have not declared national policies or priorities to make aquaculture a significant factor in food production or in the realization of export revenues".

B. Advantages of fish

Although the culture of fish is at present well behind the culture of terrestrial livestock, it is likely that the gap will decrease as development proceeds. This is because many of the techniques used in intensive agriculture can be readily applied to aquaculture, and already some farming of salmonids bears a close resemblance to the broiler house production of chickens and other animals.

A major difference concerns the lack of genetic development in aquaculture, but Wilkins (1981) in a review of the application of genetics to aquaculture has emphasized the advantages of high genetic variation, high fecundity, external fertilization and plastic sex determination (Price, Chap. 5, this volume) which characterize fish and other aquatic organisms. Genetic variation is measured in terms of heterozygosity, the proportion of polymorphic loci and the number of alleles per polymorphic locus, and these can presumably be regarded as components of reproductive tactics.

Thus although genetic manipulation in fish is still in its infancy, it is clear that fish do have several inherent advantages, once the problems of getting them to spawn in captivity are overcome. These advantages are such that fish may be seen to bear more resemblance to the plants rather than the animals of agriculture, and this partly reflects an earlier viewpoint of Steele (1974) that fish and trees occupied equivalent positions in their respective ecosystems.

C. Seed supply

The drive to culture a species is usually generated by market demand and the possibility of realizing high profit margins. Many of the species are of high market value and the demand often arises from a scarcity in yields from capture fisheries, in turn arising from natural causes, pollution, habitat destruction or overfishing. Thus the species in use and of potential use in aquaculture are likely to include both those whose seed is readily obtainable and those whose seed is more difficult to harvest or produce. In other words species are not usually chosen because their seed is available, but conversely the culture of an otherwise desirable species may be constrained if seed is not readily available.

The two alternative sources of seed have already been considered and enough has been said to indicate the considerable range from species which readily spawn in captivity to those which at the present time will not spawn and whose seed must be obtained from the wild. However, in general, the real constraint is not getting the adults to spawn but in rearing the larvae (Nash and Kuo, 1975; Pullin and Kuo, 1981) and this is currently acting as an effective bottleneck in marine aquaculture. Normally the problem involves rearing the larvae from the time when exogenous feeding begins, but an exception is in *Scophthalmus maximus* hatcheries where most mortality occurs during egg incubation and the 20 days after hatching (Gillespie, pers. comm.).

The list of species which have spawned spontaneously or have been induced to spawn in captivity continues to grow. Undoubtedly in some cases the reproductive tactics, perhaps at the level of endocrine function, are inhibiting the utilization of certain species, and in turn, the differences between species in this respect are intriguing in that they are presumably adaptive in the natural environment. Unfortunately real differences between species may be obscured by differences in captive conditions and husbandry skills: it is clear that stress is a very important factor in determining whether or not a fish will spawn successfully.

D. Influence on system design and operation

Two examples will be given here. The first concerns the ranching of salmonids whose success depends on the anadromous spawning migration of ripening adults to home rivers. Without this particular component of reproductive tactics it is difficult to imagine that ranching would be possible. According to Thorpe (1980) $2 \cdot 8 \times 10^9$ juvenile *Oncorhynchus* salmon were released into the North Pacific in 1978, and in the same area 70 000 t yr^{-1} of returning fish were harvested. This figure represents 20–30% of the total world catch of *Oncorhynchus* and indicates the large scale of the ranching industries. Ranching has been attempted with various marine species (e.g. *Pleuronectes platessa* and *Gadus morhua* in Europe; *Sparus major* in Japan) but here, although it has been more difficult to assess the benefits of releasing hatchery produced seed into the natural environment there has not been the success experienced with salmon. This must be at least partly due to differences in reproductive tactics.

The other example concerns the way in which spawning requirements may affect the design of broodstock holding facilities and this is best seen in the arena system for *Sarotherodon* designed by Haller and Parker (1981).

E. Species selection

Nash (1974) and Webber and Riordan (1976) have examined the criteria which they consider to be important when selecting suitable candidate species for aquaculture development. Of these criteria, some are biological, and some of the biological ones are associated with reproduction. Nash (1974) for example listed as desirable characteristics: high fecundity, ease of collection of eggs, juveniles and adults; natural spawning in captivity; ease of induced spawning; and early maturity. On a point system these accounted for about 40% of the total and showed much more variation between species than other characteristics relating to growth, mortality and trophic efficiency. This approach to species selection, a type of biological screening, may be of value when aquaculture development is starting *de novo* with a range of potential species, but is likely to be of most significance *within* a group such as the pleuronectids, salmonids or tilapia. Data from Jones (1972) are included in Table VI for species of British pleuronectids. These show clear differences in egg and larval size which by themselves would suggest that *Pleuronectes* and *Hippoglossus* may be the most suitable species; but a wider consideration of the economics of production indicates that *Scophthalmus* and *Solea* have the best potential in spite of small egg sizes. On this basis the two species have been selected for research and development and have begun to be used in commercial farms. The small egg size of *Scophthalmus* did give rise to problems of early feeding of the larvae, but because of the economic potential of the species there was strong impetus for overcoming the constraints imposed by reproductive tactics.

In fact it must be emphasized once again that the choice of species in aquaculture almost always arises from market desirability which in all (?) cases stems from a status acquired in a capture fisheries context. So the species used in aquaculture are those whose characteristics initially made them suitable for capture fisheries irrespective of whether they can be easily cultured. However, while as a result, certain reproductive and other characteristics may be seen as potentially disadvantageous, they are unlikely to prevent aquaculture development in a species of high market value. They may delay it, but most constraints can now be overcome by a variety of manipulations

(Section III) and in general it seems that reproductive tactics are not the most important factor in species selection.

ACKNOWLEDGEMENTS

I would like to thank Ms Sarah Helps (Israel Oceanographic and Limnological Research Ltd), Ms Nepheronia Jumalon (S.E.A.F.D.E.C., The Philippines) and Dr M. E. Gillespie (S.F.I.A. Marine Farming Unit, Ardtoe, Scotland) for providing some of the information utilized in this paper.

REFERENCES

Balarin, J. D. and Hatton, J. P. (1979). Tilapia: A Guide to their Biology and Culture in Africa. University of Stirling, U.K.

Balon, E. K. (1975). J. Fish. Res. Bd Can. 32, 821–864.

Davy, F. B. and Chouinard, A. eds (1981). "Induced Fish Breeding in Southeast Asia" Report of a Workshop held in Singapore 25–28 November 1980. IDRC, Ottawa, Canada.

El-Ibiary, H. M., Joyce, J. A., Page, J. W. and Hill, T. K. (1977). Aquaculture 10, 153–160.

Gall, G. A. E. (1975). J. Anim. Sci. 40, 19–28.

Gardner, M. L. G. (1976). J. Fish Biol. 9, 289–328.

Haller, R. D. and Parker, I. S. C. (1981). Fish Farmg int. 8 (1), 14–18.

Jhingran, V. G. and Gopalakrishnan, V. (1974). FAO Fish. Biol. tech. Pap. 130.

Jones, A. (1972). Lab. Leafl. Fish. Lab. Lowestoft No. 24.

Kentouri, M. and Divanach, P. (1982). Aquaculture 27, 355–376.

Lacanilao, F. and Marte, C. (1981). Poster No. 90: World Conference on Aquaculture, Venice, Italy 21–25 September, 1981.

Lam, T. J. (1982a). Can. J. Fish. aquat. Sci. 39, 111–137.

Lam, T. J. (1982b). Can. J. Fish. aquat. Sci. 39, 138–142.

Liao, I-C. (1981). In "Aquaculture of Grey Mullets" (International Biological Programme Handbook 26) (O. H. Oren, ed.), pp. 361–390. Cambridge University Press, Cambridge.

Lin, H-R. (1982). Can. J. Fish. aquat. Sci. 39, 143–150.

Lincoln, R. F. (1981). Aquaculture 25, 259–268.

Ling, S-W. (1977). "Aquaculture in Southeast Asia". Washington Sea Grant Publication: University of Washington Press.

McQuarrie, R. (1981). In "Salmonid Broodstock Maturation" (T. Nosho, ed.), Proceedings of Workshops held in Seattle, Washington, May 1980 and May 1981. Washington Sea Grant Communications.

Mitani, F. (1978). Actes de colloques du C.N.E.X.O. 8, 195–200.

Møller, D., Naevdal, G., Holm, M. and Lerøy, R. (1979). In "Advances in Aquaculture" (T. V. R. Pillay and W. E. Dill, eds), pp. 622–625. Fishery News Books, London.

Nash, C. E. (1974). FAO Paper (Bangkok, Thailand) IPFC/74/SYM 12, 1–11.

Nash, C. E. (1979). Food Policy (August, 1979), 204–215.

Nash, C. E. and Kuo, C-M. (1975). Aquaculture 5, 119–123.

Nash, C. E. and Shehadeh, Z. H., eds (1980). "Breeding and Propagation Techniques for Grey Mullet" (ICLARM Studies and Reviews, 3). ICLARM, The Philippines.

Nosho, T. ed. (1981). "Salmonid Broodstock Management" Proceedings of Workshop held in Seattle, Washington, May 1980 and March 1981. Washington Sea Grant Communications.

Pillay, T. V. R. (1979). In "Advances in Aquaculture" (T. V. R. Pillay and W. E. Dill, eds), pp. 1–9. Fishing News Books, London.

Pullin, R. S. V. and C-M. Kuo (1981). In "Symposium on Food Producing Systems for Arid and Semi-Arid Lands; Kuwait, 19–23 April 1980".

Purdom, C. E. (1979). In "Fish Phenology" (P. J. Miller, ed.), pp. 207–288. Academic Press, New York and London.

Sarig, S. (1981). In "Aquaculture of Grey Mullets" (International Biological Programme Handbook 26) (O. H. Oren, ed.), pp. 391–410. Cambridge University Press, Cambridge.

Smith, I. R., Cas, F. C., Gibe, B. P. and Romillo, L. M. (1979). Aquaculture 14, 199–219.

Stacey, N. E., Cook, A. F. and Peter, R. E. (1979). J. Fish Biol. 15, 349–362.

Stearns, S. C. (1976). Q. Rev. Biol. 51, 3–47.

Steele, J. H. (1974). "The Structure of Marine Ecosystems". Harvard University Press, Cambridge, Mass.

Thorpe, J. E., ed. (1980). "Salmon Ranching". Academic Press, London and New York.

Webber, H. H. and Riordan, P. F. (1976). Aquaculture 7, 107–124.

Wilkins, N. P. (1981). Aquaculture 22, 209–228.

Zohar, Y. and Gordin, H. (1979). J. Fish Biol. 15, 665–670.

17. A Comparison of the Reproductive Tactics and Strategies of Cod, Haddock, Whiting and Norway Pout in the North Sea

J. R. G. HISLOP

*Department of Agriculture and Fisheries for Scotland, Aberdeen
U.K.*

Abstract: A typical gadoid produces large numbers of pelagic eggs. There are both inter- and intra-specific differences in features such as egg size, fecundity and the size and age at which maturity is reached. This contribution deals with the reproduction of four species within a single area, the North Sea.

Norway pout are small, short-lived plankton feeders, found mainly in the deeper parts of the North Sea. Age at first maturity, absolute fecundity and relative fecundity all appear to vary in response to changes in population density. Although mortality in the adult stage is high, it appears to be relatively low during the first year of life, probably as a consequence of the offshore distribution and shoaling habit of the juveniles.

Haddock are medium sized benthic feeders whose distribution, though more widespread than that of Norway pout, is also basically offshore. Maturity is reached at three years of age. The eggs are fairly large but absolute fecundity rather low, suggesting that mortality during the early life history is comparatively low. As for Norway pout, the young fish are distributed mainly over the deeper parts of the North Sea, which may be a factor in reducing mortality. Haddock recruitment fluctuates more than that of the other three species.

Whiting are similar in size to haddock but they feed on crustacea and fish. They are widely distributed and abundant throughout the North Sea. Maturity is reached at two years of age. Absolute fecundity is high and relative fecundity very high. It is suggested that the long pelagic phase and shallow water distribution of the first year fish render whiting liable to predation, although the former habit may be an aid to the dispersal of the young fish.

Cod have a similar distribution to whiting and similar feeding habits, although they reach a much greater size and are far less abundant. Maturity is reached at four years of age, by which time the females are large, with very high absolute individual fecundities. Mortality is extremely high during the first year of life. It is suggested that the high egg production ensures widespread dispersal of the spawning products and that cannibalism plays an important part in the regulation of population numbers.

FISH REPRODUCTION
ISBN: 0–12–563660–1

I. INTRODUCTION

The gadoids are a very successful group of fishes, including species adapted to a wide variety of life styles. Although several species are of major commercial importance and have been the object of considerable research, many of the minor ones have received little attention. The geographical distribution of the gadoids is widespread, but this paper is mainly concerned with the reproduction of gadoids in the waters around the British Isles, with particular reference to the North Sea populations of cod (*Gadus morhua*), haddock (*Melanogrammus aeglefinus*), whiting (*Merlangius merlangus*) and Norway pout (*Trisopterus esmarkii*).

II. GENERAL FEATURES OF GADOID REPRODUCTION

In the northern hemisphere most gadoids spawn during the first six months of the year. The spawning season of each species tends to be rather prolonged and although in any one region the different species have individual peak spawning periods, there is much overlap. For any one species, the time of peak spawning often varies with latitude; for example whiting spawn mainly in February and March in the English Channel, in April, May and June in the northern North Sea and in May and June at Iceland.

No field observations have been made of the spawning behaviour, but in captive cod (Brawn, 1961), haddock (Hawkins *et al.*, 1967) and whiting (Hawkins, 1970), the males have been seen to perform a courtship ritual involving the erection of the unpaired fins, changes of colouration and, in the case of cod and haddock, the production of sounds. Fertilization is external but its efficiency is increased by a pattern of mating behaviour that terminates in a spawning embrace, bringing the vents of the two fish into close proximity just prior to the emission of eggs and sperm. The eggs of an individual female are ripened and shed in discrete batches, at intervals of 24–48 h, over a period that may last for several weeks, so a female has the opportunity to mate with several males during a single reproductive season. In the aquarium a single dominant male has been seen to monopolize the attentions of all available females but it is not known whether males maintain breeding territories or harems in the wild.

Almost all gadoids have pelagic eggs. Two exceptions appear to be the burbot, *Lota lota*, which is the only fresh water species, and the navaga, *Eleginus navaga*, whose eggs remain on or close to the bottom (Svetovidov, 1948). On hatching, the larvae and young O-group fish spend several weeks, or even months, in the upper part of the water column before moving to the sea bed.

Gadoid fecundities are high, ranging from tens of thousands for the smaller species to tens of millions for the largest individuals of the largest species such as cod, saithe, *Pollachius virens* (Storozhuk and Golovanov, 1976) and ling, *Molva molva* (Fulton, 1891).

The eggs have mean diameters between 0·75–1·75 mm (Simpson, 1956). The water content of the eggs is high (approximately 95%), and dry egg weights fall mostly within the range 0·025–0·100 mg (Fig. 1). Although there are considerable differences in the maximum sizes attained by the various gadoid species (10–150 cm) there is no obvious tendency for the biggest species to have the largest eggs (Fig. 2). There is some degree of association between egg

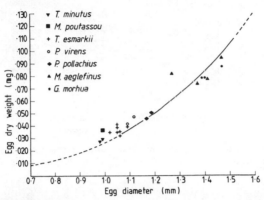

Fig. 1.   Relationship between dry egg weight and egg diameter. Curve describes relationship found for captive North Sea haddock and whiting (log egg weight, mg = 3·35 log egg diameter, mm − 1·57). Symbols represent data obtained from ripe females off the west coast of Scotland in February and March 1982.

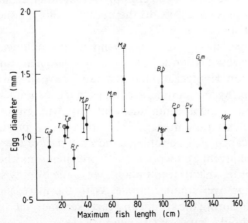

Fig. 2.   Relationship between egg diameter (from Simpson, 1956; Russell, 1976) and maximum fish length (based on Svetividov, 1948; Wheeler, 1969). Key: G.a. = *Gadiculus argenteus*; T.m. = *Trisopterus minutus*;   T.e. = *Trisopterus esmarkii*;   R.r. = *Raniceps raninus*; M.p. = *Micromesistius poutassou*; T.l. = *Trisopterus luscus*; M.m. = *Merlangius merlangus*; M.a. = *Melanogrammus aeglefinus*; B.b. = *Brosmius brosme*; Mer = *Merluccius merluccius*; P.p. = *Pollachius pollachius*; P.v. = *Pollachius virens*; G.m. = *Gadus morhua*; Mol = *Molva molva*.

size and spawning season, those species that spawn in the late winter and early spring having slightly larger eggs than those than spawn later in the year (Fig. 3). In fact Fig. 3 over-simplifies the situation, because a constant value for egg size has been assigned to each species, but, in practice egg size decreases with time, within each species, so the figure should properly consist of a set of downward-sloping rather than horizontal lines.

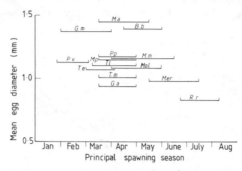

Fig. 3.   Relationship between mean egg diameter and principal spawning season in northern North Sea and off west coast of Scotland. Key as in Fig. 2.

It has been suggested that the observed seasonal decrease in egg size was due to older and larger fish, with bigger eggs, arriving on the spawning grounds earlier than the younger fish. Although this may be a contributory factor, aquarium observations of captive haddock and whiting, have shown that the diameters and dry weights of the eggs of an individual female decline as her spawning period progresses, as do the numbers of eggs shed in each batch (Hislop, 1975; Hislop et al., 1978).

Seasonal changes in egg size are by no means unique to gadoids. For instance, the egg sizes of Atlantic herring, *Clupea harengus* vary markedly with the spawning season. Hempel and Blaxter (1967) have shown that populations which spawn in spring and summer have eggs that are significantly smaller and lighter than those of the autumn and winter spawning groups.

This seasonal variation in egg size with time is presumably of some ecological significance. For example, in the early part of the year, prior to the spring outburst of juvenile copepods, small prey items may be in short supply, so that larger larvae, able to feed on a larger range of prey sizes, may have a survival advantage over smaller larvae. With the increasing abundance of juvenile copepods during the spring and early summer, the survival prospects of small larvae should improve (Bagenal, 1971).

Greater egg and larval size does not necessarily ensure a higher rate of survival. Laurence et al. (1981) found that when cod and haddock larvae were grown in mixed cultures, the growth rate and survival of the former consistently exceeded those of the latter, even though the eggs and newly hatched larvae of cod are slightly smaller and lighter than those of haddock.

There is considerable intra-specific geographical variation in the reproductive performance of gadoids. For instance, the fecundity of Baltic cod, on a length for length basis, is about 70% greater than that of cod from Iceland and the North Sea (Oosthuizen and Daan, 1974). In the North Sea more than 50% of the four years old cod are sexually mature (Oosthuizen and Daan, 1974; Daan and Kuiter, 1981; Heessen and Kuiter, 1982), whereas in the Arctic 50% maturity is not attained until an age of nine or ten years (Ponomarenko and Yaragina, 1981). In this paper, attention will be focused on four species, belonging to different genera, in a single area, the North Sea.

III. GENERAL BIOLOGICAL CHARACTERISTICS OF THE SPECIES UNDER INVESTIGATION

The life history and ecology of the four species differ considerably. Norway pout and haddock occur mainly in the deeper northern and central parts of the North Sea, both species being abundant north of the Dogger Bank but scarce to the south. Norway pout is a small, short-lived species, rarely exceeding 23 cm in length and three or four years of age. The main food of Norway pout is planktonic crustaceans, principally copepods and euphausids (Raitt and Adams, 1965). Haddock reach a greater size (60–70 cm) and age (8–12 years) than Norway pout. They feed mainly on small benthic animals, principally molluscs, annelids and echinoderms (Jones, 1954). Cod and whiting are widely distributed throughout the North Sea but are most common in depths of less than 100 m. Both species feed mainly on crustaceans and the larger epifauna when young, but their diets include an increasing proportion of fish as they grow bigger and they have cannibalistic tendencies. Whiting reach a maximum length of 50–60 cm at an age of about seven or eight years but cod grow to a length of over 100 cm at an age of nine or ten years, and they are one of the largest species of fish in the North Sea.

IV. REPRODUCTIVE CHARACTERISTICS

A. Spawning times and places

Haddock and Norway pout spawn mainly over the deeper parts of the northern North Sea (> 100 m), peak spawning occurring in March and April. Cod and whiting spawning grounds are generally in shallower water (< 100 m) and are widely distributed throughout the North Sea. The spawning time of both species depends to some extent on latitude, but in cod

TABLE I. Proportions of mature and immature cod, haddock, whiting and Norway pout of each sex and age group.

| | | Age 1 | | | | Age 2 | | | | Age 3 | | |
| | | ♂ | | ♀ | | ♂ | | ♀ | | ♂ | | ♀ | |
		Imm	Mat	Imm	Mat	Imm	Mat	Imm	Mat	Imm	Mat	Imm	Mat
Norway pout	%	87	13	94	6	3	97	0	100	0	100	0	100
	mean length (cm)	10·2	11·8	10·3	12·4	15·2	15·6	13·8	17·2		19·6		20·4
Whiting	%	83	17	96	4	7	93	10	90	2	98	1	99
	mean length (cm)	16·5	20·7	16·9	21·5	24·5	24·7	23·0	25·5	27·0	27·5	27·7	29·3
Haddock	%	97	3	100	0	55	45	80	20	19	81	38	62
	mean length (cm)	15·6	20·9	14·9		24·3	26·6	25·3	27·8	30·4	33·2	31·5	34·6
Cod	%	100	0	100	0	95	5	96	4	76	24	80	20
	mean length (cm)	20·4		20·9		34·7	42·9	35·1	38·1	49·2	58·9	50·5	59·7

| | | Age 4 | | | | Age 5 | | | | Age 6 + | | |
| | | ♂ | | ♀ | | ♂ | | ♀ | | ♂ | | ♀ | |
		Imm	Mat	Imm	Mat	Imm	Mat	Imm	Mat	Imm	Mat	Imm	Mat
Norway pout	%	0	100	0	100	0	100	0	100	0	100		
	mean length (cm)		21·4		23·2		22·5		24·5		24·2		
Whiting	%	1	99	1	99	1	99	1	99	2	98	1	99
	mean length (cm)	35·9	30·2	29·3	33·1	35·9	32·9	32·5	36·0	36·0	42·7		33·9
Haddock	%	8	92	18	82	6	94			1	99	0	100
	mean length (cm)	33·4	38·7	36·3	41·7		43·9	42·4	48·2	46·5	47·1		51·6
Cod	%	33	67	45	55	22	78	9	91	5	95	1	99
	mean length (cm)	64·1	74·9	65·6	76·7	73·9	84·5	72·0	87·2	81·2	95·8	77·5	101·3

the main season is February and March whereas whiting spawn later, and over a longer period, the season beginning in February in the south, and extending to June in the north.

B. Size and age at maturity

Data on age, length and maturity, collected during recent trawling surveys covering the entire North Sea (Daan and Kuiter, 1981; Heessen and Kuiter, 1982) are given in Table I. In cod and haddock the proportion of mature individuals increases more or less gradually with age whereas in whiting and Norway pout the transition from immaturity is more abrupt; only a small percentage of the one-year-old fish are mature but almost all have reached maturity by two years of age. In all four species the males mature at a slightly younger age and at a smaller size than the females. Within any one age group, the mature individuals of each sex are on average larger than the immatures.

The age at which Norway pout attain maturity in the North Sea appears to vary in response to changing conditions. Raitt (1968) showed that typically only a small proportion of the one-year-old fish are mature, as exemplified by the data in Table I, but he found that about 60% of the one-year-olds of the 1964 year class were mature. This year class grew up at a time when the population density of Norway pout in the North Sea was unusually low, as a result of the failure of the preceding (1963) year class. There was no change in the minimum size at which the fish attained maturity (approximately 13 cm) but the length range of the 1964 year class as one-year-olds was, at 12–17 cm, appreciably different from the average length range of one-year-olds (10–15 cm). It seems likely that conditions in 1964 and the early part of 1965 favoured above-average growth, allowing a greater than normal proportion of the one-year-old fish to reach a critical size necessary for the maturation of their gonads.

It has been suggested (Oosthuizen and Daan, 1974) that during the last 50 years there has been a significant reduction, of the order of 14 cm, in the length at which North Sea cod attain sexual maturity, even though there has been no observed change in growth rate over this period. This hypothesis has to be treated with some caution as the pre-war data quoted by Oosthuizen and Daan were obtained from only one area in a single year (Graham, 1924) whereas Poulsen (1931), who examined cod from a different part of the North Sea gives values for length at maturity that are not dissimilar to those found for recent years.

C. Fecundity

1. *Fecundity related to body length.* Relationships between fecundity and length are shown in Fig. 4. For North Sea cod and haddock there is no

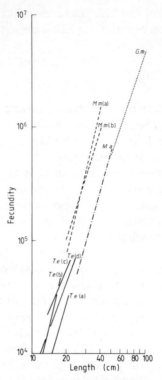

Fig. 4.   Relationships between fecundity and length. G.m. = North Sea cod (Schopka, 1971; Oosthiuzen and Daan, 1974); M.a. = North Sea haddock (Raitt, 1932; Hislop and Shanks, 1981); M.m.(a) = northern North Sea whiting (Hislop and Hall, 1974); M.m.(b) = southern North Sea whiting (Messtorff, 1959; Hislop and Hall, 1974); T.e.(a) = North Sea Norway pout – 2-year-old fish in 1964; T.e.(b) = 1-year-old fish in 1965; T.e.(c) = 2-year-old fish in 1966 (all from Raitt, 1968); T.e.(d) = mean value for Norway pout based on (a), (b) and (c).

evidence of significant year to year differences in fecundity at length [cf. the annual differences reported by Hodder (1963) for haddock from the Grand Banks of Newfoundland]. Hislop and Hall (1974) found small annual changes in the fecundity of whiting in the northern North Sea and a greater difference between the northern and southern North Sea populations. The fecundity of Norway pout appears to be much more variable: Raitt (1968), found that the fecundity per unit length of the 1964 year class, as both one-year-old fish and two-year-old fish was more than double that of the 1962 year class, at two years of age. Both of these year classes grew up in unusual, although contrasting circumstances. As discussed earlier, the 1964 year class occurred during a period of low population density. Growth was rapid and fecundity high, suggesting that food may have been very abundant. Both the 1961 and 1962 year classes were unusually strong with the consequence that the latter

TABLE II. Modal length of mature females and average fecundity at that length, together with data on minimum age of female maturity and the age at which 50% of females are mature.

Species	Modal length of mature females (cm)[a]	Approximate fecundity (thousands)[b]	Youngest age of mature females[c]	Age at which more than 50% of females mature[d]
Cod	70	1620	2	4
Haddock	30	100	2	4
Whiting	26	230	1	2
Norway pout	17	30	1	2

[a] From Daan and Kuiter (1981) and Heessen and Kuiter (1982).
[b] Estimated from relationships: Cod $F = 3.81 \ L^{3.05}$; Haddock $F = 0.40 \ L^{3.65}$; Whiting $F = 5.85 \ L^{3.25}$; Norway pout $F = 12.98 \ L^{2.72}$.
[c] Oosthuizen and Daan (1974), Hislop and Shanks (1981) and Table I of the present paper.

grew up during a period of high population density, when it might be expected that the food available for growth and reproduction would be limited.

It is apparent from Fig. 4 that the fecundity length relationships of cod, haddock and Norway pout (mean value) are rather similar, with respect both to slopes and intercepts but the fecundity of whiting is approximately double that of the other species, length for length.

When comparing the fecundities of the different species one must of course take into account not only the relationship between fecundity and length, but the length of an average-sized spawning female. Table II gives data, obtained from the 1981 and 1982 International Young Fish Surveys of the North Sea (Daan and Kuiter, 1981; Heessen and Kuiter, 1982) on the modal length of the mature females of each species, and the estimated fecundity at that length. The fecundity of an average-sized mature female cod is 16 times as high as that of a whiting and 100 times that of a Norway pout. The fecundity of an average haddock is eight times that of a Norway pout.

It is possible to make an estimate of the total egg production of the North Sea populations of cod, haddock and whiting using data on stock numbers derived from virtual population analysis (Anon., 1981a). Unfortunately, no reliable data on total stock size are available for Norway pout. The data are set out in Table III. It can be seen that the estimate of the total egg numbers produced by cod and haddock are rather similar; although cod have very high individual fecundities the number of spawning females is comparatively small whereas the much lower fecundity of haddock is compensated for by their much greater abundance. Whiting, by virtue of their high abundance and rather high fecundity produce a far greater total number of eggs than both cod

TABLE III. Estimated total egg production of North Sea populations of cod, haddock and whiting.

	Age	Mean population size (millions) 1963–1977[a]	Proportion of mature females[b]	Number of mature females (millions)	Mean length of mature females (cm)	Eggs produced per mature female (millions)	Total egg production (10^9)
Cod	1	235·6	0	0	—	0	0
	2	139·0	0·019	2·6	38	0·25	650
	3	52·4	0·09	4·7	60	1·01	4747
	4	20·0	0·25	5·0	77	2·16	10800
	5	9·0	0·36	3·2	87	3·14	10048
	6+	7·4	0·55	4·1	101	4·94	20254
						Grand total	46499
Haddock	1	2159·4	0	0	—	0	0
	2	1065·2	0·10	106·5	28	0·08	8520
	3	429·8	0·32	137·5	35	0·17	23375
	4	124·1	0·42	52·1	42	0·34	17714
	5	43·2	0·54	23·3	49	0·59	13747
	6+	18·7	0·53	9·9	52	0·73	7227
						Grand total	70583
Whiting	1	2217·5	0·02	44·4	22	0·13	5772
	2	1313·8	0·47	617·5	26	0·23	142025
	3	448·2	0·44	197·2	29	0·33	65076
	4	111·3	0·46	51·2	33	0·50	25600
	5	34·5	0·46	15·9	36	0·67	10653
	6+	13·7	0·57	7·8	43	1·19	9282
						Grand total	258408

[a] Data derived from virtual population analysis (Anon., 1981a).
[b] From Daan and Kuiter (1981) and Heessen and Kuiter (1982).

and haddock. There are pronounced between-species differences in the age groups making the largest contribution to egg production. In whiting the two-year-old fish produce most eggs, in haddock it is the three-year-old fish whereas in cod the oldest fish (6+) make the largest contribution.

It should be remembered that these species are the objects of considerable fisheries in the North Sea and the relative importance of the various age groups to the egg production of the population is very much influenced by the rate at which the stocks are exploited.

2. *Fecundity related to body weight.* Table IV gives, for each species, mean diameter and dry weight of eggs, relative fecundity (defined as the number of eggs produced per g of wet, gutted body weight) and a measure of reproductive effort, expressed as the weight of dry egg matter produced per unit of wet, gutted body weight.

TABLE IV.   Mean egg diameter, egg dry weight, relative fecundity and reproductive expenditure for North Sea cod, haddock, whiting and Norway pout.

Species	Mean egg diameter (mm)[a]	Mean dry egg weight (mg)[b]	Relative fecundity (mean no. of eggs per g of wet gutted fish wt)	Reproductive expenditure (dry egg wt, mg, per g of wet gutted fish wt)
Cod	1·37	0·075	475[c]	36
Haddock	1·45	0·094	550[d]	52
Whiting	1·16	0·044	2000[e]	88
Norway pout	1·07	0·034	(1) 475[f]	16
			(b) 1110[f]	38

[a] Taken from Simpson (1956).
From relationship: log dry weight, mg = 3·35 log egg diameter, mm −1·57 (Fig. 1).
[c] From predictive regressions given by Schopka (1971) and Oosthuizen and Daan (1974).
[d] From Raitt (1932) and Hislop and Shanks (1981).
[e] Hislop (unpublished data).
[f] D. F. S. Raitt, unpublished data (a: 1962 year class in 1964; b: 1964 year class in 1965).

The relative fecundities of cod and haddock are similar, whilst that of whiting is higher by a factor of four. The relative fecundity of Norway pout can vary from the level found for cod and haddock to double this value.

When egg weights are taken into account, the differences between the reproductive expenditure of the species are less marked; whiting still has the highest value, approximately double those of cod and haddock, but the values for Norway pout are comparatively low, as a consequence of the relatively small, light eggs of this species. As will be discussed in the concluding section reproductive expenditure should perhaps be seen as a dynamic, rather than an instantaneous process.

D. Distribution, relative abundance and mortality during the first year of life

Information on distribution and abundance is available from two sources: a series of midwater trawling surveys of the northern and central North Sea in June/July, during which O-group gadoids were sampled at an age of two to three months, whilst they were still leading a mainly pelagic life (Holden, 1981) and a series of demersal trawling surveys, covering the whole North Sea, in the period late January-early March, when the youngest age group was approximately one-year-old (Anon., 1979b). Long-term catch rates per ICES statistical rectangle are given for the two series in Figs 5 and 6. It should be noted that Fig. 5 is based on geometric mean catches, and Fig. 6 on arithmetic means. The main areas of abundance of pelagic O-group Norway pout (Fig. 5d) and haddock (Fig. 5b) are over the deeper (> 100 m) parts of the northern North Sea, between Norway and the Shetland Islands whereas cod (Fig. 5a) and whiting (Fig. 5c) are more generally distributed throughout the North Sea. The results of the pelagic survey probably do not properly represent the distribution and abundance of cod and whiting, because the shallower parts of the southern North Sea, where these species are likely to be relatively abundant, were not covered by the surveys, partly because of the difficulties experienced in using the midwater trawl in shallow water.

The data for fish at the end of their first year of life are given in Fig. 6. The main area of abundance of 1-group Norway pout (Fig. 6d) is in the deeper (> 100 m) parts of the North Sea, as was the case for the pelagic O-group phase. Haddock (Fig. 6b) are more widely distributed throughout the north-western North Sea, mainly in depths of 50–200 m. Whiting (Fig. 6c) occur mainly in relatively shallow water (< 100 m), being particularly abundant in the central and southern North Sea and in Scottish coastal waters. Cod (Fig. 6a) are also found mainly in the central and southern regions; the shallow waters (< 50 m) near the coasts of Denmark, Germany and the Netherlands are important nursery areas for young cod.

If one accepts that demersal trawl catch rates are representative of relative fish abundance, it appears that by the end of the first year of life there are marked differences in the abundance of the four species. Arithmetic mean catches per rectangle within the main area of distribution of each species, averaged over the surveys of 1970–1981 are 4880, 535, 503 and 34 for Norway pout, haddock, whiting and cod respectively (Anon., 1981b).

For cod, haddock and whiting the virtual population analysis (VPA)

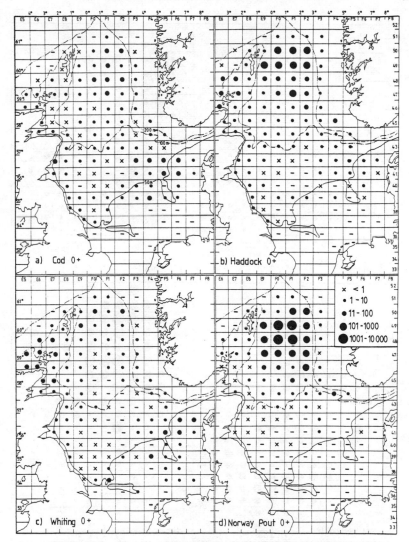

Fig. 5. Geometric means of the number of pelagic O-group (a) cod, (b) haddock, (c) whiting and (d) Norway pout caught per one hour haul in each statistical rectangle during the ICES International O-group Gadoid Surveys, 1973–1978 (Holden, 1981).

technique provides an estimate of actual, rather than relative, numbers of fish alive in the sea at the end of their first year of life. The data in Table III suggest that the number of eggs needed to produce a surviving one-year-old fish and by implication the degree of mortality that must occur during the first year of life, increases in the sequence haddock→whiting→cod.

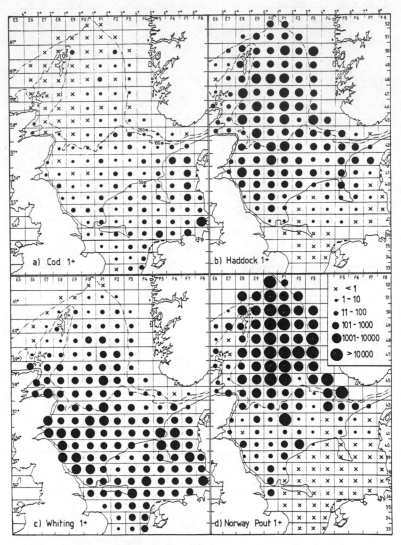

Fig. 6. Arithmetic means of the numbers of demersal 1-group (a) cod, (b) haddock, (c) whiting and (d) Norway pout caught per one hour haul in each statistical rectangle during the ICES International Young Fish Surveys, late January–early March 1974–1979 (Anon., 1979a).

V. DISCUSSION

It will now be attempted to relate these different reproductive strategies to the positions of the four gadoids in the ecosystem.

Norway pout is a small short-lived, plankton-feeding species, whose growth rate, age at first maturity and fecundity, both relative and absolute, can vary markedly in response to changing environmental conditions. Compared with the other three species each Norway pout produces a small number of eggs in a season and this fact, taken in conjunction with the short life span of the fish, which means that few adults spawn more than once in their life-time, suggests that the survival rate to maturity is higher than that of the other species. There are several features of the early life history of Norway pout that may tend to reduce mortality. First, the majority of the O-group fish are found over deep water (Fig. 5d) where they make pronounced diel vertical migrations (Bailey, 1975), coming to the surface as darkness falls, and descending to the bottom at dawn. This combination of habitat and behaviour might make young Norway pout less vulnerable to potential predators such as birds and pelagic fish. Secondly, juvenile Norway pout grow less rapidly than the juveniles of the other three species. Food requirements and foraging rates are presumably correspondingly lower and this may confer a survival advantage. Thirdly, O-group Norway pout frequently occur in much denser aggregations than O-group cod, haddock and whiting, and it is generally believed that shoaling confers a survival advantage. The length range of O-group Norway pout at the end of the first year of life, at 7–15 cm (Daan and Kuiter, 1981; Heessen and Kuiter, 1982) is narrower than that of the other species. Although this narrow length range is in part a reflection of the lower rate of growth and eventual size attained by these fish, it also suggests that the spawning season of Norway pout may be of comparatively short duration. A short spawning season which has the advantage of producing young that can aggregate in shoals of similar-sized individuals, carries two penalties. First, it will tend to limit the number of eggs that can be produced by a female in a season, as the energy for reproduction will have to be drawn very largely from stored resources. Secondly, if the spawning season is short, varying environmental conditions at spawning time are particularly likely to cause large fluctuations in year class strength. The data in Table V, although not directly comparable with those for the three other species, suggest that year class strengths of Norway pout fluctuate much more than those of cod and whiting (although less than those of haddock).

Haddock are medium-sized, benthic-feeding fish, maturing at about three years of age. The absolute fecundity of an individual female is fairly low (although, because haddock have rather large eggs, their investment in reproductive energy is relatively greater than that of cod and Norway pout). The comparatively low fecundity suggests that, as with Norway pout, mortality during the early stages is low compared with that of whiting and cod. It may be significant that the distribution of the pelagic young haddock (Fig. 5b) is very similar to that of Norway pout, mainly over deep water and that Bailey (1975) also observed diel vertical migration in O-group haddock, although not on the same scale as seen in Norway pout.

TABLE V.   Numbers of fish (millions) recruiting to spawning populations of cod, haddock and whiting in the North Sea (Anon., 1981a) and catch rates of Norway pout at age 1·5 years in Scottish research vessel trawling surveys of the North Sea (Anon., 1979b).

Species	Period	Age	Minimum recruitment (A)	Mean recruitment (B)	Maximum recruitment (C)	C/A	A/B	C/B
Cod	1963–1977	4	9	20	32	4	0·4	1·6
Haddock	1960–1977	3	15	430	2830	189	0·03	6·6
Whiting	1960–1977	2	233	1314	3164	14	0·2	2·4
Norway pout	1960–1978	1·5	6	98	329	55	0·06	3·4

The data in Table V suggest that reproductive success in haddock varies more than in the three other species. Haddock recruitment in the North Sea has fluctuated dramatically in recent years, outstandingly strong year classes being born in 1962, 1967 and 1974 and very poor ones in 1963 and 1968, but the causes of this variability are not yet understood. Annual differences in the food available to the larvae would seem to be one likely explanation [experimental work by Laurence (1974) has shown that both the percentage survival and the growth rate of haddock larvae are positively correlated with the density of planktonic prey encountered at the stage of yolk sac resorbtion] but why these should affect haddock more than other gadoids is not easy to understand. It might be that because the young stages of the haddock have a relatively restricted spatial distribution (Fig. 5b) they are particularly vulnerable to local annual fluctuations in food supply. The same argument could also be applied to Norway pout, whose pelagic young also have a relatively restricted distribution (Fig. 5d).

The life styles of whiting and cod are broadly similar. Both feed mainly on crustaceans and fish and the proportion of fish in the diet increases with the size of the predator (Jones, 1954; Daan, 1973). Both of these active, predatory species appear to have adopted a reproductive strategy involving high fecundity and high mortality, although the tactics employed are different.

Whiting mature relatively early, at about two years of age. Fecundity per unit length and per unit weight are very high, compared with those of the other species. The spawning season of whiting is more prolonged than that of most other gadoids; in the northern North Sea the whiting population begins spawning in March and continues well into June. An individual female whiting kept in an aquarium has been seen to spawn at regular intervals, for as long as 13 weeks (Hislop, 1975). Judging by aquarium observations, whiting continue to feed during the spawning season, so that the relatively large amount of energy expended by whiting on reproduction is not all drawn from stored reserves; some is obtained, as food, during the reproductive season. One possible benefit from a reproductive strategy that produces eggs that are widely distributed both in space and time is that fluctuations in year class strength due to local fluctuations in food supply will tend to be damped. Table V shows that whiting year class strengths are considerably less variable than those of haddock and Norway pout.

The large number of eggs produced by an individual implies that mortality during the first two years of life, before the attainment of maturity, is high. It may be of significance that whiting have a longer pelagic phase than most other common gadoids in the North Sea. While this may have the advantage of ensuring that the young fish are widely dispersed, it may make them more vulnerable to certain predators. [It is interesting that the only O-group gadoids that were found to make an important contribution to the food taken to their young by puffins, *Fratercula arctica*, from the waters round the northern part of the British Isles were whiting and rocklings, which both appear to have a prolonged pelagic phase (Harris and Hislop, 1978).] Once they have become demersal in habit, young whiting are most commonly found in relatively shallow water where predation by birds, mammals and fish, including whiting, may be heavy.

In the case of cod, the numbers of fish recruiting to the adult stock fluctuate less than in the other three species (Table V). Maturity is not attained until the fish have reached a considerable size, at an age of about four years, by which time the number of spawners has become comparatively small. The absolute fecundity of an individual is very great with the consequence that the population fecundity of cod in the North Sea is approximately the same as that of haddock (Table III). By the end of the first year of life the numbers of cod are apparently much smaller than those of the other species (Fig. 6, Table III), implying that mortality during this period is much higher. Laurence et al. (1981) showed that in aquarium experiments the growth of cod larvae, like that of haddock, is positively correlated with zooplankton abundance, but that unlike the situation in haddock, there is an inverse correlation between food density and survival. These authors, and Ellertsen et al. (1981), put forward the hypothesis that cannibalism might be responsible for reducing the number of cod larvae, although in neither study was cannibalism confirmed by observation. There is some evidence that cannibalism may play a part in regulating cod numbers during the early part of the demersal stage. Daan (1975) found that the extent to which cod preyed on other cod varied markedly from year to year; in the southern North Sea cannibalism was particularly prevalent in 1970 and 1971 when two unusually abundant year classes (those of 1969 and 1970) were present, but was virtually non-existent in 1966, 1968 and 1969. The fact that demersal O-group cod live in shallower water than 1-group cod (although the latter also have an inshore distribution) would seem to provide an ideal opportunity for this type of population control mechanism because the small fish, as they disperse from the spawning grounds to the nursery grounds, have to run the gauntlet of the larger, older individuals.

The different reproductive strategies of the four species appear to be related to differences between their general ecology. Haddock and Norway pout, whose spawning grounds and main area of distribution are in the deeper parts of the North Sea, have relatively low fecundities, associated with relatively low mortality during the immature phase. Their year class strengths show large fluctuations, particularly in the case of haddock. Whiting and cod, on the other hand are both active, predatory species, whose spawning grounds and young stages occur in shallower water, on grounds that are distributed throughout the North Sea. In both of these species individual fecundities are high (in the case of cod, this is a reflection of the large size of the spawning females but in whiting the fecundity per unit length and per unit weight are both very high) suggesting that mortality during the early part of the life history is also high. Year class strengths of whiting and cod appear to fluctuate less than those of haddock and Norway pout. The long spawning season of whiting may serve to damp these fluctuations, whereas in cod it appears that cannibalism may act as a damping mechanism, at least in certain years.

ACKNOWLEDGEMENTS

The author is grateful to Mr R. Jones and Mr B. B. Parrish of the Marine Laboratory, Aberdeen for their helpful comments on the manuscript.

REFERENCES

Anon., (1979a). *ICES* CM 1979/G:35 (mimeo).
Anon., (1979b). *ICES* CM 1979/G:26 (mimeo).
Anon., (1981a). *ICES* CM 1981/G:8 (mimeo).
Anon., (1981b). *ICES* CM 1981/H:10 (mimeo).
Bagenal, T. B. (1971). *J. Fish. Biol.* **3**, 207–220.
Bailey, R. S. (1975). *J. mar. biol. Ass. U.K.* **55**, 133–142.
Brawn, V. M. (1961). *Behaviour* **18**, 177–198.
Daan, D. (1973). *Neth. J. Sea Res.* **6**, 479–517.
Daan, N. (1975). *Neth. J. Sea Res.* **9**, 24–55.
Daan, N. and Kuiter, C. J. (1981). *ICES* CM 1981/G:71 (mimeo).
Ellertsen, B., Moksness, E., Solemdal, P., Tilseth, S., Westgard, T. and Oiestad, V. (1981). *Rapp. P.-v. Reun. Cons. int. Explor. Mer* **1978**, 260–267.
Fulton, T. W. (1891). *Rep. Fish. Bd Scot.* **9**, 243–268.
Graham, M. (1924). *Fishery Invest. Lond.* (2) **6**, 1–77.

Harris, M. P. and Hislop, J. R. G. (1978). *J. Zool. Lond.* **185**, 213–236.
Hawkins, A. D. (1970). *Scot. Fish. Bull.* **33**, 16–18.
Hawkins, A. D., Chapman, C. J. and Symonds, D. J. (1967). *Nature, Lond.* **215**, 923–925.
Heessen, H. and Kuiter, C. (1982). *ICES* CM 1982/G:66 (mimeo).
Hempel, G. and Blaxter, J. H. S. (1967). *J. Cons. int. Explor. Mer* **31**, 170–195.
Hislop, J. R. G. (1975). *J. Cons. int. Explor. Mer* **36**, 119–127.
Hislop, J. R. G. and Hall, W. B. (1974). *J. Cons. int. Explor. Mer* **36**, 42–49.
Hislop, J. R. G. and Shanks, A. M. (1981). *J. Cons. int. Explor. Mer* **39**, 244–251.
Hislop, J. R. G., Robb, A. P. and Gauld, J. A. (1978). *J. Fish. Biol.* **13**, 85–98.
Hodder, V. M. (1963). *J. Fish. Res. Bd Can.* **20**, 1465–1487.
Holden, M. J. (1981). *ICES* Coop. Res. Rep. 99.
Jones, R. (1954). *Mar. Res. Scot.* **1954** (2), 1–34.
Laurence, G. C. (1974). *J. Fish. Res. Bd Can.* **31**, 1415–1419.
Laurence, G. C., Smigielski, A. S., Halavik, T. A. and Burns, B. R. (1981). *Rapp. P.-v. Reun. Cons. int. Explor. Mer* **178**, 304–311.
Messtorff, J. (1959). *Ber. dt. Wiss. Kommn f. Meeresforsch N.F.* **15**, 277–334.
Oosthuizen, E. and Daan, N. (1974). *Neth. J. Sea Res.* **8**, 378–397.
Ponomarenko, I. Ya and Yaragina, N. A. (1981). *ICES* CM 1981/G:22 (mimeo).
Poulsen, E. M. (1931). *Meddr. Kommn. Danm. Fisk.-og Havunders., Fisk.* **9** (1), 148.
Raitt, D. S. (1932). *Fish. Bd Scot. Sci. Invest.* **1932** (1), 40.
Raitt, D. F. S. (1968). *Mar. Res. Scot.* **1968** (5), 24.
Raitt, D. F. S. and Adams, J. A. (1965). *Mar. Res. Scot.* **1965** (3), 28.
Russell, F. S. (1976). "The Eggs and Planktonic Stages of British Marine Fishes". Academic Press, London.
Schopka, S. A. (1971). *Ber. dt. Wiss. Kommn. f. Meeresforsch N.F.* **22**, 31–79.
Simpson, A. C. (1956). *In* "Sea Fisheries: Their Investigation in the United Kingdom" (M. Graham, ed.), pp. 487. Edward Arnold, London.
Storozhuk, A. Y. and Golovanov, A. V. (1976). *Annls. biol., Copenh.* **31**, 107–109.
Svetovidov, A. N. (1948). "Fauna of the USSR, Fishes". IX, No. 4, *Gadiformes.* Israel Programme for Scientific Translations Jerusalem, 1962.
Wheeler, A. (1969). "The Fishes of the British Isles and North West Europe". Michigan State University Press, East Lansing.

18. Allocation of Resources to Gonad and Soma in Atlantic Herring *Clupea harengus* L.

T. D. ILES

Marine Fish Division, Fisheries Research Branch, Department of Fisheries and Oceans, Canada

Abstract: Changes in somatic fat, water and "protein" were followed for North Sea herring over most of the growth and reproductive season. Comparison was by means of "partial condition factors" which are length-independent and change with time.

Somatic fat and protein increase during May and June, peaking at the onset of gonad maturation. The subsequent decline of somatic protein implies translocation to the developing gonad. Once the gonads are ripe, somatic protein levels fall very slowly, conserving protein above a basic overwintering level. This decline is only one eighth of that predicted by the von Bertalanffy growth theorem.

The cycles of metabolic components are evaluated in relation to the known seasonality of feeding and growth and a scheme of seasonal hormonal control of metabolism is derived. Stocks differ in the timing of their seasonal cycles, but these differences cannot be entirely explained by differences in the production cycles of their food. Year to year differences are examined.

The results explain the absence of a "gonad effect" on somatic growth and are incompatible with the concept of a reproductive cost. This has important consequences for life-history theories which rely on this concept.

The results are inconsistent with the assumption (in the field of energetics) that the calorific value of food provides sufficient information on which to base theoretical models.

I. INTRODUCTION

Seasonal changes in the percentages of fat, water and "crude protein" in North Sea herring were interpreted as the result of active transport of water between the fish and its medium (Iles and Wood, 1965). This was considered one aspect of an adaptation to maintain a net negative buoyancy when the summer accumulation of fat, with a lower specific gravity than sea water, would otherwise give positive buoyancy; at the same time, the protein/water

FISH REPRODUCTION
ISBN: 0–12–563660–1

ratio varies only between physiologically acceptable limits. Iles and Wood (ibid.) emphasized that changes in the percentages of the three major components of somatic herring tissue do not necessarily reflect changes in their absolute amounts. These depend also on concurrent weight changes resulting from both increases in length, defined as somatic growth, and variation in "condition". This variation in condition reflects the accumulation and elimination of somatic material over and above that involved in permanent changes in length.

In this communication these weight changes are taken into account. The seasonal changes in the individual somatic components fat, water and "protein", are followed by choosing a basis of comparison that is valid for different times of the year and over the length range of the population being studied. The changes in somatic components are then related to concurrent changes in the gonad and in somatic metabolism.

II. MATERIALS AND METHODS

A. Partial condition factors

A suitable standard of comparison is basic to the study of the variation in any quantity whose determination involves the sacrifice of individuals. In following the seasonal changes in the biochemical composition of some common cirripedes Barnes et al. (1963) compared groups of individuals of the same valve size throughout the year; this effectively eliminated seasonal growth. Idler and Bitners (1958, 1959, 1960) in a series of papers on the biochemistry of sockeye salmon during its spawning migration, chose individuals from a single homogeneous "run" at different states of its ascent. Each individual represented a "standard" fish (Idler and Bitners, ibid.). The data could then be treated as approximately closely to what would be expected if a fish could be captured, analysed and then returned to the river. Growth of sockeye salmon is known to have ceased by the time the river ascent begins, and is not a complicating factor. Energy changes in the soma and ovaries of perch in Lake Windermere were measured by Craig (1977) in fish large enough to show but little net somatic growth.

In this communication the comparison is based on the term K in the equation, $K = W/L^3$, where W is the weight and L the length of individual fish. This "simple condition factor" for the whole fish is partitioned into separate elements each referring to a single component. These are somatic fat, somatic water and somatic "protein" (Iles and Wood, 1965) on the one hand, and the whole gonad on the other. The maturation of the gonad represents a major expenditure of proteinaceous material for the adult fish, and seasonal changes in the somatic components over the period of maturation and spawning should allow insight into the quantitative and qualitative nature of the interaction of soma and gonad. All material entering the gonad must pass through the soma and must be processed, and partitioned or allocated, by somatic metabolism.

The condition factors calculated for each component can be called "Partial Condition Factors" (PCF) and are defined as follows:

$$K_{W(ater)} = \frac{\text{Weight of somatic water}}{L^3} \times 10^5$$

$$K_{F(at)} = \frac{\text{Weight of somatic fat}}{L^3} \times 10^5$$

$$K_{P(rotein)} = \frac{\text{Weight of somatic protein}}{L^3} \times 10^5$$

$$K_{G(onad)} = \frac{\text{Weight of gonad}}{L^3} \times 10^5$$

$$K_{T(otal)} = K_W + K_F + K_P + K_G$$

$$K_{(T-G)} = K_W + K_F + K_P = \text{somatic condition factor.}$$

Weight is measured in grams and length in centimetres (total length, caudal fin extended).

These equations emphasize the fact that the total condition factor of an individual fish can be affected by any independent changes that may occur in individual components; conversely, any change in the total condition factor cannot be interpreted as a change in any single component unless those in other components can also be accounted for. It is emphasized that the percentage of any single component is affected by changes in any other component, quite independently of the way it varies itself.

The methods to be used are dictated to a large degree by practical considerations. The dissection out of individual organs and tissues such as muscle, liver, kidneys, etc. and their separate analysis is feasible, but tedious and leads to inaccuracy when the results are combined for the whole fish. The maceration of whole herring, after removal of the gonad and elimination of any stomach contents, is a simple and rapid procedure allowing sampling of populations at a relatively high level of intensity. Analysis for somatic fat and water [and by inference "protein" (Iles and Wood, 1965)] would be expected to isolate those components whose interactions represent the most important aspects of seasonal changes.

B. Condition factors and length–weight relationships

Hickling (1930) used the simple condition factor to follow seasonal changes in hake and estimated partial condition factors for liver, gonad and flesh although he did not use the term. Scott (1979) calculated a somatic condition factor (equivalent to $K_{(T-G)}$ above) which, he maintained, was an estimate of change in somatic weight. However, he retained the use of the gonadosomatic index (GSI) as a basis for comparison of gonad weight.

There has been considerable discussion and even confusion in the past about the significance and validity of "condition factors" (Hile, 1936; Le Cren, 1951; Rounsefell and Everhart, 1953). An analysis of "condition" in relation to "length–weight" relationships is underway (Iles, in prep.), and it is necessary here, merely to make the following point. In this study cyclical changes are being investigated in components which do not necessarily make any contribution to permanent changes in structure or form. One, fat, is an energy-rich storage material whose proportion varies widely over the year from a seasonal minimum of near zero (Wood, 1958); similarly large changes are represented by the maturation of the gonad and the eventual liberation of gametes. Variations in neither of these are length dependent in the sense implied by a length–weight relationship of the type $W = aL^n$; nor are their seasonal cycles necessarily in phase with that of growth in length. Their levels at any one time are the result of complex interacting metabolic mechanisms, the organization of which is the problem under study.

The herring used in this analysis are the same individual herring from which the fat/water relationship was derived – the methods of preparation and analysis have already been discussed (Iles and Wood, 1965). Figure 1 shows the area of study. For each individual, the weight of somatic fat, water and protein was estimated from its measured percentage and the body weight. Condition factors for each component were calculated as indicated above.

C. Herring stocks of the North Sea

Two main groups of herring are recognized in the North Sea. The Banks group, spawns in the central and northern areas in late summer and autumn, and the Downs group, spawns in the English Channel in winter (November–January) (Cushing, 1955; Cushing and Burd, 1957; Zijlstra, 1958; Parrish and Saville, 1965). Subdivisions of both of these spawning groups have been proposed (see Parrish and Saville, 1965 for a review) but there is no consensus as to the status of the subdivisions or their interrelationships (but see Iles and Sinclair, 1982). These subdivisions will not be discussed in detail here; it is sufficient to point out that the distinction between Banks herring and Downs herring is generally agreed to be biologically significant (Cushing, 1966; Zijlstra, 1963).

The samples of herring from which these data are derived contain members of both the Banks and the Downs groups. Sampling at the Lowestoft laboratory began in May from the North Shields fishery, exploiting herring

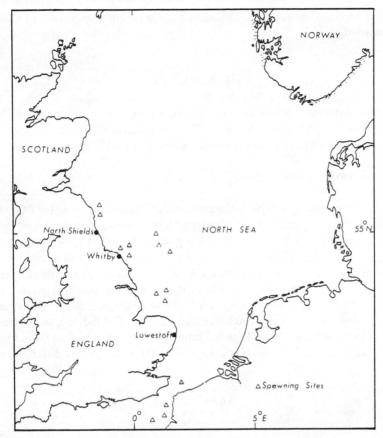

Fig. 1.   The North Sea area.

feeding off the northeast coast of England. These are considered to be a mixture of both Banks and Downs fish (Burd, 1962; Cushing, 1962), although the proportions may vary. During July and August there is a shift in the fishery to the Whitby area, where pre-spawning and spawning concentrations of autumn-spawning herring are fished close inshore. These concentrations are of Banks type fish (Burd, 1962; Cushing, 1962). The East Anglian fishery is defined as beginning in October in an area south of Smiths Knoll. This is to exclude fish taken (mostly in September) from the Haisborough and Dowsing grounds off the Norfolk and Lincolnshire coast. These are mainly autumn spawning fish with a proportion of Downs fish passing through the area towards their spawning grounds (Burd, 1962; Cushing, 1962). The East Anglian fishery is based predominantly on full ripe fish of the Downs group. From December on, fishing takes place at or near spawning areas in the

Channel itself and besides ripe fish, spawning or recently spawned individuals are sampled.

III. RESULTS

Sampling in the year 1956 was at a high level which was maintained from May throughout the year and into early 1957. This covered the major part of a single full seasonal cycle and is conveniently dealt with separately.

A. The seasonal water cycle

Figure 2 shows changes in both the percentage water and the water PCF(Kw) from May 1956 to January 1957. The trend line is fitted as a moving average of three. Kw increases from May to reach a peak in June declining thereafter till mid-September. The discontinuity in October represents a difference in the timing of the cycle between autumn (Whitby) spawners of the Banks group and winter (East Anglian) spawners of the Downs. This is estimated at about 42 days which is only about one third of the difference in spawning time; Whitby fish spawn in early September and East Anglian fish in late December (Burd, 1962; Cushing, 1962). Figure 3 emphasizes what is evident from Fig. 2, that the seasonal cycle of the percentage of water is completely different from

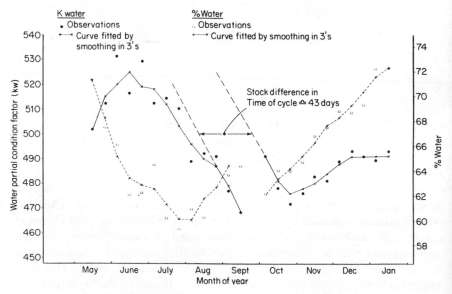

Fig. 2.   North Sea herring 1956–57. Water cycle as partial condition factors and as percentage.

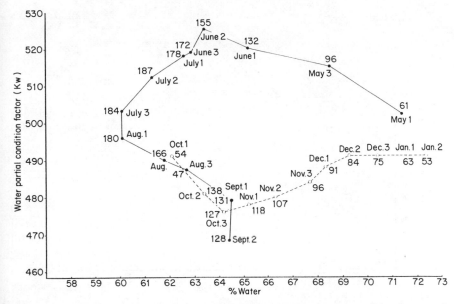

Fig. 3.   North Sea herring 1956–57. The relation between water partial condition factor and percentage water. (Solid line: autumn spawners; broken line: winter spawners.) Values for K_F are given at dates.

that of Kw. It must be emphasized that changes in Kw are independent of somatic growth in length; water is accumulated and then eliminated as a "net" process. The water content returns to a relatively low and stable level over winter.

B. The seasonal fat cycle

The seasonal cycle of the fat PCF (K_F) is shown in Fig. 4. During May and June there is rapid accumulation of fat to a maximum level in July, after which levels decline steadily. In the East Anglian data the decline is continuous from October onwards; the time difference between Autumn and Winter spawners is estimated to be 42 days. Figure 5 compares the fat percentages with values for K_F throughout the year.

Figure 6 compares the water and fat cycles for the period May–Sept. As higher levels of fat are achieved in late June and into July water is eliminated. This confirms a feature of the Iles and Wood (1965) hypothesis on the significance of the fat-water relationship. Initial compensation to the increase in buoyancy caused by fat deposition is achieved by reduction of swim bladder volume, but the degree to which this is possible without losing the function of the swim bladder is limited. Final accommodation is by the elimination of "negative ballast" with water (Brawn, 1969).

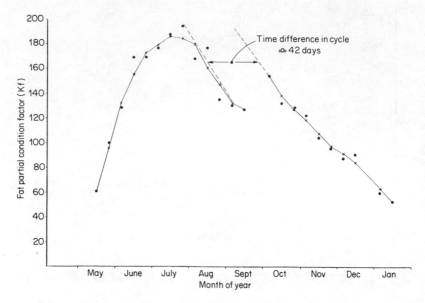

Fig. 4.   North Sea herring 1956–57. Fat cycle.

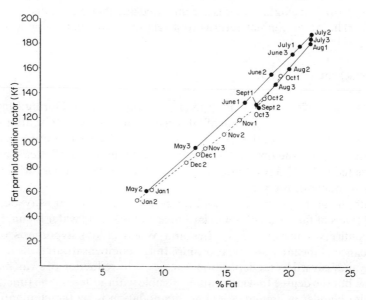

Fig. 5.   North Sea herring 1956–57. The relation between partial condition factor and fat percentage. (Solid line: autumn spawners; broken line: winter spawners.)

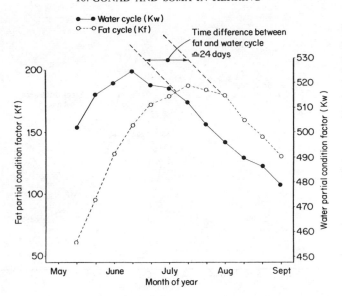

Fig. 6. North Sea herring 1956–57. Fat cycle and water cycle compared.

C. The seasonal somatic protein cycle

The seasonal somatic protein cycle is shown in Fig. 7. There is a net increase in crude protein over May and June to a July peak; thereafter somatic protein declines relatively rapidly to September. The East Anglian data shows a rapid decline from the beginning of October, but subsequently through November, December and January, the rate of somatic protein loss is very low. The stock difference in timing for protein is again estimated as just over 40 days. A comparison of protein percentage and of protein PCF (K_p) is given in Fig. 8. If time of year is ignored, the relationship is obscure; if the seasonality is taken into account then a complex relationship becomes obvious.

Seasonal changes in these somatic components must be interpreted in relation to feeding, growth and maturation.

D. Feeding and growth cycles

By May the herring of North Shields are feeding voraciously on zooplankton but from then onwards the feeding rate declines and reaches a low level by August (Savage, 1931, 1937); it has been established that feeding rate declines more rapidly seasonally than does zooplankton biomass (Savage, ibid.) and these "appetitive" changes are discussed fully by Iles (1974).

The high levels of PCF's compared to those in January suggest feeding has

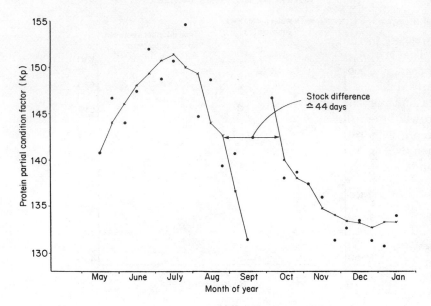

Fig. 7.   North Sea herring 1956–57. "Protein" cycle.

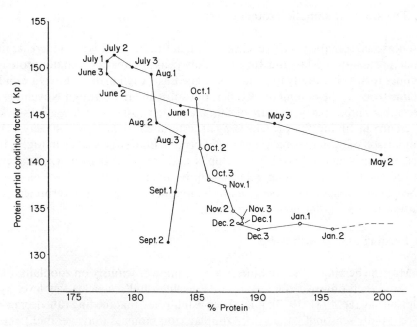

Fig. 8.   North Sea herring 1956–57. The relation between partial condition factor and percentage protein as a function of time.

been going on for some time; it can be inferred that the feeding season begins by early March (see below, and Iles, in prep.).

That growth has also been going on for some time is demonstrated by the appearance of a new growth zone outside the winter check in fish caught in early May (Lea, 1910; Hodgson, 1925). It is estimated that about a third of the seasons complete length increment has been completed by mid-May and that growth in length continues through June and July (Hodgson, 1925; Iles in prep.). Thus both somatic fat and protein are accumulated at a greater rate than they are being metabolized. The likely fate of the accumulated protein can be followed by considering the gonad maturation cycle.

E. Gonad maturation and somatic protein

1. *North Shields–Whitby Data.* It has been shown that the major part of gonad maturation occurs later in the year than does somatic growth (Iles, 1964). The seasonal increase in gonad size in the North Shields–Whitby area for the year 1956 can be determined from data on the maturation stages provided by samples from the fishery. (See Iles, 1964 for details of the methodology.)

The results are given in Table Ia and Ib and in Fig. 9 where the data for gonad growth are compared with the changes in the somatic protein. The period of major gonad growth corresponds well with that of loss of somatic protein; in addition the rates are similar from July onwards, as is shown in Table II. The rate of increase of the PCF (gonad) is $+1.56$ units per day, this is for total gonad weight. Gonad tissue contains between 20 and 25% protein (Bruce, 1924), so that this rate is equivalent to between 0.31 and 0.38 units per day, close to the estimated rate of decline in somatic crude protein. This suggests that the protein accumulated earlier in the soma during the growth season is subsequently translocated to the gonad. This tends to be confirmed by data collected in 1959 in June and July. These were deliberately chosen to cover the full range of maturation stages in the population. Gonad weights for individual females that were maturing in 1959 were compared with their somatic protein condition factors. The correlation was significant ($r = -0.712$, $df = 16$ $P < 0.001$); the slope of the regression at 0.52% of the gonad weight per unit of somatic K_p is close to that expected if translocation occurs (see Table I).

2. *East Anglian data.* (a) East Anglian Protein. The initial decline in the somatic protein PCF parallels the rate of decline shown from July in the North Shields data. It has been suggested that maturation of the gonads of East Anglian herring may not be complete by the time the fishery begins (Iles, 1964)

TABLE Ia. Gonad weight as a percentage of fish weight for stages I–VI of gonad maturation in *Clupea harengus* (Iles, 1964).

Stage	I & II	I–III & II–III	III	III–IV	IV	IV–V	V	VI
% of fish weight	0·1	0·5	3·1	6·2	9·7	14·3	19·8	22·9

TABLE Ib. Estimated *K* Gonad, North Shields fish, 1956.

	May			June				July			August		
Date	13	22	26	2	10	17	26	3	13	27	7	14	21
Mean gonad as % body weight	0·30	0·24	0·14	0·70	1·41	2·51	2·57	1·70	4·78	6·38	12·00	10·32	12·92
Mean *K* total	700	741	763	781	812	833	850	855	860	840	815	800	870
Mean *K* gonad	2·1	1·8	1·1	5·5	11·5	10·9	21·8	19·5	41·1	53·6	97·8	82·6	100·8
Smooth mean	2·1	1·7	2·8	6·0	9·3	14·7	17·4	27·5	3·16	64·2	78·0	93·7	100·8

TABLE II. Daily changes in partial condition factors for somatic protein (K_p) and gonad (K_G) for *C. harengus* from July onwards.

	Degrees of freedom	r	b (units of condition per day)
K_p (Somatic protein)	5	−0·893	−0·322 ($P < 0·01$)
K_G (Gonad)	5	+0·961	+1·555 ($P < 0·01$)

r: correlation coefficient; b: regression coefficient; P: probability.

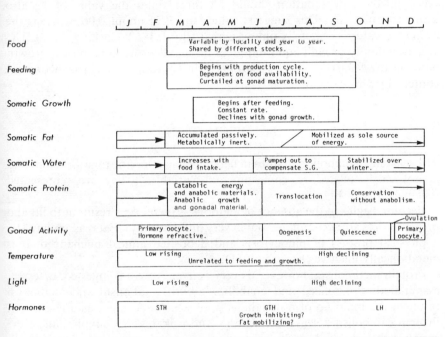

Fig. 9. Seasonal interaction of herring and environment. (S.G.: specific gravity; STH: somatotropic hormone; GTH: gonadotrophic hormone; LH: lutenizing hormone.)

which is consistent with this. However, the important feature is the subsequent low rate of protein loss from mid-October to January. The regression of K_p on time gives the equation:

$$K_p = 138·90 − 0·063X$$

where X is the number of days from the beginning of October ($r = 0·781$, $df = 7$, $P = 0·01$).

If the value of $K_p = 138·9$ is taken to be a standard for the beginning of the overwintering period then this rate is equivalent to about 17% per year. At this rate, by the beginning of March by which time feeding would be expected to begin (Savage, 1934, 1937), less than four units of protein PCF would have been lost. This represents a marked degree of conservation of protein that is considered to be an adaption to overwintering starvation.

Over this period feeding and growth has ceased (Iles, 1971) and the conditions therefore correspond closely to those under which the rate of basal nitrogen degradation should be calculated (Gerking, 1962). On theoretic grounds this should be simply related to the parameter K of the von Bertalanffy growth equation (Beverton and Holt, 1957). The annual rate of basal nitrogen degradation should be three times the value of K, also estimated annually. This suggests values for K of about 0·06, whereas the estimated value is about six times as great (Burd, 1962; Cushing, 1962). The von Bertalanffy growth equation gives an excellent fit to empirical growth data, on an *annual* census basis (Iles, 1971); it is not supported in its theoretical content by *seasonal* empirical data.

IV. DISCUSSION

The seasonal metabolic activities in herring have a specific time structure that is not easily related to environmental variables. They are represented schematically in Fig. 9.

Feeding begins in the absence of anabolic growth. As a result both fat and protein stores are accumulated but in very different ways. Fat is assimilated by a physical process of pinocytosis and deposited almost unchanged; it is metabolically inactive (Lovern, 1951).

Protein metabolism, however, is very active. Protein is ingested, digested, assimilated, catabolized and anabolized; both catabolism and anabolism result in the build up of a metabolic pool which is evident as a rise in K_p. Protein catabolism releases free energy and it is this that supplies all of the metabolic energy needs, including those generated by increased bodily activity in the search for and capture of food.

Any waste heat that is produced is eliminated by the highly efficient heat exchange mechanism represented by the gills (Miller, 1979).

Some little while after feeding and protein metabolism begins, somatic growth is initiated as an anabolic process. The preparation of protein sub-units for subsequent gonad maturation continues, so that somatic growth and gonad growth differ only in the timing of the use of material prepared at the same time by the same, parental metabolic processes.

Later in the season there is a fairly short period over which anabolic growth is decelerated to zero and translocation of protein to the gonad begins. This coincides with a marked reduction in appetite resulting in the cessation of feeding (Iles, 1974). The final stages of maturation, certainly, involve only the translocation of prepared materials. By implication these are of a great range in size and complexity; for example they must include enzymes, or their precursors, that are needed for the metabolic aspects of development following successful zygote formation (De Petrocellis and Monroy, 1974).

The cessation of feeding and growth represents a switch from protein catabolism to fat catabolism and the mobilization of fat reserves for all energy requirements. The largest non reproductive source of protein loss, represented by the maintenance of an active epithelium in the alimentary canal, is avoided by cessation of feeding and other activities involving protein synthesis, for example haemoglobin synthesis (Wilkins and Iles, 1966), are curtailed. The process of gonad maturation, leading to the ripe, competent gonad is quite distinct from that of spawning, the two stages being separated by the event of ovulation (Holliday, 1960a,b; Iles, 1964).

A. Differences between stocks

Stock differences do occur, and are of two kinds. Some gonad developmental stages, such as the "full" stage, may be prolonged. For example, individual spring-spawning herring may spend several months in the "ripe" stage; in other instances, maturation stages may be resumed after having stopped for a period (Iles, 1964). There is evidence for example that autumn spawners (and by implication, summer spawners) resume feeding and growth after spawning (Iles, in prep.). This has been shown also for summer spawning sprat (Elwertowski and Maciejczyk, 1960).

B. Hormonal control of seasonal cycles

The hormonal events that mediate and control these metabolic (and behavioural) events cannot yet be described in detail, but the important kinds of hormonal activities that might (or must) occur can be suggested. These include the production of STH (Somatotropic Hormone) and of GTH (Gonadotropic Hormone) (Holliday, 1960a,b; Iles, 1964) but these are not dealt with here. What can be asserted is that the seasonal events in herring suggest that, rather than acting as transducers of environmental stimuli to the relevant metabolic activity (Scott, 1979), hormones are endogenously controlled to integrate physiological processes within quite strict time constraints. They represent an adaptation to average seasonal conditions and the individual can ignore year to year variability as "noise", as long as it is of not too excessive an amplitude.

These results imply also that the idea of surplus energy, applied to the ordering of priorities of different "needs", is not the only basis for conceptual models of fish physiology. It has been maintained, for example, that minimum requirements for work and repair "head the line" when food input is limiting; these support anabolic processes for structural maintenance and catabolic basal or standard metabolism (Miller, 1979). Any excess can then be made available for gonad maturation, accumulation of stores and somatic growth, in that order of priority (Miller, ibid.).

Almost all of the ideas and concepts implicit or explicit in this statement are challenged by the facts of herring seasonality. The fact of appetite changes, that lead to cessation of feeding while food is plentiful, establishes food availability as being under endogeneous control (Iles, 1974). It also suggests that competition for food is not a major ecological factor for herring, once the density dependent stage is past (Iles, 1980).

It can be claimed, also, that overwintering herring do not undergo "structural maintenance", but are anabolically inert and, instead conserve protein loss rigorously. This throws doubt on the concept of basal metabolism which is re-inforced by consideration of the physiological state during the active feeding and growth period. It is difficult to dissect out a basal process amongst this intense activity. It has already been pointed out that this feeding and growth stage begins when the seasonal water temperature is very low and ends when it is at its highest (Iles, 1974). This virtually eliminates temperature as a dominant ecological factor.

The key point to emphasize is that the animal is to a remarkable degree independent of the environment. At no time is the metabolic activity, or even levels of the metabolic pool, entirely dependent on incoming material; metabolism has been effectively decoupled from assimilation and it is this decoupling that defines the true function of the hormonal system.

In addition, there seems to be no justification in using the calorie, the basal unit of energy, as if it were the accepted coinage for all metabolic processes. The time-structuring of metabolism is such that at no instant is one calorie of protein equivalent to one calorie of fat, for example. Indeed, to convert one component to the other would involve the use of the most complex of metabolic pathways and at a calorific cost that no one has yet estimated.

REFERENCES

Barnes, H., Barnes, M. and Finlayson, D. M. (1963). *J. mar. biol. Ass. U.K.* **43**, 185–211.
Beverton, R. J. H. and Holt, S. J. (1957). *Fishery Invest.* Ser. II **19**, 5–33.
Brawn, V. M. (1969). *J. Fish. Res. Bd. Can.* **26**, 2077–2091.
Bruce, J. R. (1924). *Biochem. J.* **18**, 469–485.
Burd, A. C. (1962). *Fishery Invest.* Ser. II **23** (5), 1–42.
Craig, J. F. (1977). *J. Anim. Ecol.* **46**, 617–632.
Cushing, D. H. (1955). *J. Cons. perm. int. Explor. Mer* **21**, 44–60.
Cushing, D. H. (1962). *Fishery Invest.* Ser. II **23** (5), 43–71.

Cushing, D. H. (1966). *Fishery Invest.* Ser. II **25** (1), Part I, 1–62.
Cushing, D. H. and Burd, A. C. (1957). *Fishery Invest.* Ser. II **20** (11), 31.
De Petrocellis, B. and Monroy, A. (1974). *Endeavour* **33**, 92–98.
Elwertowski, J. and Maciejczyk, J. (1960). *ICES*, CM 1960, Sardine Comm. **67**, 3.
Gerking, S. D. (1962). *Ecol. Monogr.* **32**, 31–78.
Hickling, C. F. (1930). *J. mar. biol. Ass. U.K.* **16**, 529–576.
Hile, R. (1936). U.S. Dept. Commer. Cur. Fish. Bull. Bur. Fish. (No. 19) **48**, 211–317.
Hodgson, W. C. (1925). *Fishery Invest.* Ser. 2 **7** (8), 36.
Holliday, F. G. T. (1960a). *ICES*, C.M. 1960 Herring Comm. **38**, 4.
Holliday, F. G. T. (1960b). *ICES*, C.M. 1960, Herring Comm. **39**, 4.
Idler, D. R. and Bitners, I. (1958). *Can. J. Biochem. Physiol.* **36**, 793–798.
Idler, D. R. and Bitners, I. (1959). *J. Fish. Res. Bd. Can.* **16**, 235–241.
Idler, D. R. and Bitners, I. (1960). *J. Fish. Res. Bd. Can.* **11**, 113–122.
Iles, T. D. (1964). *J. Cons. perm. int. Explor. Mer* **29**, 166–168.
Iles, T. D. (1971). *J. Cons. int. Explor. Mer* **33**, 386–420.
Iles, T. D. (1974). *In* "Sea Fisheries Research" (F. R. Harden Jones, ed.). Paul Elik, London.
Iles, T. D. (1980). *Rapp. P-v Réun. Cons. int. Explor. Mer* **177**, 315–331.
Iles, T. D. and Sinclair, M. (1982). *Science, N.Y.* **215**, 627–633.
Iles, T. D. and Wood, R. J. (1965). *J. mar. biol. Ass. U.K.* **45**, 333–366.
Le Cren, E. D. (1951). *J. Anim. Ecol.* **20**, 201–219.
Lea, E. (1910). *Cons. perm. int. Explor. Mer* Publ. Circonstance **53**, 7–174.
Lovern, J. A. (1951). *Biochem. Soc. Symp.* **6**, 49–62.
Miller, P. J. (1979). *Symp. zool. Soc. Lond.* **44**, 1–28.
Parrish, B. B. and Saville, A. (1965). *Oceanogr. mar. Biol. Ann. Rev.* **3**, 323–373.
Rounsefell, G. A. and Everhart, W. H. (1953). "Fishery Science Its Methods and Applications". John Wiley, New York.
Savage, R. E. (1931). *Fishery Invest.* Ser. II, **12** (3), 88.
Savage, R. E. (1937). *Fishery Invest.* Ser. II, **15** (5), 57.
Scott, D. B. C. (1979). *Symp. zool. Soc. Lond.* **44**, 105–132.
Wilkins, N. P. and Iles, T. D. (1966). *Comp. Biochem. Physiol.* **17**, 1141–1158.
Wood, R. J. (1958). *J. Cons. perm. int. Explor. Mer* **23**, 390–398.
Zijlstra, J. J. (1958). *Rapp. P-v. Réun. Cons. perm. int. Explor. Mer* **143**, Part II, 134–145.
Zijlstra, J. J. (1963). *Rapp. P-v. Réun. Cons. perm. int. Explor. Mer* **154**, 198–202.

19. Fitness of Different Reproductive Strategies in Teleost Fishes

D. M. WARE

Dept of Fisheries and Oceans, British Columbia, Canada

Abstract: The fitness of two reproductive strategies under two mortality regimes, which impose an explicit survival cost on reproduction, are explored for age structured populations of teleosts. Strategy A assumes that the age-specific reproductive rate $R(X)$, defined in units of energy yr^{-1}, is an increasing function of the supply of surplus energy. The alternative, strategy B, assumes that $R(X)$ is determined strictly by body size at each age. Numerical simulation suggests that strategy A ought to confer a higher fitness in iteroparous species that experience a low natural mortality rate after maturation; whereas strategy B usually results in a higher fitness when the adult mortality rate is high. This result may help explain the disparate reproductive characteristics of some fishes: in a short-lived species like stickleback, the reproductive rate is solely a function of body size at the beginning of the inter-spawning interval, whereas in a long-lived species like haddock the reproduction rate depends on the supply of surplus energy, except when feeding conditions are very poor. For less extreme life history types, the fitness of each strategy depends on the exact parameter values and form of the juvenile and adult mortality rates. The management ·implications of these findings are discussed.

I. INTRODUCTION

Recent models of life history phenomena have considered the consequences of different fecundity and survival schedules with respect to the evolution of semelparity (single massive reproduction) and iteroparity (repeated repro-duction). Schaffer (1974) argued that an optimal life history maximizes the reproductive value at all ages, and showed that when fecundity and post-breeding survival are concave functions of reproductive effort (E, defined as the proportion of available resources allocated to breeding) iteroparity is usually optimal. Conversely, when these characteristics are strictly convex functions of E semelparity is most likely to evolve. For more realistic fertility and growth-survival curves, Schaffer and Rosenzweig (1977) found that there

FISH REPRODUCTION
ISBN: 0–12–563660–1

can be multiple evolutionary steady states, depending upon the number of age classes in the population.

By extending the concept of energy allocation to age structured populations, Charlesworth and Leon (1976) showed that low adult mortality, continuing adult growth in size or reproductive efficiency, a low rate of population increase, and a high sensitivity of survival and growth to reproductive effort all favour an increase in the latter with age. Alternatively, they concluded that reproductive effort may decrease with age if a population experiences high density dependent mortality or reduction in individual growth rate.

The idea that breeding has an associated price which must be paid in terms of future survival and reproductive performance is not new (see review by Calow, 1979). Indeed, Beverton and Holt (1959) observed that in short-lived fishes where there is an abrupt end to the lifespan death usually occurs at or soon after spawning. In iteroparous forms there is a circumstantial link between reproduction and mortality as both rates often increase with age (and body weight) during the latter stages of the life cycle. Recent reports by Mann and Mills (1979), Bell (1980), and Hirshfield (1980) offer more convincing evidence of a reproductive cost in fishes, though the exact form of the relationship for any specific population is still speculative.

Most theoretical studies of alternative reproduction and survival patterns have concentrated on the evolutionary implications of the equilibrium state and have largely ignored the transient dynamics, which are an important concern of management agencies. Many fish populations fluctuate in abundance and the characteristic time they take to return to a stable equilibrium after some environmental disturbance depends on the specific regulatory mechanism of the population: the return time can either increase or decrease in response to changes in the exploitation rate (Shepherd and Horwood, 1977). In a related context, Levin and Goodyear (1980) examined the dynamics and stability properties of a striped bass population, and concluded that age structured models are so sensitive to life history parameters that any attempt to simplify the dynamics by fitting the behaviour of the population to a simple stock-recruitment equation is risky.

So far experimental biologists have discovered two reproductive patterns in teleosts: in some species such as haddock, the reproductive rate is sensitive to the available energy resources (Hislop et al., 1978), whereas in sticklebacks reproduction appears to be strictly an increasing function of body size (Wootton and Evans, 1976). This paper considers the time-dependent and equilibrium population characteristics produced by these two reproductive patterns and asks: which strategy confers a higher individual fitness under different life history conditions? The model is based on the principle of energy allocation; it is age structured, assumes density dependent survival during the juvenile phase of the life cycle, includes a maturation delay and has an explicit survival cost associated with spawning.

Before proceeding perhaps it is worth clarifying that although the word "strategy" usually denotes some purposeful plan enacted by an individual this is not the spirit in which it is used in life history studies. Instead it is recognized that the way individuals allocate resources to reproduction under different circumstances is a heritable trait which is subject to natural selection in the same manner as any other characteristic determining the production of successful offspring. The term "reproductive strategy" is therefore a convenient, if not strictly correct, way of expressing this idea (Wootton, Chap. 1, this volume).

II. DISCRETE TIME MODEL

A. Preliminaries

The empirical energy allocation model outlined by Ware (1980) can be generalized to an age structured population to examine the fitness of different reproductive patterns. Specifically, consider an iteroparous species that produces offspring simultaneously at the end of each calendar year, so these additions to the population form a well-defined age group (X). The annual rate at which individuals at each age expend energy for various vital functions has the dimensions of power $(J \cdot yr^{-1})$. For convenience, power will be defined in units of $g \cdot yr^{-1}$ since weight has an energy equivalent, where 1 g of somatic tissue (wet) equals about 3860J. Both sexes are assumed to be the same size and have identical power supplies and allocations at each age. The environment is assumed to be constant. Though these assumptions are expedient, they are not necessary for the approach can be extended to include sexual variations and environmental effects when these factors are known, or suspected, to be important.

In energetics studies the power supply remaining after an individual has paid all its metabolic and activity costs is called surplus power, which represents the fraction of ingested energy diverted to growth and reproduction (Ware, 1982). In fishes the surplus power $(S(X,T),g \cdot yr^{-1})$ available to an individual in year T increases with body size $W(X,T)g$ and often decreases with the abundance of other individuals of the same age $N(X,T)$. As an approximation this relationship can be expressed by:

$$S(X,T) = \delta W(X,T)^{\zeta} \text{EXP}(-A_2 N(X,T)) \tag{1}$$

where the parameters δ, ζ and A_2 are assumed to be constant during the life span. Eq(1) is attractive not only because it is conceptually simple, but more importantly, because it seems to work empirically (Ware, 1980). If some size and density-dependent process like this operates throughout the pre-recruit phase of the life history, the mean body weight (g) at recruitment $W(r,T+r)$, can be approximated by

$$W(r,T+r) = W_\sigma \text{EXP}(-A_1 N(r,T+R)) \tag{2}$$

where W_σ is the maximum possible weight at age r and A_1 is the density dependent growth exponent during the pre-recruit stage. Hereafter recruitment is taken to be identical to the age of maturity ($r=4$ yr), though in practice, the approach can be adapted so these two events occur independently at any age.

At some time in the life history individuals begin to invest part of their surplus energy to produce young. We will consider the consequences when all the members of a population adopt one of two plausible options. For strategy A suppose the age-specific reproduction rate ($R(X,T)$,$g \cdot yr^{-1}$) is an increasing function of the surplus energy available in year T. Specifically let

$$\text{A.} \quad R(X,T) = \xi S(X,T)^\eta \tag{3a}$$

where ξ is a constant and η a power which tends to be ≥ 1 (Ware, 1980). Alternatively for strategy B suppose the age-specific reproduction rate is a power function of the body weight in year T:

$$\text{B.} \quad R(X,T) = c\theta f W(X,T)^\phi. \tag{3b}$$

where θ is the average egg weight, and c and ϕ are constants. Here f is a dimensionless coefficient which accounts for the higher energy density of reproductive tissue (i.e. $J \cdot g^{-1}$ gonad tissue divided by $J \cdot g^{-1}$ somatic tissue); measurements by McKinnon (1972) and Wootton and Evans (1976) indicate that f is about 1·2. To insure that the reproductive rates associated with each strategy are identical when the density dependent exponent $A_2 = 0$ in Eq (1), the parameters in (Eq 3a) can be defined more explicitly so $\xi = c\theta f \delta^{-\eta}$ and $\eta = \phi/\zeta$.

For each reproductive strategy the annual egg production of the population $N(O,T)$ is given by:

$$N(O,T) = \sum_{x=4}^{X_T} \frac{R(X,T) N(X,T)}{2\theta f}. \tag{4}$$

where X_T represents the terminal age and the factor 2 in the denominator implies an equal sex ratio.

The problematical details concerning how survival changes during the pre-recruit stage can be circumvented by assuming that the instantaneous mortality rate is a linear function of year-class abundance at any time

(Beverton and Holt, 1957). The number of survivors that eventually recruit to the mature segment of the population r years later is therefore

$$N(r,T+r) = ([\psi/N(O,T)] + \gamma)^{-1}, \tag{5}$$

where ψ and γ are constants.

It follows from the definition of surplus power that the supply remaining after spawning represents the annual increase in body weight. Thus, at the beginning of year $T+1$ the weight of an individual at age $X+1$ is

$$W(X+1,T+1) = W(X,T) + S(X,T) - R(X,T). \tag{6}$$

To account for natural mortality we make the usual assumption that $dN/dT = -MN$, so

$$N(X+1,T+1) = N(X,T)\text{EXP}(-M(X,T)) \tag{7}$$

where $M(X,T)$ is the age-specific instantaneous mortality rate. Notice that the time step of 1 yr is implicit in the exponent in Eq (7).

B. Reproductive cost

In lightly exploited fish populations mortality often increases more or less exponentially with age either at, or shortly after maturation (Beverton and Holt, 1959). We will consider the implications of two functions which are in broad agreement with this observation. For the type I case suppose $M(X,T)$ rises exponentially as proportionally more surplus power is allocated to reproduction instead of growth at any age and time:

$$M(X,T) = M_2\text{EXP}(M_1 S(X,T)/G(X,T)), \tag{8a}$$

where $G(X,T) = S(X,T) - R(X,T)$ is the annual growth rate, and M_1 and M_2 are constants.

For the type II case we impose a modified reproductive cost and include an additional factor to account for the observation that the mortality rate of young and middle aged fish usually decreases with body size (Cushing, 1975):

$$M(X,T) = M_2 W(X,T)^{-M_1}\text{EXP}(S(X,T)/G(X,T)). \tag{8b}$$

In this case the death rate is presumed to be determined by two opposing forces: a food chain or predation risk factor which diminishes with body size, and a reproductive cost factor which rises with size and age. Notice that the quotient $S(X,T)/G(X,T)$ in equations 8a and b can be rewritten as $1 + R(X,T)/G(X,T)$, so the survival cost is an explicit rather than implicit function of the trade-off between reproduction and growth. As an example, the shapes of the resulting age-specific mortality curves are illustrated in Fig. 1 for both mortality functions and reproductive strategies.

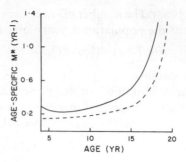

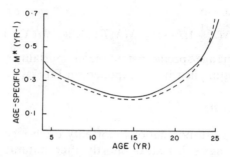

Fig. 1. Age-specific mortality rates at equilibrium produced by reproductive strategies A (broken line) and B (solid line) for the nominal parameter values listed in Table III. Upper panel, type I mortality; lower panel, type II mortality.

C. Fitness

To determine the value of different reproductive patterns we require some objective measure of fitness. Charlesworth and Leon (1976), and more recently Goodman (1982) have suggested that in density-dependent situations an evolutionarily stable life history will tend to maximize the net reproductive rate when the population is at a stable equilibrium. Thus, for our purposes, fitness can be defined in terms of the egg production of the population when it follows either strategy $A(N_A^*(O))$ or $B(N_B^*(O))$ and the population density in each case is at equilibrium (N_A^* or N_B^*). The expression

$$F_A^* = N_A^*(O)/N_B^*(O) \tag{9}$$

therefore measures the relative fitness of strategy A for a given set of initial conditions. This definition is appealing because the reproductive pattern which yields the highest equilibrium density produces the most eggs and recruits, except when N_A^* and N_B^* are very similar (see Table III below). For the life history variations outlined above the trends in N_A^*/N_B^* and $N_A^*(O)/N_B^*(O)$ in relation to different parameters are consistent so either criterion could be used to evaluate fitness.

D. Implementation of the model

This completes the general description of the model. Though it is not intended to mimic any particular population, to insure some sense of reality the nominal values chosen for the 13 parameters and initial abundance and size-at-age are based on the southern Gulf of St Lawrence cod population (Ware, 1980; Lett, 1978). A computer was assigned the task of keeping track of the abundance and energy budgets of 22 age-groups (ages 4–25) for a simulated period of 220 yr. Briefly, the algorithm starts with a matrix defining the abundance and mean weight of the members of each age group at the beginning of year T. Equation (1) specifies the surplus power available to each individual at age X, so the reproductive rate at the end of year T can be calculated using Eq (3a) or (b), as appropriate. Equation (4) defines the initial abundance of age group X; whereas the subsequent abundance and body weight at age 4 (recruitment) are obtained from Eqs (5) and (2), respectively, and are catenated into the appropriate position in the abundance and weight-at-age matrix in year $T+4$. To begin the next loop, $W(X+1, T+1)$ and $N(X+1, T+1)$ are computed for each age group according to Eq (6) and (7), respectively (where $M(X,T)$ is specified by Eq (8a) or (b), as appropriate), etc.

The sensitivity of the population to variations in a particular life history parameter was examined by systematically changing its nominal value while the rest were held constant. As a convention, to identify the various combinations of reproductive and mortality functions, the notation $A(I)$ indicates the population response when it adopts reproductive strategy A and experiences a type I mortality process.

III. POPULATION RESPONSE CHARACTERISTICS

A. Transient response

The equations governing the dynamics of the population contain two density dependent processes common to both strategies, namely the surplus power supply and juvenile survival, and an additional density dependent factor which regulates the reproductive rate for strategy A. If the feedback for this control system is stable the response of the population to an input (the initial abundance and body weight of each age group) will contain a steady state solution and a transient response which decays exponentially to zero as T approaches infinity. For first and second order underdamped systems the transient terms have the form $R(O)\text{EXP}(-\alpha T)$ and $R(O)\text{EXP}(-\alpha T)\cdot(\text{COS}\omega T + A)$, respectively (Milsum, 1966). In both cases the decay is determined by $\text{EXP}(-\alpha T)$. In this context, the predominant time constant (τ) is a useful concept since it measures the ability of the population to reach equilibrium after perturbation, and is defined as the time required to make the exponent $-\alpha T$ equal to -1; hence $\tau = 1/\alpha$. A large time constant therefore implies that the population takes a long time to return to a steady state.

In the simulations the changing structure of the population often produced a complex transient response in abundance and size-at-age where the oscillations resembled, but were not exactly sinusoidal in nature (Fig. 2). When this occurred a minimum estimate of the predominant time constant was obtained by calculating the exponential decay in successive minima of the transient response according to the equation:

$$R(T) = R(O)\text{EXP}(-T/\tau)$$

where $R(O)$ is the non-dimensional response in year 0 (Fig. 3). An analysis of the maxima usually produced a higher value.

From this brief discussion it is not surprising that the time constant is sensitive to the number of mature age groups (K) in the population. We will restrict our attention to the recruitment response. For case $A(I)$ and the nominal parameter values the recruitment time constant exhibited a local maximum when $K = 6$ (ages 4–9) and a local minimum when $K = 13$ (Fig. 4). The time constant and period eventually stabilized when $K > 17$.

Any factor which alters the mortality rate will naturally change the population age structure, but not in the dramatic way implied by Fig. 4, which illustrates the response of a truncated population where the mortality rate of age-group $K + 4$ is infinite. When the mortality parameter M_1 (or M_2) was allowed to vary, the recruitment time constant for a type A population rose to a maximum at an intermediate mortality rate, while the period of oscillation

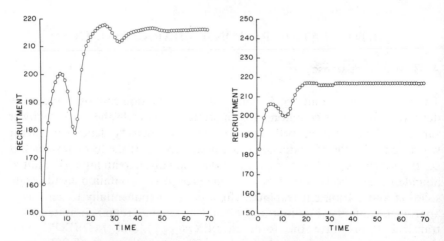

Fig. 2.   Time-dependent change in recruitment of age 4 fish in a type A (left panel) and type B (right panel) population when the life history parameters have the nominal values in Table III, and experience type I mortality. Only the first 70 yr of the simulation are shown. Notice the change in the vertical scale in the right panel.

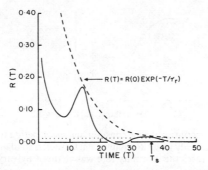

Fig. 3. Method for estimating the predominant time constant (τ_r) of the non-dimensional recruitment response, $R(T)$. The transient response shown above was obtained by transforming the values $R'(T)$ shown in the left hand panel of Fig. 2, so $R(T) = 1 - R'(T)/R^*$ where R^* is the equilibrium value. The settling time (T_S) represents the time required for the initial response to reach and remain within a specified percentage of R^*. Thus for a unit response where $R(O) = 1$, it will take $4.61 \tau_r$ yr for recruitment to return to within 99% of the equilibrium value. In this example $T_S = 35$ yr.

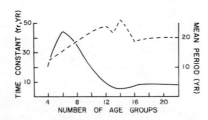

Fig. 4. Relation between the number of age groups in a type A(I) population, the recruitment time constant (solid line), and the mean period of oscillation (broken line).

generally decreased in relation to M^* (mean mortality rate at equilibrium) for both mortality functions (Fig. 5). Notice that the type II mortality regime was more effective in stabilizing recruitment and therefore produced a smaller time constant, a richer age distribution and hence a longer period between large year-classes.

The sensitivity of the population was also closely linked to the density dependent exponent A_2 in Eq (1). As this parameter increased in value the population moved through the familiar stability domains: (1) a monotonic approach to equilibrium recruitment (R^*), (2) a damped oscillatory approach to R^* (i.e. Fig. 2), (3) an overshoot and damped oscillatory decline to R^*, (4) undamped stable limit cycles where the time constant was infinite, and finally (5) chaotic behaviour characterized by irregular oscillations and periodicity. Figure 6 shows that reproductive strategy $B(I)$ produced smaller time constants over a wider range of values in A_2; however, it exhibited stable limit cycles at lower values of A_2 than case $A(I)$.

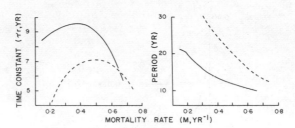

Fig. 5. Variation in the recruitment time constant and mean period of oscillation in relation to the average age-specific mortality rate at equilibrium. Case $A(I)$ solid line; case $A(II)$ broken line. In both cases the mortality rate was changed by varying M_1.

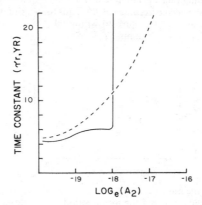

Fig. 6. Effect of the density-dependent exponent A_2 on the recruitment time constant. Notice that reproductive pattern $B(I)$-solid line-exhibits stable limit cycles when $\log_e A_2 > -18$. In contrast, reproduction pattern $A(I)$ did not produce stable limit cycles until $\log_e A_2 > -14$. At the other extreme, notice that the time constants for both reproductive patterns converge as A_2 approaches 0.

Sensitivity analysis of reproductive pattern $A(I)$ indicated that an increase in the value of all the parameters, except c, caused the recruitment time constants estimated from the decay in successive minima and maxima to either increase ($+$ sign) or decrease ($-$ sign) in the same direction (Table I). The time constants were most sensitive to changes in the surplus power and reproductive power exponents ζ and ϕ, and least sensitive to variations in the growth parameters A_1 and W_σ, and the reproductive rate constant c. I should caution that the implications of this comparison may be misleading in practice, because ζ and ϕ seem to vary by less than a factor of two between different stocks and species, whereas A_1, A_2, W_σ, and c might vary by an order

TABLE I. Sensitivity of the recruitment time constant to various life history parameters.

Parameter (Y)	Nominal value	$\Delta\tau_r$ (min) (%)	$\Delta\tau_r$ (max) (%)
A_1	$6\cdot2 \times 10^{-9}$	$+0\cdot9$	$+1\cdot1$
A_2	$9\cdot2 \times 10^{-9}$	$+2\cdot6$	$+1\cdot7$
M_1	$4\cdot1$	(1)	(1)
M_2	$2\cdot8 \times 10^{-3}$	(1)	(1)
θ	$2\cdot3 \times 10^{-4}$	$+2\cdot6$	$+0\cdot6$
C	$9\cdot3$	$-1\cdot2$	$+9\cdot3$
ϕ	$1\cdot4$	$+20\cdot7$	$+32\cdot9$
δ	$14\cdot5$	$-8\cdot5$	$-6\cdot1$
ζ	$0\cdot6$	$-33\cdot4$	$-43\cdot9$
W_σ	1000	$-1\cdot0$	$-3\cdot6$
ψ	4×10^4	$+2\cdot9$	$+7\cdot1$
γ	4×10^{-9}	$-2\cdot6$	$-5\cdot6$

(1) The time constant is a complex function of Y (Fig. 5).

$\Delta\tau_r$ indicates the percent change in the time constant; estimated from successive recruitment minima $\Delta\tau_r$ (min) and maxima $\Delta\tau_r$ (max), produced by a 10% increase in the nominal value of the parameter.

of magnitude or more (Ware, 1980). The latter parameters, therefore, may be far more important in determining the predominant time constant in natural populations than Table I suggests.

To sum up we can make the following general observations about a population's transient response characteristics: reproductive pattern B produces small abundance and size-at-age time constants because the reproductive rate is not affected by changes in density. On the other hand, a type II mortality function yields small time constants because the mortality rate is a decreasing function of body size, so the potential instability produced by large recruiting year-classes is effectively damped by density dependent growth. The combination of a type A reproductive pattern and type I mortality process therefore produces the greatest instability in abundance and size-at-age, whereas the converse is true for the combination $B(II)$. So far as the action of specific parameters is concerned, an increase in the density dependent exponents A_1 and A_2, the reproductive parameters θ and ϕ, and the recruitment coefficient ψ cause the time constants to increase, while the remaining parameters (except M_1 and M_2) have the opposite effect. As a rule the period of oscillation in the abundance and mean size of all age groups varied between two to three times the mean age at equilibrium for strategy $A(I)$ and about two to four times the mean age for strategy $A(II)$.

B. Steady-state response

Recall that the time constant measures how rapidly a population returns to equilibrium following a disturbance. In the overly simplified scheme considered here there are no random environmental effects so the time constant has nothing to do with fitness, which was defined in terms of the reproductive rate of the population when it reached a stable equilibrium (Eq 9). For comparison, the steady state characteristics produced by both reproductive patterns for the nominal parameter values are summarized in Table II. The relative fitness of each strategy centres around the reproductive rates of young versus old age groups. Strategy A invariably leads to a richer equilibrium age distribution with a higher mean age and body weight. These older individuals are larger and more prolific and therefore bear most of the reproductive burden of the population. In contrast, strategy B results in a lower mean age and weight at equilibrium, so most of the egg production is contributed by the younger mature age groups which allocate a significant fraction of their surplus power to reproduction. In Table II the type A population had a lower fitness for the type I mortality case because it was unable to accumulate enough large, fecund individuals, whereas for the type II case it could. This also explains in a more general context why reproductive strategy A yields the

TABLE II. Steady-state characteristics of the adult population produced by reproductive patterns A and B for both mortality functions and the nominal parameter values.

Characteristic	Pattern A		Pattern B		A/B
Type I Mortality					
$N(O)^*$	636×10^{11}		656×10^{11}		0·97
N^*	1221×10^6		918×10^6		1·33
B^*	1382×10^9 g		797×10^9 g		1·73
X^*	7·86	yr	6·95	yr	1·13
W^*	1132	g	868	g	1·30
M^*	0·20	yr^{-1}	0·27	yr^{-1}	0·74
P^*/B^*	0·30		0·35		0·86
Type II Mortality					
$N(O)^*$	1305×10^{11}		1281×10^{11}		1·02
N^*	892×10^6		820×10^6		1·09
B^*	1351×10^9 g		1073×10^9 g		1·26
X^*	7·28	yr	7·01	yr	1·04
W^*	1515	g	1308	g	1·16
M^*	0·30	yr^{-1}	0·33	yr^{-1}	0·91
P^*/B^*	0·30		0·32		0·94

Symbols: egg production $(N(O)^*)$, density (N^*), biomass (B^*), production (P^*), mean age (X^*), mean weight (W^*), mean mortality rate (M^*).

highest fitness when the age-specific mortality rate is low. As soon as the average mortality rate exceeds some critical value, however, the advantage shifts in favour of strategy B (Fig. 7). Where this crossover occurs depends on the precise form of the mortality function. In general it appears as if strategy A is more adaptive over a wider range of mortality rates when the population experiences a mortality process which includes both a size dependent and reproductive cost component (type II).

Sensitivity analysis indicated that the fitness of strategy A was a generally decreasing function of M_1 and M_2, the recruitment parameter ψ and the growth coefficient W_σ (Table III). On the other hand, fitness was a complex function of the density dependent exponents A_1 and A_2 and the recruitment parameter γ; as there was more than one value, in each case where the equilibrium egg production of both reproduction strategies was equal (Fig. 8). In this example, the abrupt change in the fitness curves at high values of A_2 occurred when the age-specific growth patterns produced by both reproductive patterns became increasingly unrealistic. The results for extreme values of A_2 therefore should not be taken seriously because the intensity of density dependence required to produce this phenomenon is unlikely to occur in natural populations.

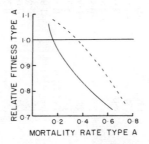

Fig. 7.   Fitness of reproductive strategy A in relation to the average age-specific mortality rate at equilibrium. The solid line indicates the fitness curve for type I mortality and the broken line, type II mortality. The mortality rate was changed by varying M_1.

In general, an increase in the mortality parameters (M_1, M_2) the reproductive rate parameters (c, θ, ϕ) the growth coefficient W_σ and the recruitment parameters (ψ, γ) decreased the mean age of both a type A and type B population. Table III shows that any parameter change which increased the mean age of a type A, relative to a type B, population tended to increase the fitness of strategy A. However, there were notable exceptions where variations in δ, ζ and W_σ produced trends in the relative mean age of A/B that were opposite to the corresponding trends in fitness. The relative mean age was most sensitive to changes in the exponents M_1, ϕ and ζ.

TABLE III. Sensitivity of fitness and relative mean age (X_A^*/X_B^*) of a type A population to different life history parameters.

Parameter (Y)	Nominal value	Type I mortality			Type II mortality		
		$\Delta F_y^*(A)$ (%)	$F_A^* = F_B^*$	$\Delta X_y^*(A)$ (%)	$\Delta F_y^*(A)$ (%)	$F_A^* = F_B^*$	$\Delta X_y^*(A)$ (%)
A_1	6.2×10^{-9}	-0.20	(3)	-0.5	$+0.14$	(3)	-0.2
A_2	9.2×10^{-9}	-0.31	(3)	$+1.0$	-0.14	(3)	$+0.6$
M_1	4.1	-10.2	4.0	-3.0	$+6.7(1)$	0.24	$+0.5$
M_2	2.8×10^{-3}	-1.7	2.3×10^{-3}	-0.9	$-1.7(1)$	0.59	-0.2
θ	2.3×10^{-4}	$+1.2$	2.9×10^{-4}	$+0.8$	$+0.2$	(2)	$+0.3$
C	9.3	$+1.1$	11.7	$+0.9$	$+0.3$	3.9	$+0.3$
ϕ	14	$+11.8$	1.4	$+5.7$	$+9.5$	1.4	$+1.5$
δ	14.5	$+1.3$	18.2	-0.5	$+2.0$	14.8	-0.1
ζ	0.6	$+11.3$	0.6	-1.9	$+10.5$	0.6	-0.6
W_σ	1000	-0.2	(2)	$+0.6$	-0.2	2150	$+0.2$
ψ	4×10^4	-0.04	(2)	-0.06	-0.01	9.0×10^5	$-0.02(4)$
γ	4×10^{-9}	-0.6	(3)	-0.2	-0.05	2.0×10^{-8}	$+0.05(4)$

(1) For type II mortality function $M_1 = 0.25$, $M_2 = 0.51$.
(2) There is no value of Y in the vicinity of the nominal value where $F_A^* = F_B^*$.
(3) Fitness is a complex function of Y, more than one value where $F_A^* = F_B^*$.
(4) Mean age is a complex function of Y.

$\Delta F_y^*(A)$ and $\Delta X_y^*(A)$ indicate the per cent change in fitness and relative mean age at equilibrium produced by a 10% increase in the nominal value of Y. $F_A^* = F_B^*$ indicates the value of Y where the fitness of both types is equal. The sign specifies whether fitness and mean age are increasing ($+$) or decreasing ($-$) functions of Y.

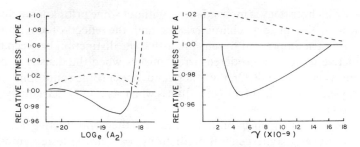

Fig. 8. Fitness of reproductive pattern A in relation to the value of the density-dependent exponent A_2 and the recruitment parameter γ. The solid and broken lines as before (Fig. 7).

IV. IMPLICATIONS

It is clear from the foregoing analysis that no single reproductive pattern is universally adaptive. Instead there is some combination of life history characteristics where each strategy confers the highest fitness. For strategy A the reproductive rate was an increasing function of the body weight and a decreasing function of the density of each age group. As the abundance of this population increased the young mature age-groups invested proportionally more surplus energy in growth than reproduction and consequently experienced a reduced mortality rate. At equilibrium, the population therefore had a high mean age because more individuals lived longer and these large, venerable fish contributed most of the offspring. For the cases examined above, strategy A produced larger time constants and a higher fitness when the average age-specific mortality rate was low. This strategy, or a variation on this theme, is therefore likely to be characteristic of a long-lived species.

By contrast, when the reproductive rate is solely a function of body weight, the young age-groups in the mature portion of a type B population invest a higher fraction of their surplus energy in egg production than type A individuals of the same size and age. This results in a higher mortality rate at equilibrium and lower mean age in a type B population. In the absence of environmental disturbances, this strategy generates small time constants so the population is inherently more stable and, at least in principle, quickly returns to a steady-state after perturbation. A constant reproductive rate in relation to body size is therefore likely to confer a high evolutionary fitness in a short-lived species.

These generalizations must be interpreted cautiously. At best they only offer a rough guide, because the fitness of each reproductive strategy is so sensitive to the energy allocation parameters and mortality process during the juvenile and adult phases of the life cycle, that it is difficult to predict with certainty which strategy is most adaptive without some prior knowledge of the population's life history characteristics and the effect of environmental factors. It is also important to remember that the distinction between the two reproductive patterns considered here vanishes when the density dependent exponent A_2 is very small. On the other hand, under some conditions, a type A strategy yields a significantly higher fitness when A_2 is only marginally greater than zero (Fig. 8).

The strong dependence of the fitness of the reproductive pattern on longevity suggests some general predictions that can be tested empirically. Specifically, in a species adopting a type A strategy, Eq. (3a) implies that individuals of the same weight should invest proportionally more surplus power in reproduction when the available supply is large. Hence for a given body weight (W):

$$R(W) = aS(W)^b$$

where $b \geq 1 \cdot 0$. Conversely, if the reproductive rate is strictly a function of body weight then $b = 0$.

Experiments by Hislop et al. (1978) indicate for a long-lived species like haddock that $R(W)$ is an increasing function of $S(W)$. A multiple regression analysis of these data which accounted for the variation in body size in the experimental animals suggested that $b \sim 2 \cdot 0$ for the five fish of similar weight fed high rations; when the largest fish (41·3 cm) was included in the regression, $b = 1 \cdot 1$. Thus, as expected $1 \cdot 0 < b < 2 \cdot 0$ for haddock. On the other hand, the five fish held on rations below, or at, maintenance level subsidized reproduction by drawing upon their somatic energy reserves. This response was not anticipated and implies that haddock may adopt a form of bet-hedging if they experience a protracted physiological stress imposed by very poor feeding conditions. Hislop et al. observed that the fish on low rations risked some of their somatic energy to reproduce, but did not deplete the soma to a potentially lethal level to maintain the same size-specific fecundity as wild fish.

In a short-lived species like stickleback the reproductive rate is determined strictly by body size at the beginning of the interspawning interval. A re-examination of Wootton and Evans (1976) data confirmed that $b = 0$ and hence that $R(W)$ was indeed independent of $S(W)$. If the available food supply is inadequate to cover the cost of egg production both stickleback and medaka (Hirshfield, 1980) lose weight to a greater extent than haddock and winter flounder (Tyler and Dunn, 1976). The former species seem to exhibit a type B strategy.

These considerations illustrate that management agencies should be aware of the life history characteristics of exploited stocks. In populations with an extended age structure, for example, a small increase in the mortality rate of the virgin stock, caused by exploitation, could shift the long term selective advantage from a type A to type B reproductive pattern (Fig. 7). Assuming there is some polymorphism for this characteristic in the population, fishing raises some important questions about possible changes in genetic composition that can affect the yield and sensitivity of the population (Shepherd and Horwood, 1977). The life history patterns considered here also imply that exploitation can decrease the average natural mortality rate (M^*) when the latter depends on either body size, growth rate or abundance. Some preliminary calculations suggest that the trade-off between fishing and natural mortality is likely to be most significant for a type I mortality function, particularly when A_1 and A_2 approximate to zero. On the other hand, M^* is very insensitive to fishing mortality if the population experiences a type II mortality process. The management implications of other suspected mortality and reproductive functions that explicitly include stochastic environmental factors should be explored. In this context, Murphy's (1967) pioneering analysis of the demise of the Pacific sardine, which failed to cope with over-exploitation and a fluctuating environment, highlights the practical significance of the problem.

ACKNOWLEDGEMENTS

I am grateful to Jeff McRuer, who wrote the computer program, and to Carl Walters, Bruce Leaman, and Jake Schweigert for their comments.

REFERENCES

Bell, G. (1980). *Am. Nat.* **116**, 45–76.
Beverton, R. J. H. and Holt, S. J. (1957). *Fish. Invest., Lond.* Ser. **2**, 19.
Beverton, R. J. H. and Holt, S. J. (1959). *In* "The Lifespan of Animals" (G. E. W. Wolstenholme and M. O'Connor, eds), pp. 142–177. Little, Brown and Co., Boston.
Calow, P. (1979). *Biol. Rev.* **54**, 23–40.
Charlesworth, B. and J. A. Leon (1976). *Am. Nat.* **110**, 449–459.
Cushing, D. H. (1975). "Marine Ecology and Fisheries". Cambridge University Press, Cambridge.
Goodman, D. (1982). *Am. Nat.* **119**, 803–823.
Hirshfield, M. F. (1980). *Ecology* **61**, 282–292.
Hislop, J. R. G., Robb, A. P. and Gauld, J. A. (1978). *J. Fish. Biol.* **13**, 85–98.
Lett, P. F. (1978). "A comparative study of the recruitment mechanisms of cod and mackerel, their interaction, and its implications for dual stock management". Ph.D. Thesis, Dalhousie University, Halifax.
Levin, S. A. and Goodyear, C. P. (1980). *J. Math. Biol.* **9**, 245–274.
Mann, R. H. K. and Mills, C. A. (1979). *Symp. zool. Soc. Lond.* **44**, 161–177.
McKinnon, J. C. (1972). *J. Fish. Res. Bd Can.* **29**, 1749–1759.
Milsum, J. H. (1966). "Biological Control Systems Analysis". McGraw-Hill, New York.
Murphy, G. I. (1967). *Ecology* **48**, 731–736.

Schaffer, W. M. (1974). *Ecology* **55**, 291–303.
Schaffer, W. M. and Rosenzweig, M. L. (1977). *Ecology* **58**, 60–72.
Shepherd, J. G. and Horwood, J. W. (1977). *J. Cons. int. Explor. Mer* **38**, 318–323.
Tyler, A. V. and Dunn, R. S. (1976). *J. Fish. Res. Bd Can.* **33**, 63–75.
Ware, D. M. (1980). *Can. J. Fish. aquat. Sci.* **37**, 1012–1024.
Ware, D. M. (1982). *Can. J. Fish. aquat. Sci.* **39**, 3–13.
Wootton, R. J. and Evans, G. W. (1976). *J. Fish. Biol.* **8**, 385–395.

20. Reproductive Strategies and the Response to Exploitation

D. J. GARROD and J. W. HORWOOD

Ministry of Agriculture, Fisheries and Food, Directorate of Fisheries Research, Fisheries Laboratory, Lowestoft. U.K.

Abstract: The life history characteristics of stocks have evolved to overcome adversity by providing growth potential and this in turn determines potential yield and the response to exploitation. The effect is most readily seen in the stock and recruitment relationship. Three categories of spawning strategy are chosen to describe the effect, "bypass", intermediate and "saturation" spawners. The major commercial resources are "saturation" spawners, the surplus yield arising through density dependent processes in the early life history, which compensate for reduced spawning potential. It is argued that the degree of compensation is related not to variations in the density dependent process as a mechanism, but from spatial and temporal heterogeneity. It is further argued that the effect has permitted the evolution of late maturity with the result that within the saturation spawning group small stocks require high compensation to overcome variability, and are therefore less sensitive to exploitation than are larger stocks, where the variability is buffered in the distributional characteristics leading to a much greater response to exploitation.

I. INTRODUCTION

We interpret a "successful" species to be one that has so far been able to ensure the continuity of its existence. In that sense numerically abundant and relatively rare species can both be seen to be successful and it is equally obvious that success can be achieved by a wide variety of life history characteristics. It is also axiomatic that success is associated with the ability to withstand some degree of adversity and that this in turn can only be achieved if a population has some "growth potential". Fisheries exploit this growth potential and sustainable harvest is synonymous with surplus production. Stocks which have little potential to overcome adversity can yield only small surplus production rates and similarly a high potential leads to a larger surplus, so the understanding of strategies used for survival and their implication for population growth potential can offer guidance to fishery

FISH REPRODUCTION
ISBN: 0–12–563660–1

managers seeking to exploit it (Ware, Chap. 19, this volume). The growth potential is most easily recognized through the stock and recruitment relationship since most of the natural modulation of population numbers in fish occurs in the early life history, but the effects are modified by differing demographic parameters such as mortality rates, growth, age at maturity, etc.

This paper identifies broad categories of reproductive strategy which can be related to growth and hence fishery potential. Stock and recruitment data from major commercial resources are reviewed to illustrate quantitatively the mechanism that generates surplus production and it will be suggested that one of the essential characteristics of the data, the density dependent compensation, may be influenced by spatial and temporal heterogeneity in the distribution of progeny. This in turn leads to the view that heterogeneity itself has a role in the evolution of life history characteristics and the mechanisms to overcome early mortality, and its variability.

II. LIFE HISTORY MECHANISMS IN RELATION TO MORTALITY

The mechanisms required to ensure "success" can be divided into characteristics which determine the number of young born (e.g. growth, fecundity, etc.) and those which influence the survival of offspring. Both aspects are of course closely related but there is a variety of combinations of characteristics that could provide the same number of offspring. It is convenient, therefore, to consider first strategies that modulate the early mortality.

Two limiting strategies can be identified in the already familiar extremes of r and K selection. Species either produce small numbers of eggs adapted for high survival and by-pass the vulnerable stage, or they produce large numbers of small eggs with low survival but enough eggs to absorb the risk. A slightly less extreme component of the "by-pass" group would include species with behavioural adaptations to protect the embryonic or vulnerable early stages (Potts, Chap. 13, this volume).

This first group as a whole is exemplified in aquatic animals by many elasmobranchs, marine mammals and, as Mann and Mills (1979) list them, Cichlidae, Cottidae, Gasterosteidae and Syngnathidae which all exhibit some degree of parental care associated with relatively low individual fecundity. The time series of data have not yet been of sufficient length or quality to permit analysis of stock and recruitment for most species within this group, but Holden's examination of the reproductive features of elasmobranchs, particularly the rays (Holden, 1977), and the protracted decline and collapse of, for example, the great whales, allow us to infer that the density dependent mechanisms are weak. Further support for this inference is provided by the ovo-viviparous *Sebastes* spp. (redfish) populations in the north Atlantic, and in the natural populations of Cichlidae which exhibit strong territoriality, and where local depletion can be rapid. In effect the rate of exploitation can rapidly exceed the rate of production leading to the periodic withdrawal of effort and an intermittent fishery. Picken's observations on Antarctic benthic invertebrates (Picken, 1980) suggest they would also fall into the same "low production" group. He records the prevalence of non-pelagic development by egg capsules, brooding and viviparity which are seen as adaptations to a variable environment, including the risk of dispersal away from suitable habitats.

The bypass type includes species with very low fecundity and others where fecundity is somewhat higher, but which exhibit special behavioural and/or morphological adaptations to provide at least some measure of protection to the vulnerable stages. The history of the fishery for *Notothenia rossi* off South Georgia suggests that they tend not to support large and sustained fisheries.

The very productive and enduring commercial fisheries are based on the second group, the highly fecund species that utilize the planktonic environment as the dispersal phase either in the egg or larval stage, or both. The larger gadoids, pleuronectids and scombrids are familiar types which achieve their success by sheer "weight" of egg numbers. These are the "saturation" spawners where the surplus available for harvest arises by taking advantage of the compensatory improvements in survival during the early life history which follow a natural or fishery induced reduction in spawning stock.

There are others whose offspring occupy a similar habitat, but which have a much lower fecundity per spawning and which must therefore exhibit some other adaptation to overcome high mortality in the early life history. Serial spawning may be regarded as one example enabling morphologically small species to boost their fecundity of eggs which are essentially the same size as those produced by saturation spawners. This has been clearly demonstrated for the anchovy (Hunter and Leong, 1981) and may be characteristic of many more (Hislop, Chap. 17, this volume).

Ware (1975) has discussed the range of variation in egg size and growth of fish larvae as it affects their survival. Typically the fecundity of species producing large eggs is lower, and they produce larger larvae which are deemed to be less vulnerable to mortality. The numerical requirement of replacement dictates this must be so. But if one considers the trajectory in numbers of a cohort of relatively small eggs, the variations in egg size could be seen as adaptations to join a more general mortality process at different points. Increase in egg size may simply delay the point of entry and there is no reason or evidence to demonstrate that the mortality rates of organisms of comparable size actually differ. The total deaths of a species producing small or large eggs will differ, but the mortality rates of a size interval may not.

The relative abundance of adjacent size groups of very young fish may be more consistent than is generally supposed, and may even be characteristic. It may also follow that the compensatory adjustments of mortality with stock size that determine stock and recruitment relationships also exhibit a degree of generality. These numerical (if not biological) mechanisms can be demonstrated in analysis of stock and recruitment data for a range of species using, for example, the Shepherd model (see below).

III. STOCK AND RECRUITMENT AND THE RESPONSE TO EXPLOITATION IN "SATURATION" SPAWNERS

Shepherd (1982) has proposed a new model of the stock and recruitment relationship which, through the inclusion of a third parameter, is less constrained than previous models by preconceived ideas on biological mechanisms involved. It is expressed as

$$R = aE/\{1 + (E/K)^\beta\} \tag{1}$$

where R is the recruitment, E the spawning stock as eggs, a the density independent variable, β the degree of compensation and K a parameter defining the stock size above which density dependent processes increasingly predominate. The log transformation of this model to

$$\ln(E/R) = \ln(1 + (E/K)^\beta) + \ln(1/a) \tag{2}$$

describes the trend of mortality, $\ln(E/R)$, in the pre-recruit phase which determines the relationship. Figure 1 (from Shepherd, 1982) demonstrates the implication of variation in the compensation coefficient β. The two forms in equations 1 and 2 are represented diagramatically in Fig. 2 where it can be seen the log transformation has been summarized as two straight line sections joined by a smooth interpolation. The density independent mortality ($\ln 1/a$) is represented by the horizontal segment: for stock sizes less than K recruitment

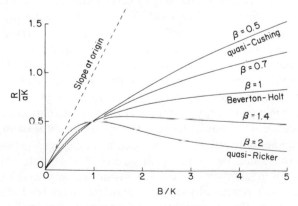

Fig. 1.   The form of the stock recruitment relationship (after Shepherd, 1982).

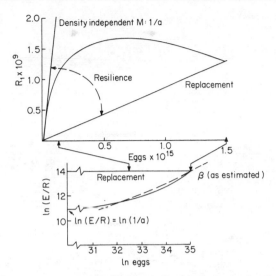

Fig. 2. Diagrammatic representation of the relationship between the Shepherd stock and recruitment model and its log transformation.

will be to all intents and purposes proportional to stock size for all values of β. The inclined segment estimates the rate of compensation of density dependent mortality with stock size (β). It also has an intercept with $\ln(E/R)$ estimated from independent egg per recruit studies following Garrod and Knights (1979), which estimates virgin stock size.

The difference $\ln(E/R) - \ln(1/a)$ reflects the scope for compensation in density dependent mortality in the early life history, or the "resilience". At the extreme, if the pre-recruit mortality is generated by density independent factors alone recruitment will be proportional to stock size, the stock would have no resilience and would eventually decline in response to any maintained level of exploitation. This is well illustrated by a recent review of the California sardine (MacCall, 1979), and reproduced in the form of the present analysis in Fig. 3a. Stocks capable of compensation can offset exploitation up to a limit determined by the resilience, but the point of maximum yield and the annual level of fishing mortality associated with it will depend on the reproductive characteristics of the stock and the age groups being exploited.

Using data from Garrod (1982) and Brander and Wood (pers. comm.) Figure 3b–d illustrates the pre-recruit mortality between eggs and one-year-old recruits against stock size as eggs for three herring, four cod, and two plaice stocks which occur in ecologically comparable habitats and which might therefore be expected to exhibit a similar response. The range of observations is not sufficient to identify all the parameters of the Shepherd model, but a minimum compensation (β) can be estimated by the coefficient of

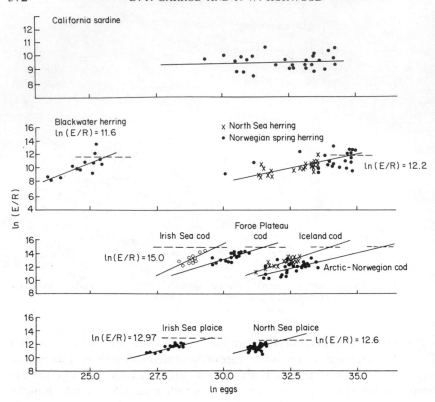

Fig. 3. Log transformed stock and recruitment data for selected stocks: (a) California sardine; (b) Blackwater, North Sea, Norwegian spring spawning herring; (c) Irish Sea, Faroe, Iceland, Arcto-Norwegian cod; (d) Irish Sea, North Sea plaice.

linear regression assuming $E \gg K$, as seems reasonable from the proximity of the data to the replacement level and the general shape of the stock and recruitment curve. These estimates of β are summarized in Table I together with estimates of the "virgin stock" size determined from the regression at the value $\ln(E/R)$ corresponding to the fecundity per recruit. Two points arise from the analysis.

The first point concerns the level of total mortality $(\ln E/R)$ of the cod and herring in the same range of stock size (as eggs). At the stock size $\exp 32 \cdot 5 = 130 \times 10^{12}$ the pre-recruit mortality of Arcto-Norwegian cod is close to $\ln(E/R) = 12 \cdot 0$, but for North Sea and Norwegian spring spawning herring it is $\ln(E/R) = 10 \cdot 0$, i.e. almost an order of magnitude higher survival. Herring are morphologically much smaller than cod and have a correspondingly lower fecundity of similar sized eggs. The stock in eggs of herring can therefore only be supported by a lower mortality, i.e. better survival. Because of the similarity of the planktonic environments of the larval stages of the two species (for Norwegian spring spawning herring and Arcto-Norwegian cod their areas coincide), it is tempting to conclude that herring achieve their abundance by an advantage conferred by the demersal egg habit. As with serial spawning the demersal egg may be an adaptation whereby some species achieve an adequate population survival from a morphologically small size.

The second point from Fig. 3 and Table I discussed below, concerns the variation of the compensation coefficient, (β) between stocks of the same species.

TABLE I. Compensation coefficients (β') and unexploited stock size in selected stocks.

Stock	β'	Virgin stock size	
		ln E	Eggs $\times 10^{12}$
Blackwater herring	1·71	25·5	0·02
North Sea herring	0·64	36·0	4226
Irish Sea cod	1·82	29·8	9
Faroe Plateau cod	1·14	33·0	215
Iceland cod	1·04	34·0	583
Arcto-Norwegian cod	0·87	36·1	4959
Irish Sea plaice	0·96	29·6	7
North Sea plaice	0·88	32·6	142

IV. SPATIAL HETEROGENEITY AND THE STOCK AND RECRUITMENT RELATIONSHIP

The data presented in Fig. 3 are not sufficient to estimate $\ln(1/a)$ or K of the Shepherd model so there may be differences in the resilience of the different stocks. It is, however, clear from Table I that the coefficient of the linear regression, β', as an estimator of β, is inversely related to virgin stock size. It is of course statistically true that β' and virgin stock size could be correlated because the two variables ln E and $\ln(E/R)$ are not independent but this feature is the same for all stocks and the interstock or species comparisons are still likely to be valid. In addition, we note the estimates of virgin stock size depend on additional biological information and for most of the stocks illustrated they fall close to the upper limit of the data. The conclusion can be put on a firmer basis by applying the same approach to other stocks (Garrod, 1982) and plotting estimates of β' against virgin stock size for a number of quite different stocks. This is shown in Fig. 4. Clearly, the smaller stocks exhibit a greater degree of compensation.

Figure 3 records the same level of pre-recruit mortality in different stocks and at different stock sizes. This suggests the mechanisms involved might be unique to each stock, but whilst this is likely to be true of the biological details, e.g. preferred prey organisms, it is not sufficient to explain the apparently systematic variation in compensation coefficients shown in Fig. 4. These point to a more general characteristic associated with stock size *per se* rather than to the biological minutae.

Table II summarizes estimates of egg and larval mortality in plaice and cod populations around the British Isles (Bannister *et al.*, 1974; Harding *et al.*, 1974; Harding and Nichols, 1977). The authors describe the trajectory of mortality in each survey by linear regression; they were unable to detect the non-linearity required to characterize density dependence in mortality *rate* within the year. We note also the mortalities in these surveys are similar to the estimate of 8% per day for Atlantic mackerel off north America recorded by Sette (1943), and indeed to the rates recorded for turbot and sole where, even under experimental rearing conditions (B. R. Howell, pers. comm.), the mortalities are characteristically very high and variable. Clearly, it is difficult to establish significant differences in the mortality in the early life history between stocks of the same species, and having in mind the evidently real variability of the process, one may doubt whether real differences do exist.

If there is no convincing evidence that the *mortality rate* of eggs and larvae (as opposed to absolute deaths) is dependent on their own density, it is then possible that the rate is a consistent property of the planktonic ecosystem, and that the compensation coefficient is a response to some other factor. The idea has its attractions because the evolution of life history

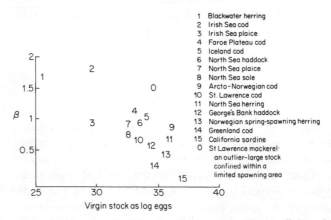

Fig. 4. The relationship between the estimator of the compensation coefficient, β', and virgin stock size.

TABLE II.   Mortality rate (Z) in the early life history of cod and plaice.

| | | Z/day | |
		Eggs	Egg stage 1 to larval stage 4
Plaice			
Southern Bight	1962	0·074	0·066
	1963	0·021	
	1968	0·071	0·068
	1969	0·074	0·021
	1971	0·118	0·067
West Central North Sea	1976	0·04	
Irish Sea	1965	0·080	0·045
Cod			
Southern Bight	1968	0·021	
West Central North Sea	1976	0·14	

characteristics requires information on the demographic consequence of a variation which persists through the life cycle of successive generations. For example, information on the relative success of different variants is necessary for the selection that has fixed spawning seasons in time (Fig. 5). It would be easier to establish that persistence if the pre-recruit mortality is a process which depends only on stochastic variation in density independent mortality and which is not subject to density dependent variation.

In the biological sense a characteristic mortality would be consistent with the ideas of Sheldon *et al.* (1977) and Pope and Knights (1982) on the apparent stability of particle size distributions in the sea. Simply from the range of choice of food organisms of the same species in different circumstances, early

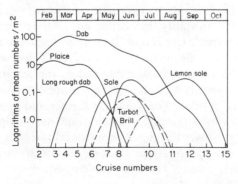

Fig. 5.   The seasonal distribution of egg production of different species off the northeast coast of England 1976 (after Harding *et al.*, in prep.).

mortality has to be a reflection of the relative abundance of particles of different sizes, predator or prey, rather than their identity. If that were so the mortality would also be a characteristic of the ecosystem.

The essential point from Fig. 3 is that the compensation coefficients may be different whilst the mortalities are the same and this requires explanation. Note, however, that in Fig. 3 stock size is expressed in absolute numbers of eggs and not as density, as would be required to identify true differences in density dependent mortality. The larger stocks occupy a larger geographical area and, frequently, a longer spawning season and the actual density of progeny may be equivalent in both large and small stocks of the same species. Indeed one would expect that to be so for reasons of adult spawning behaviour. It is not practicable to examine the data underlying Table I in terms of the relative density per unit time and space and the mortality rates per unit time and space may or may not differ between stocks. But it is evident the compensation coefficients do vary in the total environment within which the spawning takes place, and we note only that the inverse relationship between β and virgin stock size could be one result of heterogeneity in the distributions acting upon a characteristic mortality rate. At the extremes a very small stock spawning in a restricted area might generate only a single egg/larval "patch" whereas a larger stock will have preferred spawning localities within its spawning range leading to a distribution which is patchy in both time and space. This is illustrated in Fig. 6 of the distribution of plaice spawning around the British Isles. Because it is small, the Irish Sea spawning is more homogeneous than the total North Sea spawning but both are single stocks.

Heterogeneity will be a function of stock size and if spawning intensity and the local patch mortality processes were identical the average density dependent mortality over the whole stock will be lower in a larger stock than it will be in a smaller one. The rate of response to reduced stock size, as measured by the compensation coefficients, can also be expected to be lower.

We suggest that, whilst the minutae of the biological mechanisms of early mortality rates will vary, as yet there is little evidence of significant differences between stocks in the mortality they cause, and, if the hypothesis concerning mortality rate and particle size is true, there is no reason to expect significant differences at the microscale of the events involved. The observed variation in compensation coefficients might be explained by the scaling effect of spatial and temporal heterogeneity modulating the average outcome of a characteristic and fundamental process. We would go further and propose that a small stock with the saturation spawning strategy would need a highly compensated density dependent process to buffer environmental variation at the geographical scale involved, whereas the larger stock would already be partially buffered by the effect of heterogeneity. The effect has consequences for the response to exploitation.

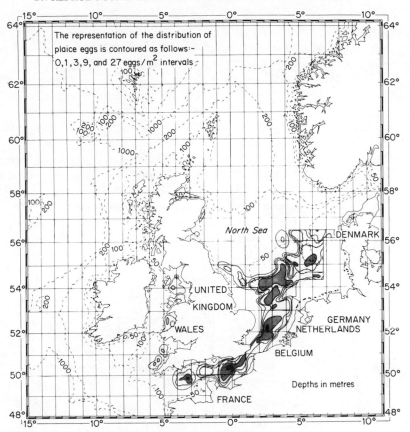

Fig. 6.   Geographical distribution of stage 1 eggs of plaice (Harding *et al.*, 1978).

V. THE EFFECT OF HETEROGENEITY ON RESILIENCE AND POTENTIAL YIELD

Figure 7 shows the stock and recruitment relationships for the cod stocks in Fig. 3, and others, retransformed but expressed in logarithmic form for convenience. For simplicity these assume the same values of $\ln(1/a)$ and with K estimated for Arcto-Norwegian cod and, for other stocks, pro-rated on the basis of the relative virgin stock size defined in Section III. These relationships can in turn be combined with the other demographic characteristics of the stocks, and the fishery, to describe the potential yield. These are shown in Fig. 8 for three stocks, the Faroe Plateau, Icelandic and Arcto-Norwegian cod, but

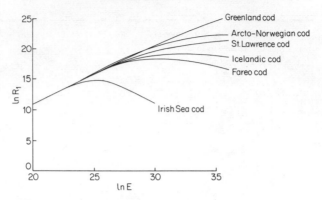

Fig. 7.   Stock and recruitment relationships of cod stocks.

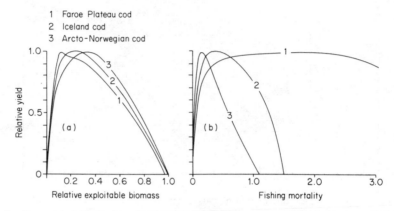

Fig. 8.   Potential yield of selected cod stocks in relation to: (a) exploitable biomass; (b) fishing mortality.

with the assumptions outlined above and exploitable biomass confined to fish of three years and older.

In the logarithmic form the estimated population fecundity per recruit $\ln(E/R))$ of the unexploited stocks are similar and with $\ln(1/a)$ assumed constant the three stocks would exhibit the same total resilience ($\ln E/R$ of the virgin stock minus $\ln(1/a)$) but with the different compensation coefficients. When combined with the other demographic characteristics, and notably growth and the age of maturity, it is clear that the larger stocks are less able to offset the proportionate effect of fishing. "Collapse" takes place at a lower level of annual fishing mortality, and at any lower level of exploitation they exhibit a greater proportional decline in stock size. The maximum yield of the larger stocks occurs at a higher relative stock size and lower level of exploitation than in smaller stocks. Indeed the Irish Sea cod was not included in Fig. 8 because at the age of recruitment to the fishery (i.e. first exploitation) taken to represent the larger stocks (three years), the proportion already mature would be sufficient to maintain the stock irrespective of the fishing mortality, i.e. without collapse and without detecting the maximum potential yield of the stock as a whole (i.e. including younger ages).

The general implication for exploitation of the relationship between β and stock size is supported by the history of these and other stocks with yields in the order $10^5–10^6$ tonnes. The Greenland and Arcto-Norwegian cod stocks have been severely depleted at an annual rate of exploitation much below that recorded for Irish Sea cod. The collapse of the California sardine has already been referred to and the Peruvian anchovetta stock almost certainly reflects the same effect. Parrish and MacCall's analysis of Pacific mackerel provides little evidence of compensation in the main body of their data (Parrish and MacCall, 1978). The North Sea mackerel collapsed very rapidly in the 1970s and recent analysis of the mackerel west of the British Isles shows its production to be rather low at 18–20% depending on stock size (Lockwood and Shepherd, in press).

The stocks that have shown a sharp response in yield, including collapse, have mainly been large ones and we do not believe this is a coincidence. We argue that being larger they will have more heterogenous distributions of progeny leading to lower compensation coefficients and a more rapid response to exploitation. It is perhaps worth noting here that Levin (1979) has shown that spatio-temporal patterns can be essential for the existence of co-dominant or sub-dominant groups and hence the stability of an ecosystem. The effect on a fish population is in many ways analogous.

Returning to the categories of strategy chosen in Section II, we can expect, in very general terms, that stocks which have adopted physiological and behavioural devices to overcome vulnerability of the early life history are unlikely to produce a substantial numerical surplus available for harvesting. Compensation coefficients can be expected to be small and the stocks sensitive to exploitation. But the argument presented above suggests that stocks which have adopted the high fecundity solution, and which have become large, *will also* tend to lower compensation coefficients and to relatively greater sensitivity to exploitation than smaller stocks with the same spawning strategy.

VI. A LINK BETWEEN HETEROGENEITY AND LIFE HISTORY CHARACTERISTICS

The discussion has so far focused on the response to exploitation arising through mechanisms in the early life history but that response is of course linked with the life history characteristics (see Section III). These determine the population growth and recovery *rates* from a perturbation: they are implicit in the stock and recruitment relationship but are not expressed until it is developed to a potential yield function. Garrod and Knights (loc. cit.) examined some general features of the influence of population growth-rates but here we are concerned with the adaptive significance of these features because the same annual egg production can be generated by a range of combination of traits. Stearns (1976) expresses the view that

> in fluctuating environments, age and size at first reproduction should be respectively lower and smaller, reproductive effort higher, size of young smaller, and the number of young per brood higher than in constant environments, where the opposite trend should hold.

But evidently some stocks with similar fecundity per gram (female) produce morphologically similar eggs and do exhibit late maturity at a larger size. What then might the selective advantage be? There is a widely held view that the age of maturity and longevity relate to the time scales of environmental change, damping out the variability. This is an attractive hypothesis, but there remains the problem of the evolutionary mechanism that could establish such a trait involving a long time lag between the adaptation and its demographic consequences. Heterogeneity may offer a way of inverting the argument with the same eventual consequences.

Horwood and Shepherd (1981) and Horwood (1982) have analysed the response of fish populations to random perturbations. If the population sensitivity is defined as the relative variance of the population per relative variance in recruitment, i.e.

$$\text{Sensitivity} = \frac{\text{var (population)}}{\text{var (recruitment)}} \times \frac{(\text{equilibrium recruitment})^2}{(\text{equilibrium population})^2},$$

if the other terms are constant then it is found that sensitivity decreases with stock (population) size increasing. If the variance of recruitment is relatively greater than the variance of the stock then the stock will not drift far from its equilibrium and its sensitivity will be low. Conversely, stocks with a low relative variance of recruitment are less responsive and therefore more sensitive to perturbation. The relative variance ratio can therefore be used to measure the influence of a particular life history characteristic.

Table III summarizes the relative variance* of a typical herring stock for a

---

* Relative variance is defined as variance (population)/(population/K)^2 per unit variance of recruitment where K is the K of the stock and recruitment relationship and is a natural scaling factor. It is, in effect, the square of the coefficient of variation of population size per unit variation in recruitment.

given compensation coefficient ($\beta = 1 \cdot 0$) and a range of age at maturity (3–15) and then for a range of β ($0 \cdot 6$–$1 \cdot 4$) at a given age of maturity (3). In all cases $\alpha = 6 \cdot 0$ and $M = 0 \cdot 1$. The full range of combinations has not yet been explored but these examples indicate that for a stock with a given β and varied maturity the ratio is very robust, but at a given age of maturity the ratio increases with

TABLE III.   Relative variance of population per $(\text{population}/K)^2$.

Age at maturity	β	Relative variance	Sensitivity
3	1	0·001465	0·051
6	1	0·001487	0·051
9	1	0·001515	0·051
12	1	0·001556	0·051
15	1	0·001614	0·051
3	0·6	0·000012	0·078
3	0·8	0·000247	0·061
3	1·0	0·001465	0·051
3	1·2	0·004718	0·044
3	1·4	0·010756	0·039

the degree of compensation. The second result arises because the equilibrium unexploited stock size is smaller at high β than at low β, and from $\beta = 0 \cdot 6$–$1 \cdot 4$ the sensitivity falls by about one half. It implies that such a stock with a high β would have a lower sensitivity and the stock would not stray far from its equilibrium. A high compensation coefficient might then offer important benefits in stabilizing a population in variable environmental conditions. The first result, that sensitivity is quite robust in respect of age at maturity is more interesting in the present context since it implies that the probability of extinction would not be sensitive to age at maturity, at least at the value of β chosen. If that is so, a stock could divert a greater proportion of the available energy to somatic growth if that offered any advantage. One might then postulate a sequence of events where individuals exhibiting a later maturity can devote more energy to somatic growth without risk to the continuity of the genepool, but thereby enhancing the stock size. If the stock enlarges further the effect of heterogeneity will tend to reduce β enabling an even larger stock size to be sustained within the carrying capacity so that the late maturity is progressively reinforced. It is therefore worth exploring the implication that it is the spatial and temporal heterogeneity which, through their influence on β, allow the development of the late maturity characteristic in saturation spawners.

This is interesting because the late maturity syndrome is frequently and loosely associated with populations at high latitudes where the environment is tacitly assumed (but not shown) to vary over longer time scales and where lower temperature could be expected to delay physiological development. In this paper we are suggesting that early maturity is associated with the need for high compensatory response in an environment which is more variable than that of the larger stock where heterogeneity buffers the variation in mortality in the early life history and has allowed the development of late maturity. The hypothesis leads to the expectation that small stocks restricted to a smaller and, in the marine environment, a more variable habitat, should mature at a younger age. This can be seen in some north Atlantic cod, viz:

	Age at maturity	Potential yield (000) tonnes
Irish Sea cod	2	5–10
North Sea cod	3	100–200
Iceland cod	6	300–400
Arcto-Norwegian cod	8	600–800

but this is compounded with latitudinal variations and exceptions come readily to mind, e.g. Faroe cod. But a similar comparison can be based on data given by Roff (1981). He established a correlation between age at maturity and reproductive life span for a number of flatfish species. These are listed in his Table IV and can be ranked according to their reproductive life span and compared with their potential or average yield as summarized in Table IV. The yield data are not very satisfactory indicators of stock size for obvious reasons, but details summarizing the trend in yield with reproductive life span are shown in Table V.

Roff's selection of stocks supports the expectation that late maturity and reproductive life span are associated with larger stock size. In another context Schaffer (1979) argues of Atlantic salmon that the length of the home river, growth at sea and fishing mortality in the marine phase are selecting fish with improved survivorship, i.e. delayed maturity. Fishing mortality at sea is of somewhat recent origin to have created an evolutionary effect but perhaps it is possible that it is the heterogeneity associated with the longer river length which has permitted the development of late maturity.

It is perhaps a semantic difference but we find it easier to understand that a given set of circumstances provides the opportunity for a set of characteristics to develop which might then enable a species to expand its "niche", rather than to suppose a particular modification is evolved to cope with the problems presented by a "perceived" set of environment constraints. In fact, rather than

TABLE IV.   Life history characteristics and average yield of flatfish stocks (after Roff, 1981).

	Age at maturity	Reproductive span	Annual yield (approx.)
Cynoglossus semifasciatus	1	1	1 000
Hippoglossoides platessoides	3	1	low
Pleuronectes americanus	3	4	?20 000[a]
Lophosetta aquosa	3·5	4·5	200
Platichthys stellatus	2·5	5·5	250
Limanda ferruginea (Newfoundland)	6·4	5·5	20 000
Pleuronectes americanus (Newfoundland)	6·5	6·5	1 000
Limanda ferruginea (New England)	2	7	30 000[b]
Isopsetta isolepsis	3	8	500
Parophrys vetulus (British Columbia)	4	13	1 000
Solea solea	3·2	13	15 000
Glyptocephalus cynoglossus	8·6	14·5	25 000
Eopsetta jordani	8	15	4 000
Hippoglossus stenolepis	11	16	25 000
Hippoglossus hippoglossus	12	17	2 500
Hippoglossoides platessoides	15·2	17	100 000
Pleuronectes platessa	4·5	26·5	120 000

[a] Overestimate.
[b] Overfished at that level.

TABLE V.

Reproductive span	Average yield (tonnes)
10 yr	9 000
10–16 yr	14 000
16 yr	75 000

being an inconvenient nuisance surrounding deterministic formulations of population processes, variability and the devices evolved to overcome it can be seen as a more potent and perhaps more fundamental force in population demography than the "geometry" of a particular niche. But there is a trade-off so far as fisheries are concerned, a stock buffered by heterogeneity which has led to a low compensation coefficient will respond rapidly to exploitation. Being large stocks they could support a high absolute yield if the rate of exploitation remained low but in these circumstances, as history shows, exploitation is especially difficult to contain. The highly productive stocks are those which exploit variability rather than overcome it.

REFERENCES

Bannister, R. C. A., Harding, D. and Lockwood, S. J. (1974). *In* "The Early Life History of Fish" (J. H. S. Blaxter, ed.), pp. 21–37. Springer Verlag, Berlin.

Garrod, D. J. (1982). *Fish. Res. tech. Rep.*, Lowestoft **68**, 22.

Garrod, D. J. and Knights, B. J. (1979). *Symp. zool. Soc. Lond.* **44**, 361–382.

Harding, D. and Nichols, J. H. (1977). *ICES* C.M. Pap. Rep. No. 1977/F:21, 9 pp.

Harding, D. W., Nichols, J. H. and Riley, J. D. (1974). *ICES* C.M. Pap. Rep. No. 1974/F:21, 8 pp.

Harding, D., Nichols, J. H. and Tungate, D. S. (1978). *Rapp. P.-v. Reun. Cons. int. Explor. Mer* **172**, 102–113.

Holden, M. J. (1977). *In* "Fish Population Dynamics" (J. A. Gulland, ed.), pp. 187–215. John Wiley, London and New York.

Horwood, J. W. (1982). *J. Cons. int. Explor. Mer* **40**, 237–244.

Horwood, J. W. and Shepherd, J. G. (1981). *Math. Biosci.* **57**, 59–82.

Hunter, J. R. and Leong, R. (1981). *Fishery Bull. U.S.* **79**, 215–230.

Levin, S. A. (1979). *In* "Studies in Mathematical Biology, Part 2: Populations and Communities" (S. A. Levin, ed.). Studies in Mathematics, 16. Mathematical Association of America, Washington.

Lockwood, S. J. and Shepherd, J. G. (1982). *J. Cons. int. Explor. Mer* (in press).

MacCall, A. D. (1979). *Rep. Calif. coop. Oceanic Fish. Invest.* **20**, 72–82.

Mann, R. H. K. and Mills, C. A. (1979). *Symp. zool. Soc. Lond.* **44**, 161–177.

Parrish, R. H. and MacCall, A. D. (1978). *Fish. Bull. Calif.* **167**, 109 pp.

Picken, G. B. (1980). *Biol. J. Linn. Soc.* **14**, 67–75.

Pope, J. G. and Knights, B. J. (1982). *Can. Spec. Publ. Fish Aquat. Sci.* **59**, 116–118.

Roff, D. A. (1981). *Can. J. Fish. Aquat. Sci.* **38**, 968–977.

Schaffer, W. M. (1979). *Symp. zool. Soc. Lond.* **44**, 307–326.

Sette, O. E. (1943). *Fishery Bull., Fish. Wildl. Serv. U.S.* **50** (38), 149–237.

Sheldon, R. W., Sutcliffe, W. H. Jnr and Paranjape, M. A. (1977). *J. Fish. Res. Bd Can.* **34**, 2344–2353.

Shepherd, J. G. (1982). *J. cons. int. Explor. Mer* **40** (1), 67–75.

Stearns, S. C. (1976). *Q. Rev. Biol.* **51**, 3–47.

Ware, D. M. (1975). *J. Fish. Res. Bd Can.* **32**, 2503–2512.

Titles of the Oral papers Presented at the FSBI International Symposium. "Fish Reproduction: Strategies and Tactics", Plymouth Polytechnic, Plymouth, Devon. July 19–23, 1982

The Breeding Strategies of *Tilapia* and Reproduction Control in Aquaculture
  J. D. BALARIN: *Baobab Farm Ltd, Box 90202, Mombassa, Kenya*

Different Patterns of Spermatogenesis and Spermatology in Teleost Fish
  R. BILLARD: *I.N.R.A., Laboratoire de Physiologie des Poissons, Campus de Beaulieu, 35042 Rennes Cedex, France*

Hormonal and Environmental Factors and the Modification of Reproduction in the Rainbow Trout (*Salmo gairdneri*)
  N. R. BROMAGE, J. A. ELLIOTT and C. WHITEHEAD: *Fish Culture Unit, Department of Biological Sciences, University of Aston, Birmingham, U.K.*

Mate Selection and Reproductive Success in Relation to Social Dominance in the Guppy (*Poecilia reticulata*)
  K. D. BROWNE and E. A. WARREN: *Life Sciences Department, Polytechnic of Central London, London, U.K.*

Survival Strategies of the Early Life-history Stages of Mackerel in Contrasting Environments
  S. H. COOMBS: *Natural Environmental Research Council, Institute for Marine Environmental Research, Prospect Place, The Hoe, Plymouth, Devon, PL1 3DH, U.K.*

Reproductive Strategies of Pike and Perch Communities
  J. F. CRAIG and C. KIPLING: *Freshwater Biological Association, Windermere Laboratory, Ambleside, Cumbria, U.K.*

Buoyancy in Marine Teleost Eggs – A Strategy for Dispersal
  J. C. A. CRAIK: *Scottish Marine Biological Association, Oban, Scotland, U.K.*

Sex Change in British Wrasse
  F. DIPPER: *Marine Station, Port Erin, Isle of Man, U.K.*

Habitat, Spawning Cycles and Competition Among *Barbus* (= *Puntius*) Species of Sri Lanka. (Pisces: Cyprinidae)
K. KORTMULDER,* S. S. DE SILVA† and J. A. SCHUT*: *Zoologisch Laboratorium, Univ. of Leiden, The Netherlands and† Department of Ruhuna Univ. College, Matara, Sri Lanka.

Strategic Differences in the Reproductive Tactics of Demersal and Pelagic Spawning Fish
T. C. LAMBERT: Marine Ecology Laboratory, Bedford Institute of Oceanography, Dartmouth, N.S., Canada

The Cost of Reproduction in American Shad
W. C. LEGGETT: Department of Biology, McGill University, 1205 Avenue Docteur Penfield, Montreal, Quebec, Canada H3A 1B1

A Reproductive Strategy for a Population of "Dwarf" Landlocked Atlantic Salmon, *Salmo salar* L., in Newfoundland
D. A. MACLEAN and A. M. SUTTERLIN: Marine Sciences Research Laboratory, Memorial University of Newfoundland, St John's, Newfoundland, A1C 5S7

The Reproductive Strategy of the Deep-sea Gonostomatid Fish *Cyclothone microdon*
N. R. MERRETT: Institute of Oceanographic Sciences, Wormley, Godalming, Surrey GU8 5UB, U.K.

Fishery-induced Changes in Population Structure and Mating Systems of Atlantic Salmon in Quebec, Canada
W. LINN MONTGOMERY and R. J. NAIMAN: Woods Hole Oceanographic Institution, Woods Hole, Massachusetts, U.S.A.

Spawning Strategies of Some Anadromous Freshwater Fishes in the Northern Baltic
K. MULLER and L.-O. ERIKSSON: Department of Ecological Zoology, University of Umea, S-901 87 Umea, Sweden

Reproduction of the Tilapias—A Study of Flexibility
A. I. PAYNE: Department of Biological Sciences, Coventry (Lanchester) Polytechnic, Priory Road, Coventry, U.K.

Reproduction and the Growth Parameters: An Optimization Approach
D. ROFF: Department of Biology, McGill University, Montreal, Quebec, Canada

Chemical Communication as a Reproductive Tactic
D. J. SOLOMON: Ministry of Agriculture, Fisheries and Food, Directorate of Fisheries Research, Fisheries Laboratory, Lowestoft, NR33 0HT, Suffolk, U.K.

Annual Cycles of Electrophoretic Patterns of Serum Proteins and Lipoproteins in *Notemigonus crysoleucas*

R. C. SUMMERFELT: *Department of Animal Ecology, Iowa State University of Science and Technology, Iowa, 50011, U.S.A.*

Physiological Tactics of Reproduction in Catfish and Carp

B. I. SUNDARARAJ: *Department of Zoology, University of Delhi, Delhi 110007, India*

Reproductive Strategies of Antarctic Fish

M. G. WHITE and A. W. NORTH: *British Antarctic Survey, NERC, High Cross, Madingley Road, Cambridge, U.K.*

Titles of the Poster Papers Presented at the FSBI International Symposium, "Fish Reproduction: Strategies and Tactics", Plymouth Polytechnic, Plymouth, Devon. July 19–23, 1982

Transfer of Passive Immunity from Mother to Young in Teleosts (Haemagglutins in Serum and Eggs of Plaice (*Pleuronectes platessa* L.)
 J. BLY: *School of Animal Biology, University College of North Wales, Bangor, Gwynedd, LL57 2UW, U.K.*

Reproduction of the Halfbeak *Hemiramphus brasiliensis* (Hemiramphidae) of the South Coast of Jamaica
 A. COOPER: *Dunstaffnage Marine Laboratory, Oban, Scotland, U.K.*

Reproduction in the Western Indian Ocean Catfish, *Arius* sp.
 A. DARRACOTT: *8, Guards Club Road, Maidenhead, Berks, SL6 8DN, U.K.*

On the Reproduction of the Macrourid (Teleostei, Gadiformes) Roughead Grenadier (*Macrouris berglax*) in Northern Norway 1981
 J. E. ELIASSEN: *Institute of Fishery Science, P.O. Box 3083, Guleng 900, Tromsø, Norway*

Sicydium plumieri (Bloch, 1786), Family Gobiidae, Reproductive Cycle of a Fish in the Mountain Streams of Puerto Rico
 D. S. ERDMAN: *Fishery Research Laboratory, P.O. Box 3665, Mayaguez, Puerto Rica, 00709*

Reproductive Tactics of Four Sympatric Sticklebacks (Gasterosteidae)
 G. J. FITZGERALD: *Department de Biologie, Universite Laval, Ste-Foy Quebec, Canada*

Ration, Body Size and Reproduction in Female Sticklebacks (*Gasterosteus aculeatus*)
 D. FLETCHER and R. J. WOOTTON: *Department of Zoology, University College of Wales, Aberystwyth, U.K.*

Gonad Maturation of Female Capelin *Mallotus villosus*
 K. G. FORBERG: *Institute of Fisheries, University of Tromso, N-9001 Tromso, Norway*

Chronic Effects of Sub-lethal Levels of Zn^{2+} and Cu^{2+} on the Reproductive Capacity of Trout and Carp
 C. A. B. GREZO, D. M. ENSOR, R. E. PARKINSON, A. PARSONS, G. DAVIS, P. SPENCER and B. SLACK: *Department of Zoology, University of Liverpool, L69 3BX, U.K.*

Reproductive Fitness in the Sand-smelt
 P. A. HENDERSON, A. W. H. TURNPENNY, R. N. BAMBER: *C.E.G.B., Fawley, U.K.*

Nutritional Level During the Reproductive Period of Partial Spawning Teleosts — The Soleidae
 F. LAGARDERE: *Station Marine D'Endoume, 17000 La Rochelle, France*

Some Effects of Food Supply on the Annual Reproductive Cycle of Female *Phoxinus phoxinus* (L.)
 K. MEHSIN and R. J. WOOTTON: *Department of Zoology, University College of Wales, Aberystwyth, U.K.*

Immunity in Fish with Free-Living Larvae
 M. S. MUGHAL and M. J. MANNING: *Plymouth Polytechnic, Plymouth, Devon, U.K.*

Environmental Control of Reproductive Timing in the Cyprinid, *Carassius carassius*, and an Hypothetical Model for Gonadal Cycling
 E. A. SEYMOUR: *Life Sciences Department, Polytechnic of Central London, London W1M 8JS, U.K.*

Measurement of Reproductive Effort
 R. J. THOMPSON: *Marine Sciences Research Laboratory, Memorial University, St John's, Newfoundland, Canada*

The Role of Environmental Factors in the Reproductive Strategies of Male Cyprinids
 D. TINSLEY, D. M. ENSOR, S. I. H. JAFRI and E. GARBA: *Department of Zoology, University of Liverpool, L69 3BX, U.K.*

Effect of Food Ration on Reproduction in the Chichlid *Cichlasoma nigrofasciatum*
 T. J. TOWNSHEND and R. J. WOOTTON: *Department of Zoology, University College of Wales, Aberystwyth, Wales, U.K.*

Are there differences in the Activity Patterns between the Nine- and the Three-spined Stickleback (*Pungitius pungitius* and *Gasterosteus aculeatus*) During the Sexual Phase?

A. VANDELANNOOTE and R. VERHEYEN: *Department of Biology, Universitaire Instelling Antwerpen, Wilrijk, Belgium*

The Annual Reproductive Cycle of the Roach (*Rutilus rutilus* L.)

A. D. WORTHINGTON, N. A. A. MACFARLANE and K. W. EASTON*: *Department of Life Sciences, Trent Polytechnic, Nottingham,* *Area Fisheries Office, Severn-Trent Water Authority, Nottingham, U.K.*

Species Index

Subject Index